Peace
JX1391 .C666 1996
Coping with conflict aft
Cold War

Contributors are Arthur J. Alexander,
Mohammed Ayoob, Nicole Ball, Paul F.
Diehl, Roger E. Kanet, Samuel S. Kim,
Edward A. Kolodziej, Edward J. Laurence,
David F. Linowes, Patrick M. Morgan,
Jack Snyder, Janice Gross Stein, and
I. William Zartman.

Edward A. Kolodziej is research professor in the
Department of Political Science at the University
of Illinois at Urbana-Champaign. Along with
Roger Kanet he is the editor of *The Limits of
Soviet Power in the Developing World* and *The
Cold War as Cooperation*, both published by
Johns Hopkins.

Roger E. Kanet is associate vice-chancellor for
academic affairs and director of international
programs and studies, as well as professor of
political science, at the University of Illinois at
Urbana-Champaign.

MURDOCK LEARNING RESOURCE CENTER
GEORGE FOX UNIVERSITY
NEWBERG, OREGON 97132

Coping with Conflict after the Cold War

Perspectives on Security
RICHARD NED LEBOW, *Consulting Editor*

Psychology and Deterrence
Robert Jervis, Richard Ned Lebow, and Janice Gross Stein

*Getting to the Table: The Processes of
   International Prenegotiation*
Edited by Janice Gross Stein

The Limits of Alliance: NATO Out-of-Area Problems since 1949
Douglas Stuart and William Tow

The Allies and Arms Control
Edited by Fen Osler Hampson, Harold von Riekhoff,
   and John Roper

International Peacekeeping
Paul F. Diehl

*Leadership Style and Soviet Foreign Policy: Stalin, Khrushchev,
   Brezhnev, Gorbachev*
James M. Goldgeier

*Khrushchev's Double Bind: International Pressures and
   Domestic Coalition Politics*
James G. Richter

Coping with Conflict after the Cold War
Edited by Edward A. Kolodziej and Roger E. Kanet

Coping with Conflict after the Cold War

EDITED BY

Edward A. Kolodziej AND
Roger E. Kanet

The Johns Hopkins University Press
Baltimore and London

MURDOCK LEARNING RESOURCE CENTER
GEORGE FOX UNIVERSITY
NEWBERG, OREGON 97132

© 1996 Edward A. Kolodziej and Roger E. Kanet
All rights reserved. Published 1996
Printed in the United States of America on acid-free paper

05 04 03 02 01 00 99 98 97 96   5 4 3 2 1

The Johns Hopkins University Press
2715 North Charles Street
Baltimore, Maryland 21218-4319
The Johns Hopkins Press Ltd., London

Library of Congress Cataloging-in-Publication Data will be found
at the end of this book.
A catalog record for this book is available from the British Library.

ISBN 0-8018-5106-8

Contents

Preface   *vii*

Acknowledgments   *xv*

INTRODUCTION

1   Coping with Conflict: A Global Approach   3
Edward A. Kolodziej and I. William Zartman

ONE | NATION-STATE ACTORS:
GREAT POWERS

2   The United States   35
Patrick M. Morgan

3   The Russian Federation   60
Roger E. Kanet

4   Japan   87
Arthur J. Alexander

5   China   110
Samuel S. Kim

TWO | INTERNATIONAL ACTORS

6   The United Nations and Peacekeeping   147
Paul F. Diehl

7   International Economic Actors   168
Nicole Ball

8 The European Community 198
Edward A. Kolodziej

9 Subnational and Transnational Actors 226
Mohammed Ayoob

THREE | CAPABILITIES, ROLES, AND
STRATEGIES

10 Communications, Signaling, and Intelligence 247
Janice Gross Stein

11 Bargaining and Conflict Reduction 271
I. William Zartman

12 Military Force and Regional Order 291
Jack Snyder

13 Privatization: Problems of Implementation and
Opportunities 309
David F. Linowes

14 The Role of Arms Control in Coping
with Conflict after the Cold War 331
Edward J. Laurance

CONCLUSION

15 Thinking about Coping: Actors, Resources,
Roles, and Strategies 363
Edward A. Kolodziej

Contributors 395
Index 399

Preface

This volume addresses one overriding question: What mix of international actors, disposing what resources and pursuing what strategies, is likely to be best calculated to ameliorate real or incipient armed conflicts between peoples and states? This question is of overriding importance today. With the end of the Cold War, the relative decline of U.S. power, and the implosion of the Soviet state and empire, there no longer exists any single state or people possessed of sufficient capabilities and will or animated by compelling national interest and ideological resolve to assume, alone, the costs and risks of leadership of the world society, as the United States and the Soviet Union strove to do after World War II. The burden of coping with conflict now reverts increasingly by default to the diverse actors of the world society, state and nonstate. If today neither a nuclear confrontation between Washington and Moscow nor a major war between the great powers appears to be a clear and present danger, the persistence of violent conflicts still racks the world society. Left unchecked, they threaten to erode the gains made so far — at great cost and much pain — in resolving differences between peoples and states through nonviolent means.

Even if regional conflicts, within or between states, may not immediately raise the prospect of a global conflagration, they are still sources of widespread material damage, tens of thousands of deaths, and untold suffering. Witness the tragedies of Cambodia, Lebanon, and Yugoslavia. Other conflicts loom in the ethnic, racial, tribal, and communal tensions now so widespread. The dissolution of the Cold War has hardly resolved the problem of armed conflicts. Its passing has merely caused this issue to be reformulated in challenging new ways.

There exist no clear rules governing the behavior of the big states to define the conditions for their intervention in a conflict where their interests may appear to be at risk and the implications of such action for great power harmony. The Russian minority problem among the former states of the Soviet Union suggests the dimensions of this problem. Nor are the major states agreed on arms control and disarmament regimes for the sale or transfer of weapons and hostile technologies to warring or incipient rivals. Peace among the great powers has to be cultivated and earned and cannot be taken for granted just because modern wars are so destructive. There is no assurance that the temporary respite from the fear of a global war occasioned by the end of the Cold War will last.

From the perspective of the world society, solutions for conflicts will have to rely on three tried but still imperfect coping instruments: the nation-state, global markets, and democratization. The two former superpowers, however much they may have differed in their vision of how to construct the postwar world society, converged on these three critical elements as global solutions to the search for order, welfare, and legitimacy. First, both affirmed the nation-state as the principal unit for political organization of the peoples of the world. By supporting nation building and state building in every region of the world, both offered constructive outlets for diverse peoples' uncompromising demands for self-determination. As a consequence, the superpower struggle facilitated and accelerated the incorporation of over a hundred new states into the United Nations. In their struggle, the superpowers channeled and checked excessive nationalism and adapted this irresistible force to the world society's need for minimal order in governing its affairs. This was no small achievement, since nationalism had heretofore been the leading cause of two world wars and hundreds of local conflicts.

Second, and from radically contrasting ideological perspectives, both converged on the principle that the demands of populations everywhere for ever greater levels of material welfare had to be solved at the global level; national solutions to satisfy national welfare demands were ruled out. Neither necessarily opposed the expansion of markets as a critical element for the solution of responding to global welfare imperatives; profound discord turned, rather, on the reliance on private property and capital as the motor force of economic growth and social development. In lieu of free markets and the unimpeded flow of investment capital to drive economic growth, Moscow favored what proved to be a flawed system of barter largely conducted between socialist states and satellites. For Moscow, capitalistic markets were the evil; for Washington, state ownership of the means of production, bureaucratic central planning, and the destruction of free markets were impediments to wealth creation, prescriptions for political oppression, and fundamental sources of conflict between peoples and states.

Finally, both sided in principle, if hardly in practice, with a mass-based, democratic test to legitimate not only domestic regimes but also the prevailing structure of geopolitical power and the economic system of the world society. The racial test of Nazi Germany and the outmoded colonialist imperialism of the European states and Japan were rejected as the legitimate basis and the institutional vehicle for the expression of popular consent in the pursuit of global order and welfare. Convergence on democracy and democratization should not obscure, of course, the profoundly different values attached to this principle by each superpower and its allies. The West promoted a model characterized by political pluralism, free association and expression, the rule of law, and limited government, disciplined and responsive to popular will expressed through periodic elections among rival candidates representing contesting party preferences. The communist solution of legitimacy—democratic centralism and one-party rule—was rationalized as a necessary step toward full popular control of the means of production and a guarantee of social justice ostensibly frustrated by free markets and capitalistic exploitation.

Few foresaw the speed with which the Western model of the nation-state, free markets, and democratization would undermine the Soviet Union and negate its proposed solutions to the problems of global order, welfare, and legitimacy. Demands for national autonomy and self-determination contributed to the demise of the Soviet empire in Eastern Europe, to the decline of its power in the developing world, and, ultimately, to the implosion of the Soviet state. The superiority of Western capitalistic markets in producing wealth, evidenced in the growing gap between East and West and between the Western developed North and the developing South, highlighted the failure of the communist experiment as a solution to popular welfare demands.[1]

These systemic outcomes of the Cold War—the nation-state, global capitalistic markets, and democratization—are the starting points for this volume. The triumph of the nation-state and the accompanying decline or elimination of former hegemons with an interest in imposing restraints on warring parties have led to the problem of coordinating national resources and will to cope with conflicts in which the interests of third-party states or their peoples outside the conflict area are not directly threatened. National self-interest and the democratization of domestic regimes conspire to limit the incentives for intervention—for peacekeeping or peacemaking—to assist divided peoples in managing and surmounting their lethal differences.

Impersonal markets are best calculated to produce wealth efficiently and effectively, yet the conditions for their operation imply a preexisting political order to facilitate the free flow of the factors of production. Once in place, such an order—the European Community, for example—reinforces the will and determination of former enemies to resolve their differences through nonviolent means. How can this experience be applied to other regions of the world society, particularly to enduring conflicts? How can genuine democracy be spread and popular governments be enlisted in coping with regional conflicts when the democratic peoples of the Western coalition, which emerged victorious in World War II and the Cold War, resist assumption of coping responsibilities today, as they did in the 1930s, because of the perceived cost to domestic peace and welfare of foreign entanglements? The discussion below provides partial and provisional responses to these questions.

These chapters, taken as a whole, respond to the question posed at the start of these introductory remarks. The discussion encourages a pragmatic, problem-solving approach to world societal order, welfare, and legitimacy issues. It argues that in a post–Cold War environment, with an increasing number of decentralized power centers around the globe, decision makers must draw on all the potential sources available to the world society and its varied actors if incentives for the resort to violence and coercive threats in fostering the resolution of differences among increasingly interdependent peoples and states are to be lowered. Hegemons, political or economic, are not likely to soon reappear to address these global problems; even more problematic is the prospect that world government will emerge as an answer. The divisions within the world society and the diffusion of power among diverse peoples and states preclude reliance on such dei ex machina solutions.

Chapter 1 specifies the need for external intervention to cope with lasting disputes and briefly explores the limits of prevailing systemic solutions, namely, the nation-state, markets, and democratization as reliable tools of conflict resolution and welfare promotion. Successive chapters explore the limits and possibilities of engaging both state and nonstate international actors in coping with conflict.

Part One, chapters 2 through 5, examines the prospects of enlisting the United States, the Russian Federation, Japan, and China in the performance of regional and global coping roles, including the preservation and development of a society of states inclined toward the peaceful resolution of conflicts and the promotion of global welfare. The news from these sources is not encouraging: they do not promise that the great powers will be equal to the coping tasks confronting the international community.

Part Two, chapters 6 through 9, explores the roles that state-based and transnational actors might play in this process. These include the United Nations, international economic actors like the World Bank, the European Community, and subnational and transnational actors, namely, Arab nationalism and Muslim fundamentalism as political movements. The authors of these chapters also caution against too much optimism about help with coping from these quarters. Preserving the advances that have been made in surmounting conflict between former enemies may be all that can be expected of these actors in the near term. These gains in conflict resolution will not be all that easy to sustain, as setbacks in Europe's movement toward political unification and the problems encountered by U.N. forces in making peace in Somalia and Yugoslavia suggest.

Part Three, chapters 10 through 14, identifies key strategies that international actors must contemplate in any attempt to promote the security, socioeconomic, and political conditions of successful coping. Chapter 10 summarizes the psychological dimensions of threat perceptions and identifies some of the ways, none of them easy, to diminish them. Chapter 11 stipulates the bargaining strategies and steps that should be employed in bringing warring parties to the negotiating table. Chapter 12 assesses the prospects of collective security among the major states and specifies the limits of the present international order in marshaling state capabilities and in defining and coordinating coping strategies to manage and resolve conflicts. Chapters 13 and 14 look at positive incentives, generated by privatization and arms control, that might be relied upon to dampen divisions and to elicit cooperation between rivals.

The concluding chapter summarizes the argument of the volume and illustrates how the approach of this volume can be applied in diagnosing conflicts and developing prescriptions for their resolution. It also makes a brief for an enlarged coping role for the coalition of states that has emerged ascendant in the post–Cold War environment. These essentially are members of the Western coalition that have the resources and, arguably, an interest in assuming much of the burden for coping with conflict today. The line of reasoning offered in the concluding chapter takes issue with the reserved positions assumed by several of the authors. The debate between contributors and the editors is drawn deliberately and aims at helping analysts and decision makers make up their minds about the issue of international security after the Cold War and what can be done to address it satisfactorily.

No effort is made in the discussion below to distinguish sharply between actor roles and strategies that might be pursued to lower local and regional hostilities. Thus, for example, relying on market mechanisms and privatization implies nonstate actors and an increased role for multinational corporations in the global coping process. The important lesson to be garnered from these chapters is that considerable flexibility must be introduced into thinking about what actors, roles, resources, and strategies must be coordinated to develop a winning combination to cope with different forms of hostile and incipiently coercive conflicts. There exists no one, all-purpose "package" of actors, roles, resources, and strategies that is suitable to all conflicts. Each needs special handling, but knowing what elements to choose for each package implies an analytic framework to guide choices.

This volume should be considered a first cut in developing such a framework. At this point in thinking about the post–Cold War world, a principal task of the volume is to open debate about the proper framework for defining local and regionally based, enduring rivalries as threats to international peace and for exploring at a global level of analysis the kinds of actors, roles, resources, and strategies that can provide practical relief to specific conflicts. Much of our intent will be achieved if the volume succeeds in putting these issues on the agenda and in stimulating others to address the problem of enduring conflicts and the feasible ways available to the world society for coping with them.

A generation ago, Thomas Schelling called for a new strategy of conflict as a prerequisite for the development of reliable policy guidelines for managing the military conflict between the United States and the Soviet Union.[2] We know now that the response of analysts and decision makers was too narrowly focused on the manipulation of force. This volume tries to avoid making the same mistake by diagnosing and prescribing for conflict coping at the broadest level of analysis. This suggests the incorporation of Schelling's call for a strategy of conflict within a more inclusive and theoretically more satisfying search for a strategy, or, more precisely, strategies, of consent to surmount armed conflicts. This volume is an initial attempt to help construct a framework of analysis that will be useful in pursuit of Schelling's laudable advice, but to do so by enlarging his challenge to seek ways to elicit cooperation more by mutual consent than by coercion. The volume does not seek to provide solutions for particular conflicts; rather, it focuses on the more fundamental problem of how to *think* about conflicts and coping per se after the Cold War. The volume identifies and explores those elements that are common to the proper diagnosis of and prescription for specific conflicts.

This volume does not lay claim to a new theory of consensual cooperation. Instead, the more modest claim is made that the authors contributing to this volume have fashioned a useful "template" to move us along toward such a theory and practice of consensual cooperation. The volume assists analysts and decision makers, as well as real or potential warring parties, to face the full agenda of the order, welfare, and legitimacy issues that define their differences. It seeks workable solutions that not only are consistent with the dominant solutions available to the world society in coping with conflicts but also, and here is the tricky part, push the limits of those solutions—the nation-state, markets, and democratization—while holding open the possibility that human ingenuity and resourcefulness will fashion better coping tools than these global instruments.

Space limitations also precluded discussion of many important dimensions of the problem and the process of coping. If more time and space had been available, the editors would have very much liked to include a discussion of the multilateral corporation, the principal instrument for investment capital, technological diffusion, and the determination of international production priorities and employment. They would also have liked to explore the use of economic incentives and associated noncoercive forms of power to encourage the peaceful resolution of conflicts. Similarly, the role of transnational groups, like Amnesty International, in promoting the rule of law, human rights, free elections, and open political processes would certainly have been incorporated into the discussion. These topics might well be pursued in the future perfection of this coping framework and the application of this "template" to specific conflicts.

NOTES

1. The rise, evolution, and demise of the Cold War is certainly a controversial subject, but this volume does not address this historical issue and the complex problems of causality that it raises. These important questions are not likely to be resolved anytime soon and are beyond the scope of this discussion. The focus here is on accepting the systemic outcomes of the Cold War struggle for an analysis of conflict coping in the post–Cold War environment simply because there is a need to rethink how armed conflicts can be moderated, managed, and resolved in a world society where rivalries persist and how others once believed solved were in fact simply smoldering, as in Yugoslavia or Somalia, only to explode with unanticipated virulence and viciousness.

2. Thomas C. Schelling, *The Strategy of Conflict* (New York: Galaxy Books, 1960).

Acknowledgments

We wish to express our sincere appreciation to all of those who made this project a possibility. The original idea of examining approaches to coping with regional conflict in a systematic manner and the resources available to the international community to deal with conflict emerged out of two earlier projects, which also involved some of the contributors to this book. In the course of carrying out the research included in an earlier volume, *The Cold War as Cooperation: Superpower Cooperation in Regional Conflict Management* (Baltimore: Johns Hopkins University Press; London: Macmillan, 1991), patterns of great power behavior across conflicts emerged. Moreover, the research on that project led the editors of this volume to reconceptualize the entire process of finding the right mix of actors, capabilities, and strategies to deal with regional conflict. This conceptualization became the framework within which the present volume evolved.

A key element in the preparation and emergence of the present study was the workshop "Coping with Regional Conflict: A Global Approach," held at the University of Illinois at Urbana-Champaign (UIUC), October 9–11, 1992. Contributors and invited guests came together to address the issues associated with regional conflict and the possible ways of coping with that conflict. The conference contributed decisively to widening the scope of this volume to include armed conflicts wherever they might arise as threats to international security, not just those between regional rivals or nation-states.

In addition to the primary contributors, who presented the initial drafts of the papers included here, several scholars served as formal commentators and provided detailed written comments on the papers. The latter included Dean Pruitt of the International Education Association and Victor Kremenyuk of the Institute for USA and Canada Studies, Moscow. Other invited participants included Robert Dekle of Boston University, Robert Russell of the International Monetary Fund, and Paul Schroeder of the University of Illinois at Urbana-Champaign (at the time a fellow at the U.S. Institute of Peace).

We are very grateful for the support provided by International Programs and Studies (IPS) and by the Program in Arms Control, Disarmament, and International Studies (ACDIS), both of UIUC. Moreover, without the substantial financial backing of the U.S. Institute of Peace (USIP), the Midwest Consortium for International Security Studies (MCISS, a program managed by the Midwest Center of the American Academy of Arts and Sciences), and the College of Liberal Arts and Sciences at UIUC, the workshop and this resulting study would not have been possible. We wish to express our special thanks to Hrach Gregorian of USIP, to the late Marian Rice and Harold K. Jacobsen of MCISS, to Larry Faulkner of the College of Liberal Arts and Sciences, and to Jeremiah D. Sullivan of ACDIS for providing that support. Of course, the opinions, findings, and conclusions contained in this book are those of the authors and do not necessarily reflect the view of the U.S. Institute of Peace, the Midwest Consortium for International Security Studies, or the University of Illinois.

We wish to express our appreciation to all the participants in the project, whose perceptive criticisms and suggestions increased the clarity and precision in the individual papers and the overall quality of the book. We also wish to thank all of the authors for their willingness to revise their chapters, taking into account the recommendations from workshop participants and sometimes stringent demands from us. The success of the workshop also owes much to the logistical support of James Alexander and Piper Hodson, graduate students in the Department of Political Science at UIUC. We also wish to express our appreciation to staff in both IPS and ACDIS—Sheila Roberts and Karen Tempel, and Mary Anderson and Merrily Shaw, respectively—for their contributions to the project; their efficient discharge ensured the completion of the final manuscript. Finally, we wish to acknowledge the indispensable roles played by Merrily Shaw as conference organizer, editor, paper prodder, and production manager.

Introduction

EDWARD A. KOLODZIEJ
and I. WILLIAM ZARTMAN

1 | Introduction

Coping with Conflict:
A Global Approach

This chapter has three purposes. The first is to underline the pervasiveness and persistence of armed conflicts as threats to the peace and prosperity of the emerging world society. The second is to define two essential requirements for successfully coping with these conflicts: the intervention of third parties and the harmonization of coping solutions at the local level with three systemic solutions — the nation-state, markets, and democratization — to solve, respectively, the problems of order, welfare, and legitimacy. The third aim is to present a conceptual template for diagnosing conflict levels and for prescribing coping solutions. The succeeding chapters develop the implications of this template, putatively applicable to the actors, roles, resources, and strategies that must be marshaled to cope with conflict.

▲ Threats to the World Society

Armed conflicts persist in the post–Cold War era. Analysts and policymakers who saw the superpower struggle between the United States and the former Soviet Union as the principal source of armed conflict have been surprised not only by the continuation of hostilities around the globe but by the eruption of renewed and deadly struggles between former rivals whose differences, as in Yugoslavia, Somalia, and Rwanda, appeared to have been long settled or on the mend. Moscow and Washington, while undoubtedly spurring regional wars and domestic strife during their Cold War struggle, also restrained local rivalries in ways that have yet to be clearly understood, much less adequately recognized by analysts.[1] Now that the Cold War is over, it is clear that the ability of the United States and the Soviet Union to compromise their differences — in southern Africa (Angola, Mozambique, Namibia, and South Africa); in the African Horn (Ethiopia and Somalia); in the Northern Tier (Iran and Afghanistan); in Southeast Asia (Vietnam and Cambodia); and, more recently, in the Persian Gulf — did not end these conflicts, even in those areas where superpower rivalries appeared to overshadow local differences. Serious conflicts persist in the Persian Gulf, the Middle East, southern and central Africa, Southeast and South Asia, and once again in the Balkans and among peoples of the former republics of the Soviet Union.

Furthermore, the end of the superpower bipolar system comes at a moment when several multiethnic, -national, -communal states — Sri Lanka, India, Ethiopia, Sudan, Rwanda, and others — are facing formidable challenges to their political integrity from minorities within their borders pressing for greater autonomy or independence or for their very survival. These conflicts are increasingly understood as deeper, more pervasive, and more intractable than the former superpower struggle. Whereas the U.S.-Soviet conflict was driven by geopolitical and ideological forces, local conflicts are more often propelled by tribal, ethnic, racial, cultural, or religious hatreds, which are less responsive to calculations of interest, rational weighing of cost and benefits, or appeals to the "shadow of the future" in compromising differences.[2] Game theorists have made much of the future, that is, of the continued interaction of opponents, as a powerful restraint on conflict. Such ahistorical evaluations bias and unduly discount the importance of the past and its reservoir of mutually remembered wrongs that have not been righted between warring groups. They have little experience and less incentive to assign much value to peaceful or noncoercive forms of cooperation with a rival. The collapse of the Soviet empire and the implosion of the Soviet Union has itself unleashed many of the forces that have transformed the former Soviet republics into warring states (Armenia and Azerbaijan) or plunged them into civil war (Russia and Georgia) and prompted anew national suspicions and tensions between peoples (Ukrainians and Russians) who had lived for centuries under a single political regime, whether czarist or communist. The "shadow of the past" hangs heavily over the future of the diverse peoples occupying the vast territory between Central Europe and the Bering Sea.

As a matter of record, most armed conflicts have occurred at a regional and local level since World War II. Most have been in the developing world.[3] These conflicts have killed millions and wreaked untold destruction. Several have threatened global peace: the Korean, Vietnamese, and Arab-Israeli wars come readily to mind. The persistence of armed conflicts and their spread today, after the Cold War, casts serious doubt on the thesis of superpower incitement to regional violence. These conflicts stem from the clash of historical imperatives unique to a region and those arising from systemic forces, like self-determination. The latter forces are associated with locally expressed popular demands for greater material welfare and for regional power balances and a world order consistent, paradoxically, with their parochial interests, values, and norms. As historical rivals are absorbed into the global modernization process, they still insist on shaping these systemic structures to suit their preferences and remembrances of things past. Thus the Iranian revolution affirms traditional Shiite Islamic beliefs and people's demands for greater material welfare, democratization, and a larger Iranian say in regional and global politics. These same contradictory affirmations of past values and a search for a better material future through modernization reappear in the civil war in Sudan and in the rising civil strife in Algeria and Egypt.

Coping with regional conflicts will require more than the cooperation of the United States and the Russian Federation, the major successor state to the Soviet Union. Neither one, alone or in alliance, is capable of or has much incentive for imposing peace on rivalries that do not immediately affect their security or economic interests. The hegemonic solutions pursued by the United States and the former Soviet Union for coping with armed conflicts during the Cold War have now devolved as responsibilities to the world community and its members to construct viable world order and welfare systems. What is not clear is whether states and other international actors are prepared to discharge these functions when their particular interests clash with the roles that may be imputed to them. Why, for example, should Americans or Europeans die for Sarajevo or Somalia any more than they were disposed to do so for Danzig in the 1930s or Kabul in the 1980s? Why should the Japanese underwrite global capitalist markets in the 1990s, as the United States did after World War II, when, alternately, they would be taxed for their efficiency in world markets and forgo the benefits of free riding?

It is by no means clear that a multipolar world, composed of an increasing number of weak and conflict-racked states and diffuse nonstate power centers, is necessarily more or less peaceful than the bipolar system that it has now supplanted. It is still too early to know whether this multipolar world will be composed of alliances, strong independent states, or some mixture of these or how these emerging new international structures, resting on shifting ethnic, national, and communal loyalties, will resist external shocks and inner stresses. Coping with conflict will require new ways of thinking and, accordingly, novel strategies that challenge a purely state-centric conception of conflict, viewed either as the primary source of hostilities or the only proper vehicle for coping with global conflict. The old formulas, based on the superpower conflict and bloc politics, no longer obtain, even if it is conceded that the East-West struggle may also have deepened and widened the sharp rifts already present in a particular region.

Before the discussion turns to the question how the global community might better cope with regional and local conflicts, stress should be placed on the difficulty of the task before the populations of the world in their quest to order their affairs by nonviolent means and to assure their welfare, and to achieve both on politically and morally acceptable terms. While the causes of armed conflict are multiple and far too numerous and complex to summarize here,[4] the dilemmas confronting the world community can perhaps be quickly grasped if we identify the principal structural impediments to conflict management and resolution. As suggested earlier, these lie at the foundation of the modern world system. At a primordial level they arise from the profound and enduring enmities nurtured by rival peoples, some preceding the modern age. These products of historical evolution, rooted in the atavistic drives associated with human behavior and rationalized, not to say often glorified, by appeals to religious authority and claims of separate and superior cultural, tribal, ethnic, or racial identity, resist incorporation into a new and internally coherent world order and welfare system.

Yet it is the construction of such peaceful and prosperous global systems that is the historically unprecedented task of the world community today. As a consequence of many factors — rapid technological progress and its diffusion; instant and increasingly dense networks of communications linking hitherto isolated peoples; ecological and economic interdependence under conditions of an exploding world population pressing toward ten billion in the next century; and the unparalleled destructive power of modern warfare, certainly among the most important factors — the imperatives of building global order and welfare systems are now inescapable, although the solutions to these problems are seldom evident or, when discoverable, readily applicable.

Indeed, the principal modern solutions to the problem of global governance and welfare — the nation-state, world markets, and the democratization of international politics — have proved wanting in resolving regional and international tensions. In almost all cases, they have contributed to regional and world division among states and peoples, even as they have been necessarily relied upon—*faute de mieux*—to relax and resolve structural conflicts within the global community. The internal contradictions inherent in these provisional solutions to conflict, as the discussion below suggests, not only hinder resolution of regional strife but also, and often unwittingly, fuel and enlarge it. A brief review of the principal lines of lethal cleavages between longtime rivals and the structural obstacles to coping with regional conflict highlight the need for new diagnostic tools and prescriptive formulas to ameliorate differences between peoples and states in the post–Cold War era, yet tools and instruments fashioned by the world's populations—principally the nation-state, global markets, and democratization—to cope with them.

▲ The Pervasiveness and Persistence of Armed Conflicts: An Overview

Regional conflicts fall into four general categories: (1) intrastate separatist or subnational conflicts for self-determination with external support, such as in Sudan, Eritrea, Cyprus, Sri Lanka, India, Yugoslavia; (2) intrastate replacement or ideological conflicts for central government control either with external support, as in Lebanon, Afghanistan, Mozambique, Angola, Chad, Zaire, Cambodia, Rwanda, Ethiopia, El Salvador, Iraq, Nicaragua, or without external support, as in Peru and Colombia; (3) intrastate rivalries over rank and relations, covering the regional context of almost all of the above; and (4) interstate claims on neighboring territories, such as in Ogaden, Kashmir, Kuwait, Sahara, Chad, Israel, and Mauritania. In the overwhelming proportion of cases, these conflicts come to the fore now either because they involve states emerging from communist control—Ethiopia, Angola, Mozambique, Yugoslavia, Czechoslovakia, Afghanistan, and Cambodia—or because they involve parties supplied and restrained closely or distantly by Cold War competitors—El Salvador, Palestine, Iran, Iraq, Peru, Colombia, Chad, and Zaire. The sources of the conflict are all homegrown, but the current form and outbreak can be partially attributable to the end of the Cold War.

Few of these have been managed or resolved by the parties alone, and the progress that has been made owes much to regional or international mediation. Intrastate separatist or centralist conflicts are most frequently resolved by victory of one side or the other. The separatists win by establishing a new state or autonomous region, the centralists by replacing the incumbents in power. Typically, neighboring states offer sanctuary and support, turning the internal conflict into a regional one. Thus, the rival factions of the Angolan nationalist movement, the government of the Popular Movement for the Liberation of Angola—with support from the Organization of African Unity (OAU), the six Front Line States of southern Africa, and the Soviet Union—and the National Union for the Total Independence of Angola (UNITA)—with support from Zaire, South Africa, Morocco, and the United States—managed their conflict through U.S. mediation in the Washington agreements of December 1988. The conflict was then transformed, albeit provisionally, from a military to a political struggle through the Estoril Accord of May 1991. This led to the elections of September 1992, whose outcome was then contested by the loser, UNITA, and not resolved until the Lusaka agreements of 1995.

In 1977 and 1978 the Zairian government, with support from Morocco, France, Belgium, and the United States, repulsed invasions of the southern province of Shaba, formerly Katanga, by dissident groups that belonged to the Angolan-supported Congolese National Liberation Front. The government then reached a reconciliation with Angola in 1979 under pressure and mediation from Zaire's Western donors and Nigeria; however, similar groups are returning to activity both on national and on provincial levels as the contest for power opens in the early 1990s. A generation later, Zaire stands on the brink of collapse and anarchy, as President Mobutu Sese Seko has outwitted the democratic opposition while at the same time destroying all national capability for self-government. Rwandan refugees living for more than a decade in Uganda returned in 1990 to contest the Rwandan government, leading to an agreement on elections in 1992. This provisional democratic solution could not resist the tribal fury unleashed by the assassination of the Rwandan president and the mass killing of Tutsis by Hutu death squads. When similar elections in neighboring Burundi brought the long oppressed Hutu majority to power in 1993, minority Tutsis in the army killed the newly elected president and massacred his compatriots.

Struggles between rival leaders or factions or even tribes over the structures and practices of future governments and their beneficiaries will not be easy to manage or resolve. Accords between feuding factions are likely to be unstable. Several examples quite aside from Rwanda and Burundi may illustrate the point. After 1990 the military dictatorship of Samuel Doe in Liberia was under attack from the National Patriotic Front of Charles Taylor, supported by the Ivory Coast and Burkina Faso, and other groups; when the Monitoring Group (ECOMOG) of the Economic Community of West Africa States (ECOWAS), led by Nigeria, intervened to preserve order, the country became divided between two competing governments led by Dr. Amos Sawyer and

Taylor. Sawyer negotiated several truces and agreements for elections through-out 1991 to 1995 under ECOWAS states' pressure and mediation, while the followers of Doe, organized as the United Liberian Liberation Movement, broadened the conflict. The southern Sudanese rebellion, which broke out in 1955, was brought to an end in the Addis Ababa Agreement of 1972, brokered by the World Council of Churches and the All-African Council of Churches; a decade later the Sudanese government reneged on the agreement, and the rebellion was renewed, now conducted by the Southern Sudanese Liberation Movement/Army, fighting not for secession but for a revolution in the en-tire Sudanese political system, with support and sanctuary from Ethiopia and Uganda.

In the 1970s ideologically based rebellions contested the Colombian gov-ernment's legitimacy, partly as a consequence of the exclusion of its members from the 1958 National Front Agreement. Step by step, in the late 1980s and early 1990s, bilateral reconciliation between the rebels and the government was negotiated on the basis of an enlarged political system. Many other simi-lar conflicts have never reach a stage of negotiation. In the near future the pressure to change nondemocratic regimes and to practice democracy is likely to provide the greatest single cause of intrastate conflict, with regional reper-cussions as antiauthoritarian movements and democratic parties find support in neighboring countries.

Boundary Disputes

Ill-defined territory provides many new states with reasons to challenge their boundaries if they will. Latin American, Asian, and African states were born under the doctrine of uti possidetis juris, whereby boundaries inherited from colonial rule were declared to be inviolable. In Latin America, many states have been fighting over the heritage of colonial boundaries ever since. In some African cases — Morocco and Somalia — colonial boundaries did not even exist, and the states expressly declared themselves to be an exception to the 1964 OAU doctrine. In many other cases, boundaries were poorly de-marcated and questionable. In other instances, new, "authentic" criteria of geography, ethnic unity, and even past history could be evoked to challenge the colonial inheritance. In still other cases, new situations, notably offshore oil deposits, required new boundaries. Finally, in another case relating to intrastate secessionist conflicts, regions of sovereign states — Slovenia, Croatia, Eritrea, Somaliland, southern Sudan, and others — used the same criteria to claim their own separate, sovereign existence, as formerly sovereign units — the

Soviet Union, Yugoslavia, Ethiopia, Somalia—broke into component pieces with contested boundaries.

Israel's border wars have been the major feature of the Middle East regional conflict since the birth of the Jewish state in 1947; each of the five wars (1948, 1956, 1967, 1973, 1982) has been punctuated by vigorous attempts at mediation. Until the dramatic and unexpected Israeli-Palestinian Liberation Organization (PLO) accord of September 1993, only the mediation efforts between Israel and Egypt of the late 1970s arrived at any conflict resolution. Still at issue are Israeli occupation of the Golan Heights and southern Lebanon and the future of Jerusalem and the West Bank. The nonexistent southern Moroccan-Algerian boundary was finally corrected by treaty in 1972, ratified by Algeria in 1973 but by Morocco only in 1989. After 1975 the two neighbors waged a proxy war over the Western Sahara, over which the Popular Front for the Liberation of Saqiet al-Hamra and Rio de Oro (Polisario Front) claims sovereignty as the Sahrawi Arab Democratic Republic. A mediated process brokered after 1988 by Saudi Arabia, Tunisia, and the U.N. Secretariat may lead to a final settlement through referendum.

Territorial conflicts and mediated attempts at conflict management have dominated the history of the Horn of Africa. The Somali-Ethiopian border remains at issue. Somalia supported the attempt of the Western Somali Liberation Front to occupy the Ogaden region of Ethiopia in the 1977–78 war; a decade later the tide was reversed, as Ethiopian-supported movements of Somali dissidents occupied much of northern Somalia and then declared it independent as Somaliland, at the same time that the Inter-Governmental Agency on Drought and Development was making some slight progress in managing the conflict. Many agencies tried to mediate between the various Eritrean groups, most importantly the Eritrean Peoples Liberation Front (EPLF), and the Ethiopian government after the latter annulled the federation in 1962. Addis Ababa had uneasily united the two areas for a decade. The only effective third-party offices proved to be those of the United States. It served as a midwife to reduce terminal violence as the EPLF and other national groups entered Addis Ababa in late 1991, leading to a confirmatory referendum on Eritrea's independence in 1993.

Delimited but still contested boundaries led to three wars between Mali and Upper Volta (now Burkina Faso), in 1963, 1974, and 1985, over a small barren strip with some meager minerals but a lot of national pride attached. Fellow members of West African regional organizations finally mediated this dispute in 1986. Maritime extensions of boundaries across offshore oil fields caused conflict between Nigeria and Cameroon in 1981, between Guinea-Bissau and

Senegal in 1988–90, and between Libya and Tunisia until 1982. The latter was settled by resort to the International Court of Justice; a similar history has marked the Libyan claims on northern Chad since the late 1960s, denied in 1993 by the Court. A succession of bilateral negotiations and trilateral awards between Argentina and Chile over their southernmost boundary reached their latest conclusion in 1985 through the Vatican's mediation.

Until the breakups in Eastern Europe, only three states—Pakistan, Malaysia, and Ethiopia—had lost any territory to a secessionist movement since World War II, and only once have two states—Tanganyika and Zanzibar in 1963—merged. This relative stability is once again open to question, as Tanzania is under stress and may revert to its former state elements. Serious territorial differences polarize Ukraine and Russia, and sustained hostilities keep Armenia and Azerbaijan from resolving their deep split. Territorial disputes loom again as major causes of regional conflicts.

It should be noted, however, that on several notable, if not numerous, occasions states have handled their boundary problems by direct negotiation, even making peaceful rectifications. The Mali-Mauritania border agreement of 1963 redrew the boundary to take into account traditional water holes. The administrative boundary between Sudan and Egypt and the submerged boundary under Lake Nasser have been agreed to peaceably—after a scare in 1958. Morocco and Algeria established a boundary where previously there had been none in 1972. Saudi Arabia negotiated border rectifications with Jordan and with Kuwait without a referendum.

As long as contested boundaries are not delimited while the heat of a crisis is off, and as long as delimited boundaries are not demarcated, even established boundaries will return as sources of conflict. As long as agreements on borders are not clearly in place between neighbors, providing mechanisms for handling inevitable incidents in the passage of border populations and the conduct or trade and mining, such incidents will either be used by policymakers to create tension and conflict or lead unwittingly to flareups just because these open wounds are allowed to fester. The reigning anarchy in Zaire inflames once cooled regional differences and may well rekindle separatist movements, like those earlier in Shaba, that could lead to the effective breakup of the state, much as in Ethiopia, Yugoslavia, Somalia, Sudan, and Lebanon.

Structural Rivalries

Structural rivalries also arise because new states have not yet worked out expectations about rank and relations among neighbors interacting within a region. Although such rivalries are not the immediate source of conflict, they make smaller disputes more significant and continue the conflict when its proximate causes have been, or could have been, resolved. Negotiations, as well as mediations, take place within the context of these rivalries as prolongations of the bi- or multilateral conflict rather than merely as attempts to resolve the immediate issue and must be understood as such. Negotiations then become more important as battles to win than as occasions to resolve, complicating their usefulness as a means of managing conflicts.

The struggle for preeminence among Egypt, Iraq, Syria, and Saudi Arabia has been the underlying regional conflict in the Middle East, with the Israeli border conflict often appearing as a mere circumstantial issue; the very question of negotiations with Israel, as much as the conduct of these negotiations when they occur, is a bone of contention within the maneuverings of the system. The Saharan dispute is a battle between Algeria and Morocco, with Libya also involved, over leadership of the Maghrib, and negotiations have been occasions for advantage, delay, and definition of regional relations. Libya's support for incursions into Tunisia and Niger in 1980 and 1982, into Sudan in 1978 and 1986, and into Chad in 1980 were part of its attempt to dominate Arab Africa, particularly against Egyptian influence, with negotiations as occasions to capitalize on momentary advances. Intervention of West African neighbors in the Liberian civil war is an act in the drama over Nigerian leadership in West Africa. Until the entry of the OAU in 1993, negotiations failed because there was no honest broker.

The Shaba invasions of 1977–78 and the Angolan civil war are events in the struggle between Angola and Zaire for predominance in the region. South Africa's incursions into Angola, Zambia, and Zimbabwe and its support for UNITA in Angola and the Mozambican National Resistance under its policy of destabilization (1978–88) were means of assuring its predominance in the region as much as they were means of destroying the foreign bases of the African National Congress. Negotiations in both cases were conflict-management means allowing the armed struggles to continue at a level that was less costly for both sides. The border disputes between Argentina and Chile and between Ecuador and Peru are incidents in the quest for position and influence in South America, where no single negotiations have ever settled either the territorial or the structural issue.

The Kashmir conflict between India and Pakistan and then the breakup of Pakistan have been chapters in the development of a power structure in the subcontinent, consolidating Indian predominance. The 1966 Tashkent agreement was a conflict-management measure mediated by the Soviet Union, but the 1972 Simla agreement was a direct, bilateral conflict-resolution measure. The struggle over the government of Cambodia among the allies of Russia, China, and Vietnam has been an ongoing contest for control of the Southeast Asian regional structure, with negotiations as well as wars serving as campaigns in the region. Such rivalries give a large structure to the many smaller conflicts on the continent, in the same way as European history was shaped over the past half-millennium or as the structural rivalry between the United States and the Soviet Union shaped world history for half a century or more. Powers external to the region are involved in these conflicts because weak states seek to borrow power from outside. During the Cold War such conflicts often escalated to the highest level, as superpowers supported local efforts to block allies of their rival. Today, in a post–Cold War, decentralized system, the management and resolution of these diverse conflicts implies external assistance from an ever broader and bewildering array of sources.

▲ Local Conflicts and Global Solutions

These self-sustaining hot points obviously will not be easily or soon cooled, a sobering prospect for those awaiting the dawn of a new world order in the post–Cold War era.[5] The security of a people ensnared in an enduring conflict is defined almost exclusively in terms of the perceived threats posed by a neighboring people, whether they are separated by a common border—itself a bone of contention—or living cheek by jowl within a state or sprawled across adjoining states, for example, the Kurds in Turkey, Iran, and Iraq. Perceived threats are steeped in mutual suspicions and cultivated hatreds. Grievances are longstanding and revolve around disputes over territories and boundaries that assume uncompromising moral significance to the warring parties. Memories are long. Past transgressions are neither forgotten nor forgiven; they simply accumulate in the minds of the embattled groups and are subsequently transmitted to new generations socialized into the conflict. The future is defined more by the search for retribution and revenge than by the pursuit of common objectives or the discovery of shared interests between rival groups.[6] The self-perceived worth of a people and their cultural heritage are woven into the fabric of hostility that they share with their rivals.

The intensity and pervasiveness of these rivalries do not dispose them to local solutions, absent the domination of one group by another. Such states and warring groups are trapped in what Barry Buzan characterizes as an immature anarchy.[7] The rivals tend to view their security relations as a zero-sum game in which the perceived gain of one side is viewed as a loss for the other. Concessions and compromises are interpreted as signs of weakness, as sellouts, or even as traitorous acts by contesting factions within a group or state in conflict with a common external foe. Governing elites and mobilized populations grow to share a common, if acquired, stake in the maintenance of a conflict. There is very little room for bargaining or negotiations between rivals or among factions within a group or state. Nonsanctioned contacts with the enemy are viewed as threats to national or group cohesion, integrity, identity, and security; they are often proscribed by law and enforced by fines, imprisonment, and even death.

Wherever enduring rivalries persist, whether in active or quiescent form, the prospects of global peace are proportionately diminished. Yet left to their own devices, these conflicts are not susceptible to local solution. They are structured by real and perceived irreconcilable group differences, resting on uncompromising claims made against each other, and nurtured by accumulated grievances that, for many who are party to the rivalry, can never be adequately compensated. The moral and political incompetence of the rivals alone to resolve their differences, as a consequence of their lasting feuds and their often limitless and absolute claims toward each other, all but preclude the possibility of purely local settlement of their discords. That Israel and the PLO have agreed to recognize each other is certainly a major step forward in reconciling their deep differences, but their accord cannot be explained solely by reference to the contesting parties.

Global forces are at work today that essentially frame a regional conflict, particularly among major population groups within the world society, in cross-regional and, in many instances, global terms. This setting transcends the narrow perspectives and interests of the warring parties. Control of these global forces to preclude their adverse widening of a local conflict must be developed in tandem with coping mechanisms to limit the damage and deaths associated with locally based enduring rivalries. The globalization of a conflict and its intensification in regional struggles are rooted in several structural sources endemic to the nation-state system. The first is simply a function of the multilateralization of arms production and transfers, including military technology, which sustain, widen, and make regional armed clashes more destructive than ever before. The processes of arms making and marketing on a global scale are partly products of modernization. The devastation wrought by a local conflict that heretofore might have been limited by the inability of hostile groups and states to gain access to advanced weapons is now facilitated by destructive capabilities that are readily available as a consequence of the efforts of other states, driven by their own security and welfare interests, to furnish these implements of war to belligerents.[8] Conversely, arms producers, particularly those capable of producing technologically advanced weaponry, can have a decisive impact on a conflict by regulating the flow of arms to opponents.

Second, as two world wars and a long Cold War attest, the incentives for foreign intervention into regional conflicts have proven compelling for many states, especially the major powers, which have tended to identify a systemic stake in regional conflicts around the globe. These incentives for intervention persist in the post–Cold War era, although in considerably reduced form, as the chapters in part one of this volume contend. There is no reason to believe that these will not grow in importance once again. Many are inherent in the nation-state system; others arise from the spread of peoples across state boundaries — Kurds in the Middle East or Russians throughout the republics of the former Soviet Union. There is also the prospect of nuclear proliferation as well as the possibility of conflict spillover from one region of the globe to another.

Today, as weak states threaten to implode, there is the perception that the outcome of a regional or local conflict will affect adversely the security guar antees and understandings that other states and peoples have reached with each other. The collapse of the Lebanese state illustrates the internationalization of civil war. Not only did it disrupt the 1943 accord between the religious communities for power sharing but it forced Lebanon's neighbors, principally Syria, Israel, and Jordan, not to mention the PLO, to recalculate their security balances to take Lebanon's disintegration into account. The extension of the Cold War to the developing world can be explained partly as a function of this prisoner's-dilemma mentality, wherein neither superpower would concede dominant influence to the other in determining the outcome of an indigenously defined conflict.

Even states that enjoy close security ties are not spared concern for each other's security behavior. The hard-won rules and norms that animate the peaceful relations of many states, like the members of the European Community (EC) and NATO, are also susceptible to disruption by their differing responses and approaches to regional conflict. The determination of the United States to undo the Iraqi occupation of Kuwait initially strained relations with Germany and Japan. Similarly, German initiative in recognizing the independence of Slovenia and Croatia forced the hand of its EC partners and the United States, which reluctantly followed Bonn's lead, but not without having stirred worries about the implications of what appeared to be a new and potentially troublesome assertiveness in German diplomacy.

If major states today demonstrate a reluctance to intervene with military force in local conflicts, like the Yugoslav and Lebanese frays, and urge peace-keeping on international organizations (if they do not otherwise try to hide), their reserve would appear to be explained less as an aversion to intervention in principle than as a response to the bloody and costly lessons learned from previous unilateral interventions into such conflicts. Unilateral or multilateral intervention attests to the perception, shared by many states, that the outcomes of local conflicts bear directly on or have long-term implications for their security and welfare interests and determine, perhaps decisively, the kind of global system of order and welfare they want and view as legitimate. If the incentives for intervention in local conflicts persist, albeit at reduced levels today, the precise forms and actor responsibility for intervention remain problematic because the immediate costs and risks of widening and perhaps exacerbating a conflict through intervention, not to mention domestic division, are acutely apparent.

Thus the terms of the dilemma confronting the global community's response to armed conflicts are joined. On the one hand, enduring rivalries must be addressed since there can be no stable, effective, and legitimate global order and welfare systems unless these products of history and long evolution are resolved. These conflicts cannot be resolved unless the power, good offices, and resources of outside actors are brought to bear on the warring contestants. Yet there can be no regional peace that is inconsistent with the principal instruments fashioned by the global community over the past several centuries to respond to its conflicting demands for order, welfare, and legitimacy. But the solutions associated with each of these imperatives—the nation-state, global markets, and democratization, respectively—are themselves flawed responses to the needs of populations everywhere in their conflicting quest for effective global governance and ever-increasing material abundance, but based, and here's the rub, on their particular and clashing assertions of moral right and political interest.

Harmonizing Coping Solutions with the Nation-State, Markets, and Democratization: Theoretical Limits

The principal solutions to the global problems of order, welfare, and legitimacy that have been fashioned by the world's peoples—respectively, the nation-state, markets, and democratization—pose, paradoxically, major obstacles to the resolution of these problems at regional and global levels. On the positive side of the ledger, for the foreseeable future the nation-state will be the principal organizing unit of the diverse peoples of the world. No other unit of organization commands the same universal acceptance, loyalty, and legitimacy by an overwhelming number of the earth's population. The notion of nationality is the most powerful unifying force of an otherwise sharply differentiated and polyglot global population. The idea of the nation has provided the principal impetus for the creation of independent states, defined by their territory and qualified by their respective political regimes. These common elements of nation, the territorial state, and governing institutions are indispensable for world order.[9] It is inconceivable that they could be ignored or designed around in the creation of the global system that is now evolving.

Many notable segments of the nation-state system have overcome the primitive or immature anarchy characterizing many enduring regional rivalries. Among the developed states, two world wars notwithstanding, there has evolved what Hedley Bull persuasively characterizes as a society of states. This artificial construction forms the basis of a mature anarchy that conforms neither to the pessimistic expectations of perpetual Hobbesian conflict nor to the optimism of Kantian or Wilsonian notions of inevitable and discoverable cooperation.[10] Such a society of state exists, as Bull argues, "when a group of states, conscious of certain common interests and common values, form a society in the sense that they conceive themselves to be bound by a common set of rules in their relations with one another, and share in the working of common institutions."[11] According to Bull, common values include the preservation of the society itself and the independence of its members; the goal of peace among participants; limitations on violence to persons and property; the keeping of promises and contracts; and respect for property.[12] That these values are often violated is less important to recognize than how pervasive and prevalent the observance of these values and the rules and norms that they imply. Similarly, the institutions of this world society—the balance of power, law, diplomacy, and war—are predicated on its preexistence.[13]

On the other hand, it is no less true that the nation-state is both a solution and a major problem for the creation of an international security community whose members trust and respect each other and are tolerant of each other's diverse interests and values. States driven by violent and virulent nationalism have accounted for much of the carnage of the nineteenth and twentieth centuries.[14] These primal forces continue to stir passions that, as the Yugoslav and Iraqi-Kurdish cases reveal, lead to the most heinous crimes against peoples and humanity. As statesmen have always recognized, the nation-state is also war-prone. Indeed, one of the driving forces resulting in the creation and final victory of the nation-state and the nation-state system has been the greater efficiency and power associated with the integral nation as the basis for a fighting state.[15] War has been the principal means by which the system was established and extended. It remains a central institution and final arbitrating instrument. At the same time, modern warfare threatens what it has wrought.

Whether war will, as John Mueller argues, shrivel and disappear as a social institution, as dueling and slavery did before it, is problematic in the foreseeable future,[16] especially with respect to the multiple rivalries with which this volume is concerned. Not without irony, as outlined earlier, the principal challenge to the nation-state and the nation-state system as a primary building block of international security arises from divisions within the state itself. These movements pressing for secession or greater autonomy raise nettling issues of status, rank, privilege, and power. In many instances, hostilities are externally supported; in all cases the implications of these enduring conflicts reach far beyond the borders of a state or region, and their sources are lodged deep within the relations of peoples and states composing the world society.

The creation of global markets, associated with the Industrial Revolution and the growth of modern science and technology, has also been the principal human instrument for the production and distribution of wealth in the modern age. Famine and poverty can now be said to have been theoretically eliminated thanks to these breakthroughs in human ingenuity and resourcefulness. As a matter of right, the enlarging segments of the world's population, increasingly conscious of the wealth-producing capacity of modern economies, global trade, and investment, are no longer prepared to submit to a future of deprivation and subsistence. The quest for ever greater material welfare, or "More Now," is as much an imperative animating the world's populations as their particular demands for national identity and independence are. The convergence of these systemic forces produces a condition of unremitting turbulence and conflict among the peoples and states of the world society.

As even the casual observer recognizes, the interdependence created by modern global markets cuts sharply against the grain of national autonomy and independence. Protectionist policies conflict with the efficiencies of the market and with product innovation as its lifeblood. Moreover, in the long run mercantilism seriously qualifies, even annuls, the productive benefits of free exchange. Yet, as socialist and Marxist thought persuasively argues, the market distributes wealth unevenly among individuals and groups and inevitably creates inequalities that are the source of social and political tensions.

While these may arise locally, they are global in their implications and repercussions. At the state level, the material distribution of wealth also results over time in a redistribution of power among states. The split between the North and the South turns primarily on the imbalanced distribution of the world's wealth. Twenty percent of the world's population controls approximately 80 percent of the world's wealth, and the gap shows no sign of being closed in the immediate future. Wealthy states are not exempt from feelings of deprivation, since welfare is defined differentially by reference to the levels of material wealth enjoyed by their populations. These welfare concerns, in turn, become major geopolitical concerns for many states since no nation can aspire to military prowess in the absence of a strong economic, scientific, and technological base.[17] Rising U.S., Japanese, and European differences over trade, interest rates, investment, and monetary policies are partly attributable to the melding of these geopolitical and welfare concerns, which have become increasingly merged in the post–Cold War world.

There is no reason to believe that the globalization of markets, left unfettered, will produce full employment. The attendant social ills associated with unemployment of those who are unable, for whatever reason, to be absorbed by the marketplace are a grave and chronic source of domestic and international strife. Technological innovation, as Paul Kennedy suggests, may actually increase unemployment in the developed and underdeveloped world.[18] The market may also serve to reinforce the nation-state split as population growth mounts in the developing world while these peoples are unable to pay market costs for the technology they need to cope with population pressures. Mass immigration is now a permanent feature of international relations, driven by a wide spectrum of separate but reinforcing causes: material betterment, personal security, escape from oppression, or the search for a new and freer way of life. The growth of the world's population and the striving for greater material welfare will continue to push people across national frontiers dividing the world community and carrying in its wake new disruptive forces.

Free, capitalistic markets, then, are powerful responses to populations everywhere for greater welfare, but they also upset stable social relations among individuals and groups and can divide states from each other. Furthermore, those states or corporations that benefit from free markets are not necessarily sensitive to the costs of the survival of markets in the form of expenditures for education, infrastructure, welfare safety nets, or the preservation of the environment. Nor can these markets be sustained in the absence of great social expenditures, whose burden falls unequally on groups and states.

Finally, democratization as the principal source of authority legitimating the pursuit of order and welfare by peoples and states can also be a two-edge sword. Increasingly, governmental policies, international institutions, and the very structure of power in the international system must meet a democratic test. The legitimacy of governmental institutions and of regional and international structures of power depends crucially, as never before, on their claim to popular support, whether identified as national or domestic populations, world public opinion, or both. Governments and governing elites around the globe have increasingly been compelled to reckon with, and respond to, public demands and to develop processes for the articulation of public sentiment and for the participation of the masses in their own governance, whether through elections, referenda, hearings, mass meetings, or the like. Democratization as a demand for self-rule essentially destroyed the colonial system after World War I. This democratization process has most recently scored victories throughout Eastern Europe, the former Soviet Union, and throughout many parts of the developing world, including South Africa, South America, and South and East Asia.[19] It can be argued that, along with nationalism, democratization was one of the primary challenges to the Eurocentric system. Certainly, it drove the American Revolution and can be said to have initially energized the French and Soviet revolutions as well as the mass movements that eventually undermined both the European and Soviet empires.[20]

But the intransigence of some mass-based democratized regimes once populations have been mobilized for war or in opposition to other groups (Arabs versus Jews) or states (Khomeini's Iran versus the United States) can also be a formidable obstacle in achieving regional harmony. The progressive rigidity of European alliances after 1848, propelled by rising nationalism throughout the continent, can be partly attributed to the democratization of domestic politics and diplomacy throughout this period, leading to World War I. Once engaged in a world war, vastly destructive to life and property, home populations were indisposed to compromise their differences with a rival portrayed as evil incarnate. These emotional obstacles to peace were further reinforced by appeals to universal purpose and moral right—the proletarian revolution or making the world safe for democracy—to justify the wholesale carnage.[21] Conversely, liberal democracies, focused on their domestic concerns and welfare needs, resist involvement in foreign conflicts where their interests and security do not appear to be directly engaged. The recent tragedies in Yugoslavia, Somalia, and Rwanda are instructive in cautioning against optimism about the likelihood of enlisting the peoples of the Western democracies in measures for coping with conflict.

Democratization can also assume ominous authoritarian and totalitarian dimensions, as in Hitler's Germany, Stalin's Soviet Union, Mao's China, and Pol Pot's Cambodia. Populations were mobilized for governmental purposes rather than consulted, and their manipulation and control were essential for the continuance of the regime. Suppressed, of course, were minority rights and civil liberties; and at risk was the very integrity of the human personality. The legitimating force of popular will has been used repeatedly to weaken and even destroy societies more tolerant of differences than the authoritarian regimes that replaced them. Under these extreme conditions, a mass-based state is more a threat than a guarantor of human rights.

▲ Coping with Regional Conflict: Standardizing Diagnoses and Prescriptions

The analysis thus far has attempted to establish the following assumptions: First, enduring rivalries and conflicts are not resolvable solely by the efforts, however well intentioned, of the principals. Second, the resources and resolve of outside actors is a necessary, if not sufficient, condition for the amelioration of these struggles. Third, with the end of the Cold War, the relative diminution of the power of the United States, the implosion of the Soviet Union, and the predominance of their domestic concerns impose the task of coping with lethal conflicts on the world community as a whole.

Fourth, the menu of prescriptions available to the world community to cope with regional and international conflict now essentially comprises three systemic solutions: the nation-state, global capitalistic markets, and democratization as, respectively, responses to the demands of the world's populations for order, welfare, and legitimacy (OWL). Coping with armed conflict at a local level implies, then, reliance on the nation-state, markets, and democratization. However, and fifth, whatever the redeeming merits of these instruments in responding to OWL imperatives, they are also flawed and can, if misguidedly applied, result in fundamentally contradictory, certainly unintended, outcomes. Unless these modernizing instruments are applied with care and conditionally, that is, in response to the specific circumstances of a regional rivalry, they can not only deepen regional divisions but set the world community against itself.

But how might local and regional conflicts be diagnosed as a prerequisite for identifying prescriptive mixes of actors, roles, resources, and strategies, consistent with modernizing trends and instruments, that promise to ameliorate a rivalry, leading conceivably to its long-term resolution? There is a need to define a standardized approach for diagnosing the severity of conflicts and for prescribing coping strategies to address them. At least three essential components can be identified that appear to be closely associated with this reconceptualization process. First, a consensually based security community has to be defined that provides a framework within which to identify, array, and analyze deviations from this ideal type. Karl Deutsch's notion of a security community—based on shared values and animated by common principles, norms, institutions, and joint decisional processes in the service of peaceful change—provides a useful paradigm.[22]

Second, the Deutschian ideal is theoretically consistent with the widely held assumption of most international relations analysts that the nation-state system is fundamentally anarchical.[23] This condition does not necessarily preclude the coordination among competing units of shared values and interests or the creation, institutionalization, and preservation of a sustainable order, as Hedley Bull, Robert Keohane, and others have argued.[24] Using Deutsch's conception of a security community as an ideal type, the analyst can array security communities, ranging from primitive to mature anarchies, within a common framework of analysis. The placement of a particular security community is essentially defined by the propensity of its members to resort to coercive threats or violence to get their way.

For purposes of this volume, *the amelioration of a conflict and the creation of a security community that moves toward the Deutschian paradigm is defined in terms of the degree of lessened propensity on the part of all rivals to resort to threats or force to get their way.* Within this context, the term *cooperation* has an elastic meaning, applicable to the quality of the security relation between diverse groups seeking their preferred order. Cooperation will range from, at one extreme, a pure coercive regime in which a hegemon or an alliance imposes its will on others by force (the Warsaw Pact) to the Deutschian ideal of consensual cooperation (the European Community, now on its way toward European Union). The aim of lessened resort to threats and violence is predicated as the immediate goal of all attempts to cope with armed rivalries; it is posited quite apart from the specific, substantive issues and values that define and sustain these conflicts. In this way, conflicts, marked by the use or threat of force, can be diagnostically standardized as the first step in devising global strategies in pursuit of world order and welfare concerns. Progress toward an international security system that better approximates the Deutschian ideal than the Cold War system or its successor depends critically on coping with these enduring rivalries.

Third, since these purposes increasingly devolve as an existential imperative, if not always as an assumed political or moral responsibility, to the actors of the world society in the post–Cold War world—and principally the great powers of the West-centric system, which have emerged as victors from the Cold War—there is an accompanying need to systematically assess the division of labor and responsibilities of these actors as well as the resources and strategies that might be adopted to cope with conflict. The post–Cold War setting excludes primary reliance on the former superpowers to perform these roles, since they lack the power, will, and acknowledgment of authority by other relevant actors, including regional rivals, to perform these roles for coping with conflict by themselves.

Diagnosing Regional Conflicts

The relative importance of a particular conflict can be evaluated along three dimensions: the tractability of the crisis, its saliency, and its historical permanency. These attributes assist in the initial diagnostic process of identifying those enduring conflicts that require immediate attention—a kind of triage—as well as assessing the level of coping challenge confronted by the international community in attempting to ameliorate the rivalry. The first is the gravity or tractability of the crisis. *Tractable* conflicts are those whose parameters, if changed in positive ways, could lead to an improvement in adversarial relations, to détente, or even to limited forms of cooperation, free of coercion and threats to ensure compliance. In other circumstances, substantial efforts may have to be exerted merely to prevent a worsening of tensions or an expansion of armed hostilities.

Past differences between the United States and England over Canada's border illustrate a tractable problem. The Rush-Bagot Treaty of 1818 helped ensure the longest demilitarized border between two countries on the globe. It was as much a step toward the creation of a Deutschian security community between the United States and Canada and, more broadly, between North America and Great Britain, as a reflection of mutual confidence and trust between the peoples of these three powers. The Israeli-Egyptian conflict was similarly susceptible to amelioration once the territorial claims of each party were compromised and the United States, as the guarantor of the accord, created incentives for both parties to observe their agreement by handsome annual grants of military and economic aid and by the extension of reliable security assurances.

On the other hand, some conflicts are so intense and profound that they are simply intractable. At best they may admit only to crisis management or some limited forms of regularization and containment. The Lebanese and Yugoslav civil wars and the Indo-Pakistani conflict fall in this category. The significance of diagnosing a conflict as tractable or not will become clearer when the discussion turns to targeting levels of cooperation that would appear to be achievable by changing the parameters of hostility and violence that define a regional conflict. Intractable conflicts require more time and effort, including the socialization of new generations to rely on noncoercive means to achieve their preferences vis-à-vis rival groups, and a gradual blurring and eventual rejection of past grievances and demands for retributions and satisfaction as a precondition for progress toward peaceful change and toward a mature security community to reflect this commitment.

Not all regional conflicts, however destructive or lamentable, are of equal importance for global stability. Some are salient to other states; others are not. Tribal warfare in Burundi has resulted in thousands of deaths but has not aroused the interest, or led to wholesale intervention, of the great powers or of the international community to end the bloodshed. Only the deaths of hundreds of thousands of Rwandans and of an unparalleled refugee crisis belatedly galvanized the international community to intervene. Terrorism in the Middle East, although it has produced far lower numbers of deaths, often stirs far more local and foreign controversy, heightens foreign media attention, and prompts impressive governmental and private efforts to limit or eliminate this mode of violence.

Finally, regional conflicts may be ranged along a time line from dormant or incipient to immediate and urgent. Some conflicts may again flare up if the conditions moderating or containing them are relaxed. The ethnic struggle between Armenians and Azerbaijanis reemerged after decades of quietude as a consequence of the well-intentioned reforms of *glasnost, perestroika,* and democratization that eventually led to the collapse of the Soviet Union and its imperial containment of these ethnic antagonisms. Although conclusive evidence is lacking, the Yugoslav civil wars are, arguably, the partial result of the end of the Cold War and the subsequent erosion of the regulatory functions of NATO and the Warsaw Pact in restraining national and ethnic self-assertion at the expense of rival groups.

Incipient conflicts, on the other hand, are those that will erupt unless there is a dramatic change in the parameters of the strife. The rise of Islamic fundamentalism in the Northern Tier and among the Asian republics of the former Soviet Union raises the possibility that regional conflict will emerge among the peoples of this region and among interested states, like secular Turkey and revolutionary Iran; similarly, the growth of separatism in Kashmir has led to the revival of Indo-Pakistani tensions, small-scale armed conflict, and the possibility of escalation. The deep rifts within China between rival factions of the Communist Party and between the gerontocracy currently in power and a rising generation signal an incipient conflict within the borders of China whose repercussions will inevitably be felt around the globe.

While hot conflicts may well attract the most attention, many now apparently dormant conflicts promise eventually to overshadow those of current moment and urgency. They need to be surveyed and included in any comprehensive review and monitoring of regional conflicts and their support structure. Many are partially rooted in enduring local divisions, but they are also the product, as in China, of modernizing trends pressing for markets and democratization. Groups and individuals associated with these processes clash with the old guard, who insist on rigid Communist Party control over all aspects of China's transformation from a traditional to a modern society. Incipient conflicts may also be cross-regional in their implications, as the pan-Islamic movement suggests, or as international migration grows as a major issue affecting the political and social integrity of particular states.

Standardizing Cooperation: Moving from Coercive to Consensual Security Systems

Six conceptually distinguishable levels of cooperation may be identified between enduring antagonists. These may be conceived as different stages of cooperative interaction of increasing scope and significance. Achievement of any one of these stages of cooperation would constitute an advance over the diagnosed status of a local conflict. At the lowest level are conflicts that have not moved very far beyond immature anarchies. The actual use of force or threats remains high, and incentives for appealing to violence or coercive intimidation to impose preferences are strong. At the upper level of the scale are enduring conflicts that are well on the way toward resolution and that evidence the coordination of values and interests and their institutionalization in joint decision making between former rivals that progressively approximate the Deutschian paradigm. These stages of conflicts may be arrayed in reverse order as (6) intractable, (5) routinized and contained, (4) stabilized and in the process of reduction, (3) resolved, (2) consolidated, and (1) institutionalized consensual cooperation. Each level may be conceived of as a rung on a Deutschian ladder leading to a security community in which, at its highest rung, differences between peoples and states are resolved through noncoercive means. A few words about each stage will clarify its relationship to those actors, capabilities, and strategies best suited to each conflict that, if employed, would offer some prospect that the conflict could be moved from a lower to a higher stage of cooperation.

An enduring conflict so polarized that security is seen to depend on the elimination of its opponent is the limiting case of an *intractable* conflict. The rivalry between Carthage and Rome is illustrative. The fervor of Balkan animosities or the struggle of Greeks and Turks over centuries have approximated at different times the conception of total warfare described by Carl von Clausewitz.[25] External actors have little room for maneuver beyond the coercive imposition of a resented order on the contesting parties if peace is to be provisionally established, much as Rome sought to bring a precarious peace to the rival tribes of Gaul and, in much lesser measure and result, what the United Nations is attempting to do in Somalia and Cambodia.

Routinized and contained conflict refers to a rivalry that falls short of the determination of each antagonist to eliminate the other. The conflict is intense and lethal, but neither side is able to prevail and a stalemate ensues. Coping efforts cover all practices that prevent such a conflict from enlarging, politically or psychologically, or from expanding with respect to the scope and intensity of armed hostilities. The best that can be done within this context is to stabilize a conflict and to prevent its further erosion, because the conditions for reaching a more ambitious level of lowered noncoercive cooperation may be neither present nor realizable in the immediate future. Stalemate keeps open future options even if the perpetuation of an armed conflict at a level of political stasis may simultaneously work against efforts to reduce or to resolve it. The long and costly military stalemate of the Cold War appears, in retrospect, to have been a necessary, if not sufficient, explanation for the cooperation between Moscow and Washington in regional conflicts around the globe preceding the demise of the Soviet Union.[26] Better a cold war between continental powers in fruitless pursuit of their imperial objectives than the risk of catastrophe evidenced in the disastrous diplomacy of the European powers before World War I.

Conflicts that are stabilized at levels of *reduced* violence or that appear to be on the way toward resolution represent more advanced stages of adversary cooperation. Reductions assume many forms, including mutual recognition by rivals of the right to exist; confidence-building measures, preliminary to more extensive negotiations on differences; political settlements of some issues; or arms control and disarmament measures. Reductions generally deal with the symptoms of conflict. The Indus Water agreement of 1960 between India and Pakistan brought about an amicable division of the world's largest integrated irrigation system. Until the provisional resolution of this issue, it certainly could have aggravated and deepened already profound divisions within South Asia and might well have been a *causus belli*.

The PLO's recognition of Israel's right to exist and Israel's acceptance of the PLO as the legitimate representative of the Palestine people represent fundamental changes in mutual perceptions by former implacable foes. These fall within the meaning of a security system moving toward progressively greater, if still modest, forms of consensual cooperation. Of course, mutual recognition of the legitimate standing of an opponent does not by itself constitute the realization of a security community based on mutual trust and dedicated to the resolution of conflicts solely by consensual means. If the Israeli-PLO accord has vaulted the bottom two rungs of an immature security community, there are still formidable obstacles in the way of progress up the rungs of the security ladder toward the Deutschian ideal. The signing of the September 1993 and 1995 accords does not eliminate coercive threats and violence issuing from many sources in the wake of these agreements. Assassinations, civil strife, terrorist bombings, and police and army skirmishes have continued despite these agreements. They are likely to be constant companions along the hard road leading to final resolution of the political status of the West Bank and Jerusalem and of Syria's claims to the Golan Heights.

Conflict reduction, management, and even a resolution of current differences between otherwise enduring rivals may not be enough to end a conflict once and for all. In the Middle East case just cited, new problems might emerge to replace old ones that have been shelved. The peace agreement will have to be *consolidated* in some fashion to create momentum for widening nonviolent exchanges and peaceful change and to ensure that the interests of all parties are satisfied in a final and comprehensive settlement. The political and economic institutions created by the Western European states after World War II were essentially conceived as a way to overcome hostilities, especially those between France and Germany. The European Coal and Steel Community, Euratom, and finally the EC were more than symbols of peaceful intent. They coordinated the economic interests and policies of the Western European democracies, sanctioned and supported by the United States, to create a community that would make it all but impossible for any one state to develop a national security policy to threaten its partners.

The enlargement and deepening of the EC, as chapter 8 and the concluding chapter detail, illustrate the most mature stage of cooperative behavior, resting on consent in lieu of coercion. If successful, it would *prevent* conflict through the pursuit of mutually shared notions of order, welfare, and legitimacy, common institutions, and joint decisional processes. Efforts are now trained both on deepening the cooperation that has been achieved and on widening and enlarging its scope to include other nations and peoples. If the EC finally achieves a single, integrated market, it will also have reached, ipso facto, an unprecedented level of political cooperation among its several parts. On that basis, with its own house resting on a solid economic foundation, the EC would then be in a favorable position to enlarge the scope of its political cooperation and to expand its contribution to reducing and resolving conflicts in Eastern Europe and in other parts of the globe. It is possible through a feat of imagination to visualize the resolution of such disputes as those over Kashmir or Jerusalem, but the intractability of these disputes suggests the need for a careful look at less ambitious strategies for moving these regional conflict to a less hostile stage.

Finding the Right Mix of Actors, Roles, Resources, and Strategies

Moving conflicts from their current status low on the Deutschian ladder, adopted by this volume for diagnosing conflicts, to a higher rung of enlarged and deepened consensual cooperation requires an understanding of who should be the relevant parties to the solution, their real or potential roles, the resources at their disposition, and the strategies appropriate to the targeted level of increased consensual cooperation. This will be a rich mixture specifically adapted to local needs and ills. Even for a particular region, it is not likely that a regional conflict will admit to just one solution in terms of achieving one or more of the desired levels of cooperation that have been outlined. Too many imponderables, such as the interest of warring groups to compromise their differences, and too many unknowns, such as, say, the reaction to terrorism, preclude definitive solutions. The purpose of the approach suggested here is to encourage the search for solutions along a wide front and to stimulate more precise thinking concerning what is known about the effectiveness of actors, roles, and resource and strategy mixes and to apply this knowledge in coping with regional and international conflicts.

Each actor brings to a conflict a different mix of resources, expertise, and capacity to play a wide range of real or potential roles relevant to coping purposes. These mixes and how they apply to a conflict will necessarily vary across regions. A common analytical framework that is sensitive to regional differences can be useful in identifying those actors that have assisted the processes of widening and deepening consensual cooperation. What the analyst and decision maker may learn in addressing conflict in one region may well have useful applications, after suitable adaptation, to other regions. The surmounting of French-German differences through economic cooperation suggests one approach that has been applied by rivals in other regions to dampen conflict. The South Asian Association for Regional Cooperation (SAARC) and the Association of Southeast Asian Nations (ASEAN) illustrate the search for greater political cooperation through enlarged economic exchange. Superpower arms control and confidence-building measures have also encouraged regional rivals to engage in the search for ways to regulate their armed hostilities. The agreement between India and Pakistan not to target each other's nuclear facilities illustrates the importance of arms control accords by regional rivals that can be said to have been inspired by previous superpower initiatives.

International actors can potentially bring a complex set of resources, expertise, and capabilities to the coping process that need to be identified and marshaled in ways that have escaped international consciousness and efforts until now. These may include the goodwill and reputation for "fair play" of one of the outside parties (Great Britain in the Rhodesian crisis); economic aid and technical know-how (Marshall Plan aid to Western Europe); military forces and advice (French troops backing the government of Chad against Libyan intervention); societal person-to-person contacts (the contacts between French Socialist and German Social Democratic parties with the Spanish socialist government, strengthening Spanish democratization after Franco); political sophistication in institution building (Eastern European legislators interning in Western legislatures); or a neutral ground for meetings between regional antagonists (meetings between Indian and Pakistani officials in Nepal under the auspices of private foundations). The list could be extended indefinitely. There presently exists no full inventory of these resources, current or potential; more importantly, there is no evaluation of their appropriateness to one or another regional conflict.

Almost certainly, the role played by a state, a group, or an organization will differ across regions. For example, the Japanese assumed a heightened political role in Cambodia, where they lent their "good offices" to facilitate peace negotiations, whereas they might be expected to play a greater economic role, say, in Central and Latin America. The Russian Federation conceivably can use its access to the Central Asian Republics of the former Soviet Union to conciliate rising Islamic claims for a revision of power relations in the Northern Tier, the Persian Gulf, and the Middle East. China's support for the United Nation's peacekeeping activities in Cambodia has been indispensable, since China had the decisive leverage over the Khmer Rouge to bring them, however reluctantly, to the bargaining table.

The roles played by external states and groups in the process of conflict management and resolution, however important, cannot, of course, substitute for the self-help efforts of regional antagonists, evidenced in the Israeli-PLO accords or in the abandonment of apartheid in South Africa. How to start and to sustain these efforts would be the principal object of third-party assistance. It would be helpful to explore the range of appropriate resources and strategies that states and nonstate forces could bring to bear on a conflict. No such effort has yet been tried; this volume attempts to give a jump-start to such an ambitious enterprise.

The mix of policy instruments and strategies appropriate to a region, combining roles and resources, is potentially limited only by the imagination of the informed analyst and the concerned decision maker.[27] The following chapters explore what roles major international actors might play in copying with conflict, as well as the roles, resources, and strategies on which they might rely.

NOTES

1. Roger E. Kanet and Edward A. Kolodziej, eds., *The Cold War as Cooperation: Superpower Cooperation in Regional Conflict Management* (Baltimore: Johns Hopkins University Press; London: Macmillan, 1991). Exceptions include Anton DePorte, *Europe between the Superpowers*, 2d ed. (New Haven: Yale University Press, 1986).

2. For a contrasting view, see Robert Axelrod, *The Evolution of Cooperation* (New York: Basic Books, 1984); and "World Politics Symposium on the Conceptual and Structural Determinants of Consensual Cooperation," reprinted in *Cooperation under Anarchy,* ed. Kenneth A. Oye (Princeton: Princeton University Press, 1986).

3. There exists no definitive summary listing of armed conflicts since World War II. Those cited below are based on different definitions of armed conflicts and serve varied and not fully compatible research aims. But however much they differ, they do converge on the general finding that most conflicts since World War II have been intrastate, not interstate. Compilations useful in developing this study include Kalevi J. Holsti, *Peace and War: Armed Conflict and International Order, 1648–1989* (New York: Cambridge University Press, 1991); G. D. Kaye, D. A. Grand, and E. J. Emond, *Major Armed Conflict: A Compendium of Interstate and Intrastate Conflict, 1720 to 1985,* ORAE Report R95 (Ottawa, Canada: Orbita Consultants, 1985); Istvan Kende, "Wars of Ten Years (1967–1976)," *Journal of Peace Research* 15 (1978): 227–41; Melvin Small and J. David Singer, *Resort to Arms: International and Civil War, 1816–1980* (Beverly Hills: Sage, 1982); and Herbert K. Tillema, *International Armed Conflict since 1945: A Bibliographic Handbook of Wars and Military Interventions* (Boulder, Colo.: Westview Press, 1991).

4. See Quincy Wright, *A Study of War*, 2d ed., 2 vols. (Chicago: University of Chicago Press, 1966); and Geoffrey Blainey, *The Causes of War,* 3d ed. (New York: Free Press, 1988).

5. Stanley Hoffmann perceptively outlines some of the fundamental stumbling blocks to the creation of a more peaceful and prosperous post–Cold War order in "Delusions of World Order," *New York Review of Books* 39 (Apr. 9, 1992): 37–43. For a more extensive treatment of the organizational disarray of the world society and its generation of a chronic turbulence in global politics, see James Rosenau, *Turbulence in World Politics* (Princeton: Princeton University Press, 1990). For additional analysis,

see I. William Zartman, "The Orders of Collapse," in *The Collapse of the International System,* ed. Zaki Laidi (forthcoming).

6. Current cooperation theory (see n. 2) ignores enduring conflicts and the powerful psychological and historical forces that produced and now sustain them.

7. Barry Buzan, *People, States, and Fear,* 2d ed. (Boulder, Colo.: Lynn Reinner, 1991), 175–81.

8. These systemic forces are explored with respect to France, a major arms producer and supplier, in Edward A. Kolodziej, *Making and Marketing Arms: The French Experience and Its Implications for the International System* (Princeton: Princeton University Press, 1987). See also idem, "Whither Militarization and Modernization: Implications for International Security and Arms Control," in *Peace, Defense, and Economic Analysis,* ed. Christian Schmidt and Frank Blackaby (London: Macmillan, 1987), 206–32.

9. Buzan, *People, States, and Fear,* chaps. 2–4, pp. 57–185. See also Samuel P. Huntington, Jr., on the political prerequisites of order and welfare, *Political Order in Changing Societies* (New Haven: Yale University Press, 1968).

10. Bull's focus on contractual relations between states contrasts with the concepts of community or traditional societies, based on history, blood ties, and ascription. The notion of modern society, based on mutually developed rules and norms and contractual accords between groups and individuals in creating society, is developed extensively by Ferdinand Tönnies but originates with many earlier writers, including Confucius. See Ferdinand Tönnies, *Community and Society,* trans. Charles P. Loomis (East Lansing: Michigan State University Press, 1963); and Hedley Bull, *The Anarchical Society* (London: Macmillan, 1977).

11. Bull, *Anarchical Society,* 13.

12. Ibid., 13–19.

13. Ibid., 23–199, extends the argument.

14. Carlton J. H. Hayes, *Essays on Nationalism* (New York: Macmillan, 1926).

15. The histories of all of the great powers of the modern age evidence these driving forces toward national integration. See, for example, Samuel P. Huntington's description of this process in Germany and Japan, along with citations, in *The Soldier and the State* (Cambridge, Mass.: Belknap Press, 1957), 98–119.

16. John Mueller, *Retreat from Doomsday: The Obsolescence of Major War* (New York: Basic Books, 1988).

17. Robert Gilpin develops these lines of analysis in his magisterial *The Political Economy of International Relations* (Princeton: Princeton University Press, 1987).

18. Paul Kennedy, *Preparing for the Twenty-First Century* (New York: Random House, 1993).

19. For a review of this process, see Samuel P. Huntington, *The Third Wave* (Norman: University of Oklahoma Press, 1990).

20. See Gordon S. Wood, *The Creation of the American Republic: 1776–1787* (Chapel Hill: University of North Carolina Press, 1969), on the American Revolution.

21. These themes are pursued in Robert E. Osgood and Robert W. Tucker, *Force, Order, and Justice* (Baltimore: Johns Hopkins Press, 1967); and Walter Mills, *Arms and Men: A Study of American Military History* (New York: New American Library, 1956).

22. Karl Deutsch et al., *Political Community and the North Atlantic Area* (Princeton: Princeton University Press, 1957).

23. The most widely quoted statement of this position from the perspective of contemporary international theory is Kenneth Waltz, *Theory of International Politics* (Reading, Mass.: Addison-Wesley, 1979). Hedley Bull makes a parallel argument in Bull, *Anarchical Society.*

24. Robert O. Keohane, *After Hegemony: Cooperation and Discord in the World Political Economy* (Princeton: Princeton University Press, 1984); Bull, *The Anarchical Society;* Alexander Wendt, "Anarchy Is What States Make of It," *International Organization* 46 (spring 1992): 395–421.

25. Carl von Clausewitz, *On War,* ed. and trans. Michael Howard and Peter Paret (Princeton: Princeton University Press, 1976), esp. bks. 1 and 8, pp. 75–126, 577–640.

26. Kanet and Kolodziej, *Cold War as Cooperation.*

27. In recent cases, the University of Illinois mounted a project that, among other things, listed more than seventy confidence-building and arms control measures that might be applied to the problem of nuclear proliferation in South Asia; these have been taken up by both governments in current negotiations over the Kashmir dispute. The Johns Hopkins University School of Advanced International Studies organized a National Reconciliation Workshop for the warring factions in Liberia that laid out goals and purposes for a future Liberia so that parties could focus beyond the conflict; the agenda has been carried back to Liberia for use in ongoing talks.

ONE

Nation-State Actors

Great Powers

.MURDOCK LEARNING RESOURCE CENTER

PATRICK M. MORGAN

2 The United States

In chapter 1, Edward Kolodziej describes regional conflicts as a profound concern of the world community. He offers ways of "diagnosing" such conflicts and a list of broad responses that may be employed to get them under control. This paper considers roles the United States has played and might play.

Regional conflict is meaningful only within a concept of a global system in which there can be a regional subdivision. Otherwise it is simply conflict. Envisioning a global system and regional systems can employ various perspectives. The Kolodziej approach is functionalist, specifying adequate performance of certain functions as vital for system stability. This invites a focus on resources for systemic management to ensure that the functions are performed in an effective fashion.

Concern about management has normally drawn attention to the most impressive concentrations of resources available, the great powers.[1] The rub comes in finding attractive and feasible ways to associate them with effective and acceptable management. The problem has not normally been seen as finding states willing to bear the burdens. The term *great power,* or *superpower,* has been associated with an active, directive, manipulative orientation toward the system, a desire to dominate and manage. Wanting to influence developments around the world, including regional conflicts, has been seen as an intrinsic part of being a great power.[2] The great powers are frequently depicted as having their reach exceed their grasp, testimony to their ambitions to dominate. Modelski depicts the "World Power" as inevitably experiencing a growing gap between its capabilities and its responsibilities; Paul Kennedy cites "imperial overstretch" as a characteristic problem.[3]

Another assumption has been that great powers manage the world, when they can, in an imperial fashion, pursuing their interests at the expense of others. Many governments saw the Cold War as producing altogether too much superpower "management" of regional conflicts. Much of international politics, in the traditional view, turns on *avoiding management* of this sort.

The expectation that great powers will act selfishly and that management by one will be resisted by the others, leading to conflict and violence, has often led to considering great powers as the prime *targets,* rather than the proper purveyors, of any systemic management. Controlling them becomes the key to peace, for instance, or to reductions in global inequalities. This leaves great powers as at once the most plausible and the most improper source of management.

Given this view, sustained and effective management, even for functions vital for stability of the system, is unlikely. Explaining how it sometimes occurs or might occur is a major task.[4] Effective management can hardly be undertaken without the consent and participation of the great powers, but how can the concerns about their motives be assuaged?

This brings us to the role of the United States. Its distinctive potential contributions derive from its superpower status. Kolodziej identifies six levels of cooperation for coping with regional conflicts, and in most the special contribution the United States can offer is directly related to its unique resources. For instance, effective *crisis management* normally requires the capacity either to apply great pressure on the antagonists or to pose as a disinterested but legitimately concerned party. (What gives the U.N. Security Council its impact, when operating properly, is that it combines the two.) The United States is certainly experienced in and equipped for crisis management, but not uniquely so. What is unusual is its ability to apply pressure either unilaterally or with others with military forces that, in conflicts against some antagonists, are unmatched for the purpose. It also has the finest intelligence resources for fast-breaking conflicts.[5]

The same is true of *routinization and containment,* Kolodziej's second category. The United States has much experience with this around the world. But its capabilities permit a distinctive contribution. It is particularly experienced in discouraging destabilizing military postures among antagonists and designing steps away from them. The United States has given more thoughtful attention than anyone to these matters via nuclear deterrence and the pursuit of arms control. In addition, routinization and containment sometimes involve intervention beyond the capacity of international organizations or smaller states. Then it is best carried out by one or more great powers, and the United States can play a dominant role here if it wants.

With regard to *conflict reduction* and *resolution,* the United States is deeply committed to these pursuits and quite willing to take the lead or participate in other ways. Apart from its experience — the Camp David accords, the Angola-Namibia agreements, and so forth — and its relatively atypical belief that many conflicts can be resolved, it is difficult to see what is distinctive about its potential contribution, with one exception. Where significant side payments or special services to the parties can contribute to reaching a settlement, the United States has advantages. A good example is the U.S.-operated early warning stations in the Sinai, which made its reversion to Egypt acceptable to Israel.

Institutionalized reconciliation and *conflict prevention* seem to depend primarily on the parties that are directly or potentially in conflict. However, where U.S. military commitments contribute to regional stability, the United States can maintain them to facilitate reconciliation and prevention, a role again derived from its superpower stature, and one widely endorsed today.

However, we must recall the fears about great-power management. The most important contribution the United States can make today is to ease fears of great-power domination. Any realistic possibility that global management of regional conflict can be perceived now as relatively benign results largely from the image of the United States. This image is such that there is no widespread desire either to do without such management or to treat the great powers as its targets. It is widely believed that the United States is not bent on imperialism and that its management will be shaped accordingly, giving it something of the stature of an "honest broker." Since other great powers, except China, are associated with the United States or are attempting to be so, world attitudes are unusually acceptant. To an unusual extent, there is a surplus of demand for great-power management rather than a desire to evade it.

If great-power rivalry can be avoided, particularly in regional conflicts, and if the great powers' behavior credibly conveys an image of representing the common good, then prospects for dampening or resolving regional conflicts are enhanced. This does not seem possible unless the United States retains its favorable image and the confidence of others that it is willing to tackle those conflicts.

This will require sensitivity to others' fears. The United States is not a burgeoning hegemon, but that is not how it always looks in Beijing or Paris. Russian conservatives see Washington dictating to Moscow. Asian and African regimes resent preaching on human rights and worry about U.S. intentions. The United States is more acceptable than other great powers, but it is not a leader by acclamation.

▲ The U.S. Conception of World Order

The United States is emerging from an era of *managerial internationalism* on a *global* scale. For years it perceived regional conflicts as crucial. They were approached from a domino-theory perspective: without U.S. involvement, many states would bandwagon with the enemy.[6] This perspective was reinforced by viewing commitments as highly interdependent, so that a commitment in one conflict was deemed crucial to the credibility of others.[7] While allies were important, the United States viewed itself as indispensable to order and management and viewed its alliances as blending lesser forces with superior U.S. resources and leadership. The nation had not only the will and resources but, it was said, an obligation to play this role. Hence the United States "repeatedly sent troops and resources overseas for the purpose of resisting aggression, even in situations where the probability of an attack was remote and where the states they were defending did not always see fit to contribute proportionately to their own defense."[8]

The same was true for *welfare*. Management was undertaken globally, with many regions deemed economically vital either directly or for demonstrating the superiority of free enterprise. The United States saw itself as an indispensable source of welfare, through aid, trade, investment, and international financial management, and felt obligated to provide it.

Regarding *democratization,* the self-perception was equally global, if somewhat less managerial. Washington pressed democratization on Europe and Japan and attempted this elsewhere. But it frequently was willing to actively support undemocratic systems useful in the Cold War and unwilling to accept largely democratic systems that appeared useful to the other side, as in Chile.

The United States has been consistent in its conception of what international politics should be, a conception associated squarely with the approaches to order, welfare, and legitimacy (OWL) that Kolodziej identifies as dominant—the nation-state, an interdependent international economic system, and democracy. In this sense, quite apart from its extraordinary resources and responsibilities, the United States is at the heart of international politics. It espoused these solutions years ago and has seen their influence rise precipitously as the century closes.

It has consistently upheld the concept of sovereignty and has never been associated with the idea of a world government. President Bush coupled references to a new world order with assertions that this was not meant to eliminate sovereignty. This concern shaped U.S. designs for both the League of Nations and the United Nations, yesterday's new world orders.

However, the United States accepts departures from this. National self-determination is one approach to sovereignty, but the United States does not support dissolution of existing states for that purpose.[9] It did not officially advocate this for the Soviet Union and was reluctant to endorse the breakup of Yugoslavia. It did not support Biafra or Bangladesh. It has done nothing to encourage Quebec separatists and was never a champion of dividing Cyprus. Thus the sovereignty it supports is associated with existing states. In one region only, precisely to contain regional conflict, did it accept and sponsor a retreat from sovereignty. It was an early advocate of European integration and has endorsed every advance of the European Union (EU) as the way to put aside the destructive wars of Europe's past.

Thus the U.S. version of a proper international system consists of sovereign states not regularly subject to intense separatist pressures, with sovereignty cherished but with due regard for the need to submerge traditional rivalries within the EU. Added is a liberalist insistence that there are no inevitable conflicts among nations that must lead to war, plus a belief in economic development and democracy as the best ways to lessen internal conflicts. Conflict and war are not "natural" adjuncts of sovereignty in this view.[10]

The United States has long endorsed the idea that states can effectively abandon war: a league could exist in which members promised not to make war (the League of Nations), states could renounce war among themselves (the Kellogg-Briand Pact), and states can set up a regional system in which war is unthinkable, like the Conference on Security and Cooperation in Europe (CSCE). However, this endorsement has been combined with enough concern about states' behavior to maintain various forms of insurance. In 1945 this meant arranging a Security Council to preserve peace and the U.N. Charter provision for regional self-defense as well. Currently, it includes retaining NATO and maintaining significant U.S. forces. Presidents wish for harmony but know it is not just around the corner.

With respect to *welfare*, the United States is the champion of global free enterprise with minimal national restrictions on flows of goods, capital, technology, and, within limits, people. While not immune to protectionism, it opposes this abroad and has resisted it at home.[11] It dislikes trade preferences for developing countries and has had stiff disputes with Asian neomercantilist systems. It has pressured the EU not to construct a closed economic space. Again, Washington was willing to countenance exceptions during the Cold War. It pressed for stronger barriers to trade and investment with the East than its allies wished. It accepted departures from free trade and related policies among its allies to help cement its anticommunist coalition. It helped create oligopolistic management of global oil resources. However, while it preserved some politically sensitive aspects of its economy from foreign competition, it also used access to its economy as an instrument to gain cooperation from others and urged them to follow suit.

While not always comfortable with interdependence, the United States remains certain that a global capitalist system will maximize everyone's welfare and do much to contain or eliminate conflict. Great inequalities are not inevitable under a liberal economic order, and the way to eliminate them is to further liberalize national economic practices. This has meant a marked retreat, starting in the 1970s, on foreign aid. U.S. assistance today is minimally aimed at development and continues to shrink as a percentage of the gross national product. This also meant opposition to the New International Economic Order pressed by developing countries.

Finally, with respect to *legitimacy,* the U.S. commitment to democracy as the only sound basis for political stability has survived numerous departures from it in the name of national security and now appears stronger than ever.[12] It is nourished today by the view that democracies are very unlikely to fight each other, so that spreading democracy enhances peace.[13] Left unexamined is the possibility of ethnic fragmentation in many states, with violent conflicts driven by popular nationalisms expressed through democratic institutions— common enough in the nineteenth century and disturbingly present today. The democracy the United States has in mind remains rooted in political structures that reflect the popular will, as opposed to the notion that important human rights can be pursued via many political structures. Thus, targets of U.S. pressure are primarily violations of political rights. Social justice is something democracy can be counted on to bring about and is not to be pursued at the expense of political freedoms.

The argument to this point can be summarized as follows. The United States is clearly committed to OWL and has much experience in conflict management, including efforts to deal with regional conflicts. Its major contribution now would be to remain a dominant but relatively nonthreatening state, allowing it to lead in generating a global management, primarily collective, on regional conflicts.

But how much leading should it do? The current debate in foreign policy is not about what to stand for—on that there is consensus—but about when and how (and how far) to actively promote U.S. preferences. The spectrum of opinion is roughly as follows. The minimalist view, often called *neoisolationism,* reflects classic conservative and leftist views that were earlier swamped by the Cold War and have now come to life.[14] Conservatives who feared that foreign involvements would create an overly extractive and intrusive government pursuing objectives that were unrealistic adopted instead a globalist anticommunism that spawned military interventions, heavy defense spending, and security-related encroachments on citizens' lives.[15] For the Left, containment was just a rationalization for militarism, the support of reactionary regimes, witch hunts against leftists, subsidies for business at the expense of social justice, and protection of foreign investments in the name of the national interest.

Now conservatives endorse "putting America first" by defining the national interest narrowly and by minimizing foreign obligations, burdens, and activities. For the Left, the recipe is much the same: eliminate foreign bases, eschew military interventions, slash defense spending. Why? From both perspectives the domestic situation deserves more resources (via lower taxes or funding for social programs), little that happens in the rest of the world can seriously harm the United States, and the United States cannot realistically do much to give people elsewhere freedom, safety, and prosperity. According to conservatives, multilateral endeavors will not work—they are inept and often corrupted by the nature of the member states—while U.S. friends and allies are mainly free riders rather than real supporters. For many on the Left, however, multilateral endeavors hold the promise of more global management so that burdens on the United States can be much reduced.[16]

Deriving from traditional realist perspectives, the *neorealists* are mostly moderate to liberal Republicans and conservative Democrats.[17] The neorealist view rests on skepticism about how much the United States can do abroad combined with a perception of numerous actual and potential threats. U.S. interests and responsibilities around the world are seen as substantial, as well as threatened, requiring U.S. engagement and leadership. The nation must maintain much of its political, economic, and military strength in order, some say, to retain its dominance or, others say, to sustain a proper balance globally and in key regions. But this power must be used in a hardheaded fashion, by appreciating its limits and not taking the pursuit of U.S. objectives, especially democracy or welfare, to foolish lengths.

The central liberal position, often labeled *neoliberal internationalism,* includes people who earlier defected from Cold War internationalism because of Vietnam plus classic supporters of détente, arms control, increased East-West trade, and a liberal international economic order.[18] They see the United States as having a good deal of power, so that well mounted efforts by the United States, and especially in conjunction with others, can significantly enhance democracy, welfare, and security elsewhere. This is deemed the crux of the national interest. Thus the stakes are very high, and this calls for a determined U.S. effort at global and regional management. Conflict among and within nations is not inevitable, and the world is not intractable; progress can be made. For much that needs doing the traditional elements of national power may be of limited utility, but when they are relevant they should be used—in interventions, blockades, sanctions. Finally, multilateral action is to be greatly preferred, not only in order to share costs and make intervention an easier sell domestically but because multilateral action is in itself an important contribution to the building of the regional and global community, which is the ultimate U.S. foreign policy objective.

▲ The United States and Global Management

How can these differing views be translated into action? The United States seems to have arrived at a working compromise. A neoliberal rhetorical posture is being combined with a neorealist concern about national capabilities, while both are augmented by a neoisolationist response to any regional situation that seems likely to involve a costly and difficult intervention. This fits the U.S. response to Bosnia, the eventual response to Somalia, much of the response to Haiti, and the Clinton decision on China and human rights.

How might this compromise fit into an overall strategy? There are at least three patterns within which the U.S. might define its role in detail, three fundamental orientations to the problem of order. Some are more congenial for the Kolodziej framework than others, and all have been given serious consideration recently.

Regional Power Balancing

Regional power balancing deals with regional conflict by attempting to manipulate it in order to contain threats to the United States and global stability. This is not Kolodziej's "routinization and containment," that is, efforts by external actors to ease or eliminate conflicts because they are unfortunate and unwelcome. Power balancing assumes that regional conflicts are often unavoidable, harmful only under certain circumstances, and best kept contained. They might even be encouraged; attempting to resolve them could even be counterproductive.

This strategy fosters or helps sustain competitive regional power distributions. It curbs the participants and their conflicts and may also help maximize U.S. influence, just like Britain's fostering of power balances on the continent was meant to preserve its influence as well as preclude direct threats.

One argument for this approach is that the world is becoming multipolar, which will lead to more balancing behavior by major states, including interventions in the Third World to sustain spheres of influence.[19] Another is that it is the way to get the most out of U.S. resources while trimming obligations.[20] Thus it can appeal to both conservatives and neorealists.

Power balancing was important in the original (Kennan) approach to containment and was often employed during the Cold War. The best recent example is the Iran-Iraq War. The United States hoped neither side would win and maneuvered to ensure a stalemate in order to maintain the regional balance. The United States currently sees itself as the key to a balance in Asia that maintains order and stability; without its military presence and commitments there would be greater insecurity and greater chances of war.[21] Notice the range of possibilities in power balancing. The Iran-Iraq War involved maneuvering to keep states at odds, with limited direct intervention. In Asia, by contrast, the United States is allegedly the key to the regional balance.

These examples also illustrate possible objectives. In the first, the United States was not trying to stop the war, but just keep it in hand. In the second, the United States is involved directly in a region so that others will find it rewarding to mute conflicts rather than pressing them to extremes. The first is not compatible with the Kolodziej framework; the second is much more so. For instance, the United States is now using its leverage to urge a more multilateralist security environment in Asia.[22]

There are drawbacks to manipulating regional balances. This strategy is best suited to an aggressively hegemonic state that prizes dominance and wants to preclude challenges, enough to devote the resources and interventions such a strategy can involve. However, "Americans have no interest in conquering the world and little interest in running it."[23] The United States is not now aggressively hegemonic and is unlikely to become so in the absence of a grave threat.[24] It is now in deliberate retreat from its superpower status and residual hegemonic inclinations, the Gulf War notwithstanding. It will not *unilaterally* impose OWL on troubled regions even when it has the capacity to try, and its capacity for trying in many places is now declining.

It will skirt hegemonic tendencies and not rigorously pursue power balancing in various regions, because they cannot command public support. This extends beyond a reluctance to have U.S. forces under fire. The government cannot consistently convince citizens to ignore the domestic complexion of a foreign government for regional power-balancing purposes.[25] This was hard when the Cold War supplied a justification; now it will be nearly impossible. When the Bush administration, after the Iran-Iraq War, continued tilting toward Iraq, it had to hide this. In the Gulf War, the decision not to seize Baghdad was meant to keep the regional balance in kilter, but permitting Saddam Hussein to survive has had little public support.

The problem with directly participating in a regional balance is evident in Asia. Many governments there want U.S. forces to remain lest they fall to quarreling. This means protecting U.S. friends from each other and spending more on defense so the friends will not. Both are difficult to justify at home, and rightly so. If Japan boosts its forces, how does the United States "balance" its ally? If China and Vietnam fall to fighting again, what role does the "balancer" play? The role is hollow for a government little inclined to realpolitik, and this will be apparent if Asia heats up again.

Finally, this approach too readily lends itself not to the Kolodziej conception but to its antithesis. Observers who care about regional conflicts for the reasons he suggests will urge intervention in many more cases and in far different ways than power balancing requires. Instead, power balancing would be used precisely so interventions need not be undertaken, with regional conflicts often allowed to fester and even grow worse.

Collective Great-Power Management

Another approach would have the United States in league with other major states in a concert. Numerous analysts feel that a great-power concert is the most plausible route to international security[26] and often cite regional conflict management as one objective. They can hardly cite anything else. A concert occurs only if the great powers have no conflicts that preclude collaboration; it cannot resolve fundamental rivalries among them. This leaves regional conflicts, among or within lesser states, as the primary target.

A concert has the appeal of oligopoly in a market.[27] Conflict and rivalry impose great burdens on states. At times, particularly after a very costly war, leading states may agree on a collective management that not only meets their needs but finds support among weaker states—everyone expects to benefit from a stable and ordered environment. The assumption is that leading states are eager to operate the system and that the concert merely gives this a collective form.

Many view the United States as the suitable leader of any concert. It has more prestige and stature as a leader, and fewer liabilities, than Japan, Germany, or Russia. It has more resources more suitably arranged, especially in flexible power-projection capability. It has unmatched experience in thinking and acting regionally on the basis of global considerations. There is also appreciation at home and abroad that the United States will not or cannot simply act on its own in most cases. This is reassuring to other major states, offering them continuing influence in system management, even a veto, due to the pragmatic necessities of the politics involved.[28] Perhaps the major role the United States can play, therefore, is to lead a great-power concert as the global community's ultimate resource for coping with regional conflict.

We should be clear about what is necessary. The great contribution of a concert would be to act when *costly, even forceful, intervention* is needed. A lesser degree of management via U.N. resolutions, nonrecognition, limits on trade, curtailed arms transfers, international aid efforts, and the like, is already available but often of marginal utility.

Despite its appeal, there are serious difficulties with such a concert. The notion that collective management cannot persist is a cornerstone of the international relations field. Barriers to it are traced to the anarchy of the system, the natural incompatibility of the great powers, or the selfish conceptions of their interests, which they inevitably pursue.

Thus, a possible constraint on a concert is that the members will not get along. We cannot be certain Russia will remain a congenial partner. A most unsuitable regime might yet emerge there. China is an awkward member of the club. Being unlike the others politically, it is wary of the uses to which management might be put, is often disinclined to cooperate, and is now the only member engaged in a military buildup. Thus, it is possible that the members will soon fall out. The Bush administration struggled to sustain good relations with Beijing precisely to gain its cooperation on many problems but faced heavy domestic pressure against this, as has the Clinton administration.

A way to avoid regarding such conflicts as inevitable is to postulate a liberalist, not realist, relationship among the great powers. This view is encouraged by the triumph of the democracies in the Cold War and their strong inhibitions on making war against each other. "In light of the very different behavior of liberal democracies towards each other, it is clear that the realist or realpolitik model of international relations is in serious need of reexamination."[29] If the great powers (nearly) all become liberal democracies, then their conflicts should be muted. Cooperation would be promoted by mutual interest and a growing sense of community. Thus, it should be possible to get joint military action on regional conflicts in the short run and cooperation to foster welfare and democratization as solutions for the long run, with the United States as the logical leader.[30]

Can we expect high-powered management by a concert of great-power democracies? Actually, this is probably not feasible. The first problem is that liberal democracies are not typical great powers. This is one implication of the fact that they do not go to war with each other. They do not naturally seek active domination of the international system and will not readily take opportunities to dominate, even collectively, under normal circumstances. When it comes to security management, a number of things suggest this is the case. The United States long resisted the burdens of great-power status, and there is evidence that the Soviet threat had to be deliberately overblown to get it to accept them after 1945. In the 1930s, rather than pay the price of confronting Hitler in typical great-power fashion, Britain and France pursued appeasement. After the war former great powers, some of which were new democracies, consistently lacked domestic support for the burdens of retaining or regaining that status. They had to give up global reach capabilities. They could not contribute to their defense on a scale commensurate with their resources. They objected to supporting the United States in costly ways in conflicts around the globe. In the West today there is even less interest in many facets of traditional great-power behavior, while in a more democratic Russia there is a retreat from globalist aspirations.

Such behavior has long been explained by references to something other than democracy. There is the "free rider" tendency of states in alliances or under hegemony. There is the legacy of the past for Germany and Japan that causes self-imposed limitations on their foreign policies. There was U.S. isolationism in the 1930s and the Vietnam Syndrome in the 1980s. There was the weakness of the British and French economies after 1945, and there is the collapse of the Soviet-Russian economy now. And so on.

These factors are not irrelevant. But it is more suitable to stress the onerous difficulties of sustaining a consensus in a democracy for interventions that are costly, get citizens killed, and seem unlikely to be effective because regional conflicts are usually deep-seated, endlessly complex, and highly emotional. Officials know that an intervention that drags on, with significant costs and casualties, and is hard to sustain with a clear sense of direction will soon forfeit public support. And not just due to the costs. There is also distaste in democracies for the means associated with normal great-power behavior.

The second problem is a disjuncture between the natural order of a liberalist view of the world and the envisioned imposition of order via a concert. In the liberalist view, the emphasis in achieving peace and order is not on directive management but on securing the better conduct of states. The idea is that democracy can alter how states behave, so that the need for enforcement is minimal. Better regimes mean peaceable states, and peaceable states can eliminate the security dilemma among themselves.

The problem is that this provides for peace among democracies but not for intervention to curb conflicts elsewhere. Thus, vigorous enforcement of OWL by a concert is incompatible with the restraint democratic states display, with what they normally accept as suitable ways to pursue the national interest. It clashes with their reluctance to use force on a large scale or to do other costly things unless the necessity is formidable.

What if the great powers have no major conflicts among themselves, co-operate on many matters, and regard regional conflicts as unfortunate or harmful but display a collective unwillingness to bear serious burdens in regional conflict management? And what if this is due to their being democratic, with citizens and elites that, given half a chance, will not support military interventions, big aid programs, costly economic sanctions, and the other serious tools for grappling with regional conflicts? This means that if a costly intervention was needed to control a nasty conflict, an effective great-power concert of liberal democracies would be almost a contradiction in terms.

The ideal approach to regional security among democracies is a pluralistic security community within which the uses of force is unacceptable and inconceivable. That makes protection of everyone from attack within the community unnecessary; a good thing, too, because it would be difficult for the members, as democracies, to rouse domestic support for costly responses to misbehavior.

Consider the West's reaction to the crisis in the Balkans. Europeans, in the CSCE framework, are trying to construct a pluralistic security community that embraces the continent. Hence there is no institutional arrangement for a collective response to the use of force. The Serbs, then others, systematically violated the understandings on which the security community rests. And the reluctance of the democracies to adopt a costly response—with success quite uncertain—was palpable.

We know almost nothing about how such a community "should" react to conflicts in the *outside* world, but the available evidence is not encouraging. Even during the Cold War Europeans showed little interest in "out-of-area" problems and preferred to narrowly define the circumstances that required a strong, and costly, intervention elsewhere. Why should a pluralistic security community encompassing the great powers behave differently?

In a concert of democracies, the less glaring the impact of a conflict on their citizens, the less likely their direct intervention. The more vicious and intractable the conflict, the less likely their intervention. And in an intervention a significant rise in costs, especially casualties, sharply increases the chances of its termination. One thinks of Lebanon, where a modest Western intervention collapsed with the first fatalities.

The only obvious way for these limitations to be overcome is for the United States to serve as the activist leader of the concert, around which the others can coalesce in ways that suspend their inhibitions. The clear example is the intervention against Iraq. If the United States will not lead with vigor, other candidates for the role are unlikely to emerge. Many commentators endorse just this solution to the problem of order today.

However, the domestic situation in the United States is incompatible with leadership of this sort. U.S. reservations cannot, for once, be ascribed to an election year. The national malaise is overwhelming and has been building for years. One component is the belief that the nation must concentrate on domestic problems, that foreign burdens must be reduced or ignored.[31] With no consensus on how to fix things at home, on which sacrifices to make, further pruning of the resources for foreign affairs is unavoidable to secure some fiscal purchase on domestic problems.

Little of this is classic isolationism. Polls show strong support of "good" causes abroad, of the United Nations and a strong national defense, of NATO and keeping U.S. troops in Europe.[32] Even so, the public only marginally endorsed opening the war with Iraq, and congressional approval was a close thing. Support for war was quite limited even in the upper echelons of the administration. Today there is far less support for intervention in a disastrous domestic situation—Yugoslavia—that has many parallels elsewhere.[33] (The thirty-four violent conflicts in the world in 1993 were internal wars.)[34] The rules for participation in multilateral interventions adopted by the Clinton administration will make vigorous intervention very difficult to contemplate in most instances.

In short, the United States is in no mood to lead, and its leadership seems vital for an effective concert. The absence of a consensus for active intervention within the democracies, coupled with a lack of vigorous leadership, seems likely to mean a collective paralysis. But is this just temporary, and can we be more optimistic about the future? At least two grounds for pessimism can be cited. It is hard to anticipate fixing the problems at home soon. If this means little U.S. leadership, then regional conflicts will receive scant attention. The second is that there is little evidence that the United States will behave differently when its domestic house is in order, absent an overwhelming threat. Democratic states, the United States included, are likely to settle for a system in which they need not immerse themselves in the quarrels among obscure peoples and lesser states. In the past we ascribed the paralysis of collective institutions to great-power political conflicts or the impact of anarchy. Now we have to cite the democratic character of key states.

To this point we have considered management that might involve a substantial military reaction to conflicts. However, a highlight of the Kolodziej framework is its emphasis on the roots of regional conflicts in inadequate welfare. The assumption is that a regional system cannot be stable if mass demands for More Now are not addressed. This calls attention to a long-running example of great-power management, the concert in charge of international trade and finance though the Group of Seven (G-7), the World Bank, the International Monetary Fund (IMF), and the General Agreement on Tariffs and Trade (GATT). Four generalizations appear appropriate. First, management has indeed involved readiness to penetrate deeply into national economies. The structural realignments demanded by the World Bank and IMF as the price for their assistance, with bilateral aid and private investment usually predicated on the clients' acquiescence, are potent examples of concert management at the expense of national sovereignty. Second, the amount of management in recent years has been limited when the costs and burdens involved have risen. There has been much cost avoidance and wrangling over burden sharing.

Third, management in later years has consistently been conducted to minimize burdens on the leading states, paralleling their reluctance to bear heavy costs for security management. The requirements set for clients are clearly considered alternatives to massive assistance via direct aid, trade concessions, and the like. This has shifted much of the burden of resolving the debt crisis, insufficient trade balances, and general underdevelopment to the weak.

Fourth, there is little evidence of highly beneficial effects. The past two decades brought terrific declines in Third World living standards and an outflow of resources from the poor to the rich. A few countries have done well, and there have been more reasons for the failures than concert management, but the reverse flow of economic resources between North and South is impossible to justify in a Kolodziej framework.

And the role of the United States? There is little doubt that it has been largely responsible for these policies and practices. It has resisted calls for cancellation of Third World debt, cut foreign aid, cut its contributions to international aid agencies, and so forth. Its primary recipe for dealing with the world's welfare problems is a more open and competitive international economy.

The record of great-power collaboration to deal with problems in Eastern Europe is a case in point. Here the United States has deferred to others, officially the EU, when it came to leadership. Economic advice has followed familiar lines: privatize, hold the line on government spending, permit bankruptcies and throw people out of work, decartelize, and so forth, no matter how painful and politically unrealistic such policies are. Intervention in the form of financial flows has been notable, particularly the German contributions, but well short of Marshall Plan dimensions and is now faltering. The EU has been very sparing in trade concessions on Eastern European products. The restrained U.S. contribution is an accurate reflection of public sentiment, which supports some assistance and trade concessions but not a large direct aid program. Conspicuously absent is support for costly new economic initiatives abroad, even ones manifestly relevant to national, regional, and global security.[35]

Finally, we can consider concert management in terms of legitimacy, on democratization. This is where the great powers have had the least experience in collective intervention. However, there has been a general escalation in ambitions recently. Human rights advocates in the United States and other democracies have harassed policymakers on Iraq, Yugoslavia, and Haiti, pressing for intervention to punish and remove offensive regimes. What have been the results?

An important example is Iraq. The Security Council has taken unprecedented steps to cripple that government's domestic repression, with limited success. Washington has been in the forefront, supporting the Kurds and trying to bolster the Shiites. This is largely a great-power concert approach within the context of the United Nations, and it has been carried to the brink of ignoring national sovereignty.

However, the unwillingness of the great powers, including the United States, to go further and militarily oust a highly undemocratic regime has also been displayed. The Security Council acted as it did not because of the domestic situation in Iraq but because of the Iraqi government's highly dangerous ambitions and desire for weapons of mass destruction. The expressed concern for human rights was partially a rationalization. No general principle of intervention for human rights has been established. We do not yet have an instance of the sort proposed back in the worst days of the Khmer Rouge, the outright ouster of an unacceptable regime. The old Concert of Europe was willing to undertake such a task or to acquiesce in its being done by one of its members, so it is not impossible, but such a willingness does not exist now and I know of no proposal by the great powers to return to it.

To many contemporary critics anything less is morally disgraceful. But such pressure can keep the great powers from going as far as they did in Iraq and make even lesser interventions more unlikely. Why get into such situations, officials may feel, if there is never enough support for the costly steps to eliminate offensive regimes but failure to go that far evokes condemnation for doing too little?

Robert Art suggests that the United States undertake interventions to support democracy only when the target nation is small and weak, its population is supportive, the costs are low, and the probability of success is high. This is how all the democracies will likely behave, and the instances where these conditions are met will be few.[36]

The United States and Broader Collective Management

The United States has done much to foster multilateralism in the second half of this century. Multilateralism can simply mean employment of groups of nations, usually through international organizations, to address common problems. However, it is better to think of a continuum of multilateral endeavors running from a periodic coordination of states' policies to the elaborate interdependence that grew up in the West during the Cold War.[37]

In the West, as the United States led the way, participants came to see themselves as a community with shared values and purposes, eventually with comparable political systems. They operated on the basis of expectations of diffuse reciprocity, so decisions did not require repeated quid pro quo negotiation. This made it possible for nations that remained sovereign to coordinate policies in an unusually intimate way. The result was an alliance far beyond the traditional marriage of convenience, as well as a degree of interplay on political, economic, intellectual, and other matters that both reflected and strengthened the community. Such an arrangement cannot operate entirely on the basis of a hegemonic structure or a concert, though those elements were initially present. The consensus must extend to all the members.

The United States might proceed on this basis in regional conflicts today. A weaker, more hegemonic multilateralism developed earlier in the Organization of American States (OAS) might now be operated in order to enhance the weight of Latin members. The United Nations might be used in a way that downplayed the great-power concert in the Security Council by broadening the council or making more use of the General Assembly. The United States now seeks multilateralism in East Asian security, and this might be expanded in the future. Success in the Middle East negotiations will probably be linked to multilateral security arrangements.

Washington has participated recently in several multilateral efforts to ameliorate conflicts, for example, the use of the United Nations to broker agreements to end the fighting between Iran and Iraq and in Afghanistan or the ambitious incursion in Kampuchea. The settlements on Namibia and, tenuously, in Angola were of a different sort in that the United Nations had a role but the United States was the dominant party. These examples, where multilateralism legitimizes a great power's crafting of the outcome, show the United States involved in multilateral conflict management in a variety of patterns. The United States is now far more inclined to proceed in this fashion or via a great-power concert than unilaterally. It has gone so far as to accept, in principle, its forces serving under an international command.

As with the earlier patterns, we must ask how effective this one is likely to be. Full-blown multilateralism U.S.-style is not easily developed and cannot easily be extended. This is the difficulty in trying now to align Eastern Europe and Russia with the West. Thus, it is an unlikely model for the U.S. role in regional conflicts elsewhere.

Lesser efforts seem more promising, and the United States is well equipped to take part. These would eschew highly expensive and dangerous interventions and thus need not arouse the concerns discussed earlier. (Unfortunately, they normally are not useful in situations requiring a large response.) Washington has had vast experience in international institutions, and there is strong public support for participation in these efforts.

The constraint in limited multilateralism will often be felt when the United States tries to secure the necessary international consensus. The United States has unmatched experience in international consensus building. Yet its achievements are matched by a long string of so-so successes and outright failures. And the global system is now more fragmented than ever, with even more members.

Management Forced By Events?

Pessimism about future collective management is unwarranted if the United States can be compelled to lead or at least lend strong support.[38] It could be driven to do so by intolerable contingencies, and several possibilities come to mind.[39] The first is that the war with Iraq signals that outright, blatant aggression in various regions will provoke a direct U.S. and collective response — Bush's New World Order. This is unlikely but not impossible. Open interstate wars are becoming rarer, perhaps meaning that an international norm against them is building. If so, other invasions might be treated by Washington and others as equally intolerable.

Another intolerable contingency might be proliferation of nuclear and other weapons of mass destruction, especially when married to delivery systems that provide greater range and potential for surprise attack. In a curious way, this is considered a global problem, not a "regional" one, even though the search for a nuclear capability is the result of regional conflicts. This makes it more difficult for the United States to dismiss proliferation as someone else's responsibility.

Related examples include large transfers of sensitive conventional weapons or the fear that dangerous technologies could fall into the hands of terrorists. The confrontation with Iraq raised all these concerns simultaneously, which is one reason why a coalition could be mobilized so quickly and maintained so long. However, these reasons are unlikely to ever be as compelling as nuclear proliferation. They have not been treated as such in the past.

The United States is a leading proponent of international management to deal with nuclear proliferation. Cold War considerations often watered down its commitment—the Pakistan case, for example—but now these have disappeared. However, the vigor in the U.S. position was due in large part to forceful prodding by Congress. The concern has not been as strong on the part of other governments, and the potential suppliers of the relevant technologies are multiplying. Officials often fear that a tough stance will bring loss of leverage rather than good results, particularly in conventional arms transfers. Hence the Bush administration surreptitiously armed Iraq after the Iran-Iraq War, resisted congressional pressure for sanctions against China for arms transfers, and ultimately approved a major arms sale to Taiwan. Britain joined in the hidden arms sales to Iraq, the German record on sensitive arms or technology transfers is deplorable, and the French have an intense arms sales program. Bringing Russia, with its current financial problems, into a strict regime on arms transfers seems improbable at this time.

Thus, effective management of this aspect of regional conflict seems implausible. The end of the Cold War encouraged management, but this is more than offset by the increased surpluses in great-power arsenals available for sale, the reduced credibility of great-power alliances with regional actors that have big security problems, and the diminished likelihood of great-power intervention to contain regional conflicts due to a reduced fear of escalation.

Still, management may just be an innovation awaiting a suitable disaster. Down the road may lurk a rude shock that will propel the United States into management. A striking feature of the situations in Iraq and Somalia has been the chorus of calls, mainly on Op-Ed pages, for formidable global intervention capabilities.[40] There has been a marked increase in proposals by Americans for a true U.N. military capability, either a permanent force or designated national units on standby. The unease evoked by Iraq's progress toward nuclear weapons and the longstanding concern in Congress about proliferation suggest the possibility of broader public support for reacting to regional conflicts than the earlier discussion suggests. Americans have been lambasting Europeans for inaction on Bosnia and suggesting that the United States should contribute forces for an intervention. Many have proposed shaping U.S. force reductions in order to retain the capability for such interventions.[41] That potent combination of idealism and pragmatism, which treats many features of the human condition as problems to be solved, not tolerated, is still with us. It is flourishing now in much of the rhetoric about the world's trouble spots. The question is whether it is sustainable in the face of the potentially large costs and painful burdens of a serious intervention in a place like Bosnia.

Rising interdependence offers a second category of intolerable contingencies that might provoke U.S.-fostered management: economic or ecological disasters. The Kolodziej approach suggests that interdependence can have this effect because of both positive and negative factors. Without greater management, interdependence means that standard, highly desirable interactions become excessively costly, difficult, and unreliable, and undesirable developments in any one place have nasty consequences everywhere else. On the positive side, interdependence breeds mutual interests in security, welfare, and the like that impel greater management.[42]

However, interdependence will probably have an uneven impact in this regard. As a general rule it not only affects great states less than smaller ones but it tends to redistribute power and influence in their favor. Contrary to earlier expectations, the interdependence of the Organization of Petroleum Exporting Countries (OPEC) and the West has not enhanced the former's leverage; rather, the reverse has been true. Rising interdependence can have quite mixed results in terms of management. The Third World debt crisis moved the great powers to do "something" lest it erode the international financial system; it did little to get them to address Third World impoverishment. This mirrored the overall shift in the global economic system in the 1980s: a prior decade of rising interdependence that promised to enhance Third World bargaining power produced a Third World economic collapse amid minimal multilateral management to prevent it.

There are, once again, potentially offsetting contingencies, and they may have a particularly large impact on the United States. It supports international arrangements that maximize economic interactions. Its academics are leading proponents of the inevitability of interdependence and its virtues. Its citizens, if not always its government, are among the foremost supporters of global approaches to environmental problems. Added to this is the immense power of the media. A standard response to proposals that the United States exploit, OPEC-style, its dominant position in world food production is that this would be impossible because shortages abroad would mean that viewers would see foreigners starving to death on TV. The case of Somalia seems very much in this vein, an intervention generated in large part by graphic television images of people dying of starvation literally next door to massive food supplies.

When fear about the ozone layer, tropical rain forests, whales, and oil spills have become items on the foreign policy agenda in large part because of media attention, it is impossible to suggest that there are no grievances or catastrophic problems, especially economic ones, that can provoke a greater U.S. commitment to management for a "global community."

▲ Conclusion

This attempt to survey the possible roles of the United States in efforts to cope with regional conflicts results in a mixed assessment. There is much discussion now about how the great powers, most likely under U.S. leadership, might collectively act to make a safer world. While it is too early to be certain, the initial evidence is not encouraging. We may turn out to be unable to regard such conflicts as truly the responsibility of a global community and to effectively marshal the resources of the United States in conflict management.

The reasons are the same liberalist impulses that make the United States appealing as a great power. In effect, to create a vigorous great-power concert or strengthen multilateral organizations, the United States would have to accept commitments, with associated burdens and costs, that a democratic society is likely to find intolerable. Instead, it is almost certain to combine liberalist rhetoric and a realist maintenance of respectable military and other intervention capabilities with an almost isolationist aversion to serious burdens for the sake of managing regional conflicts.

This will clash, however, with the evidence that there are serious problems out there, that the United States might be able to help, and that if it leads, others might be induced to follow. However, action would have to be sustainable in the face of serious costs in order to bring the most dangerous and difficult regional conflicts under control.

This applies even to actions short of military intervention. The United States can do the most by helping to organize and coordinate major interventions to deal with inadequate welfare around the world. The question is whether it will if there is no clear and compelling threat and the costs are daunting. It is more compatible with U.S. values, traditions, and institutions to urge the impoverished to import capital and practice free enterprise.

However, it is a bit early to dismiss the alternative. The magnitude of the challenge to order, welfare, and legitimacy is only now becoming clear. We are still in the early stages of disentangling the U.S. stake in these matters from the Cold War. An urgent and intense U.S. commitment to action is not impossible, just unlikely.

NOTES

1. A good example is Hedley Bull, *The Anarchical Society* (London: Macmillan, 1977).

2. See, e.g., Robert Gilpin, *War and Change in World Politics* (New York: Cambridge University Press, 1981).

3. George Modelski, *Long Cycles in World Politics* (Seattle: University of Washington Press, 1986); Paul Kennedy, *The Rise and Fall of the Great Powers* (New York: Random House, 1987).

4. See Kenneth A. Oye, ed., *Cooperation under Anarchy* (Princeton: Princeton University Press, 1986); and Robert Keohane, *After Hegemony: Cooperation and Discord in the World Political Economy* (Princeton: Princeton University Press, 1984).

5. On American intelligence and peacekeeping or peacemaking see David L. Boren, "The Intelligence Community: How Crucial?" *Foreign Affairs* 71 (summer 1992): 52–62.

6. See Robert Jervis and Jack Snyder, eds., *Dominoes and Bandwagons: Strategic Beliefs and Great Power Competition in the Eurasian Rimland* (New York: Oxford University Press, 1991).

7. Patrick Morgan, "Saving Face for the Sake of Deterrence," in *Psychology and Deterrence,* ed. Robert Jervis, Richard Ned Lebow, and Janice Gross Stein (Baltimore: Johns Hopkins University Press, 1985), 125–52.

8. John Lewis Gaddis, "Toward the Post-Cold War World," *Foreign Affairs* 70 (spring 1991): 112.

9. For a criticism of this U.S. policy see Michael Lind, "In Defense of Liberal Nationalism," ibid. 73 (May–June 1994): 87–99.

10. Thus, "every President since Eisenhower . . . [has had] the persistent hope of ultimate harmony—the belief that if only the evil system could change or disappear, Americans and Soviets might cooperate" (Stanley Hoffmann, "American's Heritage," in *America's Roles in a Changing World,* Adelphi Papers No. 256 [London: International Institute for Strategic Studies, winter 1990–91], 13).

11. This led to strong U.S. pressure for completion of the Uruguay Round. However, this reflects the dominance of the establishment view. In polls the public continues to be quite solidly protectionist.

12. On promoting democracy as the core of foreign policy see Larry Diamond, "Promoting Democracy," *Foreign Policy* 87 (summer 1992): 25–46. On U.S. efforts in Latin America see Abraham F. Lowenthal, ed., *Exporting Democracy: The United States and Latin America,* 2 vols. (Baltimore: Johns Hopkins University Press, 1991).

13. See, e.g., Francis Fukuyama, "Democratization and International Security," in *New Dimensions in International Security*, Adelphi Papers No. 266 (London: International Institute for Strategic Studies, winter 1991–92), 14–24; and Michael Doyle, "Kant, Liberal Legacies, and Foreign Affairs," *Philosophy and Public Affairs* 12 (summer 1983): 204–35.

14. Patrick Buchanan laid out the conservative view in the Republican primary campaign in 1992. The writings of Doug Bandow, such as "Avoiding War," *Foreign Policy* 89 (winter 1992–93): 156–74, and "Keep the Troops and the Money at Home," *Orbis* 35 (fall 1991): 552–61, touch on all the conservative themes, as do those of Alan Tonelson, notably "What Is the National Interest?" *Atlantic Monthly*, July 1991, 35–81. Or see George F. Kennan, "American's Duty to the Wide World Starts at Home," *International Herald Tribune*, Mar. 14, 1994. The best examples of a modern leftist approach to security matters are in the publications of the Center for Defense Information, such as "The U.S. as the World Policeman?" *Defense Monitor* 20, no. 1 (1991); "1995 Military Spending: The Real Story," ibid. 23, no. 5 (1994); and "Does the United States Need Nuclear Weapons?" ibid. 22, no. 10 (1993). A critique of these views that suggests they are widely held by mainstream Democrats as well is Edward Alden and Franz Schurmann, "Neo-Nationalist Fallacies," *Foreign Policy* 87 (summer 1992): 105–22.

15. George Kennan's version of containment was the ultimate refinement of this view in foreign policy for the Cold War era: the United States would have to be involved but should do so with a close eye on the limits of U.S. power and wisdom plus the need to tend to its own needs at home.

16. A good example is the view offered by Randall Forsberg. See her articles in the *Boston Review* in recent years.

17. Examples would start with the Bush administration's foreign policy and the Defense Department's Draft Planning Guidance for FY 1994–99, which called for the United States to spend in order to forestall the emergence of any military equal for years to come. Harry G. Summers, Jr., "How to Be the World's Policeman," *New York Times Magazine*, May 19, 1991, calls for maintaining ample military strength within the context of a conservative view of the world. Henry Kissinger writes consistently about the need for U.S. involvement on the basis of a constant appreciation of global and regional balances of power. Other examples would include Samuel P. Huntington, "Why International Primacy Matters," *International Security* 17 (spring 1993): 68–83; the view of the American role in David Abshire et al., *The Atlantic Alliance Transformed* (Washington, D.C.: Center for Strategic and International Studies, 1992); and James Schlesinger, "Quest for a Post–Cold War Foreign Policy," *Foreign Affairs: America and the World, 1992/93* 72, no. 1 (1993): 17–28.

18. Examples are Senator Joseph Biden's view of the Bosnian situation and Senator George Mitchell's views on human rights in China. Columnists with this view of events in Europe include William Pfaff and Anthony Lewis. The writings of Joseph Nye are often cited, especially on the effects of nonmilitary forms of international influence. Other examples are Warren Zimmermann, "Why America Must Save Bosnia: Our Interests Demand Intervention," *Washington Post*, May 2–8, 1994, national weekly edition, 23–24; David Gompert, "How to Defeat Serbia," *Foreign Affairs* 73 (July–Aug. 1994): 30–47; Morton H. Halperin, "Guaranteeing Democracy," *Foreign Policy* 91 (summer 1993): 105–22; James P. Grant, "Jumpstarting Development," ibid., 124–37; and Ameri-

can Assembly, *U.S. Intervention Policy for the Post–Cold War World: New Challenges and New Responses* (New York, 1994).

19. See John J. Mearsheimer, "Disorder Restored" in *Rethinking America's Security: Beyond Cold War to New World Order,* ed. Graham Allison and Gregory Treverton (New York: W. W. Norton, 1992), 213–37, esp. 234.

20. Good examples of this argument are Alberto R. Coll, "America as the Grand Facilitator," *Foreign Policy* 87 (summer 1992): 47–65; and William Odom, "Military Lessons and U.S. Forces" in Allison and Treverton, *Rethinking America's Security,* 337–48.

21. Typical of the sentiments of the Association of Southeast Asian Nations (ASEAN) is Yeo Ning Hong, "America Should Maintain Its Asia-Pacific Presence," *International Herald Tribune,* Dec. 10, 1992. The official U.S. view is endorsed in A. James Gregor, "The United States and Security Issues in East Asia," in *National Security: Papers Prepared for GAO Conference on Worldwide Threats* (Washington, D.C.: GAO, 1992). On alternative roles for the United States as a "balancer" see R. J. Ellings and E. A. Olsen, "A New Pacific Profile," *Foreign Policy* 89 (winter 1992–93): 116–36.

22. For a nonofficial but establishment case for multilateralism see the Carnegie Endowment National Commission on America and the World, *Changing Our Ways* (Washington, D.C.: Carnegie Endowment for International Peace, 1992).

23. William Kaufmann, *Assessing the Base Force: How Much Is Enough?* (Washington, D.C.: Brookings Institution, 1992), 23.

24. Should it attempt regional hegemony, there would be much opposition along the lines of Robert W. Tucker and David C. Hendrickson, *The Imperial Temptation: The New World Order and America's Purpose* (New York: Council on Foreign Relations Press, 1992).

25. "To many Americans the most objectionable feature of the balance of power is its apparent moral neutrality," Henry Kissinger, "Balance of Power Sustained," in Allison and Treverton, *Rethinking America's Security,* 242.

26. See John Mueller, "A New Concert of Europe," *Foreign Policy* 77 (winter 1989–90): 3–16; and Charles Kupchan and Clifford Kupchan, "Concerts, Collective Security, and the Future of Europe," *International Security* 16 (summer 1991): 114–61.

27. Michael Mandelbaum, *The Fate of Nations* (New York: Cambridge University Press, 1988).

28. Jean Francois-Poncet argues that the United States would not have acted in the Gulf without the support of other states and that this will hold true in the future ("Toward a Directorate of Continents," in *In Search of a New World Order: The Future of U.S.-European Relations,* ed. Henry Brandon [Washington, D.C.: Brookings Institution, 1992], 64–65).

29. Fukuyama, "Democratization and International Security," 18.

30. Michael Doyle, "An International Liberal Community," in Allison and Treverton, *Rethinking America's Security,* 307–33.

31. A good example of this view is Tonelson, "What Is the National Interest?" 35–52; or see Peter Peterson with James K. Sebenius, "The Primacy of the Domestic Agenda," in Allison and Treverton, *Rethinking America's Security,* 63.

32. Richard Cattani reviews many polls in "America in the World," *Christian Science Monitor,* Mar. 4, 1992; or see R. W. Apple, "Majority in Poll Fault Focus by Bush

on Global Policy but Back New Order," *New York Times*, Oct. 11, 1991. On what public opinion will and will not support see Ronald H. Hinckley, *People, Polls, and Policy Makers: American Public Opinion and National Security* (New York: Lexington Books, 1992); or William Schneider, "The Old Politics and the New World Order," in *The New World Order: Rethinking America's Global Role*, ed. Carol Rae Hansen (Flagstaff: Arizona Honors Academy Press, 1992), 117–49.

33. See Bruce W. Jentleson, "The Pretty Prudent Public: Post-Vietnam American Opinion on the Use of Military Force," *International Studies Quarterly* 36, no. 1 (1992): 49–73. On contemporary internationalism, see Eugene R. Wittkopf, *Faces of Internationalism: Public Opinion and American Foreign Policy* (Durham, N.C.: Duke University Press, 1990).

34. Peter Wallensteen and Karin Axell, "Major Armed Conflicts," *SIPRI Yearbook 1994* (Stockholm: Stockholm International Peace Research Institute, 1994), 81–95.

35. Richard Morin, "Most in Poll Reject Giving Soviets Cash," *Washington Post*, Aug. 29, 1991; John Benson, "Caution Still Much in Evidence," *Christian Science Monitor*, Sept. 27, 1991.

36. Robert J. Art, "A Defensible Defense: America's Grand Strategy after the Cold War," *International Security* 15 (spring 1991): 5–53.

37. See John Gerard Ruggie, ed., *Multilateralism Matters: The Theory and Praxis of an Institutional Form* (New York: Columbia University Press, 1993).

38. A more optimistic analysis is Steven Weber, "The United States, the Soviet Union, and Regional Conflicts after the Cold War," in *Beyond the Cold War: Conflict and Cooperation in the Third World*, ed. George Breslauer, Harry Kreisler, and Benjamin Ward (Berkeley: Institute of International Studies, 1991), 382–410.

39. Edward Luck suggests that military intervention could be triggered by outright aggression, a governmental collapse that brings chaos and violence, genocidal behavior, or "rogue behavior" on nuclear proliferation or terrorism (see "Making Peace," *Foreign Policy* 89 [winter 1992–93]: 137–55).

40. See Bandow, "Avoiding War."

41. Examples include Ashton Carter, William J. Perry, and John D. Steinbruner, *A New Concept of Security* (Washington, D.C.: Brookings Institution, 1992); Roger Morris, "From Clinton the World Needs a Radically New Foreign Policy," *International Herald Tribune*, Dec. 10, 1992; and Carnegie Endowment National Commission on America and the World, *Changing Our Ways*.

42. As envisioned in the classic functionalism literature, Gorbachev's "new thinking," and in Robert Keohane and Joseph Nye, *Power and Interdependence: World Politics in Transition* (Boston: Little, Brown, 1977).

3 | The Russian Federation

The revolutionary changes of recent years that resulted in the end of the Cold War, the collapse of the Soviet empire in East-Central Europe, and, finally, the very dissolution of the Soviet state have had a major impact on the role of the Russian Federation, the primary successor state to the Soviet Union, in coping with regional conflicts. While for most of the postwar era Soviet leaders viewed regional conflicts mostly as an opportunity to strengthen their position in the global competition with the capitalist West, the leadership of the new Russia has taken a very different approach. As part of the effort to be accepted as a "normal" world power, Russia's leaders have generally played a supportive role in cooperating with the United States and other Western states in the effort to contain regional conflict.

However, there exist within Russia strong voices opposed to this policy of accommodation. They see it as a form of subservience to the West and contrary to Russian interests. Moreover, the policies of the Russian Federation toward regional conflicts differ depending upon whether the conflicts occur in the territory of the former Soviet Union, elsewhere in Europe, or in the developing world. Russia has indicated a growing willingness to engage in unilateral intervention in the first group of cases when intervention is viewed as necessary to pursue Russian interests. However, in conflicts in the territory of the former Soviet Union Russian intervention is likely to exacerbate conflict rather than contribute to its successful resolution. Elsewhere, in Europe and in the developing world, where Russian interests are less immediately engaged, Moscow's role in coping with regional conflict will likely remain less central but more positive. In the conflicts in former Yugoslav territory the Russian government has, owing to substantial domestic pressure, shifted from virtual full support for Western policy to a policy more balanced among the protagonists and, thus, more supportive of Serbia. But overall the Russian role has been coordinated with Western policy. In the developing world Russia has not been extensively involved in formal peacekeeping activities, although it has supported U.N. operations. However, in an effort to generate hard currency earnings, it has committed itself to a resumption of the export of military equipment, an activity viewed in the United States as a major challenge to long-term stability in parts of the developing world.

The degree to which the Russian Federation will be able to play a positive role in coping with conflict in Europe and in the developing world will depend to a substantial degree on domestic political and economic developments in Russia itself and on the outcome of the conflicts occurring in former Soviet territory. The ability of the current coalition of forces, headed by President Yeltsin, to retain political power is an important factor; this, in turn, is closely tied to its ability to create a functioning economy and a stable political system. This is especially important because of the continuing, although reduced, commitment of Yeltsin and his supporters to integration into the Western-dominated world community. Russian nationalists, were they to emerge dominant in the domestic power struggle, would likely take a much less cooperative approach vis-à-vis the West. However, even if extremist forces do not come to power in Russia, domestic factors will limit substantially the freedom of action of any Russian government in some of the areas associated with the problem of coping with international conflict.[1]

The future role of the Russian Federation in the long-term process of coping with conflict is not clear, either in the territory of the former Soviet state or elsewhere in the world. The collapse of the Soviet Union has meant the disintegration of the security regime stretching from central Europe to the Pacific that was created and maintained by the Soviet Union. It has brought, as well, a whole set of challenges to the very existence of the new Russian state and to its security, defined increasing to include the welfare of ethnic Russian populations resident in the near abroad.[2] While other major state actors will be discussed in this volume in terms of their likely contributions to the containment of regional conflict, the Russian Federation must be seen as much as a potential contributor to or source of regional conflict as it is as a possible facilitator in coping with conflict. Perhaps the most to be hoped for is that Russia and the other Soviet successor states will be able to solve their own problems without continually resorting to military action and without dragging other members of the world community into conflict situations.

▲ The Emerging Russian View of a Future World Order

Of central importance for the behavior of the Russian Federation toward regional conflict will be the general view of Russian leaders concerning the type of world order that they prefer, Russia's place in that world, and the means they must employ to accomplish their objectives. To this point the Russian foreign policy leadership, headed by President Boris Yeltsin and Foreign Minister Andrei Kozyrev, has emphasized its commitment "to secure Russia's entry into the civilized [world] community" and "to enlist maximum support for efforts toward Russia's transformation."[3] In their view a major objective of foreign policy is the preservation and expansion of the emerging democratic institutions in Russia. Cordial relations with the West have been expected to bring relief from Cold War burdens and to provide access to Western financial and technical assistance and an entree into the international economic institutions seen as important for the economic rehabilitation and long-term development of Russia. Russia's new leaders also committed themselves to base their relations with other former Soviet republics on a full recognition of mutual independence.[4]

To a great degree the foreign policy of Kozyrev has built on and extended that of Eduard Shevardnadze, the architect of Gorbachev's foreign policy in the late 1980s. Kozyrev and the liberals who have staffed important positions in the Russian Ministry of Foreign Affairs believe that Russia must end its decades of isolation from the Western world. To do this requires the establishment of effective institutions that will support and nurture the emerging democracy and market economy, which they see as an integral part of a new Russia. Relationships with the outside world, whether with former enemies from the capitalist world or with the newly independent states that shared with Russia the experiences of the twentieth century as part of the Soviet Union, must be based on mutually beneficial contacts, not on coercion or threats of coercion. Both Yeltsin and Kozyrev have emphasized on many occasions the desire for Russia to become a "normal" great power, not just a military power.

Kozyrev has noted his concern about the reemergence of the search for enemies and scapegoats, which he believes will undercut "Russia's integration into the democratic world."[5]

The concrete expression of this foreign policy line meant initially a foreign policy of moderation in relations with other members of the Commonwealth of Independent States (CIS) and the Baltic states (although threats and even forms of intervention have also occurred),[6] a continued emphasis on strengthening the new economic and political ties with the West, and overall support for U.S. and Western policy initiatives. However, by mid-1993, in part as a result of domestic pressures, Russian policy had become more assertive and less accommodating to the West. As relates to regional conflict, the Western-oriented foreign policy of Yeltsin and Kozyrev has centered on active participation in efforts to strengthen the role of the Conference on Security and Cooperation in Europe (CSCE)[7] and alignment on Western-oriented policies in the United Nations. This new role has led Russia to condemn Serbian policy in the civil war in former Yugoslavia and to follow U.N. agreements on the economic blockade of Serbia and Montenegro. Throughout the territory of the former Soviet Union this policy shift has meant that Moscow has taken a more assertive role.[8]

A central component of Russian foreign policy has been support for U.N. efforts at international peacekeeping and conflict resolution. This policy builds on the reassessment of international politics and the place of the United Nations that occurred under Gorbachev, who outlined a plan in late 1988 that included an "all-encompassing system of security" tied into the network of the U.N. system.[9] In this speech and on other occasions, Gorbachev and his major advisers called for an alternative world order with fewer weapons and, ultimately, for a system of largely disarmed states. Gorbachev and Shevardnadze repeatedly stressed the need to search for a future order of peace, for principles and mechanisms of international conflict resolution, and for means to settle international problems in the postnuclear age. In this system, the dominant role for military and political security would fall upon the United Nations.

The Soviet reevaluation of the United Nations called for increasing the effectiveness of major organs, especially a heightened role for the Security Council and the expansion of U.N. peacekeeping operations; the creation of new subsidiary organizations to deal with issues such as disarmament, arms trading, environmental degradation, and so forth; and bolstering the financial base of the organization. The Soviets admitted that in the past they had not contributed to maintaining an effective international peacekeeping organization. They also announced that they would henceforth cooperate more fully with U.N. economic and social organs and become involved in other specialized U.N. organizations of which they had not been members. After 1988 the Soviet Union did expand its contacts with these organizations and paid off its outstanding debts accrued over the decades by the Soviet Union as a consequence of its refusal to pay for U.N. operations that it opposed.

Evidence of the impact of the shift in Soviet policy became clear when the April 1988 agreement on the Soviet troop withdrawal from Afghanistan and the armistice of August 1988 in Cambodia included provisions for the dispatch of U.N. peacekeeping forces or observers to the two regions. Since 1988 the United Nations has played an active role in peacekeeping and peacemaking in a number of conflicts. Especially important was the role of the United Nations in the 1989 settlement on Namibia, where it helped to broker negotiations and provided buffer and police forces and election monitors. The United Nations has played an active role at various levels of involvement in Central America, the Western Sahara, and Cambodia.[10] The shift in Soviet policy and the willingness to join with the United States and other Western countries in dealing with regional conflicts have been essential to the expanded security role of the United Nations. After the joint U.S.-Soviet resolution of November 2, 1989, calling for the expansion of practical peace efforts, cooperation between the two countries became a central element of the environment in which the United Nations was operating.

The crisis that broke out in August 1990, after the Iraqi invasion of Kuwait, tested the strength of this new cooperative relationship. Immediately after the invasion Soviet Foreign Minister Shevardnadze provided Soviet political support for joint U.N. operations. Not until after Shevardnadze's resignation in December did Soviet policy shift away from complete cooperation with the United States.[11] Evgenii Primakov, a key figure in Gorbachev's foreign policy establishment, attempted at the last moment to forestall the attack on Iraq by convincing Saddam Hussein to be more compliant. But the attempt failed, and Moscow supported U.S.-led policy to the point where U.N.-backed joint action against Iraq was possible.

The point of this brief discussion is to emphasize the fact that during the period leading up to the collapse of the Soviet state there was a dramatic shift in Soviet foreign policy. The Soviet leadership now saw the United Nations as an instrument through which to facilitate the achievement of foreign policy objectives, which now included the resolution of regional conflicts, and as a forum in which to push its new conception of a global order based on the peaceful resolution of international disputes.

During the first two and a half years of its existence the Russian Federation pursued a policy toward the United Nations and toward regional conflict resolution that was largely in line with that developed during the last years of the Soviet state. Speaking before the Security Council in January 1992, for example, President Yeltsin called for the strengthening of the organization's capacity to deal with significant international problems, including peacekeeping. He recommended the formation of rapid response mechanisms to permit the United Nations to deal with military conflicts, as well as the creation of institutions to permit the United Nations to play a role in global economic and social processes.[12] However, given the demands placed on the limited resources of President Yeltsin's government to deal with conflicts throughout former Soviet territory, Russia has had relatively limited direct involvement in peacekeeping operations in the developing world. The establishment of bilateral and multilateral relations with other former Soviet republics and the attempt to deal with conflicts in former Soviet territory have forced a shift in emphasis in Russian policy. However, it is an indication of the importance of the role of the United Nations in peacekeeping that Russian troops were part of the U.N. peacekeeping forces sent to Croatia in spring 1992 and Russia voted for sanctions against rump Yugoslavia in late May 1992.[13]

At the official level the foreign policy of the Russian Federation was built upon the foundations laid by Gorbachev and Shevardnadze from 1987 to 1991. The vision of a future world that has informed Russian foreign policy has been one in which Russia is a full member of an international community dedicated to the peaceful resolution of conflict. President Yeltsin and Foreign Minister Kozyrev have been committed to a policy of binding Russia firmly to the West on the basis of policies of democratization, demilitarization, and deideologization. This priority in Russian policy has been determined largely by the recognition that it is an essential condition for the successful stabilization and restoration of the country's economy.[14]

Simultaneously, however, elements of an expansionist orientation have also been evident in Russian policy toward some of the other new states. The foreign policy of Kozyrev and Yeltsin has come under severe attack by those who advocate a more assertive, nationalist approach to dealing with both the near abroad and the West. The pressure exerted by these forces has had an impact not only on the general orientation of Russian policy but also on Russian behavior in specific regional conflicts, in particular on the manner in which Russia responded to conflicts along its periphery and in former Yugoslavia. Any substantial increase in the influence of extreme nationalism on domestic and foreign policy will likely mean that Russia will be more a problem than a solution either in reconciling differences between the various peoples of the former Soviet Union or in assisting with coping efforts in conflicts elsewhere.

▲ Russia and the "Near Abroad": Regional Conflict in the Former Soviet Union

One of the largely unexpected results of the end of the Cold War and the implosion of the Soviet Union has been the outbreak of a series of regional, largely ethnically based conflicts in territories of the former Soviet Union. All across the southern reaches of former Soviet territory, from Moldova in the West to Tajikistan in Central Asia, people have been dying in the violence associated with the effort to create new states, often on land inhabited by ethnic groups with historical animosities toward one another or territory claimed as part of the patrimonial homeland by more than one ethnic group.[15] For a number of reasons the Russian Federation has been intimately involved in most of these new regional conflicts.

First, there is the fact that at independence twenty-five million ethnic Russians instantly became members of minorities in fourteen of the fifteen Soviet successor states. Some of these Russian minorities are directly involved in a number of the crises. This is most evident in eastern Moldova, where the Russian minority, with the open support of the Russian Fourteenth Army, has established a breakaway regime in the so-called Transdniester Republic, and in Crimea, where a Russian majority favors a return of the district from Ukrainian to Russian control.[16] Elsewhere, in northern Georgia and Central Asia, for example, fighting among local competitors for power challenges the security of substantial numbers of Russians resident in the area. The fact that Russians are involved, directly or indirectly, in many of the recent conflicts is a major factor in the concerns expressed in Moscow for their safety and for active Russian policies to protect them. In addition, however, the issues involved in some of the conflicts have already spilled over into the territory of the Russian Federation itself. Fighting has occurred in the northern Caucasus, where the border between Russia and Georgia cuts across extremely complex ethnic boundaries, in a region where many mutually hostile ethnic communities are currently vying for political identity and some form of political autonomy or even independence.

A second factor, which differs somewhat from the first, is the concern in Moscow about the possible emergence of radical Islamic regimes in Central

Asia. The Russian Federation has signed agreements with the governments of several of the countries in this area to provide them with security assistance, and Russian troops have played an important role in supporting the current government in Tajikistan, composed largely of holdovers from the communist regime, against Islamic and democratic forces committed to toppling it. In one of the major ironies of the postcommunist world, Russian troops are now challenged in Tajikistan by Mujahidin based in Afghanistan. The broader concern, however, is the emergence of revolutionary Islamic regimes along Russia's borders that might attract the significant Muslim population of Russia itself.

A third factor of relevance in explaining the interest of Russia in the conflicts that have broken out along its new southern borders is the view, openly expressed by many Russian leaders, that Russia, as the successor of the Soviet Union, has a responsibility to assure stability throughout the entire territory of the former Soviet state. The claim for the special role of Russia in assuring regional security can easily lead to efforts aimed at reestablishing Russian dominance in a region most of which was under Russian or Soviet control for centuries. This is precisely the charge made by President Leonid Kravchuk of Ukraine and the leaders of several other Soviet successor states, as well as the stated objective of many Russian political figures.

Immediately after the dissolution of the Soviet Union and the emergence of fifteen independent successor states, the leadership in Moscow was especially cooperative on issues related to regional conflicts as it focused its foreign policy efforts on normalizing relations with the West. Negotiations, efforts at mediation, and the provision of peacekeeping forces only in cooperation with others characterized official policy. However, parallel to this official policy and in line with the strong criticism of Yeltsin and Kozyrev's foreign policy mentioned above have been the charges of former vice president Rutskoi and others that the Russian government has abandoned the legitimate interests of the Russian state and of the millions of ethnic Russians living outside the borders of Russia. They have called for a much more assertive Russian policy and have, in fact, engaged in direct intervention on behalf of one faction or another in several of the regional disputes. Because of the weakness of the central government and its inability to control the military, an occurrence of major relevance in this area has been the independent action of local military commanders. Regardless of officially stated policy, for example, Lt. Gen. Aleksandr Lebed, former commander of the former Soviet forces still present in Moldova, intervened directly in the civil war in the eastern part of that country. In Abkhazia local Russian troops have engaged in fighting with Geor-

gian National Guard forces that were sent to the area to put down the secessionist movement. Moreover, Russian forces have reportedly provided equipment to the Armenians fighting the Azeris in and around Nagorno-Karabakh.

It is important to recognize that Russian policies toward the various conflicts in former Soviet territory are occurring within the context of emerging
new relationships among the former Soviet republics as they jockey for position in the regional and global community. While Russia, even the Russia of
foreign policy liberals such as Yeltsin and Kozyrev, attempts to establish its
paramount position in the complex regional system(s) emerging out of the
former Soviet system, leaders in the Baltic states, in Ukraine, and elsewhere
are attempting to assert their sovereignty and independence from Moscow. In
some cases this has resulted in increasing hostility in the relationships among
the new states of the region. In the Baltics the issues concern the continued
presence of Russian troops, on the one hand, and the treatment of the large
Russian minorities, on the other.[17] The expanding list of issues that divide Russia and Ukraine concern the degree to which the latter will be able to function
as a truly independent state. The specific issues of Russia's claims to Crimea,
of Ukraine's refusal to transfer to Russia long-range nuclear weapons based on
its territory, and of ownership of the Black Sea Fleet must all be understood
as part of the politics of national self-assertion. It must also be recognized that
the growing frictions between Russia and its new neighbors can contribute to
an increasingly hostile environment in which Moscow's policy is being made
regarding the conflicts in the near abroad.

One of the tasks to which the members of the fledgling CIS committed
themselves after the organization's creation in December 1991 was the creation
of mechanisms to facilitate the resolution of conflict among and within the
members states. At a meeting of CIS foreign and defense ministers held in
Tashkent in July 1992 agreement was reached on the creation of a CIS peacekeeping unit. Several days later Russian Defense Minister Pavel Grachev announced that some Russian troops would be trained specifically as peacekeeping forces for possible deployment with U.N. and CIS peacekeeping units.[18]
However, despite some achievements resulting from Russian pressures, the
CIS has not proven to be an effective organization. For the most part agreements signed are merely that, with little, if any, follow-up by the signatories.
In January 1993 the heads of state of the CIS member states met in Minsk
for their eighth summit, at which seven of the countries — excluding Ukraine,
Turkmenistan, and Moldova — agreed to a draft charter to be submitted to
their respective parliaments for ratification. The agreement called for greater
cooperation in economic matters, especially the creation of a CIS interstate

bank. There was far less progress made on security matters, although there was general agreement on the creation of an interstate court to adjudicate interethnic and interstate disputes.[19]

After a period during which the CIS did not seem to be evolving into an effective integrative organization, especially in the security area, important breakthroughs occurred during 1993 and 1994. These resulted largely from Russian economic and military pressures on the other members of the organization. At a meeting of CIS defense ministers in May 1993 Russia opposed two draft agreements that called for the creation of unified CIS military forces, although five other CIS states supported the proposed security organization. The Russian representative explained that Moscow's opposition was in part due to the fact that Russia would have to bear the brunt of the costs of such a force.[20] Finally, all pretense at military coordination within the CIS was dropped in early summer 1993 when Marshal Evgenii Shaposhnikov, the commander in chief of the CIS joint armed forces, resigned to take a high-level position in the Russian government. Several days later, on June 15, 1993, it was announced in Moscow that the CIS joint military command had been abolished.[21] However, less than a year later Russia announced plans for the signing of bilateral military agreements with all CIS members except Ukraine for the establishment of some thirty military bases throughout the CIS.[22]

Within the territory of the former Soviet Union, Russian efforts to deal with regional or local conflicts have occurred at three major levels. Most of Russia's involvement has been at the bilateral level as, for example, it has attempted to work out arrangements with both Georgia (concerning the fighting in South Ossetia and Abkhazia) and Moldova (concerning the secession of Transdniester) to bring a halt to the fighting and to work out a settlement of the issues in dispute.[23] Russia has also attempted to work through the CIS to deal with some of the conflicts occurring in former Soviet territory. In Tajikistan, for example, Russian forces guarding the Tajik-Afghan border, in accord with a bilateral security agreement, have been joined by a battalion of five hundred men from each of the four other Central Asian states that signed a collective security agreement within the framework of the CIS in 1992.[24] Finally, Russia has also attempted to deal with the more intractable conflicts in collaboration with other, outside states. This has occurred, for example, in the conflict between Armenia and Azerbaijan over the issue of Nagorno-Karabakh, where the efforts of both the central Soviet government of President Gorbachev and, more recently, both Russian President Yeltsin and President Nazarbaev of Kazakhstan have failed. In mid-May 1993 a CSCE-sponsored plan for the resolution of the conflict in Nagorno-Karabakh was submitted to the governments of the two countries involved. The plan, which had been worked out by representatives of the United States, Turkey, and Russia, was immediately accepted by Azerbaijan and taken under consideration by Armenia, but it was rejected outright by the self-proclaimed Nagorno-Karabakh Republic.[25] Russia has continued its efforts in conjunction with the CSCE to develop a workable peace plan for Karabakh.

Any discussion of the role of the Russian Federation in conflict resolution or peacemaking in the territory of the former Soviet Union must take into account the friction mentioned previously in the emerging relationships between Russia and the other successor states. Despite official disclaimers that Russia has no desire to reestablish dominance over the newly emerging states, Russian leaders have had problems adjusting to the new reality, in which they are required to negotiate as equals with elites in Kiev and Almaty (Alma-Ata) instead of merely issuing instructions, as they would have done in the past. This is part of the much larger psychological problem of "redefining Russia's statehood and establishing a new concept of Russian identity." [26] Members of the political opposition in Moscow are clear in stating that Russia's legitimate interests extend to developments internal to the affairs of the other post-Soviet states. Even President Yeltsin, who maintains that Russia has no intentions of resurrecting its imperial past, has problems distinguishing between Russia's interests within the Russian Federation and its interests in the near abroad. In February 1993, for example, he stated that "the time has come for authoritative international organizations, including the United Nations, to grant Russia special powers as guarantor of peace and stability in this region" of the former Soviet Union.[27] This and later efforts by Yeltsin and his officials at the United Nations and within the CIS to gain approval for what would amount to the right of unilateral intervention by Russia received a very hostile response in Ukraine and in several other new states and a cool reception at the United Nations.[28]

However, public expressions by high-ranking officials of the goal of recreation of a Russian-centered Eurasian great power continue to be heard in Moscow. In early July, for example, presidential adviser Sergei Stankevich noted that except in the Baltics, leaders of the former Soviet republics who had pushed for independence were being replaced, with improved prospects for future reunion with Russia. Russia's current task, he asserted, is to stabilize itself within its current borders and then pursue a policy of gradual "economic and cultural expansion" into the near abroad.[29] This is precisely the type of policy feared by leaders in Kiev and other capitals in the near abroad.

Russian policy on regional unrest along its borders is increasingly likely to come into conflict with the interests of neighboring states and with the perceptions of acceptable policy in the West, including the United States. The motivations in Moscow for a more direct and assertive Russian response to what is perceived as growing chaos along, and even spilling over, its borders are clear. Since negotiations have proven to be ineffective in most of the ongoing military conflicts, according to one Russian analyst, the view has become widespread among Russian political elites, even those around Yeltsin and Kozyrev, that the bloodshed in "lands which simply can't qualify as 'foreign territories' must be halted, even if that means the direct use of Russian military force."[30] There is also the view, strongly held within the military, that the establishment of rapid deployment forces and their successful suppression of regional conflict would help to restore the prestige and status of the military. There is the added concern that the failure of Russia to act forcefully to deal with regional conflicts will invite others to intervene. Turkey, Iran, and especially the United States are among those most actively poised to act, Marshal Evgenii Shaposhnikov, former commander in chief of CIS Joint Armed Forces, argued in December 1992.[31] Others, especially opponents of Yeltsin and Kozyrev, have expressed concern about the possibility of U.N. intervention. This explains, in part, their strong opposition to military intervention against Serbia, which might then serve as a precedent for future intervention in former Soviet territory.[32]

Taken together, these factors explain why the Russians have sought support for their role as guarantor of security in the region. However, Russia is not a disinterested bystander in most of the conflicts: witness the role of Russian troops in Moldova, Abkhazia, Tajikistan, and even Nagorno-Karabakh. Regardless of Russia's motives—and neoimperialist designs simply cannot be discounted, Kozyrev and Yeltsin's claims notwithstanding—some of Russia's neighbors have responded very negatively to the prospects of expanded Russian military involvement throughout the region. Discussions have already taken place concerning the establishment of a common security system for Eastern Europe that would include the former western republics of the Soviet Union and the former Central European members of the Warsaw Pact. According to Dmitry Volsky, a liberal Russian commentator, "The anti-Russian direction of the planned association of East European states is absolutely clear."[33] He attributes the plans to nationalist political forces in Ukraine. Although Volsky is correct that nationalists in some of the new states are motivated by anti-Russian attitudes, those attitudes cannot but be reinforced by statements by high-level Russian officials, including the president, that imply a desire to recreate aspects of the old Russian-Soviet empire. In other words, the

Ukrainians and other Eastern and Central European leaders are responding to views expressed in Moscow—and to Russian behavior patterns that they see as threatening.

Besides the talk of a special security role for Russia, there is the fact that Russia has been able to use its dominant economic and political position in the region to pressure or elicit cooperation from neighboring countries. In Belarus former "president" Stanislav Shuskevich unsuccessfully opposed what he viewed as a gradual reabsorption of Belarus into the Russian sphere; in fact, his opposition was a key factor in his removal from power prior to the elections of 1994, which brought pro-Russian forces to power in Belarus. Interpreters of the power struggle in Azerbaijan in June 1993 have seen the rise to leadership of Heydar Aliyev, a former KGB chief in Azerbaijan and Moscow Politburo member in the mid-1980s, as possible evidence of Russian involvement and of a future enhanced Russian role in that country. The special relationship between Russia and the Central Asian states that has emerged since independence has created a virtual patron-client relationship between Moscow and the unreformed governments of the region.[34]

It is evident at this point that the security interests of Russia, especially since they are likely to be defined for the foreseeable future as including the welfare of ethnic Russians in the near abroad, will increasingly come into conflict with the interests of at least some neighboring states. In other words, Russia can be viewed, in some cases at least, as a likely contributor to regional conflict. This is especially true given the relative weakness of the government in Moscow and its inability to control the statements and actions of leading political and military figures. However, even those who are supposedly committed to establishing relations based on mutual recognition of national sovereignty have often sounded like Great Russian chauvinists.

The unilateral large-scale introduction of Russian military forces, especially in the conflicts in the European and Caucasian areas of the former Soviet Union, would without doubt exacerbate rather than mitigate regional tensions. From a Western perspective this is highly undesirable. However, given the apparent intractability of some of the conflicts, the concerns in Russia about their outcome, and the probable inability or unwillingness of the United Nations or other international security organizations to deal effectively with regional conflict in former Soviet territory, the alternatives to a "special" Russian security role seem very limited. To this point efforts at institution building among the Soviet successor states that might serve to mitigate tensions and facilitate problem solving have had very limited results. This has been true in virtually all areas, from interstate trade and customs cooperation to more broadly based economic and political cooperation. The scores of agreements in these areas that have been signed by CIS representatives have simply not been implemented. Obviously the inability of the states in the region to work out mutually beneficial relationships in the economic and political arenas does not bode well for their ability to solve security-related problems.[35]

▲ Peacekeeping in Europe: The Russian Role

As already mentioned, Russian policy on international peacekeeping has been built on the foundations created during the final years of the Soviet state. Russia has generally supported Western initiatives, in some cases actually committing Russian personnel to U.N. operations. In Europe the United Nations is currently involved in two operations. These include twenty-two hundred personnel in Cyprus since 1964 to supervise the cease-fire and the demilitarized zone between Turkish and Greek Cypriot forces and more than fifteen thousand troops in Croatia since spring 1992 to serve as a buffer between Serb and Croat forces. The mandate of the Croatian operation has been expanded to include the provision of humanitarian aid in Bosnia-Herzegovina. Although there has been much discussion within the United Nations and without about the creation of an international buffer force for Bosnia-Herzegovina, as of August 1994 it remained quite limited.

Russia's direct role in peacekeeping operations in Europe has been limited. However, in May 1993 Russia cast its first U.N. Security Council veto, the first Soviet or Russian veto since 1984, on the issue of the financing of the U.N. peacekeeping troops in Cyprus. In explaining the Russian position on the 14 to 1 vote, Russia's permanent representative to the United Nations, Iulii Vorontsov, explained that the vote was made on purely practical grounds, implying that Russia could not afford the additional $2 million contribution called for in the resolution. Thus, the U.N. operation, which costs $31 million per year, will continue to be financed by voluntary contributions.[36]

Russia's involvement in the conflicts that have torn apart the former Yugoslavia has been more extensive and complex. With the outbreak of fighting in Slovenia and Croatia in 1991, Russia supported the Western position. Besides committing troops to the U.N. peacekeeping force in eastern Croatia, the Russian Federation also supported the Security Council sanctions against rump Yugoslavia because of the latter's role in the fighting that had by then broken out in Bosnia-Herzegovina. This vote occurred after Foreign Minister Kozyrev's visit to Yugoslavia earlier in the month in an attempt to broker a peace settlement.[37] The policy came under immediate attack in the Russian parliament, where Kozyrev was accused of ignoring, even selling out, Russia's interests in an attempt to curry favor in the West.[38] Despite the strong opposition and a vote of the Russian parliament against sanctions, President Yeltsin signed decrees in mid-July that imposed strict sanctions on Yugoslavia in line with the U.N. resolutions. During the remainder of 1992 the issue of sanctions against Yugoslavia became an integral part of the general debate on Russian foreign policy. Indications of a possible shift in the Russian position occurred in late summer, when Russia, along with four African states, abstained on a U.N. General Assembly vote calling on the Security Council to take "further appropriate measures" to put an end to the fighting in Bosnia-Herzegovina.[39]

In December the Russian parliament approved, by a vote of 151 to 5, with 13 abstentions, the Resolution of the Russian Federation toward the Yugoslav Crisis, which outlined policy changes viewed as essential. It called for sanctions against all three warring parties in Bosnia-Herzegovina, Russia's use of its veto should the U.N. Security Council entertain the idea of military intervention in Bosnia-Herzegovina, and the sending of humanitarian aid to rump Yugoslavia.[40] These and later efforts of the parliament to shift official policy have not succeeded, yet they no doubt have influenced the position of the Yeltsin government on a number of issues directly related to U.N. involvement in former Yugoslavia.

On the one hand, Russia has actively opposed the introduction of international troops into Bosnia-Herzegovina as either peacekeepers or peacemakers. While Russian conservatives have opposed such a move as anti-Serbian, Foreign Minister Kozyrev has emphasized the dangers of becoming entrapped in a quagmire comparable to Afghanistan. On the other hand, Russia was quick to support efforts at a negotiated settlement and even promised to commit Russian troops as part of a U.N. multinational force committed to implementing the Vance-Owen proposals for a resolution of the conflict in Bosnia-Herzegovina should agreement be reached on that or any other peace plan.[41]

Overall, the policy of the Russian Federation has not been directly disruptive to Western efforts to deal with the crises in Yugoslavia. In fact, to a substantial degree Russia has been supportive of U.N. operations, despite the widespread and vitriolic criticism of Russian policy from those associated with the so-called national patriotic movement, discussed below. Yet, given the strength of domestic attitudes concerning the special relationship between Russia and Serbia, the Russian government has served as a brake on whatever pressures existed in the West for military intervention in Bosnia-Herzegovina. Added to this have been the charges that Russian volunteers have been fighting on the side of the Serbs in Bosnia-Herzegovina and that Russia has supplied weapons to the Serbs. Although the Russian government denies these reports, there is evidence that such unofficial activities might well have taken place.[42]

▲ Regional Conflicts in the Developing World: The Russian Role

During the Cold War the vast majority of the regional conflicts that challenged international security occurred in developing countries.[43] Throughout that period and until the mid-1970s the Soviet Union was increasingly involved in the major regional confrontations. With few exceptions, the Soviets were allied with local forces in conflict with Western-supported governments or movements. With the rise in the 1970s of communist-oriented governments in the developing world, however, the Soviets increasingly found themselves supporting governments that were under attack, as in Angola, Afghanistan, and Cambodia. One of the major developments in the "new thinking" on foreign policy that characterized the Gorbachev years was the reassessment of both the feasibility and the cost-effectiveness of Soviet policy objectives in the developing world. The result was an increasing Soviet disengagement from the Third World that, by late 1991, had resulted in a virtual renunciation of earlier Soviet commitments to radical client states and movements — as in Afghanistan, Cuba, and Cambodia — and a substantial reduction in overall Soviet involvement in the developing world where it was not overtly beneficial to Soviet economic interests.[44]

The most dramatic illustration of the revolutionary shift in Soviet policy occurred during the Gulf Crisis and War of 1990–91. Although a fundamental improvement in U.S.-Soviet relations had occurred over the course of the prior three years or so, the crisis represented a real challenge to these new relations. They required the U.S.S.R.'s abandoning a longstanding ally, Iraq. Even though the U.S.S.R. committed no troops to the Desert Storm operation against Iraq and did attempt initially to push for a more conciliatory policy toward Saddam Hussein, its general support of the invasion and its political support in the United Nations were crucial successfully driving Iraqi troops out of occupied Kuwait.

Thus, when the Russian Federation launched its independent foreign policy at the beginning of 1992, it inherited a reduced set of ongoing commitments and involvements in the developing world. As part of its objective of cooperation with the world community in facilitating conflict resolution, the Russians have continued backing for various U.N. peacekeeping operations. Most significant has been the ongoing support for U.N. operations in Iraq. Russian technicians have been included among the U.N. weapons inspectors engaged in finding and destroying Iraqi weapons of mass destruction, in accord with the terms of the cease-fire agreement. Moreover, two Russian warships were sent to the Persian Gulf in fall 1992 as part of the U.N. effort to pressure the Iraqi government into observing human rights and fulfilling the terms of the U.N. resolutions.

Elsewhere throughout the developing world the Russians have supported U.N. peacekeeping and humanitarian operations, as in Angola, Cambodia, and Somalia, each of which, at one time or other, had been a close ally of the former Soviet Union. In none of these cases, however, have Russian troops or other personnel been directly employed in peacekeeping operations.[45]

Although Russian policy within the United Nations has supported efforts to deal with regional conflict in the developing world, one aspect of overall policy, the resumption of arms exports, has been received in Washington with significant concern. What is particularly disturbing is that these exports have been motivated almost exclusively by a desire to generate hard currency income and not by any concern about the policies of the purchaser or the uses to which the armaments might be put. The United States has been especially concerned about the export of submarines to Iran and rocket fuel to Libya.[46]

Since independence Russian trade has dropped precipitously, as did Soviet trade in the prior year. Arms exports were a major item in Soviet trade, generating an estimated two-thirds of all hard currency earnings by the early 1980s.[47] In constant 1990 prices, Soviet arms sales (not all for hard currency) were estimated at $17.75 billion, or 38.7 percent of total world armaments exports. Four years later sales had dropped to less than $4 billion, only 17.7 percent of a much smaller market.[48]

The Russians have emphasized the costs to their economy, at a time of deep depression, of the various U.N. embargoes to which they are a party. Libya, Iraq, and even former Yugoslavia were all important hard currency markets for Soviet weaponry. According to the minister of foreign economic relations, U.N. sanctions cost Moscow an estimated $16 billion in lost revenues during 1992.[49] This decline is especially detrimental to the Russian economy, where an estimated 37 million people are tied to the defense sector.[50] During 1992 major efforts were made to expand Russian arms exports, with China, India, Iran, and Turkey as the major purchasers. In summer 1994, however, Russian military exports remained very limited. The hope among some officials is that Russian arms exports will rise to $20 billion per year. This income is expected to go far to keep the defense industry operating and to finance the conversion of the remainder of the industry.[51]

Stated objectives for long-term arms exports are unrealistically high: the market to permit such growth simply does not exist. In addition, any unrestrained increase in the export of sophisticated weaponry from Russia would conflict with U.S. objectives and could jeopardize Western trade and assistance. An interesting aspect of this likely conflict is that the Russians have already accused the United States of a double standard. They note that the U.S. percentage of international arms exports has increased dramatically—to ten times the percentage of Russian sales to developing countries in 1992—and raise the question whether the United States is attempting to freeze Russia out of the international arms market.[52] Given the domestic political and economic importance of arms exports for Russia, it is unlikely that the issue will soon disappear. In fact, it will probably continue to represent an area of concern in Russia's relations with the United States.

▲ Conclusions and Projections

What emerges from this discussion is a picture of Russian foreign policy and, especially, a likely future role of the Russian Federation in regional conflicts that is far from clear. Central to the lack of clarity is the fact that there does not yet exist a clear definition of Russian interests and Russian foreign policy agreed to by a broad cross section of the Russian political elite. While policy to this point has been based largely on coordination with the West, that policy has been increasingly challenged by a substantial portion of the political elite. Many call for a much more assertive Russian policy, even including unilateral intervention in conflicts occurring along the Russian periphery. The result of these challenges to the initial policies of Yeltsin and Kozyrev has been a gradual but visible shift in Russian policy, a policy that now claims a special Russian role in former Soviet territory, is less cooperative in the Bosnian conflict, and will probably generate growing friction with the West in parts of the developing world.

The Western-oriented foreign policy vision of Yeltsin and Kozyrev has come under a great deal of criticism from others who do not share this perspective, either in full or in part. Included among the opponents are many who hold positions of influence within the governmental structures of the Russian Federation. In many respects Kozyrev's opponents have charged that he, like Soviet Foreign Minister Shevardnadze before him, has been so enamored with the West that he has abandoned Russia's national interests. He has been charged with helping to dismantle Russia's military power and with pursuing a foreign policy based on weakness, both in relations with the West and in relations with the other Soviet successor states. Former Russian Federation state adviser Sergei Stankevich, one of President Yeltsin's hand-picked advisers, has argued that much of the blame for the problems in Moldova and elsewhere derives from "ballroom diplomacy," that is, a policy based not on considerations of power but on smiles and good wishes. He concludes that "the policy of ostentatious weakness and endless ritual conversations . . . is suffering one obvious failure after another. Today, as never before, Russia needs people who are able to understand, formulate, and defend its true interests." Stankevich has called for the direct intervention by Russian troops in both Moldova and South Ossetia in order to save lives, especially those of Russians, and he envisions the reemergence of a Russian-led Eurasian power.[53] While still in office, former vice president Rutskoi took similar, even stronger positions on the secessionist struggle in Moldova, as did former Supreme Soviet speaker Ruslan Khasbulatov on the fighting in both South Ossetia and Abkhazia.

Between summer 1992 and early 1993 Foreign Minister Kozyrev and his ministry faced serious challenges from the parliament, which is dominated by those calling for a more assertive policy. The parliament, under the leadership of Khasbulatov, threatened to strip the ministry of responsibility for relations with the near abroad by creating a separate ministry for CIS affairs.[54] Another challenge to the authority of the Foreign Ministry came from the State Security Council and its former chief, Iurii Skokov. Members of the council, created by President Yeltsin, were among the strongest critics of the policies of the foreign minister.[55]

During 1992 several distinct factions emerged in Moscow whose views on foreign policy differed substantially from those of the Democratic Russia group associated with Kozyrev. The "national patriots" included a growing number of former democrats who had abandoned Kozyrev and Democratic Russia on the issue of Ukraine. For them the concept of a Ukraine separate from Russia is unthinkable. The national patriots differ from the democratic liberals primarily on the issue of the reestablishment, in some form, of the old empire — at least its Slavic portion. As the philosopher Iurii Borodai, a spokesman for this group, put it: "I can say frankly that I am an imperialist. . . . I believe in the resurgence of the Russian empire after Golgotha."[56]

The differences over foreign policy within the Russian political system have been matched by great differences on domestic policy and by the power struggles between Yeltsin and his opponents that culminated in the referendum of May 1993. Civic Union, the political faction that initially focused its disagreements with Yeltsin on economic policy, has called for a Russian foreign policy that is much more assertive in protecting Russian minorities and in forcing Ukraine, Belarus, and Kazakhstan to turn over their nuclear weapons.[57] To the right of Civic Union are the truly authoritarian and nationalist groups, which oppose the rapid introduction of a market economy, favor an authoritarian political system, and advocate the reestablishment of the Soviet Russian empire. The confrontation peaked in the attempted coup against Yeltsin orchestrated by the parliamentary leadership in September 1993 and in its forceful suppression by forces loyal to the president. The elections of December 1993 brought into the new parliament a majority supportive of nationalist and neocommunist policies. Yet, throughout 1994 President Yeltsin managed to pursue a largely presidential foreign policy that was influenced by the more nationalist demands of parliament but not determined by them.

Overall, however, the attacks on the Yeltsin government have had an impact on foreign policy, as is witnessed by the general hardening of Russian policy positions on issues associated with both the "far" and the near abroad.[58] By early 1993 Russian policy had shifted perceptibly on a number of issues, especially those related to peacekeeping. On the matter of the fighting in former Yugoslavia, the Russians raised the issue of possible sanctions against Croatia and strongly opposed any international intervention against Serbia. As part of an effort to get Iraq to pay its outstanding debt to Russia, Yeltsin instructed the Ministry of Foreign Affairs to improve relations with Iraq and to work to reduce tensions in U.S.-Iraqi relations.[59] On the issue of regional conflict in the new states along Russia's borders, Yeltsin and Kozyrev mounted a campaign to gain world recognition for Russia's special role in resolving these conflicts. Moreover, by early 1993 Russia was taking a much more assertive position in its disputes with the Baltic states over the issue of Russian minority rights.

Perhaps more important even than these specific modifications in Russian policy has been the emergence of a changed foreign policy framework. The Foreign Ministry's revised foreign policy concept, first published in early December 1992 and submitted in final form to the parliament in March 1993, gave much greater significance to relations with the near abroad and to the status of ethnic Russians than earlier official foreign policy proclamations did. It also emphasized far more the significance of Asia in future Russian policy and downplayed somewhat the emphasis on relations with the West, which President Yeltsin also did in a speech in early 1993.[60]

By now it should be evident that the policies of 1992, a year when the Russian leadership focused almost exclusively on relations with the West and on cooperation with the United States, were only temporary. Although the concept of Russian statehood and of the nature of Russia is an issue of major debate in Moscow, it is likely that any government in Moscow will be much more nationalist and assertive in the future than was the case during the first year of independence.

Already by early 1993 Moscow's policy had shifted rather significantly on a variety of issues. In most cases the shifts were viewed with concern by Russia's neighbors and indicated, at a minimum, a lack of sensitivity among Russian leaders to the security concerns of these countries. As one Western analyst has stated of the democratically oriented forces in Russia, "The danger is that Moscow's efforts to prevent conflict in the 'near abroad' may simply provoke it. Just as the Westernizers of the nineteenth century did not conceive of Russia as anything other than an empire, today's democratic Russian leaders still appear to distrust instinctively the eligibility for independence and statehood of much of the 'near abroad.' " [61]

Although the United States is likely to accept a "leading" role for Russia in Central Asia because of U.S. concern about Islamic fundamentalism and the potential political influence of Iran in the region, Europe is not likely to do the same. Russian efforts to impose settlements in Moldova or Georgia or Russian attempts to coerce the Baltic states or Ukraine are likely to be opposed by the United States and its Western European allies. Already by summer 1993 a *New York Times* editorial called upon Western governments to make clear to Russian nationalists "that continued military meddling in the politics of non-Russian republics could lead to economic isolation. There is no future in dreaming about the past." [62]

Elsewhere in the world Russia's interests will probably diverge increasingly from those of the United States and other Western states. The historical ties to Orthodox Serbia and the desire to profit from armaments sales to Iran and Libya and to improve relations with Iraq—these and other issues may introduce friction into Russian-U.S. relations. This is not to argue that confrontation of the sort that characterized the global competition between the Soviet Union and the United States is likely to reemerge. What it means, however, is that the U.S. image of a new world order, if such an image still exists, is likely to be challenged by a resurgent Russia even if democratic forces remain in control but especially should strongly nationalist-oriented political groups attain power.

The place of the Russian Federation in regional international peacekeeping depends, then, on Russian domestic political and economic developments. Unless the economy is turned around, the democratic forces are likely to face greater challenge from the nationalists, who, should they come to power, would likely pursue a much more aggressive foreign policy, one that might be committed to reestablishing Russia as a global counterweight to the United States and might attempt to recreate a political unity of large parts of former Soviet territory. Yet, even a more democratically oriented Russian leadership is likely to be less cooperative with the United States than the leadership in the first year and a half of Russian independence has been. Russian interests as perceived in Russia will take precedence over deference to the West, which is in part the result of expectations of aid, in determining the orientation of Russian policy. These interests will very probably diverge from those of the West in a number of important areas.

Russia will focus most of its foreign policy energies on the near abroad, where it may well be as much a source of conflict as a contributor to conflict resolution. Russia's ability to play a constructive role in coping with regional conflict beyond the boundaries of the former Soviet Union will depend upon the success of Russia and the other Soviet successor states to solve their own problems associated with state building in multiethnic environments, with creating the constitutional and legal contours of postcommunist polities, and with restructuring functioning and competitive economies out of the legacy of the collapsed centralized economy of the former Soviet Union.

NOTES

An earlier version of this chapter appeared as "La résolution des conflits: Le rôle de la Fédération russe," *Revue d'Études Comparatives Est-Ouest* 25, no. 1 (1994): 5-32.

1. Samuel P. Huntington discusses the likely continuing divisions between Russia and the West in his recent article "The Clash of Civilizations," *Foreign Affairs* 72 (Apr. 1993): 22-49.

2. *Near abroad* is the term used widely in Russia to refer to the other new states that emerged out of the collapse of the Soviet Union. On this issue see Jeff Checkel, "Russian Foreign Policy: Back to the Future?" *RFE/RL Research Report* (hereafter *RFE/RL*) 1, no. 41 (1992): 17-18.

3. Boris Yeltsin, speaking on Russian television, Feb. 13, 1992, cited in Suzanne Crow, "Russian Federation Faces Foreign Policy Dilemmas," *RFE/RL* 1, no. 10 (1992): 15. See also the interview with Yeltsin in a major Polish daily, where he stated that "Russia's foreign policy objective is to gain an honorable place in international society and become an open and honest partner for states and peoples in the creative and peaceful activity of all mankind" (*Rzeczpospolita*, May 22, 1992, translated in *Foreign Broadcast Information Service—Central Eurasia* [hereafter *FBIS-CE*], June 4, 1992, 16-20).

4. Andrei Kozyrev, "Russia: A Chance for Survival," *Foreign Affairs* 71 (Jan. 1992): 1-16.

5. See *Nezavisimaia gazeta*, Mar. 5, 1992, and *Izvestiia*, Mar. 31, 1992, cited in Suzanne Crow, "Russia Debates Its National Interests," *RFE/RL* 1, no. 28 (1992): 46.

6. Original membership in the Commonwealth of Independent States included eleven new countries: Belarus, Russia, Ukraine, Moldova, Armenia, Azerbaijan, Kaz-

akhstan, Kyrgyzstan, Tajikistan, Turkmenistan, and Uzbekistan. The three Baltic states and Georgia never joined the CIS. After its founding, however, CIS lost two of the original members, Azerbaijan during 1992 and Moldova in summer 1993. In 1994, as part of Russian conditions for its "peacekeeping role" in regional conflicts, Georgia joined the CIS, and both Azerbaijan and Moldova rejoined. On the CIS see Andrei Zagorski, "Die Entwicklungstendenzen der GUS: Von der Differenzierung zur Konsolidierung?" *Berichte des Bundesinstituts für ostwissenschaftliche und internationale Studien* (hereafter *BBoiS*) 24 (1994).

7. On the activities of the CSCE in various regional conflicts see Konrad J. Huber, "The CSCE and Ethnic Conflict in the East," *RFE/RL* 2, no. 31 (1993): 30–36.

8. See Alexei Arbatov, "Russian Foreign Policy Priorities for the 1990s," in *Russian Security after the Cold War*, ed. Teresa Pelton Johnson and Steven Millers (Washington, D.C.: Brassey's, 1994), 1–42.

9. See President Gorbachev's speech to the United Nations in *Pravda*, Dec. 8, 1988. The following discussion of Soviet views and policy vis-à-vis the United Nations draws on Günther Unser, "The United Nations Revaluated," in, *The Soviet Union, 1990/91: Crisis—Disintegration—New Orientation, Foreign Policy*, ed. Gerhard Simon (Cologne: Bundesinstitut für ostwissenschaftliche und internationale Studien, 1992), 118–33.

10. As of November 1992 U.N. peacekeeping operations were active in thirteen countries and proposed for an additional eight countries. Eight of the existing peacekeeping operations began after the shift in Soviet policy. See U.S. Central Intelligence Agency, Directorate of Intelligence, *Worldwide Peacekeeping Operations, 1993*, EUR 92-10027 (Washington, D.C., 1992).

11. See Gerd Linde, "Soviet Policy in the Kuwait Conflict as an Indicator of a New Mid-East Conception," in Simon, *The Soviet Union, 1990/91*, 165–77.

12. See *New York Times*, Feb. 1, 1992, international edition, 5.

13. See Suzanne Crow, "Russia's Response to the Yugoslav Crisis," *RFE/RL* 1, no. 30 (1992): 31–35. See also idem, "Russia Adopts a More Active Policy," ibid. 2, no. 12 (1993): 1–6.

14. For an excellent discussion of Russian foreign policy, in which these points are developed more fully, see Heinz Timmermann, "Profil und Prioritäten der Aussenpolitik Russlands und der Jelzin," *BBoiS* 21 (1992).

15. A 1992 study carried out by the Institute of Political Geography in Moscow estimated the existence of 180 territorial disputes within the borders of the former Soviet Union (*Moscow News* 5 (1992): 6. See also Uwe Halbach, "Ethno-territoriale Konflikte in der GUS," *BBoiS* 31 (1992).

16. Over the objections of President Yeltsin the Russian parliament asserted in July 1993 that the Crimean city of Sevastopol belonged to Russia, not to Ukraine. See Suzanne Crow, "Russian Parliament Asserts Control over Sevastopol," *RFE/RL* 2, no. 31 (1993): 37–41.

17. In both Latvia and Estonia laws have been passed that make it extremely difficult, if not impossible, for the vast majority of Russians to gain citizenship. The Russian delay in withdrawing the remnants of Soviet troops from these countries has been directly tied to the Russian minority issue, as has Russia's periodic economic pressure against the Baltic countries. A recent example of the latter occurred in late June 1993, when all gas exports to Estonia were stopped. In condemning Estonia's citizenship laws,

President Yeltsin reminded Estonia of "some geopolitical and demographic realities" (cited in Celestine Bohlen, "Russia Cuts Gas Supply to Estonia in a Protest," *New York Times*, June 26, 1993, 4).

18. *RFE/RL* 1, no. 31 (1992): 59–60.

19. These issues are discussed in some detail in Ann Sheehy, "Seven States Sign Charter Strengthening CIS," ibid. 2, no. 9 (1993): 10–14. Two modestly optimistic assessments of the future development of the CIS can be found in Jan S. Adams, *Will the Post Soviet Commonwealth Survive?* (Columbus: Mershon Center, Ohio State University, 1993) and Yuri Zhilin, "A Future for the Commonwealth," *New Times* 7 (1993): 13–16.

20. *RFE/RL News Briefs* 2, no. 21 (1993): 21. On more recent strengthening of the CIS see Zagorski, "Die Entwicklungstendenzen der GUS"; Suzanne Crow, "Russia Promotes the CIS as an International Organization," *RFE/RL* 3, no. 11 (1994): 33–38; and Bruce D. Porter and Carol R. Saivetz, "The Once and Future Empire: Russia and the 'Near Abroad,'" *Washington Quarterly* 17, no. 3 (1994): 75–90.

21. See *RFE/RL News Briefs* 1, no. 26 (1993): 7; see also Stephen Foye, "End of CIS Command Heralds New Russian Defense Policy?" *RFE/RL* 2, no. 27 (1993): 45–49.

22. Cited in *RFE/RL Daily Report*, Mar. 1, 1994.

23. On the situation in Abkhazia see Elizabeth Fuller, "Abkhazia on the Brink of Civil War?" *RFE/RL* 1, no. 35 (1992): 1–5; on developments in Transdniestr see *New Times* 34 (1992): 13.

24. *ITAR-TASS*, Jan. 25, 1993, cited in Sheehy, "Seven States Sign Charter," 13.

25. See *RFE/RL News Briefs* 2, no. 22 (1993): 8, 9.

26. John Lough, "Defining Russia's Relations with Neighboring States," *RFE/RL* 2, no. 20 (1993): 53. See also Lough's earlier article, "'The Place of the 'Near Abroad' in Russian Foreign Policy," ibid. 2, no. 11 (1993): 21–29; and two recent essays by Andrei Zagorski, "Russlands Beziehungen zum 'fernen' und 'nahen' Ausland" and "Die Gemeinschaft Unabhängiger Staaten: Entwicklungen und Perspektiven," *BBoiS* 46 and 50 (1992), respectively.

27. In a speech to members of Civic Union (*ITAR-TASS*, Mar. 1, 1993; cited in Suzanne Crow, "Russia Seeks Leadership in Regional Peacekeeping," *RFE/RL* 2, no. 15 [1993]: 28).

28. Crow, "Russia Seeks Leadership in Regional Peacekeeping." See also Arkady Chereshnia, "Big Brother as an Equal," *New Times* 17 (1993): 12–13.

29. *Novaia ezhednevnaia gazeta*, July 7, 1993, cited in *RFE/RL News Briefs* 2, no. 29 (1993): 5.

30. Chereshnia, "Big Brother as an Equal," 13. This statement was written before the Russian invasion of Chechnia in December 1994.

31. *Radio Rossii*, Dec. 11, 1992, cited in Crow, "Russia Seeks Leadership," 31.

32. *INTERFAX*, Dec. 17, 1992, cited in Crow, "Russia Seeks Leadership," 31. See also Suzanne Crow, "Ambartsumov's Influence on Russian Foreign Policy," *RFE/RL* 2, no. 19 (1993): 36–41.

33. Membership supposedly would include Ukraine, Hungary, Poland, the Czech Republic, Slovakia, Romania, Bulgaria, the Baltic states, Belarus, Moldova, and possibly Georgia. See Dmitry Volsky, "Eastern Europe — Counterbalance to Russia?" *New Times* 21 (1993): 22. For a more extensive discussion of this Ukrainian security initiative

see Roman Solchanyk, "Ukraine's Search for Security," *RFE/RL* 2, no. 21 (1993): 1–6.

34. See "Russia and Eurasia: Political and Economic Update, May 21, 1993," *Bulletin, The Atlantic Council of the United States* 4, no. 3 (1993): 4; "Pressure Grows on Azerbaijan Leader to Quit," *New York Times*, June 23, 1992, A3; Elizabeth Fuller, "Azerbaijan: Geidar Aliev's Political Comeback," *RFE/RL* 2, no. 5 (1993): 6–11; and Bess Brown, "Regional Cooperation in Central Asia?" ibid., 32–34.

35. On these issues see Philip Hanson, "The End of the Ruble Zone?" *RFE/RL* 1, no. 34 (1992): 46–48.

36. Suzanne Crow, "Russia Uses UNSC Veto," *RFE/RL News Briefs* 2, no. 21 (1993): 4.

37. See Crow, "Russia's Response"; and Olga Alexandrova, "Russland und die Jugoslawien-Krise," *BBoiS* 34 (1992).

38. The chairman of the Supreme Soviet Committee for International Relations, Evgenii Ambartsumov, argued this in an article in *Izvestiia* on June 27, 1992. Earlier, during the fighting in Croatia, opponents of official policy had called for support for Russia's historical Slavic and Orthodox ally, Serbia. See Eduard Limonov, "Russia Is Repeating the West's Mistakes in Assessing the Yugoslav Conflict," *Pravda*, Jan. 13, 1992, 4, cited in *Current Digest of the Post-Soviet Press* (hereafter *CDPSP*) 44, no. 2 (1992): 17.

39. "Yeltsin Signs Decree on Freezing FRY Relations," *ITAR-TASS*, July 17, 1992, and "Orders 'Stiff' Sanctions," *INTERFAX*, July 17, 1992, both translated in *FBIS-CE*, July 17, 1992, 92–138.

40. *INTERFAX*, Dec. 27, 1992, cited in Crow, "Russia Adopts a More Active Policy," 3.

41. For Kozyrev's statement see *Stern* 7 (1993): 190, cited, along with other relevant materials, in Crow, "Russia Adopts a More Active Policy," 4. Kozyrev's implied commitment of up to two thousand Russian troops to an international peacekeeping force was seemingly contradicted by Russian Defense Minister Pavel Grachev, who ruled out the introduction of Russian troops (see *RFE/RL New Briefs* 2, no. 22 [1993]: 4).

42. For documentation on this issue see *RFE/RL News Briefs* 2, no. 22 (1993): 5.

43. While the term *developing countries* is inadequate to categorize the very different states of Asia, Africa, and Latin America, in the absence of a better term, I shall use it to refer to these countries. Despite the explosion of ethnicity-based conflict in formerly communist countries since 1989, the list of countries in which ethnic or religious conflict is a serious problem is still dominated by countries in Asia, Africa, and Latin America. For example, of forty-eight countries included in a recent listing, all but eight are in the developing world (see David Binder, with Barbara Crossette, "As Ethnic Wars Multiply, U.S. Strives for a Policy," *New York Times*, Feb. 7, 1993, 12).

44. For an overview of Soviet policy toward the developing world see Roger E. Kanet, "The Evolution of Soviet Policy toward the Developing World: From Stalin to Brezhnev" and "Reassessing Soviet Doctrine: New Priorities and Perspectives," in *The Limits of Soviet Power in the Developing World: Thermidor in the Revolutionary Struggle*, ed. Edward A. Kolodziej and Roger E. Kanet (London: Macmillan, 1989), 36–61, 397–425; and Roger E. Kanet with Garth T. Katner, "From New Thinking to the Fragmentation of Consensus in Soviet Foreign Policy: The USSR and the Developing World," in *Soviet Foreign Policy in Transition*, ed. Roger E. Kanet, Deborah Nutter Miner, and Tamara J. Resler (Cambridge: Cambridge University Press, 1992), 121–44.

45. See *New Times* 37 (1992): 5.

46. One Kilo-class submarine was delivered to Iran in November 1992 despite strong U.S. protests, and the sale of another two was confirmed in May 1993 (*RFE/RL News Briefs* 2, no. 20 [1993]: 3). In June 1993 the United States threatened legal sanctions against the Russian Federation and the cancellation of plans for space cooperation because of the shipment of rocket fuel from Russia to Libya, a shipment that was held up in transit by the Ukrainian government at the time of writing (Michael R. Gordon, "U.S. Warns Moscow on Sale of Key Rocket Fuel to Libya," *New York Times,* June 23, 1993, A1, A5).

47. See Roger E. Kanet, "Soviet and East European Arms Transfers to the Third World: Strategic, Political, and Economic Factors," in NATO — Economics Directorate, ed., *External Economic Relations of CMEA Countries: Their Significance and Impact in a Global Perspective* (Brussels, 1984), 171–94, esp. 185.

48. Thomas Sachse, "Russische Rüstungsexporte 1992: Umfang und Organisation," Bundesinstitut für ostwissenschaftliche und internationale Studien, *Aktuelle Analysen* 13 (1993): 1–8; see also his longer article "Russische Rüstungsexportpolitik 1992: Umfang, Organisationsstrukturen, Perspektiven," *BBoiS* 4 (1993).

49. *INTERFAX,* Jan. 20, 1993, cited in Stephen Foye, "Russian Arms Exports after the Cold War," *RFE/RL* 2, no. 13 (1993): 61.

50. *Rossiiskie vesti,* May 22, 1992, cited in Keith Bush, "Russia's Latest Program for Conversion," *RFE/RL* 1, no. 35 (1992): 33.

51. See Sachse, "Russische Rüstungsexportpolitik," 15–17; and Foye, "Russian Arms Exports," 62.

52. See Foye, "Russian Arms Exports," 66. For current data on arms sales see Richard F. Grimmett, *Conventional Arms Transfers to the Third World, 1985–1992,* CRS Report 93-656F (Washington, D.C.: Congressional Research Service, 1993).

53. Sergei Stankevich, "Viewpoint: The State Made Manifest," *Rossiiskaia gazeta,* June 23, 1992, 1, translated in *CDPSP* 44, no. 26 (1992): 1–2; See also Stankevich's direct response to Foreign Minister Kozyrev, "So Far, No One Has Succeeded in Completely Eliminating Force from the Arsenal of Politics," *Izvestiia,* July 7, 1992, 3, translated in *CDPSP* 44, no. 27 (1992): 10–11.

54. See Pavel Golub, "The Creation of a Separate Ministry for Commonwealth Affairs May Be a Political Mistake," *Izvestiia,* July 24, 1992, 7, translated in *CDPSP* 44, no. 30 (1992): 1.

55. In the wake of his victory in the May 1993 referendum President Yeltsin fired Skokov, who had strongly opposed many of his policies. In June 1993 Marshal Shaposhnikov, former commander in chief of joint CIS forces, was appointed to head the council (see Foye, "End of CIS Command").

56. Iurii Borodai, "Totalitarianism," *Nash sovremennik,* July 1992, 130, cited in Vera Tolz, "The Burden of the Imperial Legacy," *RFE/RL* 2, no. 20 (1993): 43. For a categorization and analysis of forms of Russian nationalism see Astrid S. Tuminez, "Russian Nationalism and the National Interest in Russian Foreign Policy" (paper presented at the annual meeting of the American Political Science Association, Washington, D.C., Sept. 2–5, 1993).

57. See Alexander Rahr, "Russia: The Struggle for Power Continues," *RFE/RL* 2, no. 6 (1993): 1–9.

58. Evidence of this shift can be seen in Yeltsin's announcement in December 1992

that de facto control over Russian foreign policy would be placed in the Foreign Policy Commission of the Russian Federation Security Council (see Suzanne Crow, "Processes and Policies," *RFE/RL* 2, no. 20 [1993]: 50). Moreover, Evgenii Ambartsumov, chairman of the parliamentary Committee for International Affairs and Foreign Economic Relations and one of the harshest of Kozyrev's critics, noted in March 1993 that it was no longer necessary to replace Kozyrev as foreign minister, since he was pursuing policies supported by the parliament (*ITAR—TASS*, Mar. 13, 1993, cited in Lough, "Defining Russia's Relations," 57. For an assessment of Ambartsumov's role in Russian foreign policy see Crow, "Ambartsumov's Influence").

59. See Crow, "Processes and Policies," 50, 52.

60. See "Foreign Policy Concept of the Russian Federation," translated in *Foreign Broadcast Information Service—USSR-93-037*, Mar. 25, 1993, 1–20. On the "near abroad" see 3–5; on the importance of Asia see 12–14. Yeltsin's speech was on Russian television, Jan. 25, 1993, and is cited in Crow, "Processes and Policies," 52.

61. Lough, "Defining Russia's Relations," 60.

62. "A New Russian Empire?" *New York Times,* Aug. 1, 1993, 14. The Council for Foreign and Defense Policy, a private but influential body in Russia, issued theses on Russian foreign policy that included the call for the creation of a new union on the territory of the former Soviet Union (see *Nezavisimaia gazeta,* 27 May 1994).

ARTHUR J. ALEXANDER

4 | Japan

▲ East Asia and the Logic of Regional Stability

The central logic of the opening chapter of this book holds that attaining regional order, welfare, and legitimacy must be consistent with the principal instruments available to the global community, that is, the nation-state, markets, and democratization. Each of the three instruments is said to be linked one-on-one to a specific objective: order depends on the nation-state, welfare on markets, and legitimacy on democracy. But, the argument continues, each of these instruments is flawed. However, the Japanese experience, and, more broadly, the East Asian experience, is inconsistent with this logic. Although the instruments may be defective, they have done a remarkable job. Moreover, just one of these instruments—competitive markets—has promoted all three objectives. Successful economic growth produced both security and legitimacy in addition to material welfare. Authoritative regimes in Korea, Singapore, Taiwan, and China gained legitimacy because they delivered the economic goods. More than that, in all these countries the market organization of the economy seems to have led to a reduction of authoritarian rule and a gradual but undeniable move toward true democracy.

Economic success altered the tradeoffs confronting regimes throughout East Asia as they considered the economic losses that would be produced by domestic and external violence. The shift in the relative terms of trade between economic and political goals has dampened the level of conflict in the region. The East Asian experience, among others, also refutes the assertion that "the market distributes wealth unevenly among individuals and groups and inevitably creates inequalities that are the source of social and political tensions."[1] Such effects are not a universal characteristic of markets per se or of their role in all developing countries. A prerequisite for equality is that wealth-producing assets be equally distributed; these assets can be land, political power, military rank, caste or other privileges of birth, or education. The uneven distribution of these assets is not a matter of markets; it is a matter of politics and policies, of criminal and incompetent regimes, of naked power, and of the preservation of accustomed rights.

The degree of concentration is not a result of economic performance in open competitive markets. It is much more commonly a result of arbitrary, nonfunctional, historical factors creating special advantages. Concentration of ownership has been reinforced over long periods by effective exclusion of much of the population from opportunities to raise their earnings and acquire capital and skills. The reluctance of the people who have controlled these societies to invest in education and creation of opportunities for the poor has been a powerful factor helping to keep market forces acting in favor of the few.[2]

The East Asian experience challenges the view of necessary links between per capita income growth and increases in inequality. From 1960 to 1981 the four fastest growing East Asian countries—Korea, Hong Kong, Japan, and Taiwan—exhibited a 6.7 percent annual growth in per capita income. The comparable growth of eight Latin American countries was only 2.7 percent. The average income share of the richest 10 percent of the population in the East Asia sample was 5.6 times that of the poorest 20 percent, whereas in Latin America the richest received 18.3 times the income of the bottom 20 percent. Education is the asset most closely associated with income equality. Differences in the distribution of educational attainment explain these disparities; secondary school enrollment rates in the East Asian countries averaged 86 percent, compared with 49 percent in Latin America.[3]

▲ Japan's Regional Role

Japan's economic growth policies have been the models for Asian states from Singapore to China. Moreover, the lure of Japanese trade, aid, and investment often has subordinated these nations' political goals in favor of economic objectives. In giving up some degree of flexibility in exchange for growth-enhancing policies, the region has been marked by a relative degree of political stability.[4] By inspiring its neighbors to embrace policies of economic growth, Japan has made a fundamental contribution to the region.

Japan's performance, though, has tended to be more passive than active. Asian growth has occurred without the support of formal economic or political structures designed and implemented by regional powers. Indeed, the principal actors in this transformation have been individuals and firms acting in their own interest within the market structures of national economic programs.

Through a Darwinian process of competing economic species, the competitive market method of organizing economic activities has demonstrated outstanding success. Through the force of example, Japan has provided governments and their leaders the information to make better rather than worse choices. Masaru Tamamoto notes that we tend to think of international relations in terms of competition between states and the need for hegemonic leadership to bring international order. The example of Asia provides an alternative where the market, not the hegemon, delivers peace and prosperity.[5]

Unfortunately, we cannot say that Japan has now done its job and can collect the congratulations of the international community. Listing "economic model" on one's resume is insufficient to get one the job of modern economic power. Security objectives can not be automatically assured through the agency of economic development.

The success of Asian economic growth in satisfying multiple needs has been attained within a security framework that guarantees the political stability of an open international economic system.[6] That security framework is now provided in Asia by the United States through bilateral security arrangements. Future security will likely involve Japan as a more active participant with the United States, although the shape of that participation will have to be compatible with the fundamental nature of Japan as a civilian power. Japanese activism in security affairs will impose new kinds of burdens on Japanese society.

Japan possesses serious deficiencies in the three instruments identified as the essential, and only, tools for promoting regional security and welfare: market, state, and democratic structures. The nation's economy remains relatively closed to imports and investment, and its support of multilateral trading institutions remains halfhearted. Japan's political structure does not allow it to engage actively in international affairs when this could adversely affect identifiable members of the public or when uncertainty could bring risk to the bureaucracy. Finally, Japan's relations with the rest of the world are skewed and incomplete, marked by Japan's reluctance to exercise its civilian power actively.[7] For Japan to move forward, passive methods will have to give way to active policies, markets will have to be further perfected, democracy made more mature, and the nation-state completed. Correcting these deficiencies will allow it to take the more responsible and active role in international affairs that its present stature as a near great power leads the world to expect. Such policies will not only require spending national resources but also impose sharp costs and pain on the uncompetitive and hitherto protected sectors of Japanese society, including its politicians and government ministries. Pain of this type can only be accepted if the domestic political system is transformed. Given the scale of the required transformation, the transition to responsible global actor could take decades.

U.S. postwar policies of selfish altruism imposed direct costs on the U.S. population through expenditures on defense and economic aid. The United States also absorbed the indirect costs of dislocation as many U.S. producers lost out to foreign competitors. The U.S. public, by and large, accepted the arguments of the political leaders that these policies contributed to the national welfare. However, bitter congressional battles and constant reiteration of basic themes by a succession of presidents attested to the great effort and attention needed to maintain public support for policies from which few could expect near-term results.

An overwhelmingly dominant country, as the United States was for much of the postwar period, could carry much of the load in maintaining international order while allowing others to be free riders. The United States was willing to take on this burden for the global public good because it also benefited from the results of the policies. However, a shift is now in train from bipolarity and U.S. dominance to multipolarity and interdependence. Global transformations of this scale require adjustments by both the United States and Japan, and both are finding them difficult. A more multipolar world with diffused power and a high degree of interdependence requires that others join with the United States and share the responsibilities and costs of sustaining the global economic and security systems.

The Japanese ambassador to the United States, Takakazu Kuriyama, incisively noted that the international order is not maintained by an invisible hand. "Maintaining world peace and prosperity demands that there be countries willing to accept the responsibility for forging and maintaining the world order and willing to pay the necessary political, military, and economic costs that this entails."[8] The basic question is whether Japan will contribute to the production of international public goods at the expense of identifiable near-term costs to specific domestic parties in exchange for likely long-term benefits to the broader national and international interests.

▲ Japan's Support of the Global Economic System

The Struggle between Openness and Protectionism

Trade and growth create losers as well as winners; businesses, industries, entire geographic regions, and countless numbers of individual workers suffer from the continuous process of change in a dynamic economy. The forces of regionalism and protectionism counter the nationwide benefits of an open, global economic system. Nations want to have the absolute benefit of an open trading regime, while they seek to increase their own relative gains through special arrangements, including protection and managed trade, that will shield potential domestic losers and maximize the rewards to the winners.[9] In this dialectical race between openness and protectionism, Japan is a confused participant. Its external relations and rhetoric favor the former, while its domestic politics and internal bureaucratic interests put it on the side of the protectionists.

Japan's very existence as a modern, technologically advanced nation depends critically on access to the materials, supplies, technologies, and products of other countries and on the ability to market its own output abroad. However, Japan has tended to see free trade as "freedom to export" and not as the freedom of others to export to Japan.[10]

The Closed Nature of the Japanese Economy

The Japanese economy is saddled with a network of government regulation, controls, guidance, and customary business practices that have created protected sectors in banking and finance, retail and wholesale trade, transportation, communications, agriculture, and other industries and products. Legally registered cartels as well as formally illegal but formerly accepted collusive practices in such areas as construction further protect many businesses from the full force of competition, domestic and foreign. As might be expected, these protected sectors, which have been estimated to account for as much as 40–50 percent of national income, are considerably less productive than many of their foreign counterparts. Recent studies conclude that, outside of manufacturing, Japanese productivity is 30–70 percent below U.S. levels.

Opening these markets to competition would place the Japanese participants at severe risk. Japanese domestic politics works to support the status quo and to protect accustomed interests and privileges.

Domestic Politics and Closed Markets

The structure of domestic politics has been a barrier to any market openings that would harm constituents. Multimember parliamentary districts avoided the bitter disputes that would have arisen within the dominant Liberal Democratic Party (LDP) by redistricting. Instead of district lines' being redrawn to reflect relative population shifts, the preferred solution was to grant more seats to districts that gained population. As many as six members represented a single geographic district. A typical election saw six to ten candidates representing the various factions of the LDP and opposition parties. A winning candidate, therefore, could win with only 10–15 percent of the votes. Candidates directed their strategies to appeal to very narrow groups and special interests; politicians did not have to appeal to the broadly based views of the entire district or the even more abstract notion of national interest. Additionally, rural regions and small towns had been overweighted in the Diet. Agriculture, small shops, local banking, and small-scale industry were favored over the interests of city-dwellers, international business and industry, foreign trade, and global finance.

Japanese politics required great sums of money. Regulation and oversight of the political financing laws was particularly weak and ineffective, as one scandal after another has demonstrated. The combination of multimember districts, overrepresentation of rural interests, and unrestrained political financing gave great power to narrow groups and made it extremely difficult to generate change that imposed costs on specific players regardless of the broader national welfare.

The social and political strains implicit in the stagnant political structure grew more severe over time. A combination of events in 1993 led to the downfall of the LDP and the election of a coalition government whose main platform was political reform. Redistricting, single-member districts, and the beginning of political finance reform were the central elements of the reform legislation. One feature of the reform is a combination of proportional representation plus first-past-the-post selection methods. Until several elections have taken place, it will be difficult to predict how the evolving party structure and proportional representation will affect the dynamics of representation and whether broader issues will feature in local elections. Nevertheless, the 1993 elections mark the beginning of a political transformation that should remove many of the impediments to a more active global role for Japan.

Gradual Market Openings

Despite the resistance to change, the Japanese market has, in fact, opened up considerably since the early 1980s. Significant portions of banking, transportation, and telecommunications have been deregulated and privatized. Under pressure from the United States and others, many product areas have been opened to international competition. A Congressional Research Service study found that for twenty-seven products subject to negotiations between 1986 and 1990 the annual export growth rate was 25.2 percent, compared with an 18 percent rate for all U.S. exports to Japan. For the ten classes of manufactured goods the results were even more dramatic: 30 percent growth for negotiated products.[11] It is difficult to identify a single product, industry, or sector that is more closed today than it was in 1980.

A Japanese Role in Supporting Global Openness

It is important for Japan to open its economy and support more broadly an open global economic system. First, the balance between the forces of openness and protectionism is as yet uncertain. Regionalism, fragmentation, and a breakdown of the free trade system are not inevitable, although the highly visible domestic costs of openness push governments in these directions. The European Community, for example, has not become "fortress Europe," despite its erecting barriers to many Japanese products.

Second, opening Japan's markets would support the economic development of many Asian and other countries. These countries typically are most competitive in agricultural products and those that are less technologically advanced, such as textile, clothing, and simple manufacturing products. Japanese barriers to these and other products reduce their sales and profitability and slow economic growth. Japanese support of further WTO (World Trade Organization) negotiations to reduce global trade barriers would work to the same ends. Active moves by Japan to reach agreements by throwing its own markets on the table would aid the developing countries through greater access to the Japanese markets and through the further opening of other developed economies.

Third, for Japan to take a hand in shaping affairs, it must behave in a manner that elicits other countries' willingness to accept Japan's ideas and diplomatic efforts as well as its exports and investments. Acceptable behavior includes explicit attention to "fairness" in its international relations, especially increasingly open markets for foreign goods and investment.

Fourth, many Japanese internationalist business leaders now recognize that corporate Japan's efficiency, competitiveness, and drive for global markets have led to protectionist policies abroad. What seems to be demanded by foreign governments is for Japan to place more of its own markets, firms, managers, and workers at risk of potential dislocation from unrestricted foreign access. The very real changes that have already taken place are deemed to be insufficient. The remaining patterns of insularity do not inspire confidence on the part of other members of the world economic community that Japan is serious in its support of a liberal trade regime.[12]

▲ Japan's Support for Global and Regional Security

Japan's Postwar Strategy

As Japan emerged from its traumatic defeat and occupation in the early 1950s, its economy was shattered, its democracy fragile, its security threatened by highly visible antagonistic regimes on all sides, and its regional objectives distrusted by its neighbors. To achieve its top-priority goals of economic reconstruction, international rehabilitation, and security, Japanese leaders adopted a two-pronged strategy. First, they would concentrate on expanding foreign markets, while nurturing domestic industry. Trade was especially important for economic growth because of Japan's dependence on foreign inputs for its industry; to pay for the imports, Japan had to export.

Second, Japan would minimize military expenditures and maintain a low international profile, relying on the United States to guarantee its security. The architect of this strategy, the first postwar prime minister, Shigeru Yoshida, was reluctant to participate in a multilateral Pacific security pact that would draw Japan into Cold War politics and dangers, force it to devote resources to remilitarization, risk enmity from its neighbors, and delay economic recovery. Moreover, the United States, found Japan's policies congenial to its own objectives. Japan was a bulwark against communism and a showcase of market economics and democratic politics. Japanese leaders viewed as fundamentally important the U.S. role of facilitating access to markets and technologies and providing protection against foreign threats. The U.S.-Japan Mutual Security Treaty codified the basic interests of both parties. Yoshida recognized from the beginning that Japan eventually would have to engage actively in international politics and security affairs. Nevertheless, the Yoshida doctrine governed much of Japan's postwar domestic and international relations.

The Routine Quality of Behavior

With the success of Japan's postwar policies, its institutions, politics, and deeply entrenched vested interests evolved into an almost unbudgeable status quo. The Japanese government rarely has assumed positions of global leadership, responsibility, and innovation. However, the sheer volume of routine activity of an economy as large as Japan's, with its often overwhelming global presence, lends it an extraordinary quality. To borrow from Lenin, quantity has a quality all its own.

The routine quality of much of Japan's world behavior left a gap between what was expected and what was delivered. The world now looks to Japan to take a more active role in (1) regional diplomacy and security; (2) supporting the global trading system; (3) economic assistance; and (4) solving transnational problems, such as protecting the environment, combating terrorism, assisting in natural disasters, and fighting disease. In fact, Japan is engaging in all these areas, but significant impediments restrict its ability to act more heroically.

Security Roles for Japan

Japan is constrained by its constitution, by the attitudes of its citizens, and by its neighbors from taking an active military role, especially one that carries with it the potential for offensive action. Asian nations, especially China, will also be wary of a Japan that tries to assume military or other leadership of an Asian bloc. Future policies must recognize and be consistent with the constraints imposed on behavior, while also noting that many of the constraints can be loosened by vigorous Japanese leadership at home and abroad. Even within these constraints, though, Japan has many opportunities to work for greater order, security, and peace. The principal tools at its disposal are diplomacy, enhanced by economic levers; unarmed military actions; and the application of civilian resources.

A more active diplomacy inevitably will expose Japan to criticism and the risk of failure, neither of which Japanese government officials are accustomed to. Domestic political reactions to international activism would require energy and struggle by government leaders. Neither the bureaucracy nor the political system is adept at dealing with this kind of adversity. All parties seem to be desperately in search of "no surprise" ventures with little exposure to risk.

In this light, the 1991–92 political debate over the law to allow the overseas deployment of Japanese peacekeeping forces was a watershed experience that introduced the Japanese public, the Diet, and the political parties to the new international realities that had hitherto been recognized only by a small internationalist elite. Since then, there has been a seemingly greater willingness by Japan's government to participate in a wide range of diplomatic activities, especially in Asia. Internationalist professionals and knowledgeable politicians had desired such an approach earlier, but the peacekeeping debate seemed to release them to act with somewhat greater freedom. Although still hesitant in putting forth innovative leadership on major issues, Japanese diplomats have moved with some skill in supporting joint U.S.-Japanese interests and in taking the initiative in using the incentives of investment and aid to motivate recalcitrant parties. However, whether Japan can engage in high-stakes games with a potential for loss to domestic parties will depend on the reform of domestic politics and the construction of new or at least revised institutions.

With the collapse of the Cold War, some, but certainly not all, of the rationale for U.S.-Japanese security cooperation has disappeared. Likewise, the pressure for Japan to continue to strengthen its force posture has diminished. The prevalent belief is that the key to conventional deterrence in the Asia-Pacific region is having U.S. forces in and around Japan, with the initial defense of Japanese territory the responsibility of the Self Defense Force. Although there is no single view in Washington, the U.S. government position seems to favor a continuation of present arrangements, but with Japan carrying more of the load and being ready to accept wider roles, such as its sending mine-sweepers to the Gulf in the aftermath of the war against Iraq.[13] Japan gradually has absorbed more of the costs of supporting the U.S. military presence in its country. By the mid-1990s these contributions will amount to almost 100 percent of the stationing costs, so that it will be cheaper for the United States to keep forces in Japan than to return them to the United States.

The Asia-Pacific region is unlikely to see the creation of a security organization similar to NATO. The region is too diverse in terms of types of government, levels of economic development, and security concerns. Democratic, authoritarian, and Stalinist-communist governments coexist. The ratios of GNP per capita varies among the states of the region by factors of more than ten to one. And not only is there no shared threat to bind the region together but some of the putative members of proposed security regimes are the main threats to other members. For these reasons, we are likely to continue to see security arrangements in the form of bilateral agreements with the United States and loose arrangements among the various regional states.

The use of military forces in enhancing security does not necessarily require the use of arms. Logistics support, intelligence, communications, reconnaissance, mine clearing, road building, transportation, and the provision of medical services are functions for which most military organizations are equipped and trained. Such services can be used in peacekeeping operations, disaster relief, and humanitarian operations. Japanese forces could provide these services without doing damage to Japan's constitutional constraints on the use of military force or to neighbors' sensibilities. Civilian organizations could also perform many of these services. For a country with as competent an industrial sector as Japan's, there is little excuse for not contributing to the amelioration of international problems except for lack of will.

▲ Impediments to International Political Involvement

Organizational Underdevelopment

Many of the institutions and the processes required for an active and independent Japanese foreign policy have gone undeveloped.[14] Organizations geared toward intelligence gathering and analysis, strategic thinking, crisis management, and policy implementation have been stunted. Japan's Foreign Ministry, for example, is smaller than Canada's and one-half the size of Great Britain's. Recognizing this deficiency, a government-appointed advisory com mission recommended that the Foreign Ministry be expanded significantly, but implementation has proceeded slowly.[15] Japan is also underrepresented in key multilateral organizations. In 1991, for example, Tokyo provided more than 11 percent of the regular budget of the United Nations, but Japanese made up less than 4 percent of the staff.

Preference for the Status Quo

In domestic politics, the efforts by several prime ministers to alter the Yoshida doctrine were unsuccessful because, according to former prime minister Yasuhiro Nakasone, "public opinion had become blindly committed to pacifism as the best way to preserve their livelihood."[16] Mr. Nakasone has called for strong political leadership to wean the Japanese people from the politics of "willful political innocence, . . . prevarication, escapism, and ostrich-like pacifism."[17] When governments tried to implement policies for a more activist Japanese international role, they were attacked by all sides: by the bureaucracy for overriding its prerogatives and narrow policies; by conservatives, who clung to the Yoshida doctrine; by the Left, which saw the constitution being undermined; and by hard-line nationalists, who regarded the government's plans as too deferential to the United States.[18]

A low posture in international affairs and a concentration on economic growth enabled Japan to avoid the extreme political divisions that an active foreign policy would generate. Japanese politics saw tacit agreements between conservative and left-wing parties that avoided the divisive issue of rearmament and collective security. These tacit agreements not to raise divisive international issues helped to marginalize the Left, as it had the luxury to withdraw from realistic thinking and the advancement of viable alternative policies. The nonparticipation of the major opposition parties in international affairs left the field open to the centrist groups of the LDP, who assiduously continued to follow the Yoshida line. However, the participation of the socialist parties in the coalition government of Prime Minister Hosokawa in 1993–94 introduced them to the world of political reality. Many observers claim that this loss of innocence has fundamental, long-term importance for both domestic and international politics.

Internationalist Stirrings in the LDP

In the 1970s, however, another view gained credence among the "nationalist right" of the LDP. The leaders of this loosely knit group, which includes former prime minister Nakasone and political kingpin Ichiro Ozawa, called for a reevaluation of the Yoshida policies. This group continues to believe that Japan must shed its obsession with the past and its fear of involvement in international politics.[19]

Security and Relations with Neighbors

Japan's participation in world affairs, however, is not solely in its own hands. In the Asian region especially, Japan's history places constraints on its actions. Korea, China, and parts of Southeast Asia have bitter memories of harsh wartime and occupation experiences from World War II, and in the case of Korea, from hundreds of years earlier. But not all the historical memories are negative. Cultural links between China, Korea, and Japan go back nearly two thousand years. Japanese support of anticolonial movements in Indonesia,

Burma, and Thailand were positive experiences. Japan's behavior also created a dualism within many of the countries. Japanese often cultivated nationalist leaders while drafting citizens for dangerous projects. There sometimes arose a distaste for Japan among the population at large accompanied by elite-level cooperation.[20]

Although there is tolerance for greater Japanese activism in Asia, there also is criticism of suggestions that Japan assume a greater security role. A powerful reason for continued suspicion not only in Asian countries directly affected by Japan's wartime behavior but in the United States, Europe, and elsewhere is Japan's reluctance to face up to its past. Japanese journalist Yoichi Funabashi has explained, "Its feeble efforts to educate its people about this history generate deep suspicion and mistrust all over Asia. This reluctance also creates complacent and self-indulgent views among Japanese themselves."[21] Many in Japan believe that Japan behaved no worse than many other powers. Also, most Japanese regard themselves as victims of the same military clique that imposed suffering on other nations. As a result of these beliefs and for other complex reasons, many observers contend that Japan has not done enough to atone for its misconduct.[22] As argued by Hanns Maull, Japan has benefited less than Germany from a reappraisal of its wartime behavior because Germany's postwar political transformation was more profound and its integration into regional security and economic webs more varied. This was in part because Germany's leaders adopted as a central postwar policy the offering of numerous strong apologies to the victims of its abuses as well as exposure of German youth to wartime atrocities and efforts to understand their causes. "Thus, the burden of Japan's past seems more of a political impediment than is the case with Germany; Japan's domestic political transformation . . . seems less complete."[23]

Social and Cultural Factors

Japanese analysts have identified the hierarchical nature of their society, in which rank is the basis of order, as a source of difficulty in international relations. Japan's history shows an inability to accept equality of sovereignty as a basis for relations among states, according to Tamamoto. This kind of equality, even among states of vastly different size and power, is the cornerstone of Western concepts of international law and order.[24] The combination of overdependence on its U.S. ties and the accustomed role of deep-rooted hierarchical relationships in Japanese society produced a psychology of dependence in global affairs.[25]

Japan's sense of being the junior member in a hierarchical relationship was reinforced by its wartime and postwar experience. Japan prospered while following the lead of the United States, which provided both national security and a market for Japanese products. For many Japanese the lesson was clear: "A strategy of following was thus born, came to be cherished, and eventually developed into a kind of an axiom."[26] Others see a Japan that reacts to America in the way that a Japanese child reacts to a dominant parent. This Japan wants to be liked; it is U.S. norms and standards that Japan seeks to satisfy for international recognition. In this kind of relationship, Japan's anxiety is heightened by a United States that often appears irrational, unpredictable, and weak.[27]

The anxiety level is raised even further by the sense that throughout their modern history the Japanese people have felt isolated in world affairs and have been kept away from the tables where the major decisions were being taken. A sense of Japan as latecomer on the world scene contributed to a foreign policy stance of inward-looking exceptionalism coupled with desperate efforts to catch up.[28] Confined by this mindset, Japan has seldom tried to make the rules; the rules were already there. A Japanese political scientist crystallized these ideas by declaring, "The world is nothing but a 'framework' or the setting, which can change only mysteriously."[29]

A Meiji period novelist captured the Japanese predicament eighty years ago. Attempts to pursue progress, to become more open, wrote Natsume Soseki, must be accompanied by frustration, ambivalence, and emptiness because standards of progress come from the West and not from within. Each time the nation achieves a standard, a new one is imposed, and "the Japanese who do not even fully comprehend the old standard are made to feel left out."[30] According to this reading, the world is seen as something "out there" and a continuing source of unease for the Japanese. From this perspective, the staying power of the Yoshida doctrine becomes more understandable. Japan did not have to deal with "out there" but could focus inwardly. However, as Japan shifts its focus to a more global view, its level of discomfort is bound to rise. In addition to being an economic model for its neighbors, Japan is likely to become an anxiety role model for the world community.

▲ Forces for Change

Numerous forces restrict Japan from taking a more active stance in global affairs. While the power of these forces should not be minimized, it is necessary to recognize significant changes that act to encourage and motivate a more active role.

Broadened Experience

Japan now has far-flung interests around the world. It is globally involved in business and economic affairs. Japanese citizens and organizations are exposed to political instability, economic crises, violence, and terrorism worldwide. As a result, Japanese diplomacy is becoming more experienced at dealing with the countless routine issues and occasional major challenges that such exposure generates.

Whether lobbying against higher minivan tariffs in the United States or pressuring Vietnam to be more forthcoming on U.S. demands for information on MIAs, Japan's diplomacy is becoming more active. Business too is more cosmopolitan, with several hundred thousand people now working abroad at any one time. The cultural and social effects of foreign experience are showing up in Japanese society as families, children, business people, and government personnel return to Japan from life abroad. This kind of extended firsthand experience is reinforced by the 10 million or so Japanese tourists who travel outside the country each year. The entertainment media and popular culture also contribute to the broadening horizons of typical Japanese.

The effects of foreign practice are readily observed, for example, when Japanese businesses and consumers question regulations that appear to restrict behavior or impose costs. This extends from bankers who seek deregulation of financial structures after exposure to financial practices in New York, Singapore, or London to consumers who find Japanese products at lower prices in Beverly Hills than on the Ginza.

The growing awareness of alternatives has been coupled with significant shifts in Japanese society and politics. As the postwar political consensus for rapid growth eroded in the 1970s, the popular support for cost-imposing policies began to fade. Additionally, the group-oriented nature of the Japanese people was weakening as more people lived in urban centers rather than in villages, with their stronger orientation to traditional values. The slackening of group consciousness and a weakening of social networks allowed greater voice to be given to a steadily rising sense of dissatisfaction. People started to seek solutions to their immediate problems, such as long commuting times, tiny houses, high-priced goods, and environmental pollution.[31]

Forces for Market Opening

Decontrol was a central thrust of Prime Minister Nakasone's domestic strategy. Moreover, his policies were supported by powerful business forces. Major, internationally competitive industries found their costs and productivity adversely affected by the inefficient and protected domestic sectors. For example, automobile producers whose assembly operations were the most efficient in the world could find their costs increased by nonmanufacturing services: by commercial insurance that was perhaps 30 percent more expensive than competitive rates because of industry regulation and guidance by the Ministry of Finance and by industry self-governance;[32] by factory construction costs rigged by collusion among construction companies; or by regulated transportation of materials and other inputs to the factory that cost more than shipping finished cars across the Pacific. As the yen appreciated in value and as foreign efficiency and competitiveness in production rose to Japanese levels in the 1980s — largely by copying Japanese manufacturing techniques — Japan's production sector became an active voice for decontrol of the rest of society.

Other forces have also been pushing market opening. The numbers of some protected groups, such as small farmers, have fallen sharply. From 1955 to 1990 the total number of farm households declined by more than 2 million (37 percent), while those engaged full-time in farming dropped by a startling 72 percent. Moreover, in just the seventeen years from 1969 to 1986 the number of small retail establishments fell by more than three hundred thousand (20 percent).[33] Since both groups have been large and stalwart supporters of the LDP, their decline was bound to have a noticeable political effect. It is no accident that the opening of these sectors coincided with declining populations of the affected parties. For example, in the past decade the government reduced import barriers for agricultural products such as beef and citrus and revised the Large Scale Retail Store Law, which had restricted the opening of department stores, supermarkets, and other big outlets — including foreign-owned chains such as Toys-'R'-Us — that had threatened the livelihood of mom-and-pop shops. Of major symbolic importance was Japan's 1993 agreement to begin opening its rice market as part of the final Uruguay Round GATT negotiations. At least some of the explanation for this opening, which had been bitterly fought for decades, must lie with the election of the pro-reform government of Prime Minister Hosokawa.

Political Change

Japanese politics is changing because it must meet the desires of voters and the pressures of major constituencies, such as the international business sector. The Japanese electorate is becoming increasingly urban and more urbane, mobile, critical (especially women), and internationally conscious. The new electorate is more volatile and less loyal to a single political group than in the past. The aging of society and the growing attention to quality-of-life issues further deepen the dilemma over how much and what kind of reform is possible in light of the political parties' traditional small-business, small-farmer, and pro-production biases.[34]

The October 1992 resignation of LDP kingpin Shin Kanemaru from his party leadership post was a landmark event as the media, the public, and younger LDP Diet members gave loud voice to complaints over Kanemaru's involvement in a political financial scandal with links to the shady world of Japanese gangs (*yakuza*). For the first time, public outrage erupted over outrageous political behavior and had a major effect on political fortunes.

Although a detailed scenario for political reform could not be written at the time, the forces for change were clearly present in the early 1990s. As it turned out, scandal, recession, political hubris, and insensitivity on the part of the older LDP leaders, younger LDP members' disgust with the existing structure, and tactically brilliant moves by opposition groups within the LDP led by Ichiro Ozawa led eventually to the predictable downfall of the party that had governed Japan for almost forty years.

Generational Change

Former prime minister Kiichi Miyazawa, who as a youth had been an aide to Mr. Yoshida, continued to proclaim the value of the Yoshida doctrine in domestic and foreign affairs into the 1990s. Several prominent political leaders in their fifties, such as former LDP general secretary Ichiro Ozawa, are more activist-minded followers of Mr. Nakasone's line in foreign affairs. In the past several years, many of the younger LDP Diet members flocked around Ozawa, speaking openly and forcefully for the need for reform of politics and policies.

These younger politicians are matched in their desire for change by today's generation of Japanese in their twenties and thirties, who have already adopted a cosmopolitan attitude that eluded their elders. Because of their education and their exposure to other cultures, for them the world is less something "out there." This generation gradually is changing the tone of the Japanese bureaucracy as well as private behavior.[35]

▲ An East Asia Sphere

A More Vigorous Diplomacy

Although Japan's economic relations are more global than regional, several circumstances in the mid-1980s pushed Japanese government analysts into viewing East Asia as a key region for interdependence, a place where Japan could use a battery of economic and political levers to establish political leadership. The rise in the value of the yen, the deregulation of domestic and international capital flows, and foreign pressure to reduce Japan's persistent trade surplus induced Japanese businessmen to turn to East Asia. The government facilitated these moves by providing development assistance intended to underpin private investment. Concern in the late 1980s that more pervasive protectionism and renewed attention to trading blocs would restrict Japanese access to European and North American markets stimulated even greater attention to Asia.[36]

Only in East Asia does Japan have a long record of significant diplomatic activity; its willingness to exert leadership is more evident there than elsewhere around the world.[37] Japan's ability to play a role in East Asia has followed from relative U.S. neglect of the region. Japan did not have to confront active U.S. leadership or pose a direct challenge to key U.S. interests, particularly after the Vietnam War weakened U.S. interest in the area. Also, since many Japanese are beginning to think of themselves as Asian, the region is not "out there" but relatively benign.

In 1992 alone, Japan's diplomats and spokesmen were active on a number of East Asian fronts. Discussions with North Korea in cooperation with the United States included Japanese efforts to convince Pyongyang to be more forthcoming on nuclear facilities inspections. Japanese diplomacy helped to convince Vietnamese leaders to be more accommodating to Washington's requests for information on Vietnam War MIAs; Japanese diplomats argued that not only would such cooperation improve relations with the United States but it would remove some constraints on private Japanese investment. Japan also quietly intervened in Indonesia to push for a more benign approach to human rights after government forces massacred hundreds of protesters in East Timor. (Japanese diplomats argued that if Indonesia were not more accommodating, it could expect harsh economic and political treatment from the West.) In Burma, a Japanese deputy foreign minister raised the issue of democratic reform as a prerequisite for new Japanese aid and investment; this resulted in the ruling military junta's easing pressure on the country's dissidents in an attempt to address Japanese concerns.[38] Interestingly, in the Burmese case and in some of the others, it was Japanese businesses that urged their government to intervene to open up profitable opportunities.

Cambodia: A Test for Japanese Diplomacy

An important test case for Japanese diplomacy was in Cambodia, which had emerged as the best candidate for Japan's demonstration of a more vigorous foreign policy. According to Japanese government officials, "The Middle East and Eastern Europe were considered too complicated, Africa and Latin America too emotionally distant, while China, Korea and much of the rest of Asia still harbor distrust."[39] When it looked as though Japan was going to be asked to support a large part of any U.N. peacekeeping operation, the Foreign Ministry decided to seize the chance to play an active diplomatic and operational role to accompany its financial contributions.

Japan's involvement was highlighted by the assignment of several Japanese nationals to key positions. Yasushi Akashi, a longtime U.N. career civil servant, was appointed as special representative of the United Nations in Cambodia to head the entire U.N. operation. Mr. Akashi used his ties with the Japanese government to urge it to engage in greater activism and risk-taking. For example, when the peace process appeared to have stalled, Japan unexpectedly invited the parties to a meeting organized by Japanese diplomats that helped dislodge the stuck negotiations. Even though its strategy generated opposition from some of the players, it made Japan an active player and formed the foundation for further proceedings. "We considered that move bold, brave, and risky — quite atypical of Japanese diplomacy," an official in the Asian bureau of the Japanese Foreign Ministry said.[40]

In support of its Cambodian diplomacy, Japan spent more than $250 million to support the U.N. operation there and sent six hundred peacekeeping troops from the Self Defense Force. These moves came after a prolonged parliamentary struggle over the peacekeeping support legislation in which the emotional subjects of the postwar "peace" constitution and Japanese global responsibilities were central, conflicting elements.

Japan's support of the delicate and complex diplomatic maneuvers was critical to the success of the largest U.N. peacekeeping effort to date. For Japan to have done more — for example, to have applied its considerable economic leverage against Thai support of the recalcitrant Khmer Rouge — would have risked offending the Thai government, which could have damaged Japanese companies' commercial relations in that country. The final story of how Japan played out its Cambodian role will be a signal to future Japanese diplomatic trends in the region.

▲ Conclusions: The United States in Japan's Global Role

Japan's future path will depend critically on U.S. strategy and behavior because the United States continues to be the dominant economic and military power in the world. Also, the United States will continue to have a profound influence on Japan, for one thing, because that country still is both psychologically and institutionally the junior partner in the relationship. Although a new internationalist group is beginning to take shape, it is still in a formative stage. Kenneth Pyle concludes, "Except in response to outside pressure, there is not yet sufficient political will, nor the necessary institutions, nor the values and cultural resources that would impel Japan to abandon the highly successful but narrowly self-interested policies of the past and assume a self-generated role of international leadership." [41] Although the coalition governments that replaced the LDP after 1993 are trying to alter this pattern, Tokyo still faces an uphill battle as it continues to look to the United States as its security guarantor.

However, the United States has accepted more global responsibility than it is willing to support single-handedly, and Japan has the capability to take on greater burdens than it has agreed to support. It is necessary for the United States to join with others if it is to perform effectively. It is in this sense that the United States needs Japan.[42] At the same time, Japan needs the United States. As many Asians see it, the United States is essential to peace and security in the Asia-Pacific area. U.S.-based security arrangements operate to reassure Japan's neighbors that while Tokyo assumes a broader international stance, a balance of power with the United States as the balancing element keeps the region stable.

Determining common U.S.-Japanese interests and working out concrete means for pooling resources and allocating tasks are prerequisites for sharing responsibilities. Although Japan gradually is supplanting U.S. economic and even diplomatic leadership in some instances in the Asian region, the United States still is the dominant provider of security there and the primary market for Asia's exports; it still enjoys the legitimacy of leadership. The United States, moreover, remains the principal player in shaping the institutional structure

of a regional order.[43] The changing world scene means, however, that cooperation between the United States and Japan could promote economic welfare
and regional security that works to the mutual advantage of all participants.

With the demonstrated ability of successful economic policies to bring both
material welfare and order, some analysts have raised the notion of "soft"
power as replacing the outdated concepts of superpower hegemony. The new
watchwords are *cooperation* and *complex interdependence*. However, the soft-
power theorists also note that the first precondition is a security framework
that guarantees the stability of the global economic and political system.[44] The
very ability to develop and project economic and technological power depends
on a security framework based on "hard" power — in traditional military and
political terms — to back it up.[45]

The key question now is, what will be the source of the hard power? Asia is
not ready to accept Japan as a regional political or military leader. Moreover,
Japan's economic involvement is global rather than regional; it is unlikely to
cast off its global relationships in order to confine itself to its regional backyard. But given the necessity for major countries, even the United States, to act
cooperatively, Japan potentially is a key participant in any security framework,
regional or global. Yet, Japan's responsibility most likely still will be fashioned
around its alliance with the United States.

Logic suggests that Japan can make contributions by continuing its relatively passive role as a model of successful economic development and by
actively promoting broader economic structures. Tokyo also can contribute to
the support of a security framework in alliance with the United States, which
remains the essential cornerstone to Asian security in cooperation with Japan
and others. In continuing to take the lead in security, the United States follows its honored path of selfish altruism, but now with a more mature cast of
supporting players.

The tasks for Japan in supporting its global responsibilities will be difficult
to achieve, but they can be accomplished through changes in internal policies;
they place few demands on its neighbors or others. Domestic political reform
seems to be a precondition for accepting some domestic pain in exchange for
broader and longer-term goals. Among the active steps to be taken next are a
further opening up of the Japanese economy and expanded support of global
economic institutions such as GATT. The national leadership could prepare
the Japanese public for the post-Yoshida era by promoting a global consciousness and by taking up former Prime Minister Nakasone's challenge to educate
the public about contemporary realities and wean it away from romantic and
untenable ideas about the nation's international role.

The United States, for its part, could promote Japan's acceptance of global responsibilities by learning better how to participate with its most important global partner. Neither the United States nor Japan has much experience in operating in a relationship of genuine equals. Cooperation will require greater shared understanding, genuine consultation, and public and private appreciation of the gains from partnership and shared responsibility.

NOTES

1. Edward A. Kolodziej and I. William Zartman, "Coping with Conflict: A Global Approach," chap. 1 above.

2. John Sheahan, *Patterns of Development in Latin America: Poverty, Repression, and Economic Strategy* (Princeton: Princeton University Press, 1987), 320–21.

3. Nancy Birdsall and Richard Sabot, "The Accumulation and Utilization of Human Capital in East Asia," *World Bank,* Apr. 1992.

4. Masaru Tamamoto, "A New Order in Asia? Japan's Uncertain Role," *World Policy Journal,* fall 1991, 579–98.

5. Ibid., 593.

6. Ibid., 596; Hanns W. Maull, "Germany and Japan: The New Civilian Powers," *Foreign Affairs* 69 (winter 1990–91): 102.

7. Hanns W. Maull, "Civilian Power: The Concept and Its Relevance for Security Issues," in Trilateral Commission, *Working Group Papers, 1991–1992* (New York, 1991–92), 26–27.

8. Takakazu Kuriyama, "Japan–United States Relations in the New International Order: Forging a Global Partnership" (in Japanese), *Gaiko Forum,* Nov. 1991.

9. Robert Gilpin, "The Debate over the New World Economic Order," in *Japan's Emerging Global Role,* ed. Daniel Unger and Paul Blackburn (Boulder, Colo.: Lynne Reinner, 1993), 21–36.

10. Kuriyama, "Japan–United States Relations."

11. Peter L. Gold and Dick K. Nanto, *Japan-U.S. Trade: U.S. Exports of Negotiated Products, 1985–1990* (Washington, D.C.: Congressional Research Service, Nov. 26, 1991).

12. Edward J. Lincoln, "Trade and Investment Issues in Japan's Global Role," in Unger and Blackburn, *Japan's Emerging Global Role,* 133–54.

13. Kenneth Hunt, "Japan's Security Policy," *Survival* 31 (May–June 1989): 205.

14. Kenneth Pyle, "Japan and the Future of Collective Security," in Unger and Blackburn, *Japan's Emerging Global Role,* 99–117.

15. Barbara Wanner, "Reforms Eyed for Administration of Japan's Foreign Policy," *JEI Report* 3A, Jan. 24, 1992.

16. Yasuhiro Nakasone, quoted in Pyle, "Japan and the Future of Collective Security," 112.

17. Ibid., 109.

18. Pyle, "Japan and the Future of Collective Security," 110.

19. Masaru Tamamoto, "The Japan That Can Say Yes: Groping for a World Role," *World Policy Journal,* summer 1990, 501.

20. Kent E. Calder, *Japan's Changing Role in Asia: Emerging Co-Prosperity?* (New York: Japan Society, 1991), 1, 4.

21. Yoichi Funabashi, "Japan and the New World Order," *Foreign Affairs* 70 (winter 1991–92): 71.

22. Takashi Inoguchi, "Japan's Role in International Affairs," *Survival* 35 (summer 1992): 75.

23. Maull, "Germany and Japan," 97.

24. Tamamoto, "Japan's Uncertain Role," 585.

25. Funabashi, "Japan and the New World Order," 62.

26. Ibid.

27. Masaru Tamamoto, "The Japan That Wants to be Liked," in Unger and Blackburn, *Japan's Emerging Global Role,* 37–54.

28. Funabashi, "Japan and the New World Order," 60.

29. Kyogoku Junichi, quoted in ibid.

30. Natsume Soseki, quoted in Tamamoto, "The Japan That Wants to be Liked," 44.

31. Kozo Yamamura, "The Deliberate Emergence of a Free Trader: Japanese Political Economy in Transition" (paper read at the Woodrow Wilson Center Conference, "Japan and the World," Washington, D.C., Jan. 27–28, 1992), 9.

32. Arthur J. Alexander and Hong Tan, *Barriers to U.S. Service Trade in Japan* (Santa Monica, Calif.: RAND Corporation, 1984), 14.

33. Retail trade figures refer to establishments engaging one to four persons (*Japan Statistical Yearbook* [Tokyo: Prime Minister's Office, 1965–93]).

34. Kent Calder, "Japan's Changing Political and Economic System: Implications for Japan's Global Role," in Unger and Blackburn, *Japan's Emerging Global Role,* 122.

35. Tamamoto, "The Japan That Wants To be Liked."

36. Kenneth Pyle, "How Japan Sees Itself," *American Enterprise,* Nov.–Dec. 1991, 31.

37. Daniel Unger, "ODA Paradigms and Japanese Shaping of the East Asian Economy," in Unger and Blackburn, *Japan's Emerging Global Role,* 156–57.

38. Bertil Lintner, "A Yen for Self-Interest," *Far Eastern Economic Review,* May 14, 1992, 16.

39. Teresa Watanabe, "Japanese Venture into Indochina on Wings of Doves," *Japan Times,* Mar. 7, 1992.

40. Ibid.

41. Pyle, "Japan and the Future of Collective Security," 114.

42. Kuriyama, "Japan–United States Relations."

43. Ibid.

44. Maull, "Germany and Japan," 102.

45. This point is made in Tamamoto, "Japan's Uncertain Role," 596.

SAMUEL S. KIM

5 | China

Despite the momentous and peaceful changes in the global situation in recent years, regional conflicts continue to plague our increasingly interdependent and fragile planet. The demise of the Cold War and the consequent removal of East-West conflict are having both positive, liberating effects and negative, constraining ones. While the dangerous pattern of East-West conflict, characterized by global military confrontation between the two superpowers, locked in struggle for spheres of influence in every corner of the planet, has suddenly withered away with the disintegration of the socialist superpower, other embedded social, economic, and ecological conflicts have become more salient. Even in Europe, where the Cold War began and ended in a dramatic manner, both centripetal and centrifugal forces are developing in tandem.

Paradoxically, the collapse of the Soviet Union has produced the greatest leap in superpower nuclear disarmament *and* horizontal nuclear proliferation since the end of World War II. While the United States and Russia have agreed to reduce their nuclear arsenals by about three-fourths, the former Soviet nuclear superpower seems to be splitting into four nuclear powers, and potential sources of dual-use nuclear technology—Russia, Ukraine, Kazakhstan, and

Belarus. Local and regional ethnonational conflicts, previously overshadowed and repressed by the global superpower contention, are breaking out in many parts of the world. Interstate armed conflicts befitting the traditional definition of *war* have virtually disappeared. (Iraq's invasion of Kuwait stands out as the most recent conspicuous exception.) The overwhelming majority of armed conflicts today are *internal conflicts* and *state-formation conflicts*. Wars of national identity have emerged as the primary species of regional conflict in the post–Cold War setting.

To a significant extent, the post–Cold War challenge of preventing, controlling, restraining, weakening, or encapsulating regional conflicts has devolved on the global community. Thirteen of the seventeen current (as of December 1994) U.N. peacekeeping operations were established in between 1991 and 1994—more operations than in the previous forty-four years—as the U.N. Security Council expanded and deepened its coping roles and resources in relation to a series of sanguinary conflicts in trouble spots around the world, from Central America to the Balkans, through Africa and the Middle East, to Southeast Asia. Tellingly, the member states are asking the world organization to do more and more with less and less, without opening their wallets or delegating more peacemaking power or revamping the half-century-old Big Five anachronism of the Security Council.[1] At the same time, the authoritarian political lid has been lifted from several multinational states, including the former Soviet Union itself, riven with primordial ethnonationalist tensions and rivalries. Coping with regional conflict in such a setting will necessarily require both new thinking and greatly expanded intersystemic cooperation between the world community, major global actors (e.g., the United States, Russia, China, Japan, the European Community, and the Third World), and local and regional antagonists.

How does China fit into the post–Cold War challenge of establishing a more peaceful, equitable, democratic, and ecological world order? By virtue of what it is and what it does, China becomes part of both the problem and the solution. As the post–Cold War world moves toward increasing global interdependence and substate fragmentation, the risks and consequences of regional conflict, especially conflict of a military nature involving major regional powers, will be magnified. To improve the chances for avoiding, abating, containing, and resolving such regional conflicts, an understanding is needed concerning the ways regional great powers cope with international disputes and crises involving the use of military force, as well as the rationale or calculus that provides the basis for their international behavior.

As one of the Permanent Five, China is ipso facto involved in the conflict-management process of the Security Council. No major international conflict of a military, social, demographic, and environmental nature in the world at large, especially in the Asia-Pacific region, can be resolved or abated without Chinese consent or cooperation. As the world's third largest nuclear weapons power and one of the top five arms exporters, China's cooperation would be indispensable in any meaningful global and regional arms control and disarmament process. There can be little chance of stabilizing world population growth at a tolerable level unless the Chinese (and the Indians) improve their family-planning programs and services. Many scientists and environmentalists believe that China has already crossed critical thresholds of environmental sustainability and that consequently new conflicts will emerge at levels unseen in recent history.

The purpose of this chapter is to develop a broader conceptual framework by identifying one major power's national roles, resources, and strategies in the international processes of coping with conflict. The study is mainly concerned with China's response to what Edward Kolodziej calls the "three inescapable global imperatives of order, welfare, and legitimacy." For this line of inquiry, the following questions will be addressed: (1) What are the Chinese definitions of the international situation in general and a legitimate world order in particular in this turbulent, transitional time and setting? (2) What are the established patterns of Chinese conflict and cooperative behavior ,especially in relation to recent regional conflicts? What conceptions of its national role and what capabilities and strategies does China bring to the international negotiating processes for coping with conflict? (3) What is China's propensity for international cooperation likely to be?

▲ China Adrift in a Post–Cold War World

Just as Japan is sometimes seen as a wallet in search of a new global money trough, post-Tiananmen China has become an almost empty seat in the U.N. Security Council in search of a new national identity and role. Suddenly Beijing is unsure of its place in a post–Cold War world no longer dominated by superpower rivalry and hence is now in the grips of an unprecedented legitimacy/identity crisis. Not since the founding of the People's Republic in 1949 have the crises of internal and external legitimacy, in the form of the Tiananmen carnage and the collapse of global communism, been as conflated as in the past few years.[2] A measure of the leadership's acute siege mentality can be seen in its confusing and often contradictory definitions of the changing international situation. The propaganda apparatus has been releasing a flurry of accounts of China's own domestic stability and foreign policy accomplishments coupled with extensive coverage of the economic difficulties and social and political instabilities in Eastern Europe and the constituent republics of the former Soviet Union. It is claimed that China's relations with neighboring countries "have never been more satisfactory since the founding of the Republic."[3] Given the acceleration of world history and the uncertainties of post-Tiananmen Chinese politics, it is not easy to determine whether these policy pronouncements are suggestive of a rising index of China's confidence about its emerging global position in a multipolarizing world or a sort of whistling-in-the-dark posturing to be appearing confident. One thing seems obvious: international legitimation has become another way of shoring up sagging domestic legitimation.

Since 1983 Chinese analysts have often used the term *multipolarization (duojihua)* in a loose, freewheeling way. Apparently, the self-serving behavioral definition of *hegemony*—any criticism of the Chinese government or its behavior—gets in the way of Chinese global learning. Surely, multipolarization has both normative and strategic appeal inasmuch as it seems to validate the claims that the world is finally moving from superpower contention toward a more diffused, polycentric international order and that China is on the upward trajectory in the inexorable rise and fall of great powers. And yet, a multipolarizing world was seen by many Chinese strategic analysts as one bereft of the much-coveted balancing third force—the vaunted China card—in global triangular geopolitics. It was, after all, bipolarity that had served as the lodestar of Chinese global politics in the 1970s and 1980s, enabling Beijing to exploit superpower rivalry to gain its own strategic leverage, economic and trade benefits, and global weight. The structural reality of what the Chinese call the Yalta system is an answer to the puzzle of how a regional power managed to be treated as a global power without first having acquired the reach or the requisite normative and material resources. With the demise of the strategic triangle, China's permanent membership in the Security Council, coupled with its status as one of the nuclear powers, became the more visible symbolic way of legitimizing its standing as a global power.

There still remains more confusion than coherence in Chinese assessments of the multipolarizing (power diffusion) process because of disagreement about its implications for China in a rapidly changing world. As late as early 1990, one publicist, echoing an official prognostication, insisted that bipolarity, though somewhat weakened, would continue for a long time. Yet only three months later his assessment of the world structure, influenced by the collapse of the bipolarized system and the demise of the Warsaw Pact, had taken on a more pessimistic tone. A multipolar world of indeterminate form and direction was replacing the bipolar world order.[4] In Beijing's view, then, a multipolarizing world will give rise to new geopolitical alignments in the Asia-Pacific region and, concomitantly, intensified rivalry for the enhancement of the so-called comprehensive national strength (zonghe guoli). The broader point is that the comprehensive-national-strength interpretation of the world situation comes much closer to a realist-nationalist than to a Marxist interpretation of uneven development and international conflict formation.

From a post-Tiananmen perspective, the collapse of the Soviet Union and the prospects of U.S. military disengagement in East Asia represent a newer danger in the form of the rise of an unbridled Japan as an assertive regional and global power seeking to transform its enormous economic power into military and political power, as well as an opportunity for China to prevent this from happening by preemptively filling the power vacuum. Some Chinese analysts argue that Tokyo began to pursue such "superpower diplomacy" in 1991 by expanding its influence from economic to political and military fields; for example, Japan's U.N. budget assessment for the years 1992–94 shot up to 12.45 percent. A recent classified internal document offers a more revealing window into the Chinese leadership's thinking. Although one cold war has ended, we are told, two new cold wars have already started, namely, the confrontations among the imperialist powers Japan, the United States, and Western Europe and the confrontations among imperialist states, Third World countries, and socialist countries that survived the fall of Soviet communism. The central challenge of post–Cold War Chinese foreign policy is said to be threefold: "We must especially take advantage of confrontations among Western nations, strengthen ourselves and consolidate the neighboring region by giving priority to our maneuvers in Asia and the Pacific region."[5]

Once again China has demonstrated a remarkable capacity to redefine the international situation and steer the ship of state according to the changing political winds at home and in the world at large. The world military pattern is said to be shifting from global military threats to regional military threats, giving rise to "strategic no-man's-lands of various sizes in certain regions."[6] Apparently, the rise of strategic vacuums does not represent dangers to be avoided or managed through regional or global conflict-management mechanisms, but opportunities to be unilaterally exploited. We are told, as if to legitimize China's gunboat diplomacy in the South China Sea, that "various countries have universally taken the capabilities of coping with regional tensions, conflict crises, and partial wars as the major objectives of army building."[7] Beijing seems to have recovered rather quickly from the shock of the collapse of Soviet communism's turning Russia, as well as several of the other successor states, into a wholesale arms bazaar for advanced weapons systems, as evidenced by the Chinese purchase of twenty-four Su-27 long-range jet fighters worth more than $1 billion.[8]

Since mid-1984, however, a conceptual readjustment has occurred in the form of a "world peace and development line," accompanied by a more positive view of an Asia-Pacific economic community. In mid-1985 the Central Military Commission reached a strategic decision requiring the People's Liberation Army to redirect its military strategy from the preparation for general nuclear war with the Soviet Union to preparation for the more probable scenario of local and regional wars around China's periphery. The most significant effect is the gradual decoupling of local and regional conflicts from superpower rivalry. The fading of the Cold War and the disintegration of the Soviet Union have hastened this delinkage process. This does not mean that the center of normative gravity has shifted from hard globalism to soft regionalism. Instead, China's regional security policy has now become a function of its unilateralism in bilateral realpolitik relief.

With the end of the Cold War and the ensuing removal of the Soviet military from Southeast Asia and the U.S. withdrawal from the Philippines, this strategic reorientation has become a more credible and potentially actionable tableau. China today regards the disputed but oil-rich Paracel and Spratly Islands in the South China Sea in terms all too reminiscent of the Third Reich's *lebensraum* imperial policy. A recent internal Chinese document states that these island groups, some of which are situated nearly one thousand kilometers south of China's Hainan Island and most of which are subject to conflicting jurisdictional claims by Vietnam, the Philippines, Taiwan, Malaysia, and Brunei, could provide *lebensraum* (*shengcun kongjian*, literally, "survival space") for the Chinese people. According to an internal document published in the *Far Eastern Economic Review* in August 1992, "In terms of resources, the South China Sea holds reserves worth $1 trillion. Once Xinjiang has been developed this will be the sole area for replacement of resources, and it is a main fallback position for *lebensraum* for the Chinese people in the coming century."[9]

The most recent party line, as expressed by Jiang Zemin's political report to the fourteenth Party Congress, in October 1992, that bipolarity is gone for good and that the international system is heading rapidly toward multipolarity, may well signal an official closure to the debate about polarity and uncertainty about the benefits of multipolarity.[10] Multipolarity is now cast in a new light, as giving China more leverage opportunities and more perceptual and behavioral space than could be realistically considered if the predominant definition of the world situation were bipolar. First, multipolarity in which China is a major player offers more genuine freedom to be and act as a Group of One in global high politics and more diversification options to counter U.S. hegemony or "peaceful evolution" than bipolarity, in which China had more limited alignment options. Second, floating multipolarity is preferred to both tight bipolar conflict and tight bipolar collusion since as one of those newly emerging poles China by self-definition becomes a key player in global high politics. And third, multipolarity opens up the new pathway of improving Sino-Russian relations as part of a strategy of diversification, which might also allow China to enjoy any residual effects of a Russian card in Sino-U.S. relations, an option more credible now, with the demise of a Russian military threat, than ever before.

What about the Chinese image of a legitimate world order? It was not until April 1991 that the idea of world order began to receive normative and political consideration.[11] Apparently the government had issued a directive to the Chinese community of international relations scholars and research institutes to respond to U.S. President George Bush's invocation of New World Order. In a sense, then, Bush sired this grand debate, which generated in the Chinese press a flurry of programmatic essays on a new world order. What emerged, if only in rudimentary and reactive form, were Chinese notions of world order. World structure is construed as an empirical concept referring to the "correlation of global forces" in the world. World order is defined in aspirational and prescriptive terms and refers to the norms, principles, and mechanisms that should govern international relations. If world structure is an empirical and objective reality, world order is a subjective and aspirational condition some Western countries try to impose. Nevertheless, world order and world structure are said to be closely interrelated and interdependent. At the same time, global debate on the new world order is symptomatic of the contest for comprehensive national strength in which every global actor jockeys for a favorable position during the process of structural change. It is seen as a contest between the "theory of might" and the "theory of rights."

Embedded in the Chinese debate is a concern for drawing distinctions between *world* order, on the one hand, and *regional* or *international* orders, on the other. Much of the debate has focused on Bush's New World Order, which is considered a euphemism for a new U.S. hegemony and hence deeply problematic in the world of sovereign states. Whereas a world order is basically a set of world regulations (and therefore a potential threat to sovereign equality), an international order is a more benign notion, embodying the norms and regulations needed to govern interstate relations. Although theoretically a new world order and new regional orders may develop in tandem, the former remains mired in a wish list of abstract general statements, while the latter has become more concrete, realistic, and feasible. In actuality, we are told, in recent years the major powers have concentrated their efforts on the establishment of new regional orders. Against this background, the primary mission of the Chinese debate is to legitimize China's call for a "new international political and economic order" (NIPEO). Chinese international relations scholars are charged by the Party-state with the task of squaring the circle by way of a Marxist theory of world order with Chinese characteristics.

Despite the twists and turns in Chinese foreign policy over the years, the Westphalian concept remains dominant in the Chinese image of world order. Because of China's victimization during the long century of national humiliation, contemporary Chinese world order thinking still seems mired in a siege mentality that goes back to the traumatic period of unequal treaties. In the wake of the Tiananmen carnage, the Westphalian system acquired special resonance in Beijing's multilateral diplomacy, with its repeated calls for the NIPEO based on the Five Principles of Peaceful Coexistence (FPPC): (1) mutual respect for sovereignty and territorial integrity; (2) mutual non-aggression; (3) mutual noninterference in internal affairs; (4) equality and mutual benefit; and (5) peaceful coexistence. The principle of state sovereignty and the principle of state equality, the two core principles of the Westphalian world order system, are declared to be the cornerstone for international order. Since the individual is not separate from the state, human rights cannot be realized to the negation of state sovereignty. To posit human rights as the basis of international relations is to place the cart of individualism before the horse of state and to reject the essence of the international order.[12]

The irony is that the so-called *new* China is constantly invoking the shrill, blasé, and baroque principles of the *old* Westphalian international order. The content of the proclaimed *new* international order is remarkably like that of the *old* statecentric international order: how each sovereign state, including China, mistreats or even makes war on its own people and minority nationalities is none of the rest of the world's business. The question of how state sovereignty would actually protect the rights of the people and bring power and plenty in this postmodern age of global communication and interdependence is never directly or clearly addressed in the Chinese version of a legitimate world order.

▲ Roles, Resources, and Strategies

Like any major international actor, China brings to the international processes of conflict formation and resolution its own repertoire of national role conceptions, national resources, and national negotiating style and strategies.

Alternating National Roles

The starting point for understanding China's international behavior is to recognize that since the collapse of the traditional Sinocentric world order in the late nineteenth century this proud and frustrated Asian giant has had inordinate trouble in finding a comfortable niche as an *equal* member state in the family of nation-states and in recovering its "lost" territory. China stands out as one of the ten most *crisis-active states* in the international system during the fifty-year period 1929–79, with all but one of its foreign policy crises deriving from the core issue of national security and occurring along the peripheries of what it regards as "sacred home territory," whether recognized as such by others or not. In contrast with the Guomindang period, 1929–49, during the post-1949, People's Republic, era, the overwhelming choice among techniques for coping with conflict and managing crisis—in about 70 percent of its foreign policy crisis situations and in about 80 percent of its territorial crisis situations—was violence.[13] Beijing has had difficulties in maintaining enduring friendship with any Asian state, even North Korea. In the context of the Cold War years, the People's Republic established by choice or by necessity a record that no other country could possibly match: it had an alliance as well as a Cold War relationship with the socialist superpower, both of which proved to be inconclusive; it had a war and a quasi-alliance relationship with the capitalist superpower, both of which proved to be short-lived. The same can be said about China's relations with Vietnam, the so-called regional hegemon.

Indeed, in the course of its international relations, the People's Republic has succumbed to wild national-identity mood swings, slipping through a series of dramatically diverse national roles: self-sacrificing junior partner in the Soviet-led socialist world; self-reliant hermit completely divorced from and fighting against both superpowers; system-transforming revolutionary vanguard for an alternative United Nations; self-styled Third World champion for the establishment of a New International Economic Order (NIEO); system-maintaining status quo "partner" of NATO and favored recipient of World Bank largesse; lone socialist global power in a postcommunist world; and bargain shopper for advanced weapons systems in the former Soviet Union successor states.

One parsimonious explanation for such shifting and multiple role playing is that China is a relatively weak, reactive state in the treacherous waters of intense bipolar conflict, but a state with a goal of becoming a pole in and of itself. Balancing or bandwagoning alliances are required but are of necessity transient and unstable. They are required either until the primary threat cannot be conclusively identified, as in the mid-1960s, or the threat disappears or until options for genuine nonalignment against a new primary threat are available, as in the collapsed bipolar world of the early 1990s.

None of these multiple national roles have much to do with Asian regional identity. There is a vast gap between being and becoming in China's drive for status. This contradiction between regional power status and global aspirations has introduced a fundamental paradox in the prioritization of China's multiple national roles. More specifically, China's quest for national identity in a changing world can be seen as an ongoing negotiating process to enhance physical and psychological well-being, in the course of which the self attempts to secure an identity as a global power that others do not bestow, while others attempt to bestow an identity as a regional power that the self does not appropriate.[14] Indeed, China has found itself impaled on the horns of this dilemma in one of the contemporary paradoxes of power in global politics. The habitual and ritualized assault on power politics notwithstanding, China's unique status as a "poor global power" can be best explained as a triumph of its deft realpolitik. Just as the Cold War helped China extend its weight well beyond its national strength and the Asia-Pacific region, its ending seems to pose a new challenge for China's strategic behavior.

The difficulty of accurately assessing China's emerging role as a great power in the Asia-Pacific region is greatly compounded by the fact that the perception of what constitutes power has changed significantly in the wake of the demise of the socialist superpower and the multipolarizing process in East Asia. Even the North-South, or Center-Periphery, divide is more blurred in East Asia than in any other region of the world. As a result, the geopolitical and geoeconomic realities of the region are now amenable to diverse interpretations. In one sense the region is more *bipolar* today than ever before, given the overlay cast by two global and/or regional powers—the United States as the world's lone though fleeting superpower and Japan as the world's largest credit power. In another sense the region is more *multipolar* than elsewhere, especially after the emergence of China as a new independent nuclear power in 1964 and of India as another independent, quasi-nuclear power in 1974. And there is still another sense in which the region is more *unipolar* than elsewhere considering the as yet unchallenged U.S. hegemony in East Asian international politics.[15] Even the *tripolar* notion finds numerous regional and subregional variations. On the one hand, implicit in some recent assessments of the international situation is the emergence of a Sino-Japanese-U.S. tripolarity in the Asia-Pacific region. On the other, the collapse of the Soviet Union has also given rise to a debate on the possibilities of a new strategic triangle involving the United States, Japan, and Russia, with China as the weak power out.[16]

Despite some temporal variations, the track record of Chinese conduct over the years generally supports the belief that China is more seasoned in conflict behavior than in cooperative behavior. Any state's foreign policy orientation toward international conflict or cooperation depends on the interaction between actor (regime) attributes and external systemic conditions. Chinese conflict or cooperative behavior can be seen here as the outcome of an ongoing encounter between decision makers' perceptions of domestic needs, interests, and beliefs and their perceptions of the international situation, with its own constraints or opportunities. In China's case the predispositional domestic factors against international cooperation are legion: the deep and abiding sense of uniqueness and the consequent quest for national identity via civilizational autonomy and political and intellectual self-sufficiency, the so-called Qianlong complex; the notion that the outside world could not survive without Chinese help, but not vice versa; the Marxist notion of conflict as the motive force of human progress; the Maoist notion that political power grows from the barrel of guns; the festering problem of national reunification; the still unresolved irredentist claims and territorial disputes with most of its neighbors; the autocratic state defying the Kantian theory of peace-loving democracy; and the sovereignty-centered image of international order. Chinese conflict behavior—an unfaltering faith in realpolitik and the efficacy of force in conflicts defined as zero-sum, especially on territorial issues bound up with sovereignty—is even more deeply rooted in its traditional *para bellum* strategic culture than Marxism or Maoism.[17]

Despite China's much heralded entry into the United Nations in late 1971, a comprehensive network of linkages with the global community was not established until the 1980s, when Beijing joined practically all the important international organizations. China thus joined the global community with a high propensity to use threats or military force to get its way. The fact that the People's Republic has often taken the initiative in its armed conflicts with other nations strengthens the perception that conflict behavior is an integral part of the international conflict continuum from formation to resolution, especially in the Asia-Pacific region. It is this perception of assertive negative power that the Chinese leadership skillfully exploits to project the national-role conception that an engaged and strong China is an irreducible prerequisite to any legitimate and viable international order.

Nonetheless, there has been some global learning in the post-Mao era, especially in reference to the global political economy. It was the tradition of self-sufficiency and isolation, more than three centuries long and dating from the middle of the Ming dynasty, that paramount leader Deng Xiaoping specifically singled out and attacked in late 1984 as the major cause of China's poverty and backwardness. There is simply no alternative, Deng argued, to the open-door policy in the long march to the promised land of modernity.[18] The concept of global interdependence has followed, *faute de mieux,* the Leninist-Maoist theory of imperialism and the inevitability theory of war as the only theoretical justification for Beijing's growing dependence upon the capitalist world system. The Leninist inevitability theory of war had to be jettisoned as a normative and practical liability standing in the way of China's growing dependence on the keystone international economic institutions. How else could China cope with Lenin's belief that the slicing of the Chinese melon would be the final drama of imperialism as the highest stage of capitalism? According to post-Mao revisionism, the world economy is said to be an "inalienable whole" and the "global division of labor in industrial production is becoming a more and more important part of international cooperation."[19]

In short, China would now have to cooperate in the pursuit of power and plenty—national security and economic prosperity—with little trade-off in sovereign control. Deng opened Chinese doors for a specific kind of global learning, to energize China's born again modernization drive. This policy was based on two premises: first, that if China could not change the reality of a rapidly changing global political economy, there would be no choice but to adapt itself to that reality; and second, that a self-confident China could extract maximum payoffs and benefits from the global system with minimum costs and penalties to its state sovereignty. On balance, external systemic factors have changed more decisively than domestic factors in favor of greater Chinese international cooperation.

As China's protracted struggle to be admitted into the WTO (World Trade Organization) seems to suggest, however, international cooperation is still narrowly conceptualized and applied to what China can extract from the global community, to wit, aid, trade, investment, and science and technology. The Kennedyesque premise of post-Mao China's international cooperation seems simple enough: ask not what China can do for a more peaceful, equitable, and democratic world order; ask rather what the global community can do to make China a rich, powerful, and reunified country.

The Dialectics of Conflict and Cooperation

In Chinese thinking and behavior, conflict and cooperation are the two sides of a dialectical scissor.[20] As if to improve on the classical Hegelian-Marxist approach to human knowledge and society (or on the classical Chinese *yin-yang* duality), Chinese communist leaders divide every social situation into two opposing forces—negative and positive, conflictual and cooperative—that confront one another in the course of social process. Conflict and cooperation—fighting and negotiating—have become mutually complementary strategies to weaken an adversary's will. In the Maoist world-view, the basic and universal social phenomenon is contradiction. In international relations too, cooperation (nonantagonistic contradictions) is conceptualized as relative, conditional, and temporary, whereas conflict (antagonistic contradictions) is conceptualized as absolute, basic, and protracted. Accordingly, international crises are seen as intensifications of the existing contradictions, not as aberrations from the norm of international life.[21]

In the five well-chronicled armed conflicts across different historical contexts—the Korean War, 1950–53; the Sino-U.S. confrontation over Quemoy, 1958; the Sino-Indian border conflict, 1962; the escalation of the Vietnam War, 1964–65; and the Sino-Soviet border clashes, 1969—Chinese behavior showed a relatively coherent strategy of conflict management. To a significant extent, Chinese conflict behavior manifested a temporal and purposeful orchestration of maneuvers characterized by five distinct and sequential phases: probing, warning, demonstrating, attacking, and deescalating. The sudden abatement of overt hostilities and the introduction of détente measures in the fifth phase, for example, unilateral cease-fires, troop disengagements, and proposals for diplomatic negotiation, tacitly signal China's willingness to engage in cooperative measures for coping with conflict. In many instances, including the most recent China-generated South China Sea crisis, China's military moves have been closely linked to diplomatic negotiating processes. The "restraint" in Chinese conflict behavior can be said to have reflected the "coercive diplomacy" model of orchestrating the limited and controlled use of force in the pursuit of specific political objectives in a given situation.[22] Alternatively, the restraint in Chinese coercive diplomacy had to do simply with limited capabilities.[23]

Over the years China has formed cooperative relationships with both stronger and weaker states. Yet many of these cooperative relationships have been troubled, and many of them—e.g., with the Soviet Union, India, Albania, Vietnam, and the United States—have degenerated into open conflict. Paradoxical as it may seem, many of China's most intense international conflicts have been the product of the degeneration of what once seemed to be close cooperative relations.[24]

In the course of its international life, China has participated in various bilateral and multilateral diplomatic and commercial negotiating processes aimed at managing conflict. The picture that emerges from various studies is that China has indeed proved to be a frustratingly difficult and endlessly elusive partner in these processes.[25] One notable and revealing exception is an account of Secretary of State Henry Kissinger's firsthand encounter with Chairman Mao in the behind-the-scenes negotiations for the Sino-U.S. rapprochement of 1971–72. In spite of its ritualized assault on power politics, China seems at its negotiating best in the realm of realpolitik. The Sino-U.S. rapprochement of 1971–72 is, in Kissinger's words, a "classic definition of modern Machiavellism." After an extended dialogue with Mao, Kissinger offers his interpretation of the "power politics" side of the breakthrough in Sino-U.S. relations:

Mao Zedong, the father of China's Communist revolution, who had convulsed his people in his effort to achieve doctrinal purity, went to great pains to show that slogans scrawled on every wall in China were meaningless, that in foreign policy national interests overrode ideological differences. Ideological slogans were a façade for considerations of balance of power. Each side would be expected to insist on its principles; but each had an obligation not to let them interfere with the imperatives of national interest — a classic definition of modern Machiavellism.[26]

Here we see a meeting of two Machiavellian mindsets in the Forbidden City. Both Kissinger and Mao commanded the extraordinary ability to shift their personal and political alliances depending on the prevailing political winds; both towering players of realpolitik on the global chessboard were known to share such similar troublesome traits as being easily given to deceit, ruthless toward adversaries as well as close associates, and highly manipulative, paranoiac, and totalitarian. Viewed in this light, a more plausible interpretation of the Mao-Kissinger encounter is that Mao probably told Kissinger what he thought the noted practitioner of global power politics wanted to hear while following his own three principles of conflict resolution formulated in 1940 as the anti-Japanese strategy of conflict resolution: "the three principles are to fight 'on just grounds,' 'to our advantage' and 'with restraint.' By keeping to this kind of struggle, waged on just grounds, to our advantage and with restraint, we can develop the progressive forces, win over the middle forces, and isolate the die-hard forces."[27] Internal People's Liberation Army (PLA) documents explained the Sino-U.S. rapprochement in these Maoist–Sun Zi terms as a brilliant entrapment strategy: "Our invitation to Nixon to visit

China proceeded precisely from Chairman Mao's tactical thinking: 'exploiting contradictions, winning over the majority, opposing the minority, and destroy them one by one.' " [28] Here then is the dialectical penchant for trying to have it both ways as made manifest in the pattern of alternating rigidity and sudden flexibility. The public rationale for such conflict-cooperative behavior in Chinese foreign policy is "staying firm in principle but flexible in tactics" (yuanze de jianding xing he celüe de linghuo xing).

Closely connected to the dialectics of Chinese conflict-cooperative behavior is a deductive approach in political and commercial negotiations. Mao rejected the view that strategic victory is determined by tactical successes alone, "because it overlooks the fact that victory or defeat in a war is first and foremost a question of whether the situation as a whole and its various stages are properly taken into account." [29] In politics too Mao repeatedly stressed the notion that the correct line was "the key link; once it is grasped, everything falls into place." [30] In diplomatic and commercial negotiations Chinese officials constantly try to evaluate the wider implications of the issues directly involved and prod the other party to agree on "basic principles." "Seeking common ground while preserving differences" (qiutong cunyi) is touted as the code of conduct for multilateral negotiations that other states should emulate. [31]

Such a deductive approach has enabled Beijing to insinuate its own interpretation of "agreed common principles" as a way of gaining negotiating one-upmanship. These principles have later been unilaterally interpreted and constantly invoked as ways of testing the counterpart government's "sincerity" and commitment to a friendly relationship with China. In multilateral diplomacy China has shown a pronounced discrepancy between symbolic activism in the public espousing of general principles, especially the FPPC and the U.N. Charter, and substantive passivism bordering on indifference in the translation of general declaratory principles into norm-specific multilateral conventions. In conflict behavior China has almost always seized the initiative by shooting first, whereas in cooperative negotiating behavior, especially in multilateral settings, China has almost always followed up on agreed common principles with its own specific interpretations.

In terms of substantive normative initiatives in global politics, Chinese influence is marginal at best. There is as yet not a single China-sponsored or -initiated proposal for new conflict-management mechanisms, let alone a multilateral convention. The sum total of China-specific "accomplishments" in global politics comes down to two meaningless General Assembly resolutions on nuclear and conventional disarmament—this was the best Prime Minister Li Peng could come up with as an epitaph to the monument of China's growing influence in U.N. politics in his annual report on the work of the government.[32] Since 1986 China for the first time *solely* sponsored two such draft resolutions in the General Assembly that were adopted by consensus. When Beijing finally decided to accede to the Non-Proliferation Treaty in 1991, that action was promised to visiting Japanese Prime Minister Toshiki Kaifu as a kind of reward for his leadership in the Group of Seven's decision to phase out the Western sanctions as well as in Japan's decision to resume its large-scale loan program for China.

China's deductive approach is driven by two imperatives. The first is the normative imperative of legitimation challenge and response in Chinese politics. An inordinate demand is placed on Chinese multilateral diplomacy to gain absolute international legitimation to make up for growing legitimation deficits at home. The second is the longstanding imperative to make moral virtue out of weak material power. The problem with "principled foreign policy" is that virtually every declaratory statement of general principles, including the U.N. Charter and Shanghai Communiqués I and II, embodies mutually competing and even contradictory principles. Moreover, it is in the very nature of general principles, as against situation-specific norms and rules, that they are amenable to multiple readings and interpretations. The deductive approach is well suited to the Chinese style of promoting state interests in the name of defending or promoting abstract international principles but presents considerable difficulty for the conflict-management negotiating process. Consider China's three principles on global arms trade: that arms export should be made only for legitimate national defense, for enhancing regional stability, and without in any way interfering in or infringing upon any country's sovereignty.

Reflecting upon his firsthand encounter with China, in the fourteen-nation Foreign Ministers' Conference on Laos held in Geneva in 1961–62, as the head of the Indian delegation, Arthur Lall writes that "the Chinese diplomat is highly China-oriented — often jingoistically so — and is fundamentally more concerned about the needs and aspirations of China than anything else."[33] To a certain extent, this Sinocentric, realist orientation has persisted in both bilateral and multilateral negotiating contexts and explains the occasional willingness to trade security (in the 1960s) and wealth (in the 1970s) for sovereign control. The coherence of Chinese conduct across a wide range of issue areas and different historical contexts can be better comprehended by appreciating this obsession with state control.

Even during the heyday of the Sino-Soviet alliance in the 1950s, China was constantly testing the limits of the Soviet commitment to the alliance and the twin alliance dilemmas of abandonment and entrapment while at the same rejecting Soviet proposals for joint military forces. Since the Sino-Soviet split, China has shown a preference for loose, informal *alignment* linkages over tighter and more formal *alliance* relationships as a way of minimizing any trade-off in state control. Today China has only one formal alliance treaty, with North Korea. However, in light of the recent normalization of full diplomatic relations with South Korea on August 24, 1992, formally ending more than forty years of Cold War enmity, the practical meaning of this last remaining alliance treaty remains problematic. Once again, China is demonstrating its fidelity to the Palmerstonian realist maxim: China has no perennial friends or foes, only perennial state interests.

In the normative domain of global politics, the centrality of the Third World is assured by three recurring themes: that China is a socialist country *belonging* to the Third World; that support for and solidarity with the Third World is indeed a basic principle in Chinese foreign policy; and that such identification will continue undiminished even if China becomes a rich and powerful state. And yet, China has emerged as perhaps the most independent actor in global group politics, a veritable Group of One (G-1), by refusing to join the two leading Third World caucuses — the Group of Seventy-Seven (G-77) in global developmental politics and the Non-Aligned Movement (NAM) in global geopolitics. This G-1 insistence on playing the United Nations Conference on Trade and Development (UNCTAD) group politics by its own rules presented an extremely difficult procedural problem in the course of negotiating the voting structure of the Common Fund, the most divisive issue of the third session of the United Nations Negotiation Conference on a Common Fund under the Integrated Program for Commodities, held in Geneva March 12–19, 1979.[34] Despite all the changes and shifts in China's Third World policy since its entry into the United Nations in 1971, its firm stand as a self-styled independent G-1 remains, projecting the national role conception that China has its own national interests to protect and that China's cooperation even with the Third World can never be taken for granted.[35]

On the question of a post–Cold War collective security system in the Asia-Pacific region, the Chinese leadership has expressed a preference for a unilateral approach in bilateral clothing. The dogged determination to define national identity in terms of state sovereignty, state status, and state security stands in the way of responding positively to any proposal for a regional collective security system. Soviet President Mikhail Gorbachev's Pacific overtures in the years 1986 to 1988 for a comprehensive security system for the entire Asia-Pacific region were countermanded and scaled back to the bilateral negotiating level in order to pressure the Soviets to meet China's three security demands as the price for renormalizing Sino-Soviet relations. Beijing quashed all other similar Australian, Canadian, and Japanese proposals for a multilateral Asia-Pacific security conference, a sort of conference on security and cooperation in Asia. At the second international conference, "Joint Efforts for Development: Prevention of Conflicts," in Bandung, Indonesia, in August 1991, Chinese officials strongly opposed both the establishment of a multilateral regime for handling territorial disputes and the intrusion of outside powers, that is, Japan, the United States, and the Soviet Union, maintaining instead that disputes should be resolved by the relevant countries on a bilateral basis.[36] As Li Luye, director general of the China Centre for International Studies, put it: "Any attempt to copy Europe's model of collective security or to duplicate the pattern of integration of the two Germanys in Northeast Asia is not realistic and could by no means bring peace and stability to this area. It would be desirable to start establishing a security mechanism in the Asia-Pacific region, including Northeast Asia, on a bilateral basis."[37]

The multinational conflict over the Paracel *(Xisha)* and Spratly *(Nansha)* island groups in the South China Sea underlines the dialectics of Chinese conflict-making and conflict-coping behavior. While Chinese diplomats often talk about international cooperation for the pacific settlement of disputes, Chinese strategists reject the proposition that the seabed resources of disputed areas in the South China Sea should be jointly developed, while shelving the issue of sovereignty. The 1974 Chinese attack opened a Pandora's box of conflict over the Paracel and Spratly island groups. The dispute remained dormant until March 1988, when, under the pretext of setting up sea-level weather research stations sponsored by UNESCO, the Chinese took control of six islands in the Spratly group. Such gunboat diplomacy served as a reminder of Beijing's growing naval power — and of its willingness to use it if necessary — in a resource-rich area of more than 3.6 million square kilometers. The disputed Paracel and Spratly island groups have become the most dangerous flash point in the Asia-Pacific region as no fewer than six states — Brunei, China, Malaysia, the Philippines, Taiwan, and Vietnam — have competing jurisdictional claims over the potentially oil-rich Spratly Islands. The Spratly and Paracel Islands also straddle sea lanes that are vital to East Asian states, including Japan, adding a geostrategic dimension to the simmering conflict. China, Taiwan, South Korea, and Japan are also locked in dispute over the Diaoyu *(Senkaku)* Islands, farther north in the East China Sea. To possess the Diaoyu Islands, which comprise five islands some 166 kilometers northeast of Taiwan, would be to have legal jurisdiction over about 21,645 square kilometers of the continental shelf that is believed to be one of the last unexplored hydrocarbon resource areas in the world, with possibly up to 100 billion barrels of oil. Against this back-drop, on February 25, 1992, the National People's Congress adopted the Law of the People's Republic of China on Its Territorial Waters and Their Contiguous Areas, as phrased in article 1, "in order to enable the People's Republic of China to exercise its sovereignty over its territorial waters and its rights to exercise control over their adjacent areas, and to safeguard state security as well as its maritime rights and interests."

Ironically, China's gunboat diplomacy has injected new life into the Association of Southeast Asian Nations (ASEAN) as a regional organization, just when the U.N.-brokered peace settlement in Cambodia seemed to have removed Vietnam as a common thread holding the six member states together. At the July 1992 meeting all six member states gave top priority to the South China Sea conflict, calling openly for the first time on the United States to maintain a military presence in the region. A separate declaration on the peaceful resolution of the conflict was obviously addressed to China as a rally-ing point for the members of ASEAN to act together in this unsettling post–Cold War transitional setting. An assertive China's readiness to engage in a clash of arms to claim the disputed islands and thus to assert its jurisdiction over sea space and related resources has already become a matter of acute security concern in Taiwan and Japan.

For China, however, there seems little room for compromise, largely be-cause of the conflation of sovereignty, security, status, and "lateral pressure." The party line, as articulated in Party chief Jiang Zemin's political report to the fourteenth Party Congress, is crystal clear: "When it comes to issues in-volving national interests and state sovereignty, China will never concede to outside pressure."[38] This unilateralism conjures up an image of China as a determined irredentist power that has resorted to the use of force outside its existing borders in more conflicts and more often than any other East Asian state. In expounding China's concept of security, Chinese scholars and publi-cists repeatedly and categorically state that China will never occupy an inch of foreign territory nor yield an inch of Chinese territory.[39] The problem obvi-ously lies in the expansive definition of Chinese territory. In domestic politics no Chinese leader can afford to appear soft on such highly charged nation-alistic issues. Southward gunboat diplomacy may also have been spurred by the belief, on the basis of past behavior, that other claimants, as well as the global community, are unlikely to react strongly to Chinese coercive diplo-macy. Equally significant is the fact that the post–Cold War strategic environ-ment in this contested area presents a timely challenge and opportunity for the Chinese military to strengthen its blue-water naval power and for the Chinese government to create a national image as the dominant military power in the region.[40]

The preference for bilateral negotiations is a way of seeking the home court advantage in maximizing Chinese control over the international conflict-management negotiating process. Surely it was no accident that most major bilateral political and commercial agreements were negotiated in Beijing, with the Chinese controlling both the ambience and the agenda of negotiations. Such a home court advantage is nearly impossible to obtain in U.N.-sponsored multilateral negotiations given their regularized venue in New York or Geneva. Still, China has actively lobbied to be the sole sponsor of many Third World conferences and a cosponsor of multilateral forums as a way of trying to redefine the agenda of global politics, for example, the U.N. Conference on Disarmament and Security Issues in the Asia-Pacific Region, held in Shanghai in mid-August 1992, jointly sponsored by the U.N. Disarmament Office and the Shanghai Institute for International Studies. Such conference-sponsoring diplomacy also serves the purpose of beautifying China's image as an engaged participant in the global politics of arms control and disarmament without its doing anything substantive. Negotiating on home turf obviously helps internal bureaucratic communications and decision making as well as the manipulation of the press coverage.[41]

To negotiate with Beijing is to experience a Maoist protracted struggle. Chinese officials are skilled in drawing out negotiations to test the limits of their adversary's flexibility and patience and to expand the limits of the possible and the permissible for their own interests. A combination of domestic and external factors seems to have shortened the learning curve. If full normalization of Sino-U.S. relations took more than twenty-three years, full renormalization of Sino-Soviet relations took about ten years (1979–89). In the case of Sino–South Korean normalization, the flag followed trade rather quickly, with on-and-off behind-the-scenes talks taking less than two years to end symbolically the forty-year Cold War enmity in Northeast Asia. There is no evidence that Beijing even bothered to ask for any cross-recognition from Tokyo and Washington for its ally in Pyongyang. As many have learned to their chagrin, however, reaching an agreement does not necessarily mean the end of negotiations, as the Chinese frequently reopen issues that their foreign partners consider closed. Even commercial contracts are the start, not the end, of real negotiations.[42] And yet Beijing has also demonstrated a remarkable capacity for making eleventh-hour concessions for capitulation in those bilateral—and mostly Sino-U.S.—negotiations following the logic of its own cost-benefit calculus.

One of the reasons for this protracted negotiating tactic may have to do with the degree to which such international negotiations get entangled in Beijing's own intra-elite factional infighting. The paramount leader—Mao from 1949 to 1976 and Deng from 1978 to the present—has played the crucial defining role in all the key turning points in Chinese foreign policy. Likewise, the intervention of top leadership to put an end to the negotiating stalemate or the protracted process is a characteristic of the Chinese negotiating style. However, such intervention could go in either direction, with results that are positive or negative, more flexible and accommodating or more rigid and obstinate.[43]

The Maxi-Mini Strategy

Chinese conflict-coping behavior, manifest in the various domains of global politics, follows a real, if unstated, maxi-mini axiom, maximizing China's rights and minimizing China's responsibilities. In computerese this is called *multitasking* or *multithreading*, a program designed to do several things at the same time. It seeks as well to maximize state interests and minimize normative costs by making the world of international organizations safe for the drive for modernization and status.[44] The maxi-mini principle is expressed in the espousal of differentiated and proportionate responsibilities in the global arms control and disarmament (ACD) processes. We are told that since the two superpowers account for 95–97 percent of all nuclear warheads in the world, it is they who must bear the primary responsibility by drastically reducing their nuclear arsenals before other nuclear weapons states can join the disarmament process. By taking this stand, China projects its role as a constructive player in the U.N. disarmament game without constraining its own nuclear development.

At the Second Special Session on Disarmament (SSOD-II) in mid-1982 China somewhat modified its ambiguous stand: the superpowers should reduce their nuclear weapons by 50 percent before China and the other nuclear powers joined in further nuclear disarmament negotiations. Yet the 1988 Soviet-U.S. Intermediate-Range Nuclear Forces Treaty (INF) seems to have come as a rude awakening to the possibility that Beijing may have committed the cardinal sin of premature specificity. While it welcomed the INF as the first genuine disarmament treaty of the postwar era, China rather quickly relapsed into a "who, me?" refrain. A 50 percent reduction would no longer meet China's new measure of a "drastic reduction." At the same time, an old Chinese ACD line had been resurrected: while the superpowers have the special re-

sponsibility for drastic nuclear disarmament, all countries, big or small, strong
or weak, have the right to take part in any future disarmament negotiations.

"The most significant achievement" of Secretary of State James Baker's
three-day negotiation meetings in Beijing in November 1991 was reported
to be a Chinese commitment not to export M-9 missiles to Syria and M-11
missiles to Pakistan and other countries. Baker was also reported to have ob-
tained Chinese commitment to "observe the guidelines and parameters" of
the Missile Technology Control Regime (MTCR). Even this verbal commitment was contingent upon two preconditions: (1) that the United States first
lift the sanctions on dual-use high technology transfers imposed in the wake of
the Tiananmen massacre, and (2) that China continue to export nuclear technologies that are ostensibly for civilian use but could easily be converted to
nuclear weapons programs.[45] A third, implied precondition was the continuation of China's most-favored-nation (MFN) status, which generated a large
trade surplus with the United States — $18 billion in 1992.

Paradoxically, the evidence shows that between 1966 and 1976, at a time
when China was publicly supporting proliferation as a means of breaking the
superpower nuclear duopoly, Beijing in practice provided no nuclear assistance to other countries. In the 1980s, however, China's nuclear proliferation
principle and policy diverged. While it has made repeated pledges of non-
proliferation, culminating in the ratification of the Non-Proliferation Treaty
in March 1992, Beijing has been held responsible for helping, either directly
or indirectly, the nuclear weapons programs of six out of the seven nuclear
threshold states.[46] Even as Chinese diplomats habitually deny that China has
ever engaged in the nuclear arms race, Chinese military strategists at home
warn that "once an agreement is reached banning the use and testing of nuclear
weapons, we will lose our position as a nuclear power."[47]

In essence, then, Chinese ACD behavior is dictated by the maxi-mini
strategy of making a virtue out of necessity — the maximization of its security
interests free riding off superpower ACD negotiations and the minimization of
its own commitments to a few safe, or nonpriority, areas. China's participation
in the global politics of disarmament has become more engaging and deft,
to be sure, but the old nationalistic resolve persists that in a dangerous and
nuclearized world a China without the bomb does not count. Beijing's general
silence and passivity on regional ACD issues, in contrast to its activism on
global ACD issues in the United Nations, seem to reflect Beijing's acute concern that the establishment of an Asian-Pacific ACD regime would impinge
too closely on its expansive regional security zone for comfort.[48] Moreover,
there is now a new twist to the Maoist resolve to stand up in world politics,

with economic and military muscle power growing out of arms sales to trouble spots in the Third World.

The same maxi-mini principle is manifest in Chinese thinking on U.N. peacekeeping. Until late 1981 China showed a negative attitude toward such operations, even if principled opposition was expressed in the form of "non-participation in the vote" and dissociation from any financial obligations. Then came a policy change as part of Beijing's renewed identification with the Third World and its putative strategic dealignment from the United States. On December 14, 1981, China for the first time voted for the extension of the U.N. peacekeeping force in Cyprus (UNFICYP). By late 1982 Beijing safely projected itself as a champion of U.N. peacekeeping: "The more tumultuous the international situation, and the more seriously threatened are world peace and international security, the more important and pressing becomes the task of strengthening the United Nations."[49]

From 1988 to 1989, China's support of U.N. peacekeeping and the Sino-Soviet renormalization process progressed in tandem. In September 1988, with Soviet prodding and support, China formally requested membership on the U.N. Special Committee on Peacekeeping Operations, and two months later it was unanimously accepted. In China's first official statement as a new member, in April 1989, Ambassador Yu Mengjia urged the international community to give "powerful political support" to U.N. peacekeeping, because the facts had proved convincingly that it had become an "effective mechanism" in realizing the purposes of the Charter and an integral part of U.N. efforts in finding a political settlement for regional conflicts.[50]

The Gulf crisis put China on trial for its support of U.N. peacekeeping. Characteristically, Beijing's initial response was no response: China waited to see how others would react, perhaps hoping that this invasion, like Saddam Hussein's 1980 invasion of Iran, would turn out to be another international nonevent. This wait-and-see attitude was tempered by a sense of multiple dangers—the loss of Iraq as a valuable customer in its global arms trade, a vanishing antihegemonic line in the face of naked aggression of one Third World country against another, the loss of inordinate investments as sponsor of the Asian Games scheduled to be held in September, and so forth. Despite the initial vacillation and ambiguous posturing, Beijing soon awakened to the "dialectical" possibility of seizing the crisis in order to divert the world's attention away from China so that it could once again throw its weight around in global high politics. By abstaining rather than voting for or against Security Council Resolution 678 on November 29, 1990, China allowed itself ample maneuvering room for multiple interpretations of its "principled stand" but at the same time publicly demonstrated its multiprincipled diplomacy of projecting itself as all things to all nations.

In the end China managed to extract maximum payoffs from the United States with minimum support. Through its never-never fence-straddling strategy, Beijing maneuvered Washington into becoming an overly anxious supplicant seeking help. A Washington quid for a Beijing quo exemplified the maxi-mini code of conduct. The Bush administration, ignoring a then current crackdown on political dissidents, agreed to resume high-level diplomatic intercourse — a long-sought White House visit by Foreign Minister Qian Qichen was granted — and to support the World Bank's first "non-basic human needs" loan since Tiananmen. All the same, Beijing can still claim that it championed the Palestinian cause while at the same time it eagerly looked forward to sending thousands of construction workers and exporting major weapons systems to the postwar Middle East.

Despite the repeated pronouncements in the course of the Security Council proceedings that "China does not have nor wishes [sic] to seek any self-serving interests in the Middle East region, and its only concern is to maintain [the] peace and stability of that region,"[51] China's actual conflict-coping role can be better described as driven by the uglier calculations of making the best of all worlds in the pursuit of narrowly construed state interests. Until recently, China bankrolled the genocidal Khmer Rouge to the tune of $100 million per year and characterized its relations with North Korea as organically intertwined like "lips and teeth." Today Beijing is poised to fold its Pol Pot and Pyongyang cards in return for more lucrative hands with ASEAN and Seoul, thereby garnering multiple gains with two deft political moves.

In August 1992 Khmer Rouge president Khieu Samphan publicly pointed his finger at Beijing, stating that his group was resisting pressure from China to cooperate with the United Nations Transitional Authority in Cambodia (UNTAC) in the implementation of phase 2 (demilitarization) of the U.N.-brokered peacemaking process in Cambodia and implicitly accusing China of allied abandonment. In April 1992 China had dispatched forty-seven military observers and four hundred military engineers to join the UNTAC. China's decision to abandon rather than to fight for the Khmer Rouge has left the hardline Stalinist faction without any major external support for the first time in more than two decades. Unfortunately, that choice seems to have strengthened the Khmer Rouge's resolve to fight to the death rather than to compromise or cooperate.[52]

The decision to recognize and establish full normalization with Seoul underlines another aspect of the maxi-mini strategy. Foreign Minister Qian is reported to have used the metaphor "downing four birds with one" in favor of full normalization with Seoul in his report to the Chinese Communist Party central foreign affairs group. A preemptive strike, the Seoul card, would at one and the same time further isolate Taiwan diplomatically; strengthen Beijing's growing economic cooperation with Seoul, that is, increase trade surplus and its direct foreign investment; diminish Pyongyang's seemingly endless requests for more material, military, and political aid and support; and increase China's ability to defuse the mounting "Super 301" pressure from the United States to demand negotiations on unfair trade practices.[53] Above all, the Seoul connection is another way of demonstrating the indispensability of the China factor in the reshaping of a new regional order in Northeast Asia. How the Seoul connection would influence Pyongyang's international comportment remains to be seen. South Korean officials say Beijing has promised to "help" in the denuclearization of the Korean peninsula as part of the diplomatic deal.

Following such cost-benefit calculus, China has shifted with regard to the Korean and Cambodian conflicts from being part of the problem to becoming part of the solution. Yet deep down there is little concern for or commitment to revitalizing the U.N. Security Council as the principal instrument for preventing, abating, or even managing regional conflicts. Of the Permanent Five, China has already assumed the most skeptical posture toward Secretary-General Boutros Boutros-Ghali's proposals for rejuvenating the global collective security system envisioned in the U.N. Charter itself.[54] Once again, Beijing's response has been constrained or rationalized by its sovereignty-bound thinking. Apparently the secretary-general's report contained too many sovereignty-diluting features to provoke Beijing's public opposition: "UN reform should contribute to maintaining the sovereignty of its member states. Sovereign states are the subjects of international law and the foundation for the formation of the United Nations. The maintenance of state sovereignty serves as the basis for the establishment of a new international order."[55]

It is revealing as well, if not surprising, that China expressed its "shock and outrage" at Bush's decision to sell one hundred fifty F-16 jet fighters to Taiwan not only in bilateral terms, by warning of retrogression in Sino-U.S. relations, but also in multilateral terms, by threatening to pull out of the Mideast arms control talks and predicting "an inevitable, negative impact" on Chinese cooperation in the United Nations and other international organizations. China has already pulled itself out of the talks among the Permanent Five on arms control in the Middle East as a cost-effective means of retaliation. In short, Chinese "cooperation" with U.S. hegemonic manipulation of the Security Council is held hostage to China-specific most-favored-nation treatment in trade, arms sales, technology transfer, and so on. Where peace-keeping operations do not fit into such horse trading, Beijing has adopted a minimalist "know-nothing, do-nothing, pay-nothing" posture of abstaining rather than voting for or against recent conflict-coping draft resolutions, including in the case of the Yugoslav crisis. On November 27, 1991, in the course of Security Council deliberations on the situation in Yugoslavia, Ambassador Li Daoyu issued a warning that the establishment of a U.N. peacekeeping operation should not become a precedent for the future.

▲ Future Prospects

Only a few years ago most analysts and observers, myself included, offered a rather optimistic forecast for the continuity and stability of Chinese international cooperation. Whatever the prospects for a more peaceful, more democratic, and more just world order, nothing seems more uncertain today than the future of post-Deng China; thus, the answer to the essential question what role or roles Beijing will play in the post–Cold War world order remains elusive. The final shape of the transition to the post-Deng era is beyond our prediction, because it will involve a complex and shifting mixture of China's evolving national roles, values, capabilities, and interests in a rapidly changing world.

Past experience, if not forgotten, is a guide for the future—so goes an oft-quoted Chinese saying. In effect, what matters is not so much "past experience," whatever that may mean, as how what we remember of the past shapes the way we understand the present and prepare for a preferred future. Put differently, the prospect of Chinese international cooperation depends not only on *how* but also on *where* we look. To muddy the waters, the global technological and communication revolutions of our time are having paradoxical effects. On the one hand, they have made it necessary for China to engage in cooperation with the outside world for no other reason than to better defend and promote its own state sovereignty, modernize its economy, enhance its international reputation and legitimation, and increase its overall national strength. On the other hand, such revolutions have already penetrated and perforated the once formidable castle of Chinese state sovereignty to such an extent as to make that concept a paper tiger.

Still, we have no choice but to rely on past-as-prologue projections of several alternative futures. It is possible, from this general scanning of the track record, to hypothesize three plausible scenarios, one optimistic and cooperative, another pessimistic and conflictual, and still another cautiously optimistic or pessimistic and dialectical. The first scenario is based on the proposition that the saliency, scope, and density of China's enmeshment in the global political economy are such as to rule out the self-reliant exit option. Viewed against China's well-chronicled encounter with foreign (barbarian) technical, commercial, religious, educational, and military advisers, who have come and gone without making much of a dent in Chinese thinking about a world order, the People's Republic has indeed evolved, by fits and starts, toward greater association and cooperation with the outside world. The present constitution, adopted in 1982, both acknowledges and embodies a global *interdependence* theme: "The future of China is closely linked with that of the whole world." For a while it seemed as if global interdependence had become another victim of the Tiananmen bloodletting, but it soon became apparent that Stalinist fundamentalism, expressed in the assaults on the Western strategy of "peaceful evolution," was more domestic smoke than external fire. The theme of global interdependence, of opening to the capitalist world, practically vanished from the Chinese press and was briefly replaced by the idea that "only socialism can save China," only to return with vengeance in 1992.

This scenario is therefore based on China's growing dependence upon the capitalist world system, which is still dominated, though increasingly less effectively, by the United States. Today more than ever before, China has no rational alternative but to work within the existing global system, if for no other reason than to fuel its drive toward the promised land of modernization. The history of global political economy suggests that no country has yet modernized and prospered through bootstrap isolationism and self-reliance. For almost a decade, from 1980 to mid-1989, Beijing successfully applied the maximini principle of international cooperation in extracting maximum rights and payoffs while minimizing responsibilities and penalties. The rise of China's global standing in a U.S.-led hegemonic world order and its unique status as a "poor global power" entitled to special, that is double-standard, treatment can also be explained by the putative change in China's national role from that of a revolutionary, antihegemonic actor to that of a neorealist, system-maintaining, status quo actor. In any case, such interest-driven international cooperation has paid off handsomely. Since the end of 1978 China has received bilateral and multilateral aid in the amount of $52.5 billion and foreign investment in the amount of $50 billion.[56] In the process, post-Mao China established an all-time global record, doubling its per capita output between 1977 and 1987.[57]

Moreover, the impressive economic performance, coupled with the reality of perforated sovereignty, makes it virtually impossible for the center to turn the clock back to the heyday of orthodox Marxist self-reliance. Increasingly, foreign trade, especially export, is regarded as the key to economic growth and prosperity. The proportion of foreign trade to GNP was about 5 percent in the early 1970s but shot up to 9.9 percent in 1978, 31 percent in 1990, and more than 36 percent in 1991. Even if the U.S. hegemony factor in the multilateral economic institutions is discounted—notice how effectively the United States linked the Sino-U.S. trade row with China's GATT membership—the huge annual trade surplus together with the size of China's stake in the U.S. market gives Washington economic leverage over Chinese international behavior. An asymmetrical interdependence is suggested by the fact that China ships approximately one-fourth of all its exports to the United States but takes fewer than 2 percent of U.S. exports. China's external linkages may not automatically breed cooperation, but they are expected to lead to redefinitions of national interests and appropriate national means for international cooperation.

As China grows stronger economically and militarily through international cooperation, Chinese leaders become more confident that they can compete with advanced capitalist powers on an equal footing or even beat them at their own game. The enhancement of China's international reputation as a peaceful and cooperative member state in the global community is another way of making up domestic legitimation deficits. Even in the golden era of Sinocentric isolationism, "China's external order was so closely related to her internal order that one could not long survive without the other." [58] Although the Significant Other in the enactment of national identity has changed over the years, China has remained a country supersensitive to the rise and fall of the legitimating "Mandate of Heaven," and in modern times it has used international cooperation as a way of enhancing domestic legitimacy. In short, the trend toward greater international association and cooperation can be attributed to and explained by three requirements: the modernization imperative, the changing global situation, and international legitimation. To a certain extent, the first scenario embraces a third-image, or a second-image reversed, explanation of Chinese international behavior, to wit, that external systemic factors have fundamentally transformed the payoff structure of Chinese national interests.

The second, pessimistic scenario proceeds from the second-image explanation that a nation's conflictual or cooperative behavior depends more on its particular type of national government or social system or its historically rooted strategic culture than on the nature of the global system. Despite all the changes and shifts in international conduct, China remains a repressive, autocratic state rooted in a *para bellum* strategic culture. The present regime, which sustains its illegitimate power by pure violence at home, cannot be expected to be peace-loving, especially when China has been embroiled in longstanding territorial disputes with most of its neighbors. The recent Chinese conflict behavior over the Spratly dispute also seems to validate the Choucri-North second-image explanation of conflict-prone behavior: that societies undergoing transition to industrialization when they are experiencing lateral pressure stemming from rapid economic, demographic, and technological growth may be more likely to become involved in international conflicts.

There is also a weak-state argument that strengthens the second, pessimistic scenario. The sound and fury of a sovereignty-centered international order cannot belie the fact that the center no longer fully controls the peripheries, that Chinese state sovereignty is highly perforated, and that China today is a weak state. The defining and differentiating feature of a weak state is the high level of internal threats to the government's security. External events are seen primarily in terms of how they affect the state's internal stability. The idea of national security, which refers to the defense of core national values against external threats, becomes subverted to the extent that the Chinese Party-state is itself insecure. China no longer has a legitimizing and unifying ideology of sufficient strength to dispense with the large-scale repressive use of force in domestic life. The primary mission of the Chinese military is now twofold: repression of domestic dissent and safeguarding of China's territorial sovereignty and economic interests in disputed areas.[59]

The post-Tiananmen government increased its official military budget by 98 percent between 1988 and 1993, while publicly touting that China now enjoyed the best external security environment in history. A weakened autocratic state may well perceive and/or manufacture external threats to state interests and might then employ growing economic and military might to protect those interests. The current regime must now cope with the collapse of its international reputation, the virtual demise of its ideological appeal and normative power, the weakness of its scientific and technological power, the simmering territorial disputes with at least seven neighboring countries, and the growing scrutiny of its nuclear proliferation and human rights practices, factors that could combine to provoke the Chinese leadership to reassert its hegemony in the Asia-Pacific region, if not in the world at large. The tyranny of state sovereignty still looms large in foreign policy thinking, inhibiting more positive and cooperative behavior. From a late 1992 vantage point, the second, pessimistic scenario seems credible.

And finally there is the third, dialectical scenario. The central issue here is no longer whether China will cooperate but with whom, to what extent, and on what issues. In the dialectics of Chinese foreign policy behavior, as suggested earlier, there is no clear separation or choice between conflict and cooperation, or between fighting and negotiating, because the two dyads are conceptualized and implemented as mutually complementary. Still, cooperation will most likely remain the dominant side in such issue areas as aid, trade, investment, and science and technology, and conflict will most likely remain the dominant side in such issue areas as arms sales, arms control and disarmament, and regional and global conflict-management processes. It now seems virtually certain that a substantial portion of China's growing economic power will be used for the qualitative improvement of the Chinese military, especially blue-water naval and nuclear power, as a way of enhancing China's "comprehensive national strength."

Nonetheless, a full-scale resort to force in the South China Sea or any other part of East Asia is not likely. The Chinese leadership, while trying to hold together the multinational state by the full weight of repressive force at home, is more likely to resort to the Sun Zi-Maoist dialectical conflict-cooperation strategy abroad, that is, trying to win war or peace by conflict-cooperation maneuvers through a protracted coping process. Even in the Spratlys conflict Beijing seems determined to follow the maxi-mini strategy as it tries to maximize its access to maritime resources in the disputed area without risking major armed confrontations with ASEAN, if not Vietnam. Ultimately, an authoritative decision on international conflict or cooperation is not likely to come until the rise of another Helmsman in the post-Deng era or until a future fundamental regime transformation.

NOTES

I am much indebted to William Feeney and Alastair I. Johnston for their valuable comments and suggestions on an earlier version of this chapter.

1. For the secretary-general's report prepared at the request of the first-ever Security Council summit, in January 1992, to respond to the post–Cold War challenges and problems confronting the world organization's conflict-management process, see *An Agenda for Peace: Preventive Diplomacy, Peacemaking, and Peace-Keeping*, U.N. Doc. S/24111, June 17, 1992.

2. For a more detailed analysis along this line, see Samuel S. Kim, "Peking's Foreign Policy in the Shadows of Tienanmen: The Challenge of Legitimation," *Issues and Studies* 27, no. 1 (1991): 39–69.

3. In his political report to the fourteenth Party Congress (hereafter Jiang's Political Report), Jiang Zemin offered such an upbeat assessment. For a complete text of the report see *Foreign Broadcast Information Service: Daily Report: China* (hereafter *FBIS-China*), Oct. 21, 1992, 1–21, quotation from 16.

4. Wang Lin, "Looking towards the 1990s," *Guoji wenti yanjiu* (International studies) 1 (Jan. 1990): 1–4, 9; idem, "The World Situation in the Midst of Profound Changes," ibid. 2 (Apr. 1990): 1–3.

5. See *Tokyo KYODO* (in English), in *FBIS-China*, Feb. 27, 1992, 24–25; see also Nicholas D. Kristof, "As China Looks at World Order, It Detects New Struggles Emerging," *New York Times*, Apr. 21, 1992, A1, A10.

6. For a comprehensive Chinese description and analysis of the changing global military order, see five-part articles by Li Qingong in *Jiefangjun Bao* (Liberation Army daily), translated in *FBIS-China*, May 15, 1992, 20–22; May 28, 1992, 30–32; June 18, 1992, 26–27; July 23, 1992, 32–34; and Aug. 7, 1992, 20–22, quotation from *FBIS-China*, May 15, 1992, 20.

7. Ibid., Aug. 7, 1992, 20.

8. With an attractive package of high salaries, free housing, and paid annual home vacations, the Chinese government is reported to have successfully recruited several hundred senior scientists from the former Soviet Union to work on new military research and development and weapons systems (see Guocang Huan, "The New Relationship with the Former Soviet Union," *Current History* 91 [Sept. 1992]: 254).

9. "South China Sea: Treacherous Shoals," *Far Eastern Economic Review*, Aug. 13, 1992, 14–20, quotation from 16.

10. See Jiang's Political Report, 16.

11. For a more extensive discussion and documentation of the Chinese image of world order, see Samuel S. Kim, *China In and Out of the Changing World Order* (Princeton: Center of International Studies, Princeton University, 1991).

12. Yi Ding, "Upholding the Five Principles of Peaceful Coexistence," *Beijing Review*, Feb. 26–Mar. 4, 1990, 15–16.

13. A *crisis-active state*, or a *crisis actor*, is defined as "a state whose decision-makers perceive a threat to one or more basic values, finite time for response, and a high probability of involvement in military hostilities" (see Michael Brecher, Jonathan Wilkenfeld, and Sheila Moser, *Crises in the Twentieth Century*, vol. 2, *Handbook of Foreign Policy Crises* [Oxford: Pergamon Press, 1988], 2, 51, 160–64).

14. See Lowell Dittmer and Samuel S. Kim, eds., *China's Quest for National Identity* (Ithaca: Cornell University Press, 1993).

15. Though it has been somewhat altered and reformulated, I owe this multiple reading of the complex geostrategic landscape of East Asia to Richard Falk.

16. A two-day international conference on this theme held at Princeton University, May 5–6, 1992, attracted important foreign policy players from Russia, Japan, and the United States.

17. This argument is most fully and most elegantly developed and documented in Alastair I. Johnston, "An Inquiry into Strategic Culture: Chinese Strategic Thought, the Parabellum Paradigm and Grand Strategic Choice in Ming China" (Ph.D. diss., University of Michigan, 1993).

18. Deng Xiaoping, "Talk at the Third Plenary Session of the Central Advisory Commission on October 22, 1984," *Renmin ribao* (People's daily), Jan. 1, 1985, 1.

19. See Foreign Minister Qian Qichen's "state of the world report" delivered at the 1990 General Assembly plenary session, with the full text in *Renmin ribao*, Sept. 29, 1990, overseas edition, 4.

20. For an elegant non-Chinese exposition of conflict and cooperation as mutually complementary, see Anatol Rapoport, *Peace: An Idea Whose Time Has Come* (Ann Arbor: University of Michigan Press, 1992), 79–91.

21. See Davis Bobrow, Steven Chan, and John A. Kringen, *Understanding Foreign Policy Decisions: The Chinese Case* (New York: Free Press, 1979); and Samuel S. Kim, *The Maoist Image of World Order* (Princeton: Center of International Studies, Princeton University, 1977).

22. See Steven Chan, "Chinese Conflict Calculus and Behavior: Assessment from a Perspective of Conflict Management," *World Politics* 30 (Apr. 1978): 391–410; and Bobrow, Chan, and Kringen, *Understanding Foreign Policy Decisions.*

23. For such an interpretation of China's conflict behavior during the Korean War, see Thomas Christensen, "Threats, Assurances, and the Last Chance for Peace: The Lessons of Mao's Korean War Telegrams," *International Security* 17 (summer 1992): 122–54.

24. This is one of the major conclusions emerging from the collaborative project on the patterns of cooperation in modern China's international relations sponsored by the Social Science Research Council (see Harry Harding and David Shambaugh, "Patterns of Cooperation in the Foreign Relations of Modern China," in *China's Cooperative Relationships: Partnerships and Alignments in Chinese Foreign Policy,* ed. Harry Harding [forthcoming]).

25. For Chinese negotiating styles and strategies in various settings over the years, see Jaw-ling Joanne Chang, "Negotiation of the 17 August 1982 U.S.-PRC Arms Communiqué: Beijing's Negotiating Tactics," *China Quarterly* 125 (Mar. 1991): 33–54; Robert A. Kapp, ed., *Communicating with China* (Chicago: Intercultural Press, 1983), Samuel S. Kim, "Behavioral Dimensions of Chinese Multilateral Diplomacy," *China Quarterly* 72 (Dec. 1977): 713–42; idem, "Reviving International Law in China's Foreign Relations," in *Chinese Defense and Foreign Policy,* ed. June T. Dreyer (New York: Paragon House, 1989); Henry Kissinger, *White House Years* (Boston: Little, Brown, 1979), 163–94, 684–787, 1049–96; idem, *Years of Upheaval* (Boston: Little, Brown, 1982), 44–71, 678–99; Arthur Lall, *How Communist China Negotiates* (New York: Columbia University Press, 1968); Lucian Pye, *Chinese Commercial Negotiating Style* (Cambridge, Mass.: Oelgeschlager, Gunn & Hain, 1982); Richard H. Solomon, *Chinese Negotiating Behavior: A Briefing Analysis* (Santa Monica, Calif.: RAND Corporation, 1985); Shih-Chung Tung, *The Policy of China in the Third United Nations Conference on the Law of the Sea* (Geneva: Graduate Institute of International Studies, 1981); Byron N. Tzou, *China and International Law: The Boundary Disputes* (New York: Praeger, 1990); Kenneth T. Young, *Negotiating with the Chinese Communists: The United States Experience, 1953–1967* (New York: McGraw-Hill, 1968); and Zhai Qiang, "China and the Geneva Conference of 1954," *China Quarterly* 129 (Mar. 1992): 103–22.

26. Kissinger, *Years of Upheaval,* 67.

27. Mao, Tse-Tung, *Selected Works of Mao Tse-Tung,* vol. 2 (Peking: Foreign Languages Press, 1965), 427.

28. See "Reference Material Concerning Education on Situation," no. 43, issued by the Kunming Military Region, PRC; later published in *Chinese Communist Internal Politics and Foreign Policy* (Taipei: Institute of International Relations, Apr. 4, 1973), 135–37.

29. Mao Tse-tung, *Selected Works of Mao Tse-Tung*, vol. 1 (Peking: Foreign Languages Press, 1965), 183–84.

30. Mao Tse-Tung, "Summary of Chairman Mao's Talks to Responsible Local Comrades during His Tour of Inspection (mid-August to September 12, 1971)," translated in *Chinese Law and Government* 5 (3–4) (fall–winter 1972–73): 33.

31. For further elaboration of this deductive approach in both bilateral and multilateral settings, see Pye, *Chinese Commercial Negotiating Style*, 40; and Kim, "Behavioral Dimensions of Chinese Multilateral Diplomacy," 741–42.

32. See *FBIS-China*, Mar. 27, 1991, 32.

33. Lall, *How Communist China Negotiates*, 15.

34. For a more extensive discussion on this matter, see Samuel S. Kim, "Whither Post-Mao Chinese Global Policy?" *International Organization* 35 (summer 1981): 433–65.

35. For a more detailed analysis, see Samuel S. Kim, *The Third World in Chinese World Policy* (Princeton: Center of International Studies, Princeton University, 1989).

36. Xinhua (New China News Agency), in *FBIS-China*, Aug. 6, 1991, 8–9.

37. Li Luye, "The Current Situation in Northeast Asia: A Chinese View," *Journal of Northeast Asian Studies* 10 (spring 1991): 78–81, quotation from 80.

38. Jiang's Political Report, 16.

39. See Song Yimin, *On China's Concept of Security* (Geneva: UNIDIR, 1986), esp. 17.

40. The PLA, according to Jiang, "should more successfully shoulder the lofty mission of defending the country's territorial sovereignty over the land and in the air, as well as its rights and interests on the seas; and should safeguard the unification and security of the motherland." Jiang's Political Report, 15.

41. See Pye, *Chinese Commercial Negotiating Style*, 28–29.

42. See Solomon, *Chinese Negotiating Behavior;* and Randall E. Stross, *Bulls in the China Shop and Other Sino-American Business Encounters* (New York: Pantheon Books, 1990).

43. This point is well documented in John Quansheng Zhao, "Chinese Foreign Policy: Rigidity and Flexibility: The Experience of Sino-Japanese Relations" (paper presented at the conference "East Asia—The Road Ahead," University of California, Berkeley, Mar. 29–31, 1990).

44. This point is more fully developed in Samuel S. Kim, "International Organizations in Chinese Foreign Policy," *Annals of the American Academy of Political and Social Science* 519 (Jan. 1992): 140–57.

45. *New York Times*, Nov. 18, 1991, A8.

46. For thoroughgoing analysis and documentation of this point, see Jag Mohan Malik, "Chinese National Security and Nuclear Arms Control" (Ph.D. diss., Australian National University, 1990), chap. 4; and William E. Burrows and Robert Windrem, *Critical Mass: The Dangerous Race for Superweapons in a Fragmenting World* (New York: Simon & Schuster, 1994), esp. 378–402.

47. Zhang Qinsheng and Zeng Guangjun, "Long Live the Interests of State," *Jiefangjun Bao* (Liberation Army daily), in *FBIS-China*, July 29, 1988, 30.

48. See Alastair I. Johnston, "China and Arms Control in the Asia-Pacific Region," in *Superpower Maritime Strategy in the Pacific*, ed. Frank C. Langdon and Douglas A. Ross (London and New York: Routledge, 1990), 173–204.

49. "UN Should Play a More Effective Role," *Beijing Review,* Nov. 1, 1982, 11–12.

50. Xinhua, in *FBIS-China,* Apr. 13, 1989, 4. For a glowing scholarly account, see Liu Enzhao, "UN Peacekeeping Forces," *Guoji wenti yanjiu* 2 (Feb. 1989): 53–61.

51. See U.N. Doc. S/PV. 2963, Nov. 29, 1990.

52. See Nate Thayer, "Cambodia: Fighting Words," *Far Eastern Economic Review,* Aug. 20, 1992, 8–9.

53. See *Tokyo KYODO* (in English), in *FBIS-China,* Sept. 15, 1992, 12.

54. See "Agenda for Peace"; and Paul Lewis, "UN Set to Debate Peacemaking Role," *New York Times,* Sept. 6, 1992, 7.

55. This point was made in Foreign Minister Qian Qichen's major speech at the forty-sixth session of the U.N. General Assembly, which comes close to being China's annual state of the world report. For an English text of the speech, see *FBIS-China,* Oct. 1, 1992, 4–8, quotation from 7.

56. Jin Ling, "China Strives to Introduce More Foreign Capital," *Beijing Review,* Aug. 10–16, 1992, 22.

57. See World Bank, *World Development Report, 1991: The Challenge of Development* (New York: Oxford University Press, 1991), fig. 1.1 (p. 12).

58. John K. Fairbank, "A Preliminary Framework," in Fairbank, ed., *The Chinese World Order: Traditional China's Foreign Relations* (Cambridge: Harvard University Press, 1968), 3.

59. Nicholas D. Kristof, "China Builds Its Military Muscle, Making Some Neighbors Nervous," *New York Times,* Jan. 11, 1993, A1, A8; Jiang's Political Report, 15–16.

| International Actors

PAUL F. DIEHL

6 | The United Nations and Peacekeeping

The end of the Cold War has affected few institutions as much as it has the United Nations. In the Cold War era, the United Nations exhibited a declining rate of effectiveness[1] and seemed inclined to intervene in conflicts only when fighting escalated to serious levels, and then only when the superpowers were not directly involved and tolerated that intervention.[2] The post–Cold War era is in its infancy, and there is some question what level of maturity it might reach. Nevertheless, the recent experiences in Kuwait, Cambodia, and elsewhere indicate that multilateral intervention, under U.N. auspices, will replace unilateral national actions; the scope of that intervention, in terms of both geography and functions, will also likely be expanded. This chapter considers the roles of the United Nations in dealing with one important aspect of a new world order: regional conflict.

The United Nations is likely to play a central role in regional conflicts for several reasons. First, the end of the Cold War led to a retreat first of the Soviet Union and then of its primary successor state, Russia, from supplying aid and otherwise exercising influence in various parts of the world. Many patron-client relationships that once proliferated in Eastern Europe, Asia, and Africa have now disappeared. To a lesser extent, U.S. willingness and ability to intervene unilaterally has also diminished. The likely decrease in the number of U.S. troops abroad will further weaken the propensity and capacity for intervention. In this void, multilateral institutions will be asked to mediate conflicts and help promote conflict resolution.

Second, the United Nations is fresh from a series of triumphs that have enhanced the prestige of the organization and made referring disputes to it appear to be a legitimate alternative. In 1988, U.N. peacekeeping forces were awarded the Nobel peace prize for their continuing efforts to limit hostilities in many of the world's trouble spots. The United Nations also achieved several successes in mediating the end of, or the withdrawal of foreign troops from, several wars. The Soviet troop withdrawal from Afghanistan, negotiated under U.N. auspices, was the first in a series of successes. The United Nations also had a significant role in Vietnam's withdrawal from Cambodia and the provisional plan for free elections there. Perhaps the most impressive U.N. contribution at the end of the 1980s was its role in the achievement of Namibia's independence. The Namibian independence agreement between the indigenous parties and South Africa was based largely on the outlines of a U.N. plan drawn up a decade earlier. The United Nations was an active participant in the negotiations and a key player in the implementation of the agreement, including the supervision of democratic elections. Nevertheless, enthusiasm for the United Nations has been tempered by its peacekeeping problems in Somalia and Bosnia.

The United Nations is also likely to be the primary organization to carry out or coordinate new initiatives in the security area, at least in the near future. Regional organizations, such as the Organization of African Unity and the European Union (EU), generally lack provisions and often resources for dealing with threats to order in their geographic area. Furthermore, the lack of political consensus in those bodies will necessitate that some outside agency assume the leading role in the security field.[3] The United Nations is the logical institution to fill that role. The failure of EU efforts in Bosnia is an example.

Finally, beyond the increased prestige of the United Nations, states, especially major powers, may be more supportive of U.N. action than in the past. States have learned that the costs of direct intervention are high, especially in disputes that appear to be intractable. Because of this, the United Nations may be viewed as an inexpensive dumping ground for some regional conflicts. The end of the Cold War has also lessened the importance of some regional conflicts for the major powers, and they therefore may be willing to seek multilateral solutions. Of course, governments can easily blame the distant United Nations for policy failures rather than face the wrath of domestic public opinion for their own inadequacies. These are hardly altruistic reasons, but states may increasingly look to the United Nations as a mechanism for dealing with regional conflict, provided, of course, that the organization achieves some continuing measure of success in its actions.

The United Nations generally takes actions in regional conflicts only when military force has already been used or is about to be used. Therefore, unlike other international organizations or the great powers, it is not primarily involved in the preventive or management stages of cooperation noted in chapter 1. The United Nations also does not have the resources thus far to make extensive efforts in these areas. Accordingly, the organization has been, and is likely to continue to be, active in the containment, reduction, and resolution of conflict. In those capacities, the United Nations may play a variety of roles, from that of neutral facilitator to that of sanctioning agency for great-power action.

When the United Nations intervenes in a regional conflict, it essentially relies on a repertoire of techniques or strategies that fall into three categories, which, however, are not always mutually exclusive: collective enforcement, peacekeeping, and peacemaking. Collective enforcement involves the coercive use of military force to compel a state or group to abide by the dictates of the United Nations, usually as spelled out in that organization's resolutions; the Korean "police action" provides evidence of such actions. Peacekeeping involves the deployment of lightly armed, neutral troops following a ceasefire to act as a buffer or interposition force; peace observation teams are also included in this category. Peacekeeping does not involve coercion, and military force is only employed in a limited fashion for self-defense purposes. The current U.N. peacekeeping force in Cyprus is an example. Peacemaking includes the whole range of diplomatic maneuvers (e.g., mediation, good offices) that do not involve the use of military force and that are designed to achieve the resolution of a dispute peacefully. An example is the U.N.-brokered agreement for a Soviet troop withdrawal from Afghanistan.

For each of the three categories of techniques or strategies, this chapter reviews the range of options, considers the changes that the end of the Cold War has brought,[4] and assesses when those options will likely be employed as well as when they are likely to be successful.

▲ Collective Enforcement

Collective enforcement refers to instances in which the United Nations would authorize the use of military force to punish an aggressor, to aid in the defense of a victim of aggression, to restore peace and security, or in support of any other initiative of the organization (e.g., protecting humanitarian relief shipments).[5]

The concept of a global organization authorizing and directing an international military operation is hardly a new one. Provisions of the League of Nations Covenant provided for the possibility of multinational operations under League approval to respond to acts of aggression. The U.N. Charter is more explicit in its formulations. Under Chapter 7, the Security Council is empowered to solicit and direct armed forces for use in a collective security operation. Yet the vision of the founders of the United Nations that the organization would play the role of the world's policeman was never fulfilled. There have been no military enforcement actions by the United Nations along the lines envisioned in the Charter. The closest approximations were the actions taken in Korea and Kuwait. Nevertheless, in each case, instead of a truly international army, multinational forces—made up predominantly of U.S. forces—conducted the military operations. Furthermore, the control of the operations was clearly in the hands of the American commanders rather than the moribund Military Staff Committee (MSC).

Much of the failure of the United Nations to employ collective security action can be traced to Cold War animosities that precipitated a stalemate in the Security Council, even in regional conflicts. The new world order is certainly no longer constrained by those tensions. Nevertheless, this is by no means a signal that U.N. enforcement action will become commonplace. In assessing the prospects for enforcement action, it is useful to distinguish between U.N.-authorized internationally supplied and directed operations and those undertaken by collections of states with broad U.N. approval.

Internationally directed operations are those that are envisioned in the Charter, with an international army that is representative of different geographic regions and under the direction of the MSC. Increasing cooperation between the United States and Russia might seem to enhance the chances for such an operation; indeed, President Gorbachev suggested a renewal of the MSC to direct the Persian Gulf War. Nevertheless, the likelihood of an international police force to keep peace and international security is low. First, the agreements under the Charter to provide troops and material for an international force were never negotiated, and there appears to be little chance that this will change soon. Recent proposals by U.N. Secretary-General Boutros Boutros-Ghali for international troop contributions involved setting up standby forces for missions that would resemble peacekeeping duties more closely than they would enforcement ones. Beyond the lack of an international force, the current structural apparatus of the organization — unlike that of NATO — is not designed to handle such an assignment, especially on other than an ad hoc basis. Even proposals for limited planning coordination do not seem to have any momentum in the global community.

More importantly, an international force is unlikely to gain the approval of the U.N. membership at this time. U.N. members retain their reluctance to grant the organization autonomy in the vital area of security. In their view, a U.N. military operation would set a dangerous precedent. If the forces and supplies were readily available, U.N. operations might become more frequent, perhaps in opposition to member states or their allies. In particular, major-power states, such as the United States, have been, and continue to be, reluctant to grant supranational authority to any body in lieu of relinquishing their own political and military options.[6] The United Nations also has serious financial constraints, which would limit its ability to put together an international army; the organization is already more than a billion dollars in arrears from peacekeeping operations and does not seem inclined to add to that debt with a standing military force.

A multinational force operating with U.N. approval and under the general guidelines of U.N. resolutions is a more likely although far from common response to various regional conflicts. In this approach, the Security Council might authorize states to use "all means necessary" to resolve a particular dispute, with military force as the final option.[7] States, most likely led by the United States and perhaps certain regional powers, would make a coordinated effort to carry out the mandate, using military forces under national commands. This was clearly the model for the U.N. enforcement operations in Korea and Kuwait.

The end of the Cold War has certainly made the possibility of U.N.-sanctioned multilateral action more likely in regional conflicts, but as the Kuwait operation suggests, the use of such an option will be an exception rather than the rule. Several conditions will need to be fulfilled before collective military actions are approved. First, the regional conflict situation must present a clear and agreed-upon aggressor, a state or group that can be the target of any action. The absence of such an agreement will prevent approval of enforcement actions. In the Cold War period, it was often superpower animosities that prevented the Security Council from branding one side or the other as the aggressor, much less taking any action against that party.

In the Persian Gulf War, it was obvious that Iraq was the aggressor, dramatically invading Kuwait after little provocation. Yet such instances are relatively rare. It is too often the case that the identity of the aggressor is difficult to determine objectively. For example, who would be considered the aggressor in the 1967 Six Day War?[8] It is clear that Israel launched a preemptive strike, but only in response to Arab plans for imminent attack. When partisan loyalties are introduced, the prospect that the United States would take any action against Israel, even if only to stop the fighting, or that other states would turn against the Arab cause is wildly unrealistic. A look at longstanding regional conflicts, such as between India and Pakistan over Kashmir, will yield few with so unambiguous a villain as Iraq when they are thrust into the U.N. political arena.

A second necessary condition for U.N. enforcement action is the presence of a status quo ante that is worthy, in the eyes of U.N. members, of being defended.[9] In almost all cases, an enforcement action by the United Nations will involve the restoration of a status quo ante, as troops will be deployed following an attack. It is doubtful that U.N. members would sanction the use of military force to precipitate some type of new political or territorial change. In some cases, the status quo ante may appear offensive to many U.N. members, as defending white-ruled South Africa would have been. In other cases, the status quo ante is indiscernible in light of historical shifts (who really owns Jerusalem?) or domestic chaos (if the Serbians in Bosnia-Herzegovina are defeated, what situation is restored?). Thus, the second condition places another limitation on the number and type of regional conflicts that might be subject to U.N.-authorized enforcement action.

In the ideal world, any threat to international peace and security with a identifiable aggressor and a desirable status quo ante would receive a strong U.N. response. Indeed, it would be necessary to facilitate a credible deterrent, thereby rendering such action unnecessary. In reality, however, a third requirement for enforcement action is that U.N. members must view the stakes in the conflict as being of sufficient magnitude to justify such dramatic action; presumption is usually in favor of other peaceful alternatives. When Kuwait was attacked and the world's oil supply was threatened, the response was considerably swifter and more substantial than in the civil war in Yugoslavia. Enforcement actions involve substantial commitment and considerable risk. U.N. members are not willing to bear substantial costs in a regional conflict unless the stakes are significant for countries outside the immediate conflict area. This reluctance may be superseded by an international sense of conflict fatigue or outrage, as was the case in Somalia. Yet this excludes many cases of purely internal conflict and gives primacy to interstate conflicts that have global implications.

A corollary to the previous requirement is that there also must be a major power willing to organize, supply, and direct any U.N.-authorized action. In practice, this task will fall largely to the United States or some collection of EU states. These states must regard proposed military actions as being in their respective self-interests. Thus, one might expect the United Nations to be involved more in conflicts in Europe than in Africa, for example. One might also exclude certain conflicts that impinge on geographic areas proximate to the United States and China. Each power may be reluctant for the United Nations to intervene in its own backyard or, conversely, may insist on a leading role that may not be supported by other states in the region. The persistence of the veto in the Security Council and the unlikely use of the General Assembly as an alternate forum will limit the types of operations authorized.

U.N. enforcement actions in regional conflicts are likely to be limited.[10] Yet they may be quite successful under certain circumstances. In theory, a global collective action should be successful against any individual state or group of states. In practice, what may seem to be overwhelming odds against the aggressor may not translate into victory. Multinational forces operating under a U.N. mandate may easily win a conventional military encounter, as they did in the Persian Gulf War. In a civil war, it may be an extraordinary task to subdue internal elements and restore order; house-to-house fighting may drag an operation out for months or longer with significant loss of life. In the case of the Somali civil war, stopping the fighting does not solve the total breakdown of government order that has resulted from the civil war; U.N. enforcement actions have to be followed by administrative efforts to run the country. U.N.-backed actions might also face determined opponents with the capability and willingness to use advanced weaponry. This would raise the cost of the operation and perhaps alter the time frame, if not the probability, of success.

It is quite conceivable that the United Nations may authorize the use of military force in situations other than collective security and for more limited purposes. The United Nations has already agreed to allow states to use force in order to protect relief shipments to Bosnia-Herzegovina, and U.S.-led forces have entered Somalia to do the same. Force might also be necessary to protect neutral shipping in a war zone or to protect refugees or internal exile groups, such as the Kurds in Iraq. Yet these instances will be ad hoc to specific circumstances and, perhaps with the exception of protecting humanitarian shipments, are unlikely to be regularized.

That a well-developed and functioning global collective security system is not on the horizon should not imply that the United Nations will revert to its banal function as a debating forum incapable of concerted action. Instead, the United Nations will confine itself to actions within the parameters established by the international community. Nevertheless, the new world order offers many opportunities for an expansion of U.N. roles in international peace and security, as noted in the next sections.

▲ Peacekeeping

During the Cold War, collective military action of any sort, save the Korean anomaly, was impossible. The United Nations was forced to move beyond its Charter provisions to create a new strategy for dealing with international peace and security. That new strategy—peacekeeping—was born in response to the Suez Crisis of 1956. Traditional peacekeeping is the stationing of neutral, lightly armed troops as a buffer or interposition force between protagonists following a ceasefire but prior to a resolution of the underlying dispute. A variant of peacekeeping is peace observation, which has the same monitoring function as peacekeeping but usually involves a smaller number of unarmed personnel, who do not assume any interposition role.

Since 1945 the United Nations has conducted more than a dozen peace-keeping operations and the same number of observation missions.[11] In the Cold War era, U.N. peacekeeping played a small role in the spheres of influence dominated by the superpowers. Regional conflicts in Central America, for example, did not regularly appear on the U.N. agenda, and unilateral U.S. military action, such as the 1965 invasion of the Dominican Republic or the 1983 invasion of Grenada, was a substitute for concerted international action. Similarly, the territory surrounding the Soviet Union was off-limits to U.N. peacekeeping. In regional conflicts elsewhere, peacekeeping was considered an option when neither superpower had a direct interest in the conflict and the severity of the conflict prompted international attention. Thus, peacekeeping operations were sent to the Congo and Cyprus in the early 1960s.

In addition, the United Nations did send peacekeeping forces and observation teams to regions where the superpowers had close allies. Yet, in those cases peacekeeping forces were only deployed as a means to halt a war or a process of escalation that threatened to draw the superpowers into the conflict. U.N. Emergency Force II was sent to the Sinai as a part of a ceasefire agreement in the 1973 Yom Kippur War, but only after the United States and the Soviet Union put their militaries on low-level alert. U.N. observation forces were also deployed to Kashmir in 1949 amid continuing troubles between India and Pakistan.

With the end of the Cold War, virtually all regional conflicts became candidates for peacekeeping and observation missions. The United States has assumed the mantle of leadership in the Security Council, and Russia has generally supported or acquiesced in U.S. initiatives. A U.N. observation team—the United Nations Good Offices Mission in Afghanistan and Pakistan (UNGOMAP)—facilitated the withdrawal of Soviet troops from Afghanistan, the first time that U.N. peacekeepers had monitored the behavior of a superpower. In the U.S. sphere of influence, the United Nations Observer Group in Central America (ONUCA) monitored elections in Latin America. The United States and the Soviet Union also encouraged the use of peacekeeping and observation teams to resolve longstanding proxy conflicts in Cambodia—the United Nations Transitional Authority in Cambodia (UNTAC)—and Angola—the United Nations Angola Verification Mission (UNAVEM).

The authorization of peacekeeping and observation missions is considerably easier than enforcement actions. Peacekeeping and observation do not require U.N. members to label any side in the conflict as the aggressor, thereby mitigating many of the political obstacles to taking action. As neutral forces, peacekeepers are not to favor the interests of one side or the other in the conflict. Because peacekeeping mitigates some of the political cleavages in the United Nations, it became, and is likely to continue to be, the primary operational action of the organization in regional conflicts.

Conditions for Success in Traditional Peacekeeping Operations

Traditional peacekeeping operations may become more frequent in the post–Cold War era, but this should not imply that they are a panacea to any regional conflicts that might arise. Peacekeeping operations are successful under a limited set of conditions.[12] Most notably, peacekeeping operations perform better in interstate conflicts than in civil wars or internationalized civil wars. Interstate conflicts afford peacekeeping troops the ability to separate only two hostile parties, generally across identifiable borders or ceasefire lines. In a civil war, especially one with guerrilla fighting or urban warfare, it is next to impossible geographically to separate the combatants. In a civil war it is also hard to identify different partisans quickly. Peacekeepers are unable to stop sniper activity or realistically search everyone on the street in an urban area. Furthermore, stopping a civil war by means of a ceasefire and a peacekeeping force may inherently favor one side in the conflict. Thus, a rebel group may not accept the peacekeeping force or may break the ceasefire because it believes that stopping the fighting helps the beleaguered and challenged government. Finally, interstate conflicts usually have to rely on the cooperation of two parties. Peacekeeping in civil wars may involve reconciling the competing preferences of more than two states may have to be reconciled;[13] as in the case of the United Nations Interim Force in Lebanon (UNIFIL), the opposition of subnational groups and third-party states has doomed some peacekeeping operations. Such opposition has been a primary factor in the failure of past peacekeeping operations.

Beyond their greater suitability for interstate conflicts, peacekeeping forces are best deployed in regional conflicts when geographic circumstances favor their use. Peacekeeping operations function best when they are deployed in an area that (1) separates the combatants by a safe distance, (2) permits easy observation and detection of ceasefire violations, and (3) is relatively invulnerable to attack. Thus, peacekeeping forces are most likely to maintain stability when they are sent to a thinly populated area where movements are minimal (a desert area is almost ideal) and the demilitarized zone of operation is wide. Regional conflicts such as in Beirut, Lebanon, where Christian and Muslim areas are divided only by the narrow Green Line, represent the opposite of what is needed for a successful peacekeeping operation.

Peacekeeping operations are also most successful when they are perceived as neutral by the combatants. This is most often assured by composing the U.N. force of troops from neutral or disinterested states. With the end of the Cold War and its polarizing effects on the international system, this task should be easier. Yet peacekeeping operations must also continue to behave in an impartial fashion; failure to do so will lead one or more parties to break the ceasefire and possibly attack the peacekeeping force, which is ill-equipped and trained to be a combatant. The risk of biased behavior is highest when the peacekeeping forces are assigned a mandate that serves the interests of one side in the dispute at the expense of the other.

Two categories of disputes will form the majority of future threats to regional peace and security: interstate border or territorial disputes and nationalist conflicts. The former seem to be well suited to application of the peacekeeping strategy. Peacekeeping troops might be placed at a disputed border or throughout the territory in question until sovereignty over the area is settled. The geographic configuration and the limited number of actors in these interstate disputes make results more promising than in other peacekeeping scenarios.

Currently, there are approximately seventy-five interstate border or territorial disputes in the world.[14] This is not to say that all these disputes require a peacekeeping force. Indeed, most are latent disputes with only a slight prospect for war any time in the near future. Nevertheless, war in the Persian Gulf might have been avoided if a peacekeeping force had been deployed to the disputed oil fields on the border of Kuwait and Iraq, especially at the time of rising tensions in July 1990. Peacekeeping troops might also be sent to replace observers in the disputed Kashmir region between India and Pakistan, which has been the scene of heightened tensions in the past few years.

The outlook for the use of peacekeeping troops in nationalist struggles is less promising. The end of the Cold War has permitted the rekindling of nationalist passions of many peoples around the globe. On all the major continents, ethnic and racial groups are seeking greater autonomy or independence from their central governments. These are primarily civil conflicts in which peacekeeping troops have had difficulty in the past. As noted above, one must be cautious in sending peacekeeping forces to the sites of these conflicts. Nationalist conflicts best suited to peacekeeping operations would be those in which there has been an agreement among the warring parties to solve the dispute and the peacekeeping force is charged with assisting in the implementation of that agreement, for example, by supervising an election or monitoring a ceasefire in a transition period.

Short of such an agreement, peacekeeping forces should perhaps be used only when (1) the primary protagonists request a peacekeeping force, (2) the area of deployment and the population of the areas controlled by the respective parties do not include a large number of citizens of the opposite national group, and (3) there is an easily identifiable line of demarcation between the warring parties. Yet the United Nations most likely will have to deploy before agreement is reached resolving the issues in a national struggle and will have to do so in areas in which the population is of mixed ethnic character. Prospects for a fully deployed operation and, therefore, success will be much better if and when all the main protagonists agree to cooperate with the peacekeeping mission.

The internal weakening of central governments and the rise of semiautonomous and powerful subnational groups will likely make nationalist struggles an increasing problem in the future.[15] Unfortunately, peacekeeping operations cannot play a central role in all these challenges; they may best be used as an implementing mechanism when conflict resolution is attained.

New Roles for Peacekeeping Forces

In addition to traditional peacekeeping and observation, the United Nations is likely to assume new roles in international peace and security. The end of the Cold War and the perceived neutrality of the organization should make the following options viable alternatives: acting as a tripwire, election supervision, arms control verification, naval peacekeeping, and humanitarian assistance. In each case, the United Nations may deploy peacekeeping or observer teams to perform these new functions or create new agencies to perform the tasks.[16] Yet one should recognize that resource constraints will be greater and may affect the willingness to authorize new operations.

Acting as a tripwire. The first new role for the United Nations would be as a tripwire against surprise attack from either disputant. In this role, U.N. troops would be placed at or near a defined border area. The peacekeeping forces would monitor military movements in the area and serve as a mediator for any disputes that arise over a ceasefire agreement. The use of U.N. forces as a tripwire is not necessarily a new concept; indeed, this corresponds largely to the traditional roles assumed by peacekeeping missions. The difference would be that the peacekeeping forces would be deployed prior to, instead of following, the initial onset of armed conflict. In this fashion, peacekeeping forces would exercise preventive diplomacy to head off international crises rather than acting as band-aids for ones that have already occurred. In this way the United Nations could play a role in crisis management prior to the onset of armed hostilities.

Election supervision. U.N. troops, observers, and other personnel might also act as the supervising agency in elections that resolve internal conflict. U.N. forces would be charged with several tasks in the process. First, they would patrol the area in which the election was held seeking to limit the campaign violence that has become common in many parts of the world. Second, and most importantly, they would monitor the election process to ensure that fair and regular procedures were followed; in effect, they would be on hand to report, and thereby deter, any ballot tampering or irregularities on the day of the election. Peacekeeping troops served in this capacity in Namibia, and observation teams performed similar functions in Central America. UNTAC performed that function in Cambodia.

Arms control verification. Another new role for U.N. forces is in arms control verification. U.N. peacekeeping forces or other personnel have the potential to be the verifying agency for arms agreements. More conventionally, the United Nations might verify troop reductions or withdrawal within a given area. Traditional peacekeeping operations have performed this role in the past, as in the Israeli and Egyptian disengagement following the Yom Kippur War. A more innovative activity for peacekeeping forces would be on-site inspections; for example, they might supervise the destruction of weapons or verify that troop levels and weapons deployment were within prescribed limits. The most ambitious use of the United Nations in arms control verification would involve aerial surveillance, in which U.N. personnel would be equipped with their own planes, satellites, radar, and other intelligence gathering mechanisms to verify arms agreements through technical means.[17]

Naval peacekeeping. Another innovative role for peacekeeping forces is as a naval patrol. Previously, peacekeeping operations have been almost exclusively land-based, except for some instances of helicopter reconnaissance. As a naval patrol, U.N. personnel would be deployed on ships flying the U.N. flag. Duties would include escorting neutral shipping through dangerous waters during a war. This would discourage belligerents from attacking neutral shipping or conducting illegal searches and seizures in international waters. U.N. forces could also conduct minesweeping operations in the area. A naval peacekeeping force might also perform duties in the verification of naval treaties. For example, it could verify the Treaty of Tlatelolco, which established a nuclear-free zone in Latin America, by verifying that signatory states did not place nuclear weapons in the seabed beneath their territorial waters.

Humanitarian assistance. Humanitarian assistance involves the deployment of peacekeeping troops in a civil conflict. Peacekeeping forces would be responsible for delivering the food and medical supplies to the war-torn area. This might necessitate commissioning cargo planes under U.N. auspices or coordinating efforts with private relief agencies. Once on the ground, U.N. troops would guard the convoys that transport the food to the areas of greatest need. Food and medical supplies are at risk for theft or misappropriation to the black market; peacekeeping forces would be available to guard warehouses and distribution centers as well as protect the transportation system for the aid. Humanitarian assistance missions of this type were initiated in 1992 in Yugoslavia and Somalia.

The use of peacekeeping forces as a tripwire, in election supervision, in arms control verification, and as naval peacekeepers is promising. In all instances, however, existing peacekeeping institutions would have to be adapted to the task. In the case of election supervision, this might involve, for example, a dramatic increase in the number of troops needed. For arms control verification, specialized training and the inclusion of technocrats in the peacekeeping force might be necessary. New equipment and procedures would be required before a naval task force could be deployed in a peacekeeping role. In addition, each of these new roles involves certain unique risks. For example, the tripwire peacekeeping troops may be subject to attack by hostile parties. Nevertheless, these new operations have the potential to be at least as successful as traditional peacekeeping operations and could be valuable additions to the U.N. repertoire.

The other functional alternative for U.N. peacekeeping, humanitarian assistance, appears less promising. Peacekeeping forces in this role may experience problems similar to those encountered by interposition forces. Those opposing the government, especially terrorist groups, will have maximum incentive to disrupt the operation of everyday life in the country, the idea being that the resulting chaos will be blamed on the government, making it more vulnerable to a takeover or collapse. Preventing food and medicine shipments to government-held areas may force the ruling group to devote more of its own resources to humanitarian rather than to military efforts. Rebel groups also do not want to see food supplies and assistance go to those who support their opponents. The government may want to punish people who live in areas controlled by rebels (and, therefore, in the view of some, support the rebels). To the extent that the civil war mirrors ethnic, tribal, or other national divisions, the government may feel little obligation to feed its citizens. Indeed, NATO, a traditional military group, may be better suited than a U.N. peacekeeping operation for these kind of missions. This was quite evident in Somalia, where an initial peacekeeping effort was ineffective and had to give way to the use of regular military forces.

Using peacekeeping forces in unconventional ways seems to work best when some or all of certain conditions are fulfilled. First, the best functional alternatives are those that represent incremental deviations, rather than dramatic changes, from the traditional model. Naval peacekeeping and election supervision, for example, include many of the same basic activities (such as monitoring movements and detecting violations) as traditional peacekeeping, but in different forms and contexts. Second, promising functional alternatives involve deployment following a significant degree of conflict resolution. Functional alternatives that involve implementation of an agreement between the disputants, such as an arms control pact, have a good chance of succeeding. Finally, functional alternatives, much like their traditional counterparts, operate best in contexts other than civil conflict. The incentives for noncooperation by subnational actors can lead to violence and other problems for new applications of peacekeeping strategy just as easily as for traditional interposition forces.

▲ Peacemaking

Peacemaking includes the whole range of diplomatic maneuvers designed to achieve the resolution of a dispute without the use of military force. Peacemaking options might be chosen prior to, in conjunction with, following, or independently of the previous alternatives of collective enforcement and peacekeeping.

The first subset of diplomatic alternatives involves the resolution of disputes through adjudicatory proceedings. The United Nations may recommend or actually facilitate the settlement of regional conflicts by resorting to international courts or arbitration panels.[18] These alternatives are rarely utilized, and there appears to be little prospect that the situation will change in the near future. Many regional conflicts are fundamentally political disagreements without legal basis and therefore are not justiciable. In fact, only sixty cases have been referred to the International Court of Justice since the adoption of the U.N. Charter.[19] Most of these cases did not involve security issues; for example, several cases dealt with fishing and airspace rights. States cannot be compelled to submit cases to the court, and even when the court decides it has jurisdiction, any enforcement is up to the Security Council, with all the accompanying limitations. States are reluctant to put the most critical aspects of their national interests before an international body; self-help mechanisms are preferred.[20] The International Court of Justice has recently dealt with some border disputes between states, but this form of conflict management seems promising only when the dispute is in a latent phase and the prospects for escalation are low.

Arbitration has become increasingly rare since the beginning of the twentieth century. As with international courts, states will not agree to have "high politics" issues before an arbitration panel. Arbitration has only played a role as a mechanism for dealing with residual claims following a peace agreement between disputants, such as the outstanding claims by the United States and Iran after the release of American hostages in 1981.

A second set of alternatives under the rubric of peacemaking concerns the U.N. role in stimulating negotiations. In contrast to peacekeeping and enforcement, stimulating negotiations is a frequent and widespread activity of the United Nations, which often functions as an intermediary in regional conflicts and seeks to broker various types of agreements between the disputants. This role takes place at various junctures of the conflict process and has varying goals depending on the situation. Prior to the onset of military hostilities, the United Nations is intent upon devising long-term solutions to regional conflict. In the absence of significant military conflict, new peacekeeping and enforcement initiatives give way to diplomatic solutions. When a civil or inter-state war occurs, the goals of the United Nations are usually short-term: it is more concerned with stopping the fighting. Diplomatic maneuvers at this stage may be considered to be precursory to the establishment of a peacekeeping operation or observer mission. When the fighting stops, whether through U.N. efforts or not, the United Nations moves into another phase of operation where the goal is again the resolution of the underlying dispute.

U.N. stimulation of negotiations may take several forms.[21] The most limited of these is *good offices*. Good offices involve bringing together the disputants, but the organization plays no active role in the deliberations. In 1992, Secretary-General Boutros-Ghali sought to bring together representatives of the African National Congress and the de Klerk government of South Africa in order to resume negotiations and address the escalating violence in black townships. A higher level of intervention is the convocation of peace conferences under U.N. auspices. These high-profile talks may include the direct involvement of U.N. officials, or their involvement may be more limited, as in the use of good offices. Leading members of the Security Council, rather than members of the U.N. Secretariat, may conduct the conferences and work with the disputants. The unsuccessful 1973 Middle East conference, designed to address the aftermath of the Yom Kippur War, is an example.

Most U.N. negotiation efforts involve an active mediation role for the organization. Mediators bring the parties together or act as liaisons for disputants who will not agree to face-to-face talks. U.N. personnel attempt to craft agreements that are acceptable to all parties. The agreement for withdrawal of Soviet troops from Afghanistan is an example. Sometimes, a single individual may act as the mediator in a conflict. Former U.S. Secretary of State Cyrus Vance acted as the personal representative of the Secretary-General in both the Armenia-Azerbaijan and Yugoslavia conflicts. On rare occasions, the Secretary-General has assumed the mediator's role, such as when Kurt Waldheim attempted to secure the release of American hostages in Iran in 1980.

U.N. attempts to stimulate negotiations during the Cold War had mixed results. The organization was at its best in dealing with crisis situations and in achieving short-term goals such as ceasefire agreements. The United Nations generally enters a regional conflict when it reaches a boiling point, usually well after the conflict has begun. Fewer and less effective conflict management efforts take place when the situation is stable, even if the long-term stability of the region is doubtful, such as in the Middle East or along the border between

India and Pakistan. In the future, these general patterns are unlikely to change, even given the lessening of tensions between the major power. The United Nations tends to be a crisis-driven organization, and in the area of security its resources are not usually devoted to solving protracted conflicts in the absence of serious violence. There have been some renewed calls for preventive diplomacy that would be designed to deter or halt the initiation of military conflict. Yet it is not clear whether U.N. members are willing to devote the attention and resources to such an enterprise. Until that time, U.N. diplomacy will remain an option of near resort, one that is used in regional conflicts only after national efforts fail.

In the Cold War era there were few instances when the United Nations achieved resolution of the underlying sources of dispute,[22] particularly following the deployment of traditional peacekeeping troops. Once the peacekeeping operations were in place and the situation was stable, the troops had a tendency to "just sit there."[23] Long-term efforts to resolve the conflicts were either untried, redirected, or unsuccessful. The United Nations sometimes made little effort to resolve the conflict if a situation was stable and other conflicts were more salient. Thus, following the deployment of the first peacekeeping operation in the Middle East, in 1956 — United Nations Emergency Force (UNEF I) — there were few efforts at mediation. Admittedly, much of the blame can be attributed to the participants, who seemed unwilling to negotiate in any meaningful sense.

When good-faith efforts were made by the United Nations, they were often redirected to short-term concerns, such as defusing rising tensions in the area and working out disputes over provisions of the ceasefire agreements. U.N. concern with southern Lebanon after the deployment of UNIFIL has been with various ceasefire violations and with obtaining Israeli and PLO cooperation with the terms of the peacekeeping deployment. Solving the longstanding problems of that area has been put on the back burner. Finally, some past U.N. efforts were unsuccessful because the disputants would not compromise to resolve the conflict or their competing preferences were irreconcilable, despite the best efforts of the organization. U.N. peacekeeping personnel have been stationed on Cyprus since 1964, a testament to their effectiveness in keeping the peace but also an indication of the failure of many U.N. peacemaking initiatives.

With the end of the Cold War, U.N. diplomatic initiatives may be more successful. The secretary-general has shown more autonomy in his actions, moving quickly to intervene in escalating conflicts. The major powers have also been more supportive of such efforts, often pressuring the combatants to reach some accord under U.N. auspices. The peace agreements in Cambodia and Angola were achieved because the relevant major states placed their influence and power behind U.N. initiatives. U.N. negotiations also may have a brighter future because peacemaking efforts may be more closely tied to peacekeeping ones. The ceasefire and subsequent democratic elections in Namibia demonstrate how the United Nations may combine successful negotiations with multilateral assistance in implementing provisions of the agreement. This ensures greater stability in the long run and corrects many of the flaws of peacekeeping with respect to resolving the underlying sources of regional conflict.

U.N. negotiation efforts operate best under certain conditions. As noted above, crisis-driven responses yield the best results, especially in meeting short-term goals in regional conflicts. The United Nations is most successful when the disputants really desire peace; the organization cannot force states to compromise. The United Nations can, however, provide the mechanisms to facilitate an agreement that would otherwise not be negotiated directly by the disputants. Nevertheless, the United Nations may have no inherent advantage over similar efforts by regional organizations, such as the EU, or unilateral national efforts. U.N. efforts are also successful when there is external pressure on the disputants, most effectively by the major powers, to settle the conflict. Agreements in Angola and Cambodia can be attributed not only to U.N. policies but also to diplomatic intervention by the United States, the Soviet Union, and China.

Finally, the United Nations has a third alternative at its disposal: inquiry. Inquiry occurs when the organization undertakes a fact-finding mission in a regional conflict. This was a common approach to peace in the League of Nations era, when fact finding was combined with a recommendation for resolving the conflict.[24] It has largely fallen into disuse in the nuclear age. Furthermore, inquiry is not a solution in itself, because it is a precursor to further action. The mission to Yugoslavia and recommendations of a former Polish prime minister provide a contemporary example of this peacemaking technique.

▲ Conclusion

The United Nations has great potential to ameliorate or resolve regional conflicts, but it can only be as effective as its members and the disputants allow it to be. The end of the Cold War has widened some of the parameters of U.N. action, but significant limitations remain. The prospects are that the United Nations will not play a major enforcement role in regional conflicts. No international army is on the horizon, and multinational military operations operating under U.N. approval are unlikely to become commonplace. The use of the latter will be more frequent than in earlier eras, however, owing to the greater consensus in the Security Council. Yet the requirements of a definable aggressor, a desirable status quo ante, and vital stakes for the international community will necessarily narrow the scope of international actions in regional conflicts.

Various peacekeeping and peacemaking efforts should continue to be the United Nations' most prominent techniques or strategies in dealing with regional conflicts. They are likely to be used more frequently, and they may take a different form than in the Cold War period. Traditional peacekeeping operations will expand, but their effectiveness will be determined largely by their judicious use in interstate conflicts where the relevant parties support their presence. Perhaps more promising is the use of peacekeeping forces in new roles such as arms control verification, election supervision, naval peacekeeping, and as a tripwire. Diplomatic initiatives have already expanded under Secretaries-General Pérez de Cuéllar and Boutros-Ghali. These will be essential in ensuring the long-term stability of regions, as peacekeeping forces may only serve as band-aids for further regional conflict. As with other U.N. options, the support of the major powers and the willingness of the disputants to compromise and make peace will determine the outcome. If those are favorable, the United Nations can be a good mechanism for containing, reducing, or resolving regional conflicts.

NOTES

1. Ernst Haas, *The United Nations and the Collective Management of International Conflict* (New York: United Nations Institute for Training and Research, 1986).

2. Jonathan Wilkenfeld and Michael Brecher, "International Crises 1945-1975: The UN Dimension," *International Studies Quarterly* 28, no. 1 (1984): 45-67.

3. This is particularly the case with respect to peacekeeping operations (see Paul F. Diehl, "Institutional Alternatives to Traditional UN Peacekeeping: An Assessment of Regional and Multinational Options," *Armed Forces and Society* 19, no. 2 [1993]: 209-30).

4. On this subject, see Stephen Lewis, Clovis Maksoud, and Robert Johansen, "The United Nations after the Cold War," *World Policy Journal,* summer 1991, 537-74.

5. Another coercive alternative—economic sanctions—is excluded from consideration here as it does not usually involve the use of military and is addressed elsewhere in this volume (see chapter by Snyder).

6. President Bush stated that despite increased U.S. support for U.N. actions, "member states, as always, must retain the final decision on the use of their troops" ("Bush, in Address to UN, Urges More Vigor in Keeping the Peace," *New York Times*, Sept. 22, 1992, 1). President Clinton has relaxed that policy somewhat, but his administration has stated that it will retain control over U.S. troops in any enforcement operation.

7. For example, see the relevant Security Council resolutions concerning Iraq's invasion of Kuwait, especially 660 (1990), 678 (1991), and 687 (1991).

8. The United Nations has adopted a definition of aggression, but there is considerable Western dissent to that document. For the text of the document and a statement of U.S. objections, see *Department of State Bulletin* 72 (Feb. 3, 1975): 155–62.

9. See Inis Claude, *Swords into Plowshares*, 4th ed. (New York: Random House, 1971), for a discussion of aggression, status quo, and other requirements of collective security.

10. Peacekeeping troops might undertake some enforcement action under various proposals (see Bruce Russett and James Sutterlin, "The UN in a New World Order," *Foreign Affairs* 70 [fall 1991]: 69–83; and John Mackinlay and Jarat Chopra, "Second Generation Multinational Operations," *Washington Quarterly* 15, no. 3 [1991]: 113–31).

11. These figures, accurate as of June 1994, are taken from the U.N. brochure *United Nations Peace-Keeping* (New York: U.N. Department of Public Information, 1990); and New Zealand Ministry of External Relations and Trade, *United Nations Handbook, 1991* (Auckland: New House, 1991), and have been updated by me.

12. See Paul F. Diehl, *International Peacekeeping* (Baltimore: Johns Hopkins University Press, 1993); and John Mackinlay, *The Peacekeepers* (London: Unwin Hyman, 1989).

13. It may be impossible to reconcile competing preferences of more than two parties (see Kenneth Arrow, *Social Choice and Individual Values* [New York: John Wiley, 1951]).

14. This figure is calculated from Alan Day, ed., *Border and Territorial Disputes*, 2d ed. (Essex: Longman, 1987), as reported in Gary Goertz and Paul F. Diehl, *Territorial Changes and International Conflict* (London: Routledge, 1992), and updated by me to reflect post–Cold War conditions.

15. James Rosenau, *Turbulence in World Politics* (Princeton: Princeton University Press, 1990).

16. A discussion of alternatives to traditional peacekeeping roles is given in Indar Jit Rikhye, "The Future of Peacekeeping," in *The United Nations and Peacekeeping*, ed. Indar Jit Rikhye and Kjell Skjelsbaek (New York: St. Martin's Press, 1991), 171–99; Paul F. Diehl and Chetan Kumar, "Mutual Benefits from International Intervention: New Roles for United Nations Peacekeeping Forces," *Bulletin of Peace Proposals* 22, no. 4 (1991): 369–75; and Diehl, *International Peacekeeping*.

17. This use of U.N. forces is discussed in Michael Krepon and Jeffrey Tracey, "Open Skies and Peace-Keeping," *Survival* 32 (May–June 1990): 251–63; and John Tirman, "International Monitoring for Peace," *Issues in Science and Technology* 4 (1988): 53–58.

18. See Chapter 6 of the U.N. Charter.

19. This number includes cases through 1990 but does not include twenty advisory opinions (Barry Carter and Phillip Trimble, *International Law: Selected Documents* [Boston: Little, Brown, 1991]).

20. Dana Fischer, "Decisions to Use the International Court of Justice: Four Recent Cases," *International Studies Quarterly* 26, no. 2 (1982): 251–77.

21. Claude, *Swords into Plowshares.*

22. Of course, unilateral national or multinational efforts may fill the void, as in the United States' facilitation of the Camp David accord.

23. H. Hanning, "Report on Workshop," in Hanning, ed., *Peacekeeping and Technology—Concepts for the Future* (New York: International Peace Academy, 1983). See also Paul F. Diehl, "When Peacekeeping Does Not Lead to Peace: Some Notes on Conflict Resolution," *Bulletin of Peace Proposals* 18, no. 1 (1987): 47–53.

24. See David Wainhouse, *International Peace Observation* (Baltimore; Johns Hopkins Press, 1966).

NICOLE BALL

7 International Economic Actors

During the Cold War, the foreign policy concerns of the major powers fostered high military budgets, the growth of a domestic defense-industrial sector, war as a means of resolving disputes, and politically active armed forces. The costs of these policies were extremely high, although they were by and large ignored, particularly in the developing world and the former Soviet Union. The billions of dollars devoted to housing, feeding, paying, and arming unnecessarily large security forces in the poorest parts of the world produced serious imbalances between the military budget and the public-sector expenditures that were vital for sustained economic growth and development. The high priority accorded the military sector helped to prevent the emergence of accountable government, without which neither economic development nor political stability can be sustained. Internal and regional conflicts caused millions of deaths and led to bloated military budgets, further undermining opportunities for development.[1]

While it may not be surprising that the foreign and security policy establishments in the major industrial countries discounted the developmental impact of military buildups, arms races, and conflict, the Cold War severely limited the freedom of action of aid agencies and the other members of the international lending community as well.[2] Several bilateral donors, most notably the United States and the Soviet Union, frequently provided economic assistance during the Cold War specifically to enable governments to maintain military spending at levels that would not be attainable using only domestic resources. More generally, lenders ignored the fact that financing provided for nonmilitary purposes, particularly budget support and balance-of-payments funding, enables governments to allocate more to military expenses if they are so inclined.

Now, in the wake of the Cold War and the Gulf War, the members of the Development Assistance Committee (DAC) of the Organization for Economic Cooperation and Development (OECD), the World Bank, the International Monetary Fund (IMF), the Inter-American Development Bank (IDB), and several U.N. agencies have recognized that enhancing prospects for development requires achieving peace and stability. The successful pursuit of economic development, the establishment of participatory government, the protection of human rights, and the promotion of good governance practices are closely linked to conditions in the security sector.

Lenders have already taken some steps to help countries reduce the economic and political burden of their security sectors. Although policy formulation and especially policy implementation are still at an early stage, the lending institutions have begun to promote military-sector reforms in countries where internal and external security threats are minimal. The primary objective of this reform process has been to enhance development opportunities by reducing security spending. The official lenders have been considerably more hesitant to become involved in the military reform process where the security environment is not immediately conducive to reductions in the size and cost of security forces, arguing that it is more appropriate for international and national political actors to seek to resolve outstanding security issues within or between countries. While it is clear that political institutions must take the lead in resolving the political and military issues that underlie enduring conflicts and arms races, the international lending community can and should play an integral role in creating and maintaining an environment of peace.

This chapter is divided into three parts. The first part identifies the major international economic players and the types of economic activities they can employ as leverage. The second part describes the policies that one group of these actors — the international lending community — has developed and implemented to date. The third and final part suggests some specific ways in which these institutions can support efforts to resolve longstanding internal and interstate conflicts.

TABLE 7.1
International Economic Actors

TABLE 7.1
International Economic Actors

National Governmental Agencies	Multilateral Development Agencies
Aid ministries/agencies	UN bodies, e.g., United Nations Development
Foreign ministries	Programme, World Food Programme,
Defense ministries	UNICEF, FAO, ILO, UNHCR
Finance ministries	EU Commission
Trade ministries	
Export credit facilities	Multilateral Political Institutions
Legislatures	United Nations Security Council and
	General Assembly
International Financial Institutions	Regional and subregional organizations, e.g.,
World Bank and affiliates	OAU, OAS, ASEAN, CSCE, SADC, ECOWAS
Asian Development Bank	
Inter-American Development Bank	Private-Sector Institutions
African Development Bank	Corporations
European Bank for Reconstruction and	Banks
Development	Nongovernmental organizations
International Monetary Fund	

▲ Major International Economic Players

A wide variety of institutions are capable of either (1) taking actions in the economic sphere that affect the intensity and duration of conflicts, the acquisition of conventional arms and weapons of mass destruction, the creation of collective security mechanisms, or the promotion of political liberalization; or (2) making decisions that affect the behavior of the primary actors. The major international economic players can be divided into five main categories: national government agencies, international financial institutions, multilateral development agencies, multilateral political institutions, and private-sector institutions (see table 7.1). This chapter will deal solely with public-sector actors.

Each institution has unique strengths and mandates. The most obvious distinction is that some are authorized to deal with a wide range of topics, while others are primarily or exclusively concerned with economic affairs and are restricted, by law or by long-established practice, in their ability to become involved in what are defined as "political" issues. There are several methods of overcoming such restrictions to create programs that support the complex process of moving from active conflict, through crisis management, containment, and reduction, to conflict resolution and prevention. The first is to expand institutional mandates, either by formally revising legal regulations governing activities or by redefining what is permissible under existing regulations. The second is to identify institutional comparative advantage, constructing programs that include a wide variety of agencies and institutions and that enable each institution to carry out the functions for which it is best suited. In fact, both of these processes are now underway.

National Government Agencies

National governments have the most flexibility in supporting efforts to re-duce conflicts because they are involved in a broad range of economic and political activities as a matter of course. At the same time, because of their diverse interests, national governments frequently pursue contradictory poli-cies, resulting in bureaucratic wrangling that can prevent them from taking effective action or enable one department or ministry to undermine the efforts of another. During the Cold War the foreign policy and security objectives of the major powers allowed aid recipients to pursue policies that were in-imical to supporting sustainable development. It is increasingly clear that national well-being in the industrial countries is dependent upon enhanced political, economic, and military security throughout the world, although dif-ferent components of national bureaucracies may well define these elements of "national security" in quite different ways.

Aid Ministries

Of all national government agencies, aid ministries have the clearest view of how countries receiving their aid use resources, and in recent years they, along with several multilateral lending and development institutions, have taken the lead in putting military expenditure issues on the aid agenda in a growing number of developing countries.

Aid ministries have at their disposal a wide range of tools to encourage re-cipient governments to engage in policy reform. To begin with, aid ministries can engage recipients in public and private policy dialogue. The purposes of dialogue are to discuss both the need for reform and the ways such reform can serve aid recipients' interests, as well as to describe the support available to reform-minded governments.

There are essentially two strategies that aid agencies can follow to sup-port governments engaging in reforms. The first is to provide direct financial and technical assistance to specific reform programs. Within the international lending community this is sometimes called the "positive measures" approach. Financial support can help governments absorb extra costs associated with restructuring the military sector, such as compensating soldiers released from the armed forces or workers laid off as a result of rationalization of the defense-industrial sector. Technical support can provide skilled manpower or equipment to carry out tasks such as the destruction of weapons, threat analyses to support force planning and budgeting, and the privatization or conversion of military industries. The mechanics of designing and implementing programs to support military downsizing differ very little, from an organizational point of view, from many other development programs, although demobilized soldiers may have some special needs that will influence program design.

The second strategy is to reward good behavior in the security sector by according reforming governments preference in aid allocations. Here it is important for donors to define clearly what constitutes favorable behavior. This strategy is grounded upon the premise that positive reinforcement is more likely to produce behavioral change than is punishment. Although such an assessment may be valid for governments with a fairly firm commitment to reform, it is unclear how much leverage this sort of strategy provides over less committed countries.

Furthermore, desirable as it may be to offer the carrot rather than the stick, these two strategies virtually always require official lenders to shift resources from one country to another or, at a minimum in the case of positive measures, from one project to another within the same country. Aid recipients would like to see donors commit additional funding for military reform — "additionality" — over and above levels currently planned for development assistance, but a realistic appraisal of the foreign assistance budgets of the bilateral donors suggests that this is not likely. The aid budgets of most DAC members are stagnant or decreasing.[3]

If aid recipients are unwilling to make the reforms that the donor community has determined are important for the success of development efforts, aid ministries have two broad options for pressing for change. When providing structural adjustment lending, expenditure and performance targets can be set in priority development sectors that require expenditure reductions in other sectors. Through policy dialogue, recipients can be made to understand that the security sector should be reviewed for possible cuts but that there would be no formal requirement to reduce the military budget.

As a last resort, bilateral donors can make economic aid conditional on specific policy changes in the security sector to force a government to rethink a policy that is widely viewed as unacceptable; that is, they can apply conditionality. Since 1991, considerable attention has been focused on this option, often to the exclusion of others, in the discussions on the link between external financing and security-sector reform. Aid recipients have been concerned by the possibility that conditionality—which is frequently used in the economic sphere, particularly by the IMF and the World Bank—will be extended to the security sphere. They have argued that demanding reductions in security spending without reference to security needs is a dangerous exercise. In their view, only the country concerned has the capacity to define these needs and to decide how resources should be allocated to meet them. In addition, as donors increasingly seek to promote a range of activities designed to strengthen development capacities—such as participatory development, good governance, human rights guarantees, and environmental protection, as well as lower security budgets—there is fear that "conditionality proliferation" will overload the capacity of aid recipients to meet any individual objective.[4]

Aid donors agree that efforts to persuade governments that reform is in their own self-interest are more likely to succeed than demands for change, and they are wary of the potential negative effects of conditionality proliferation. They too, therefore, prefer to avoid specific conditionality. Nonetheless, they reserve the right to condition aid when governments are completely unwilling to contemplate change.

Foreign and Defense Ministries

Although foreign and defense ministries are primarily concerned with employing diplomatic and military tools to help them cope with enduring conflicts, often they also have economic tools directly at their disposal and have a strong influence over the activities of national "economic" agencies, such as aid and trade ministries.

Many defense ministries provide training to foreign security forces. This training has traditionally been oriented toward improving military skills and knowledge. More recently, security assistance programs have begun to provide training designed to enhance democratic institutions, civilian control over the military, and human rights, all of which are important components of resolving enduring internal conflicts.[5] Defense ministries can also provide financial and technical assistance for peace negotiations, regional security dialogues, and troop demobilization programs and support debt-relief measures to reward good behavior.

Aid to Eastern Europe and the successor states of the Soviet Union is frequently controlled by foreign ministries. These ministries also have an important, often determining, voice in discussions about how foreign assistance and other economic resources and tools will be employed in the developing countries. Like defense ministries, foreign ministries can also provide financial and technical assistance for peace negotiations, regional security dialogues, and demobilization programs and support debt-relief measures to reward good behavior.

Finance and Trade Ministries and Export Credit Facilities

Trade, credit, debt-relief, technology transfer, and investment policies can be designed to encourage countries to move along the continuum from active conflict to conflict resolution and prevention or to reduce arms procurement.

A number of defense technology supplier groups have been created that limit access to the know-how and materials required to produce weapons of mass destruction and ballistic missiles: the London Club (nuclear weapons); the Australia Group (chemical and biological warfare agents); and the Missile Technology Control Regime (longer-range ballistic missiles). During the Cold War, the transfer of dual-use technologies to Soviet bloc countries was regulated by the Coordinating Committee for Multilateral Export Controls (COCOM). As these regulations have been progressively relaxed in the post–Cold War period, the industrial countries have begun to debate the advisability of applying these restrictions to developing countries in an effort to stem proliferation.[6]

Civil-sector investment, credit, and trade policies can also be used to encourage governments to modify their behavior in the security sphere. Possible incentives—which can be used either as carrots or as sticks—include most-favored-nation status, trade privileges under the Generalized System of Preferences, subsidized food sales, export credits and guarantees, debt relief, free trade agreements, and collaborative programs in the areas of science and technology.

Economic sanctions are increasingly being applied by the international community. They are one of the most extreme forms of pressure and frequently are not successful in forcing governments to change policy.[7] But when governments are not at all dependent on external financing and routinely seek to circumvent restrictions imposed by supplier groups, international agreements, or international norms, the only way to influence their policy may be to restrict their economic activity. Sanctions are most effective when they are supported by all of a country's trade and investment partners and strictly adhered to by all parties.

The failure of Jordan to abide completely by U.N. sanctions against Iraq during the Gulf War and the willingness of Greece to continue supplying Serbia in the face of U.N. sanctions point up the difficulty in gaining compliance with sanctions imposed by the international community even when one country attacks another in blatant violation of international law. These cases also point up the importance of enforcement mechanisms, including, perhaps, credible sanctions against countries that defy embargoes. Uneven implementation of sanctions not only complicates efforts to pressure a government into changing its policies; it can also create a military imbalance that favors the aggressor, as the case of Bosnia clearly demonstrates.

Restrictions on economic activities can be of varying degrees of severity. A 1992 Government Accounting Office report identified three categories of sanctions. The least severe are "symbolic sanctions," which are intended, not to cause significant economic harm, but to send a message about appropriate behavior. The most severe are "instrumental sanctions," designed to block supplies of specific goods and/or financial capital. Between these two are "punitive sanctions," which are meant to produce economic costs but generally do not cut the target country off from all supplies of goods and capital.[8] Even where a large portion of the international community believes that strong, comprehensive sanctions are desirable, in some cases it may be necessary to begin with modest sanctions and progressively tighten them in order to gain the support of a major international actor that is also an ally of the party facing sanctions, for example, Russia in the case of Serbia.

Sanctions can also have a variety of targets. They can be aimed at individuals and firms that engage in certain activities, such as transferring military technology prohibited under export-control regimes. They can also be directed at governments that fail to enforce treaties or other international agreements, contravene international norms, or commit breaches of international law. One problem with comprehensive economic sanctions is that they generally hit the poorest members of society hardest, because economic and political elites are often able to take advantage of the inevitable loopholes in even the most stringent sanction efforts, thereby hampering efforts to achieve broad-based sustainable development.

Legislatures

Control over the purse gives legislatures the opportunity to shape the policies of the executive branch. In the past, at least in the United States, the tendency has been to focus on negative incentives or sanctions. Restrictions on the disbursement of financial assistance, on trade relations, and on the transfer of technology have been mandated when governments have failed to meet certain criteria, such as agreeing to negotiate in good faith with other disputing parties or adhering to international treaties such as the Nuclear Non-Proliferation Treaty or the Biological Weapons Convention. More recently, positive incentives such as creating special funds to support activities such as demobilization, training in conflict resolution techniques, or removing land mines have either been proposed or created by legislatures.

International Financial Institutions

Six major international financial institutions (IFIs) either are currently playing a role in developing strategies to resolve enduring conflicts or could be expected to do so. These include the World Bank, the IMF, and the four regional development banks — the African Development Bank, the Asian Development Bank, the European Bank for Reconstruction and Development, and the IDB.

The IMF seeks to promote balance-of-payments stability and monetary cooperation among its members and to facilitate the expansion and balanced growth of international trade, particularly by eliminating restrictions on foreign exchange. The multilateral development banks — the World Bank and its affiliates and the four regional banks — support economic and social development by providing financial and technical assistance to member governments.[9]

The IMF's primary input in terms of reforming the security sector will be in the area of monitoring and controlling expenditure. Because of the broader developmental mandate of the development banks, they can become involved in a wider range of activities designed to promote greater transparency and accountability in the security sector as well as specific projects to restructure that sector, such as demobilization and reintegration programs, efforts to improve civil-military relations, privatization and conversion of defense producers, and postconflict rehabilitation and reconstruction.

The international financial institutions have at their disposal essentially the same menu of tools as the national aid ministries: policy dialogue, financial and technical support, rewards for good behavior, economic and social expenditure targets designed to squeeze the security budget, and conditionality. It is the policy of both the World Bank and the IMF not to apply specific military-related conditions to their lending. There are, however, persistent rumors that they have in fact done so upon occasion, for example, in Pakistan in the early 1990s,[10] or that a commitment to reducing the size of the security sector has been a precondition for loans. There can be no doubt that adding the voice of the IFIs to policy dialogues with aid recipients increases the significance of suggestions that the size and cost of the security sector be reviewed.

Multilateral Development Agencies

Multilateral development agencies that either have already integrated security-sector reform into their policies and programs or could be expected to do so include the Commission of the European Communities and U.N. bodies such as the United Nations Development Programme (UNDP), the World Food Programme (WFP), the United Nations Children's Fund (UNICEF), the International Labor Organization (ILO), and the United Nations High Commissioner for Refugees (UNHCR). These institutions could employ policy dialogue, technical and financial support, rewards for good behavior, and conditionality to influence government policies in the security sector.

The projects supported by this group of institutions are likely to be oriented toward helping people, rather than governments, make the transition from conflict to peace. The WFP, for example, supplies food aid to support populations in need and to provide incentives to participate in development projects. UNICEF supports social-sector programs designed to benefit children, including child soldiers. The ILO has designed training and credit programs aimed at former soldiers, displaced persons, and returnees in countries emerging from prolonged periods of conflict. Assistance from these institutions could be instrumental in helping to settle refugees, displaced persons, or demobilized soldiers and their families following conflicts or in supporting postwar economic rehabilitation and reconstruction programs.

Multilateral Political Institutions

Multilateral institutions such as the Association of Southeast Asian Nations (ASEAN), the Conference on Security and Cooperation in Europe (CSCE), the Economic Community of West African States (ECOWAS), the Organization of African Unity (OAU), the Organization of American States (OAS), and the United Nations are playing an increasingly important role in activities central to managing and resolving conflict. For the most part, these activities are purely political in nature. In some cases, however, member states agree that economic pressure is necessary for progress to be recorded on the political level.

Chapter 7 of the U.N. Charter, which deals with "actions with respect to threats to the peace, breaches of the peace, and acts of aggression," empowers the Security Council to prescribe nonmilitary means of encouraging compliance with Security Council resolutions, including economic sanctions of varying degrees of severity. In 1985 the preamble of the Charter of the Organization of American States was amended to underscore the vital link between representative democracy and stability, peace, and development. On June 5, 1991, the OAS adopted Resolution 1080, on "Representative Democracy," which instructs the Secretary-General of the OAS to convene the Permanent Council immediately following the "sudden or irregular interruption of the democratic political institutional process or of the legitimate exercise of power by the democratically elected government" in any member state. Within ten days the council must call a meeting of either the OAS ministers of foreign affairs or the OAS General Assembly "to look into the events collectively and adopt any decisions deemed appropriate, in accordance with the Charter and international law."[11]

The adoption of sanctions by the international community can send a powerful message, particularly when they are well enforced. But as discussed above, the effectiveness of sanctions in forcing governments to change course is open to question. In October 1991, following the overthrow of Haiti's democratically elected president, Jean-Bertrand Aristide, by the armed forces, the OAS imposed an embargo on Haiti. Although European governments failed to participate, arguing that they had no legal basis to comply with an embargo imposed by an organization to which they did not belong, this action caused significant economic hardship for ordinary Haitian citizens. The elite were, however, able to remain fairly well insulated for nearly two years, and OAS and U.N. mediation efforts failed to return Aristide to power.

On June 16, 1993, the United Nations adopted a mandatory embargo on oil and arms and ordered a worldwide freeze on the overseas financial assets of Haitian government officials. On July 3 the military government and Aristide reached an agreement that, if implemented, would have returned the president to Haiti by October 30. Sanctions were lifted, but the military failed to comply with the agreement. Progressively stiffer sanctions were imposed, but ultimately it took the threat of military intervention to remove the Haitian armed forces from power in September 1994.

▲ Using Economic Tools to Press for Change in the Security Sector

In the past, the major powers frequently used economic tools, particularly economic and security assistance, to support the military sectors of client states in the developing world—to enable them to maintain large armed forces, to procure increasingly sophisticated weapons, or to intervene abroad in support of the objectives of their major-power patrons. The disappearance of the Soviet threat, the emergence of regional and local conflicts as a major source of insecurity in the post–Cold War era, and the growing recognition of the economic and political costs of failing to control the military sector have produced a change in the policies of most of the major industrial countries. They are increasingly tying economic rewards and punishments to containing conflicts, preventing proliferation, and reducing the size of the security sector.

This has been particularly true for the successor states to the Soviet Union that retain nuclear capabilities—Belarus, Kazakhstan, Russia, and Ukraine. Western governments have employed a combination of policy dialogue, conditionality, rewards for good behavior, and support for specific positive measures to encourage the governments of these states to adhere to international treaties (such as the Nuclear Non-Proliferation Treaty) and bilateral treaties (such as the Strategic Arms Reduction Talks [START] treaty), to withdraw troops from foreign countries, and to reduce the size of their defense-industrial sectors.

To some extent, these efforts have proceeded in isolation from the ongoing dialogue within the international lending community on using economic tools to promote change in the security sector of aid-recipient countries. That dialogue has focused on linking aid and other official financial flows to reductions in security spending in the developing countries in order to improve the opportunities for development. A number of governments and institutions have established and begun to implement policies in this area.

Among the major international lenders, consensus on the importance of integrating security spending and related factors in decisions about aid and official lending has grown with surprising rapidity. While it was still essentially a taboo subject in lending circles in 1990, by late 1993 the DAC had outlined the beginnings of a consensus on how to help aid recipients reduce the economic and political burden of the security sector.[12] This shift was due in no small measure to the decision in 1989 by the IMF managing director, Michel Camdessus, and the World Bank president, Barber Conable, to begin speaking out about the imbalances between security spending and resources available for economic and social development—well before the end of the Cold War, the disintegration of the Soviet Union, and the 1991 Gulf War induced the bilateral donors to confront the issue.

International Financial Institutions

At first glance, the World Bank and the IMF might seem unlikely leaders of an effort to introduce security-related considerations into the development dialogue. Their mandates are economic, prohibiting them from basing lending decisions on political criteria;[13] however, both have established convincing economic arguments for examining security spending. In his closing remarks to the two organizations' 1991 joint annual meeting, for example, Camdessus characterized the IMF's concern with identifying "unproductive or wasteful spending," including military spending, as "just an extension and intensification of our traditional work to help countries improve their macroeconomic policies." He further argued that because military budgets frequently absorb a large share of national resources, they are "a proper subject for our attention."[14]

In 1989 and 1990, World Bank and IMF activities were limited to in-house seminars and statements by senior management. In 1991 the issue gained new prominence. In April, security spending was one of the "cutting edge" issues addressed at the World Bank's annual Conference on Development Economics, when former Bank president Robert McNamara gave a major address calling for significant reductions in worldwide military spending. In September, the IMF board of directors instructed IMF staff to obtain information on aggregate security expenditures in member countries.

In October 1991, at the end of the joint annual meeting in Bangkok, Conable's successor, Lewis Preston, stated that while "it is the sovereign right of nations to decide" how much to spend on their military, "if we found a situation where defense expenditure was 35 percent to 40 percent of the [government] budget, we might wonder if it was an appropriate use for [World Bank] funds." While Camdessus was more circumspect in his comments in Bangkok, he too made clear that the IMF would be taking up its new mandate to put military spending on the table in lending discussions.[15]

In December 1991 the World Bank's senior management sent a memorandum to staff indicating that it was appropriate to raise the issue of resource allocation to the military with countries where development-related outlays were "seriously inadequate" and military budgets were high. The objective was "to raise issues of unproductive expenditures where they are significant, as part of [the Bank's] policy dialogue and public expenditure review, rather than to impose conditionality related to military expenditures."[16] Defense budgets have come under the World Bank's scrutiny in some twenty countries since about 1992.

Bank staff are also authorized to respond to specific assistance requests from member governments. Thus in mid-1991 the World Bank and Argentina began negotiating a loan to support the privatization of firms that historically had been under the jurisdiction of the Argentine military but have produced mainly civilian goods: shipyards, metallurgy facilities, and petrochemical plants. In 1992 the World Bank, in coordination with nine other donors, helped the government of Uganda devise and implement a program that may ultimately reintegrate fifty thousand demobilized troops and some one hundred thousand of their dependents into the civilian economy. It also established the Africa Region Working Group on the Demobilization and Reintegration of Military Personnel in response to member governments' requests for assistance in this area.[17] At the same time, World Bank management remains extremely reticent about adopting a proactive stance or assuming a leadership role in coordinating activities in this sphere.

Bilateral Donors

While the World Bank and the IMF initially took the lead in urging member governments to reduce the size and cost of their security sectors, several bilateral donors took note of the problem early on. In September 1990, following a meeting in Molde, Norway, the Nordic Ministers of Development Cooperation issued a communiqué stressing the importance of domestic resources for development and noting that reductions in military budgets could be an important source of additional domestic funding. Beginning in early 1991, the bilateral donors and other development agencies became increasingly active in this sphere, with Germany and Japan initially taking the lead in formulating policies linking economic assistance with behavior in the security sector.

Nonetheless, in 1991 few individuals within the development community anticipated that a common approach to the military sector would emerge in the near future. Yet, in spring 1992 the DAC held the first in a series of discussions that ultimately resulted in the December 1993 High-Level Meeting's endorsement of the *Orientations on Participatory Development and Good Governance (PDGG)*. This document describes, *inter alia*, an emerging DAC consensus on the linkage between military spending and aid policies. The key elements of that consensus are summarized below.

Policy dialogue and positive incentives are the preferred tools in linking development cooperation with military reform. There is widespread agreement that sanctions and conditions are to be imposed only when other, more collaborative efforts clearly fail. Lenders have expressed particular interest in positive measures that will assist recipient governments in reducing the size, cost, and political clout of their military sectors or support conflict resolution and postconflict reconstruction and reconciliation. Some of the most frequently mentioned programs include demobilization, veteran retraining schemes, defense-industry conversion, improved fiscal management of the security sector, enhanced civilian expertise in military affairs, and dialogues on the role of the military in democratic societies.

Donors increasingly recognize that military reform programs formulated in collaboration with recipients have a much greater chance for success than those imposed from outside. For their part, aid recipients are increasingly seeking lender assistance for these purposes. Countries such as Cambodia, El Salvador, Mozambique, Namibia, Nicaragua, Rwanda, and Uganda have sought donor assistance in developing and implementing programs to downsize the military sector, promote political reconciliation, and repair the ravages of protracted civil wars.

Improving transparency in the military budgeting process is vital. Transparency has two distinct elements: first, obtaining information on the level of security expenditure, and second, opening up the military budgeting and planning process. Fostering openness and accountability in the public sector is the best recipe for long-term control over security budgets. The development community has thus far focused its efforts primarily on collecting more accurate data with which to evaluate the economic costs associated with recipients' security sectors. Only a few projects have been undertaken to strengthen institutional capacity in the security sector.

Both strands are in evidence in the *PDGG*. DAC members pledge themselves to support efforts by organizations such as the IMF to develop "transparent, reliable, and comparable data on military expenditure patterns, uses, and trends." They also propose to identify the ways to strengthen civilian expertise in defense budgeting and appropriations.

Greater coordination among lenders and within individual bilateral donor governments will facilitate military reform. The *PDGG* places considerable emphasis on coordinating donor actions. Multilateral policy coordination is desirable because the members of the international development community have different strengths and mandates. By identifying what each member can do best, the development community can respond quickly and efficiently to recipients' needs in the area of security reform. The Uganda demobilization program, coordinated by the World Bank and supported by some ten bilateral and multilateral donors, offers a model for donor-donor and donor-government collaboration in this area.

Coordination has other benefits as well. It reduces the likelihood that the recipient governments will face conflicting demands from the international community. This in turn increases the likelihood that the desired reform will be undertaken or, in the case of conflict resolution, that the parties involved will take serious steps to resolve the conflict, although it in no way *guarantees* that the parties will in fact take such steps or that their efforts will result in a resolution of the conflict. Coordination also distributes the financial burdens among the donor countries. Given the current economic climate in many OECD countries, this is an important consideration. Additionally, collaboration among bilateral donors and the multilateral development agencies might make it easier for the international financial institutions to participate in reform efforts despite the reluctance of many IFI staff members to address this complex and politically sensitive issue.

In the United States, recognition of the value of coordinated action has led the United States Agency for International Development (USAID) to establish the Office of Transition Initiatives to, among other things, coordinate U.S. aid to countries undergoing the transition from war to peace. In the Netherlands, the ministers for development cooperation and defense jointly released a policy memorandum on humanitarian assistance in November 1993. Swedish aid officials meet on an ad hoc basis with their counterparts from the military to discuss issues of mutual concern, for example, Sweden's contribution to U.N. peacekeeping operations in the former Yugoslavia.[18] Efforts such as these should be continued and expanded.

In order to create the conditions under which military expenditures can safely decrease, it may be necessary to create or strengthen regional and global collective security arrangements and promote domestic political liberalization. While local, regional, and international political institutions must play the leading role in these areas, the international development community can also support peace-building efforts, such as civilianizing police forces and promoting regional security dialogues. The peace accords in Cambodia, El Salvador, and Mozambique were all negotiated on this premise. The international development community must now decide how commitments of this nature can be met in a period of widespread reluctance to expand aid budgets. DAC members began to explore how best to address these issues in November 1993 at an in-house seminar entitled "Peace Operations and Aid," organized by the Development Cooperation Directorate, and the *PDGG* notes the value of strengthening mutual security arrangements and regional defense agreements.

To build credibility and to avoid charges of discrimination and unwarranted interference in borrowers' affairs, lenders should be willing to accept the same norms for themselves that they apply to developing countries. The two points most frequently raised in this context in discussions among donors are, first, the need to restrain the conventional arms trade, and second, the bilateral donors' responsibility to control the proliferation of capabilities to produce weapons, particularly weapons of mass destruction.

The inconsistency in pressing aid recipients to reduce military spending while using exports to resolve the problem of excess capacity in donors' domestic defense industries was stressed in the *PDGG*. The United States, which emerged as the preeminent supplier of arms to developing countries in 1991, following the end of the Gulf War and the collapse of the Soviet Union, argues that its transfers, the vast bulk of which are now to oil-rich countries such as Saudi Arabia and East Asian Newly Industrializing Economies (NIEs) such as Taiwan and South Korea, are not economically destabilizing. Leaving aside Saudi Arabia's 1994 request to stretch out payments for the $30 billion in U.S. weapons and related services ordered since 1989 and the political and military implications of arms transfers to this wealthier group of countries, a significant volume of U.S. weapons continues to be provided to poorer countries through the Excess Defense Articles Program and traditional military assistance.[19] These transfers clearly run the risk of undermining the credibility of the United States as it moves into the mainstream of policymaking on aid and military reform.

It is not just the United States, however, that scores poorly on policy coherence. As more and more DAC members have begun to use their aid policies to promote change in the security sectors of aid recipients, it has become evident that within bilateral donor governments military reform continues to hold a rather low priority compared with traditional political and economic objectives. (One exception is the handful of cases where there are strong proliferation concerns.) As a result, aid ministries are increasingly seeking to engage in interagency dialogues in an effort to avoid having their development-oriented efforts in the security sector undermined by foreign, defense, and trade policies.

Multilateral Development Agencies

The Commission of the European Communities, the UNDP, UNICEF, the ILO, and the WFP are among the multilateral development organizations that are becoming involved in efforts to reduce military spending in the developing world. The UNDP was one of the first institutions with a membership that included developing countries to support linking economic assistance to security-sector reform. In the *Human Development Report 1991*, the UNDP proposed a three-pronged attack on the imbalances between security budgets and allocations aimed at supporting human development. First, military transfers from industrial countries need to be reduced by phasing out military bases, transforming security assistance into economic assistance, and restraining the transfer of sophisticated conventional weapons. Second, new methods of conflict resolution need to be adopted. Third, aid should be linked to efforts to reduce security expenditure.[20]

The UNDP has also become involved on an operational level. In 1992, for example, it agreed to help strengthen the administrative capacity of the Uganda Veterans' Assistance Board, which will ultimately oversee the demobilization and reintegration of perhaps fifty thousand former soldiers. Also in 1992, it coordinated technical and financial support to some eighty-six hundred encamped Frente Farabundo Marti para la Liberación Nacional (FMLN) soldiers who were awaiting demobilization in El Salvador, and in 1993 it began providing training, technical assistance, housing, and credits to ex-combatants from both the FMLN and the government forces.

UNICEF and the WFP have provided support to demobilization and postwar rehabilitation and reconstruction programs. In 1991, for example, the WFP approved a five-year, $10 million project to help resettle Nicaraguans who had fled their homes during the civil war. Food aid is being used as an incentive to reestablish agricultural production and construct social and productive infrastructure on a self-help basis. For its part, UNICEF participated in phase one of the Uganda demobilization program by helping to strengthen existing community-level social services so that they will be able to meet the increased demand imposed by the demobilized soldiers and their dependents. The ILO has contributed to the reintegration program in Mozambique by designing vocational training and small enterprise credit programs.

In November 1991 the European Community (now known as the European Union, EU) Council of Ministers approved the Resolution on Human Rights, Democracy, and Development, which stresses the importance of controlling excessive military expenditure, which, it was argued, competes with development for funding, contributes to regional tensions, and often results in the suppression of human rights. The council also observed that as donors downsize their own militaries, aid to governments whose armed forces exceed needs "will become difficult to justify."[21]

In this resolution, the EU and its members agreed to stress the negative effects of excessive military spending during policy dialogues with aid recipients, to request compliance with the U.N. arms transfer register, and to consider implementing specific programs designed to reduce military spending and expand outlays on health and education. The EU Commission has accordingly begun to support demilitarization efforts in Uganda, El Salvador, and elsewhere. In mid-1992, for example, the EU established a two-year, $18 million project designed to reintegrate some three thousand ex-combatants from both sides of the Salvadoran conflict into the civilian economy. This project includes financial and legal assistance for land purchases, agricultural and housing credits, and various kinds of training and technical assistance.

▲ Supporting Conflict Resolution

The new willingness within the international lending community to encourage aid recipients to reduce military budgets so that additional resources can be allocated to social and economic development has led some policymakers and analysts to examine the opportunities for using external financing to promote a broad range of security objectives. They have been particularly interested in identifying ways to incorporate the financial weight of the World Bank and the IMF into these efforts.

National, regional, and international political institutions will of necessity take the lead in the search for solutions to the political issues that divide societies and countries and lie at the root of enduring conflicts. Nonetheless, the international lending community can use its financial and technical resources to encourage the changes in policies and patterns of behavior that are a prerequisite for conflict management, resolution, and prevention. These would include:

- creating crisis management techniques such as hot lines, crisis centers, or rapid consultation mechanisms;
- negotiating with domestic and regional opponents to resolve outstanding disagreements and disputes;
- embarking on a process of confidence building with domestic and regional opponents in order to raise mutual levels of trust;
- engaging in regional negotiations, ultimately with the participation of arms suppliers, to reach agreement on regional levels of armament and reduce supplier pressure to procure excessive weaponry;
- implementing peace agreements and supporting war-to-peace transitions;
- evaluating postconflict security needs and restructuring security forces to match these;
- strengthening or creating domestic political structures and regional security mechanisms that will prevent future disputes from threatening internal and interstate security;

- strengthening or creating regional political and economic institutions to enhance cooperation and minimize disputes; and
- identifying and implementing conflict-reducing development policies and strategies.

Many of the activities currently undertaken by the World Bank and the IMF to reduce the negative economic impact of the security sector could contribute to conflict management, reduction, and prevention efforts even if they were undertaken in order to strengthen member governments' economies and their capacity for development. First, they and the regional development banks could engage recipient governments in dialogue about the costs of continued conflict and the benefits that could accrue from lower security budgets and fewer arms imports. These institutions could also discuss the kinds of programs they would be willing to fund once peace accords or other relevant agreements were signed. These could include demobilization, refugee resettlement, reintegration, rehabilitation and reconstruction, and defense-industry conversion, as well as standard development programs. The IFIs could also engage in dialogue with the industrial countries to encourage them to adopt policies that would help reduce the political power and economic burden of the security sector and strengthen the peace-building process. The IMF, for example, could continue to discuss the opportunities the post–Cold War era holds for reducing arms transfers, particularly subsidized sales.

Second, by insisting on greater transparency in the military budgeting process, these institutions are helping to lay the basis for successful confidence-building efforts. Secrecy not only frequently leads to the misallocation of domestic resources, thereby undermining a country's economic stability, but also hinders the development of increased trust, which is a prerequisite for the resolution of both internal and regional conflicts. Third, as part of their efforts to increase the efficient use of resources, the IFIs could go beyond dialogue to assist member governments engaged in enduring conflicts in evaluating the true economic costs of continued conflict and in incorporating these into medium- and long-term economic plans.

Lastly, it may be worth exploring whether the IFIs could, under certain circumstances, make their lending contingent on the pursuit of serious negotiations between disputing parties. If the bilateral donors agreed that a high level of military spending engendered by an ongoing conflict or the conflict itself constituted a serious obstacle to development and that only negotiations to resolve the underlying security imbalances could free up resources urgently needed by economic and social sectors, IFI action might be justifiable on economic grounds.

The bilateral donors can employ all of these strategies and more to put in place a variety of mechanisms that will help control and resolve conflicts and make their recurrence less likely. For instance, to help *manage regional conflicts,* they can facilitate the establishment and operation of confidence-building measures, such as hot lines and crisis centers, on-site inspections of force limitations, and the notification and observation of military exercises. To give just one example, funding could be made available to enable staff members of the CSCE's Conflict Prevention Center, which provides a forum for discussing "unusual and unscheduled military activities," to advise interested governments in other regions.

To help *resolve conflicts,* the bilateral donors can finance local mediation and peacemaking efforts. The U.S. Department of State has provided funds for the West African Military Observer Group (ECOMOG) in Liberia, which was involved in what may yet prove to have been a successful effort to halt that country's bloody civil war. It has also provided $1 million to support OAU mediation that attempted unsuccessfully to end Rwanda's civil war in August 1993 and contributed financially to the Neutral Military Observer Group (NMOG) force in that country. At various times U.S. officials have also acted as "honest brokers" in an attempt to facilitate dialogue among the parties to the Rwandan conflict.[22]

Bilateral donors, such as the United States and Sweden, and nongovernmental organizations, such as the Global Coalition for Africa, are seeking to strengthen the OAU's conflict resolution capacity. For example, the United States allocated $1.5 million in fiscal year 1994 to assist the OAU in developing conflict prevention and mediation measures, and the UNDP has provided $3 million in support to conflict resolution programs. The United States is also committed to developing the conflict resolution capacity of multilateral subregional bodies, such as the Southern Africa Development Community or ECOWAS, which sent the ECOMOG force to Liberia.[23]

In addition to making development assistance contingent on serious negotiations to end ongoing conflicts, the bilateral donors could make their assistance conditional on *conforming to certain internationally agreed standards.* These might include adherence to international arms control treaties and regimes or internationally recognized alternatives, support for the principles of nonaggression and nonintervention, participation in dialogues designed to increase regional security and stability, and participation in the U.N. standardized military expenditure reporting exercise and the U.N. arms transfer register. Informal discussions with representatives of aid ministries indicate, however, that their governments are currently unwilling to go beyond *urging* aid recipients to conform to such standards.[24]

There are a range of activities that must be carried out in order to *consolidate the peace* once agreements are reached. First, there is a need for peacekeeping, ceasefire monitoring, demobilization, reintegration and refugee resettlement assistance, and, following civil wars, civil rights protection. While the international community increasingly provides peacekeeping and ceasefire monitoring assistance, in some cases it may be more desirable or appropriate for these functions to be assumed by regional organizations. Not all regional organizations have the requisite financial capacity, however. Nor do they have the requisite technical capability, and much remains to be done to strengthen these institutions so that they can play this role. Bilateral donors could therefore fund regional peacekeeping efforts, much as the Japanese and German governments made financial contributions to the U.N. effort during the Gulf War and the United States did with the ECOMOG peacekeeping force. In fiscal year 1994 the United States allocated $2 million in nonassessed peacekeeping funding to strengthen the OAU's peacekeeping capacity.

Similarly, the donors could support programs that protect the civil rights of former combatants following protracted civil wars. It is clearly unrealistic to assume that civil rights abuses will cease as soon as peace agreements are signed. Rather, the parties will require a period of some years to learn the art of compromise, and they are likely to need assistance in resolving disputes in the interim. Following the end of the Nicaraguan civil war, the OAS International Commission for Support and Verification (CIAV-OAS) received some $67 million from the United States, channeled through USAID, to help resettle former Nicaraguan Resistance troops. As part of this process, CIAV-OAS created the Human Rights Monitoring and Mediation Efforts program, which investigated alleged human rights violations and brought cases to the attention of the Nicaraguan government as warranted. When political violence began to increase during 1991, the government requested that CIAV-OAS mediate between rebel groups and government officials. In El Salvador the United Nations was given the responsibility for monitoring the observance of human rights early on in the peace process. Such programs cannot, however, take the place of genuine efforts at national reconciliation among the parties to the conflict, and there is concern that this has been the outcome in Nicaragua.

The international lending community as a whole has a growing body of experience in supporting demobilization, reintegration, and refugee resettlement programs. It is important that these efforts be reviewed so that their lessons can be incorporated into future programs. The United States, for example, has recognized that providing demobilization assistance for only one party to the conflict, as it did in Nicaragua, can deepen cleavages between former antagonists. The United States has applied this lesson to its postconflict assistance to El Salvador, which is available to both former FMLN guerrillas and El Salvador Armed Forces soldiers. The Uganda demobilization and reintegration program, which received support from ten aid agencies in the first stage, underscores the importance of advance planning and donor coordination.

It is also important that the international development community commit itself to serious preplanning and create quick-disbursing funds to support demobilization and reintegration programs. Peace negotiations frequently continue for many years, but funds and technical assistance need to be in place quite soon after agreements are reached and ceasefires are put in place so that encampment and resettlement can begin. Indeed, planning for demobilization ideally would begin before peace agreements were concluded. Even peacetime demobilizations can place sudden, unanticipated demands on funders.

The international donor community has recognized the importance of tackling demobilization and reintegration as early in the peace process as possible. By mid-1994, discussions on the role of external donors had been held or were planned by organizations such as the United Nations Department of Humanitarian Affairs (DHA), the World Bank, the ILO, and the OAU. While these discussions may ultimately result in a donor consensus on how to approach the issue, at the time of this writing a considerable gap continued to exist between theory and practice. In 1994, USAID launched the first effort to plan demobilization and reintegration projects prior to the conclusion of a peace agreement in collaboration with DHA officials in Angola.

To ensure that demobilization and reintegration financing is used effectively and efficiently, a central repository for information on what has and has not worked in previous programs needs to be established by the international lending community. In view of the growing demand for demobilization assistance, the creation of such a facility should be given high priority. The World Bank's increased involvement in demobilization and reintegration programs and its coordinating role in consultative groups make it an obvious candidate to house such an information office. The Bank has taken an important first step in this direction by developing a roster of individuals and organizations active in this area.

Once conflicts are resolved, governments need to *reevaluate their security needs and restructure their security forces* accordingly. Very few governments in the developing world carry out detailed security assessments and integrate these into their force planning and military budgeting processes. In many developing countries, the planning that does occur in the security sector is controlled or dominated by the military. This situation grows out of the security forces' central role in the political process as well as the civilians' lack of expertise in evaluating security issues.

The international development community can assist civilian government officials in acquiring the technical expertise needed to assess their country's real security needs and create smaller, better-trained, and more effective armed forces. Under the Expanded International Military Education and Training Program, inaugurated in the fall of 1990, the U.S. Department of Defense provides military officers and civilian officials with training in civilian control of the military, improved military justice systems and procedures, adherence to internationally recognized human rights, and responsible defense resource management practices. It is important that the development agencies supplement these efforts in order to reinforce the message that civilians can and *must* develop the skills necessary to evaluate military programs and that the elected civilian government bears the ultimate responsibility for determining a country's security posture and force structure.

The international development community can also support programs that will *shift the balance of power between the military and civilian sectors of government*. To begin this process, communication between the military and civilian officials must be increased. The international development community can facilitate this process by sponsoring meetings and workshops at which the role of the military in democratic societies and the implications of a transition to civilian control can be examined. The United States provided financial assistance for a regional meeting in Burundi in early February 1993 that was attended by civilian and military representatives from nine countries in East and Central Africa. It was the first opportunity for many of them to discuss in a noncontroversial manner the implications of democratic transition for the military establishment.[25]

The international development community can also provide a range of opportunities for developing-country military officers to interact with their counterparts in democratic societies. Although it is important for developing-country military personnel to have contact with knowledgeable civilians from democratic societies, there may be lessons to be learned about subservience to civilian authority from interacting with appropriately trained military officers from democratic societies.[26]

In order to prevent future disputes' threatening internal or interstate peace and security, *alternatives to building up domestic security forces* must be considered. These include political liberalization, diplomacy, and collective security. Wherever possible, regional political and economic institutions need to be strengthened, or even created, so that cooperative behavior can be enhanced and confrontational behavior can be minimized. External economic actors can support all of these activities. For example, German development assistance enabled African leaders to travel to Germany to meet with Europeans who had been involved in the CSCE process. The proposal that the Africa Leadership Forum subsequently put forward for a conference on security, stability, development, and cooperation in Africa is currently under consideration within the OAU.[27] Political liberalization involving the transition to transparent and accountable democratic government, the respect for human rights, and the promotion of participatory development is strongly supported by more and more members of the international development community. The DAC's *PDGG* provides a general frame of reference for policy dialogues conducted by member governments on many of these issues.

Finally, the international lending community needs to *identify and implement development strategies and policies that reduce the likelihood of conflicts and avoid those that may promote conflicts.* Since many of the conflicts in the developing world stem from unequal access to both political and economic resources, it is important that development programs seek to redress this fundamental imbalance and take care not to exacerbate it. In the same vein, it is important to vet development projects for their potential to cause or exacerbate interstate disputes.

The attention that has increasingly been directed in recent years at focusing development efforts on the poorest members of society is clearly important, but much remains to be done. Development benefiting only a small portion of a country's population has been an important contributing factor to many of the conflicts in the developing world today. It is therefore important not only that programs be targeted at the poor but that these programs be carefully monitored to ensure that they reach their intended beneficiaries and do not merely end up by further enriching the wealthy, as has frequently happened in the past. Similarly, donors should ensure that development programs are not routinely biased in favor of particular ethnic, racial, or religious groups.

Concerns have been rising in recent years about the potential that competition for natural resources has to create conflict within or among states. This problem is not, of course, a new one. The Middle East, for example, has witnessed numerous disputes of varying severity over access to scarce water resources. Armed conflict erupted between Syria and Israel in the early 1950s over the construction of the Israeli National Water Carrier system and in the mid-1960s when Syria attempted to divert the Jordan River headwaters.

Nonetheless, in the closing years of the twentieth century, rapidly growing human populations are placing increasing pressure on agricultural land, forests, underground and surface waters, and the atmosphere. This pressure is exacerbated by the unequal distribution of resources, which forces the poorest members of society to exploit ecologically marginal lands or engage in ecologically unsound agricultural practices. Many analysts fear that the result will be more frequent conflicts over natural resources.[28] Under these conditions, it is vital that conscious efforts be made to design and implement development programs in ways that minimize conflicts over resources. It may also be the case that the development institutions can play a role in encouraging countries to reach equitable and enduring agreement on resource sharing. Syria and Turkey have had a longstanding disagreement over sharing the waters of the Euphrates River. Turkey's plans to develop one of its poorest regions, southern Anatolia, involve the construction of an irrigation system that will divert water from both Syria and Iraq. Some donors, such as the World Bank, have withheld direct funding from the project, while the Japanese reportedly withdrew their support in 1991 because of Syrian pressure. Estimates of the final cost of the project range from $23 billion to $32 billion. The Turkish government, increasingly conscious of the need to obtain external support, at the end of 1992 agreed to begin serious negotiations with Syria on sharing the Euphrates waters.

An interesting question is whether an institution such as the World Bank could assist these countries in reaching an agreement. There is a precedent for World Bank mediation over the division of water resources. During the 1950s the Bank played a central role in negotiating the Indus Waters Treaty, signed in 1960 by India and Pakistan. Not only did this agreement result in an equitable division of water resources, upon which some 50 million people depended in the 1950s, but it prevented Delhi and Islamabad from going to war over the issue. In addition to taking the lead in negotiating the Indus Waters Treaty, the Bank organized multilateral donor financing for the Indus Development Fund and undertook a long-range study for the development of the Indus waters.[29]

▲ Conclusion

The end of the Cold War has produced a significant opportunity to change relations among and within states. Democratization, conflict resolution, nonaggression, collective security, multilateralism, and compromise are becoming internationally encouraged modes of behavior. Yet many of the problems of the Cold War era are still very much with us. Not the least of these are numerous unresolved conflicts, including serious ethnic, religious, and national disputes that threaten long-term stability in many parts of the developing world, Eastern Europe, and the former Soviet Union.

From the perspective of the industrial world, the defining relationship of the 1945–90 period was the hostility between the United States and the Soviet Union. The Cold War undeniably also left its mark on many inter- and intra-state conflicts in Africa, Asia, Latin America, and the Middle East, but its influence in these parts of the world was often exaggerated. Local and regional conflicts derived from local and regional disagreements, many of which predated the Cold War and many of which have survived it.

It would be unrealistic to assume that conflict can be eradicated. It can, however, be channeled into nonmilitary avenues, and the norms defining acceptable behavior on the part of governments, both toward their neighbors and toward their own citizens, can be changed. The challenge of the 1990s and succeeding decades is to ensure that the emergent trend toward international cooperation and domestic participation is maintained and strengthened so that conflicts can be resolved and their recurrence prevented. International economic actors have a role to play in collaboration with national, regional, and international political institutions.

The costs to the major Western countries of attempting to resolve local and regional conflicts may seem high, but failure to control these conflicts now is likely to incur even greater costs in the future. These include the need to finance an ever-expanding number of humanitarian programs and peacekeeping missions, renewed threat of proliferation, lost markets in conflict areas, and, in some cases, regional instability sufficiently severe to potentially affect the stability of portions of the industrial world. The costs to the countries directly involved in these conflicts in terms of human and financial resources lost and development forgone are, of course, enormous and grow with every day that passes without a resolution to the conflict.

Resources applied to conflict resolution will be well spent if conflicts can be contained and prevented. In the absence of stability, efforts to promote sustainable economic and political development will falter. In the absence of sustainable development, efforts to establish peace and stability will become all the more difficult.

There is, however, only so much that the international community can do. In the end, conflict resolution and prevention will occur only if governments and citizens in countries involved in conflict accept the need for change. They must take a hard look at their priorities and devise policies that will promote reduced tension. This will require compromises, both domestic and among states. The international development community can provide a wide range of economic, technical, and diplomatic assistance. But it is ultimately the people and the governments of countries in conflict who must seize the opportunities presented by recent changes in the international system to create a more equitable, peaceful, and prosperous future for themselves.

NOTES

I would like to thank Milton Leitenberg of the University of Maryland for his valuable comments on an earlier version of this chapter and the Ploughshares Fund of San Francisco and the Charles Steward Mott Foundation of Flint, Michigan, for their support.

1. On conflict-related deaths and comparisons of military and social spending through 1990, see Robert S. McNamara, "The Post–Cold War World: Implications for Military Expenditures in the Developing Countries," in *Proceedings of the World Bank Annual Conference on Development Economics, 1991*, ed. Lawrence H. Summers and Shekhar Shah (Washington, D.C.: World Bank, Mar. 1992), 95–125.

2. Throughout this chapter, the terms *international lending community, official lenders*, and *lenders* are used interchangeably for both multilateral lending institutions such as the World Bank and the United Nations Development Programme (UNDP) and bilateral aid agencies such as the U.S. Agency for International Development. The terms *bilateral donors, aid ministries, aid agencies*, or simply *donors* denote either the governments that extend aid or their bilateral aid agencies. These terms do not cover private sources of external financing such as the international banking system or nongovernmental organizations.

3. Organization for Economic Cooperation and Development, Development Assistance Committee, *Development Co-operation. 1994 Report* (Paris, Feb. 1995), C5–C19.

4. Joan M. Nelson and Stephanie J. Eglinton, *Global Goals, Contentious Means: Issues of Multiple Aid Conditionality*, Policy Essay No. 10 (Washington, D.C.: Overseas Development Council, 1993).

5. U.S. General Accounting Office, *Security Assistance: Observations on Post–Cold War Program Changes*, NSIAD-92-248 (Washington, D.C., Sept. 1992).

6. For a description of these supplier groups, see Zachary S. Davis, *Non-Proliferation Regimes: Policies to Control the Spread of Nuclear, Chemical, and Biological Weapons and Missiles*, 93-237 ENR (Washington, D.C.: Congressional Research Service, Feb. 18, 1993); and Theodor W. Galdi, *Advanced Weapons Technology: Export Controls Before and After the Gulf War*, 93-22F (Washington, D.C.: Congressional Research Service, Jan. 6, 1993).

7. Gary C. Hufbauer and Jeffrey J. Schott, *Economic Sanctions Reconsidered: History and Current Policy* (Washington, D.C.: Institute for International Economics, 1985), provides a useful survey of the success and failure of efforts to impose sanctions since World War I. See also Margaret Doxey, *International Sanctions in Contemporary Perspective* (New York: St. Martin's Press, 1987).

8. U.S. General Accounting Office, *Economic Sanctions: Effectiveness as Tools of Foreign Policy*, NSIAD-92-106 (Washington, D.C., Feb. 1992), 8–9. See also Douglas McDaniel, *Economic Sanctions: Issues Raised by the Sanctions against Iraq*, 92-370F (Washington, D.C.: Congressional Research Service, Apr. 17, 1992).

9. The World Bank Group comprises the International Bank for Reconstruction

and Development (IBRD) and its three affiliates, the International Development Association (IDA), the International Finance Corporation (IFC), and the Multilateral Investment Guarantee Agency (MIGA). For a description of the functions of these institutions, see World Bank, *Annual Report, 1992* (Washington, D.C., 1992), 4–5.

10. "IMF-IBRD Assistance Conditional on 9 p.c. Defense Cut," *Dawn* (Karachi), Sept. 14, 1991.

11. Organization of American States, *Representative Democracy,* AG/RES. 1080 (XXI-0/91), June 5, 1991.

12. This process is described in Nicole Ball, *Pressing for Peace: Can Aid Induce Reform?* Policy Essay No. 6 (Washington, D.C.: Overseas Development Council, 1992); and idem, *Development Assistance and Military Reform,* Policy Focus No. 3 (Washington, D.C.: Overseas Development Council, 1993). On the DAC consensus, see Organization for Economic Cooperation and Development, "Reducing Excessive Military Expenditures," *DAC Orientations on Participatory Development and Good Governance,* OCDE/GD (93) 191 (Paris, 1993): 19–21.

13. Section 10 ("Political Activity Prohibited") of Article IV of the World Bank's Articles of Agreement states, "The Bank and its officers shall not interfere in the political affairs of any member; nor shall they be influenced in their decisions by the political character of the member or the members concerned. Only economic considerations shall be relevant to their decisions, and these considerations shall be weighed impartially in order to achieve the purposes stated in Article 1" (IBRD, *Articles of Agreement* [as amended effective Feb. 16, 1989], Washington, D.C., 13).

14. Board of governors, 1991 annual meeting, Bangkok, press release no. 64, Oct. 17, 1991, 2.

15. Paul Blustein, "World Bank, IMF to Press Defense Cuts: Institutions Hint at Withholding Loans," *Washington Post,* Oct. 18, 1991.

16. World Bank senior management, memo, cited in Jonathan E. Sanford, *Multilateral Development Banks: Issues for Congress,* IB87218 (Washington, D.C.: Congressional Research Service, Mar. 13, 1992), 13.

17. For a description of the Uganda program, see Nat Colletta and Nicole Ball, "War to Peace Transition in Uganda," *Finance and Development* 30 (June 1993): 36–39. The Working Group has produced the most comprehensive review of demobilization and reintegration efforts to date (see World Bank, *Demobilization and Reintegration of Military Personnel in Africa: The Evidence from Seven Country Case Studies,* Africa Regional Series, Report No. IDP-130 [Washington, D.C.: Oct. 1993]).

18. The Dutch policy memorandum is *Humanitarian Aid between Conflict and Development* (The Hague: Ministry of Foreign Affairs, Nov. 1993). Information on Sweden is from a private communication with Carin Norberg, Assistant Director-General, Swedish International Development Authority, Mar. 17, 1994.

19. J. Lancaster and J. Mintz, "Strapped Saudis Seek to Stretch Out Payments for U.S. Arms," *Washington Post,* Jan. 7, 1994, A1, A15.

20. UNDP, *Human Development Report 1991* (New York: Oxford University Press, 1991), 82–83. See also idem, *Human Development Report 1992* (New York: Oxford University Press, 1992), 84–86, and *1994* (1994), 47–60.

21. General Secretariat, Council of the European Communities, *Cooperation for Development,* Brussels, press release 9555/91 (Presse 217), Nov. 28, 1991, 15.

22. See "Testimony of the Assistant Secretary of State for African Affairs Herman J. Cohen on Peacekeeping and Conflict Resolution in Africa before the House Foreign Affairs Africa Subcommittee" (Washington, D.C.,Mar. 31, 1993, mimeographed); and "Statement by James L. Woods, Deputy Assistant Secretary of Defense (African Affairs) to the United States House of Representatives, Committee on Foreign Affairs, Subcommittee on Africa — Peacekeeping and Conflict Resolution in Africa" (Washington, D.C., Mar. 31, 1993, mimeographed).

23. George E. Moose, "U.S. Commitment to Conflict Resolution in Africa," *U.S. Department of State Dispatch,* June 20, 1994, 412–13.

24. As noted earlier, the one exception involves some of the nuclear proliferators, such as Ukraine and North Korea.

25. African-American Institute, *The Bujumbura Conference. Democratization in Africa: The Role of the Military* (New York, 1993).

26. It is of course crucial to recall that military officers who participated in U.S. training programs in the past have been responsible for serious human rights abuses, for example, forty-five Salvadoran officers implicated by the United Nations in massacres of unarmed civilians during the 1980s. It is therefore imperative to proceed with caution when proposing the use of U.S. military forces in these roles (see R. Jeffrey Smith, "Pentagon Reviews Foreign Military Aid to Address Human Rights Concerns," *Washington Post,* June 9, 1993).

27. Africa Leadership Forum, Secretariat of the Organization of African Unity, and Secretariat of the United Nations Economic Commission for Africa, "The Kampala Document: Towards a Conference on Security, Stability, Development, and Cooperation in Africa" (n.p., May 19–21, 1991, mimeographed).

28. See Thomas F. Homer-Dixon, Jeffrey H. Boutwell, and George W. Rathjens, "Environmental Change and Violent Conflict," *Scientific American,* Feb. 1993, 38–45; and Astri Suhrke, *Pressure Points: Environmental Degradation, Migration, and Conflict,* and Sanjay Hazarika, *Bangladesh and Assam: Land Pressures, Migration, and Ethnic Conflict,* both in Occasional Paper No. 3 (Boston and Toronto: Project on Environmental Change and Acute Conflict/University of Toronto and American Academy of Arts and Sciences, Mar. 1993).

29. Edward S. Mason and Robert E. Asher, *The World Bank since Bretton Woods* (Washington, D.C.: Brookings Institution, 1973), 610–27.

EDWARD A. KOLODZIEJ

8 | The European Community

What are the limits and potential scope for expansion of the European Community's (EC) role in coping with conflict? This is a daunting question. So many dynamic factors, exterior and interior to the EC, shape its behavior that predictions about its future as an agent for peace must be problematic. Past attempts have been confounded by its evolution.[1] The EC has become neither a supranational body, capable of exercising unfettered authority over the states and peoples comprising its membership, nor simply an intergovernmental agency subject to the dictates and restraints of its member states.

These cautionary observations warrant a few words to clarify this chapter's aims and assumptions. First, it focuses on the competence and actual behavior of the EC as an international actor, charged with developing and executing the policies of its treaty signatories. Distinguishing between the EC and the environment with which it interacts, especially its member states, is critical in attempting to project the possible expansion of the EC's role in managing and resolving conflict.

The restraints on EC development are often slighted. These include the limits posed by other states, principally the United States, and international organizations. Their intervention in EC affairs directly or through their access to member governments may limit the ability of the member states to reach common policies. On security problems, the Atlantic Alliance and NATO, the Western European Union (WEU), the Conference on Security and Cooperation in Europe (CSCE), and the United Nations will have an important, if differential, say in defining Europe's future security roles. On economic matters, impersonal market forces, expressed in the globalization of trade and of monetary and financial markets, also constrain the EC's autonomy and integrity in pursuing shared aims such as monetary union. The global stock market crash of fall 1987 and the monetary crisis five years later, in September 1992, illustrate the EC's sensitivity to market forces. Additional constraints are posed by international organizations, such as the World Trade Organization (WTO) [formerly GATT] and the International Monetary Fund (IMF).

Internal constraints also limit or slow the evolution toward European economic and political union. Public opinion is still anchored by habit, culture, and political loyalties to national electorates. The failed Danish referendum on the Maastricht Treaty, France's near rejection, and party splits in the United Kingdom over European union reflect public and elite resistance to further EC development. Member states bring the baggage of their histories to the bargaining table. These differences in perspective reinforce real and perceived conflicts of interest and ideology over how the EC's powers might evolve and over the scope of its policy concerns. Even under the best of circumstances, when European governments may agree on goals, national governmental bureaucracies and Eurocrats in Brussels can be expected to compete over power sharing in the pursuit of European objectives.

Finally, while this analysis necessarily emphasizes the development of the EC's competence to cope with conflict, it is important to recognize that an assessment of the EC's global contribution to international security can be restricted neither to Europe nor to a narrow definition of security associated with traditional, nation-state geopolitical concerns and military power. With the end of the Cold War and the collapse of the Soviet state and empire, there is widened recognition among analysts and governmental policymakers of the crucial importance of the economic and political determinants of national and international security.[2] As one noted defense analyst observed at a transatlantic seminar devoted to defining Europe's post–Cold War role: "Threats to a future security system can be defined not only just in military terms — or the need to be able to discipline a rogue state — but also in political, economic and social terms. One need only look back to the 1930s to see the parallel: the Great Depression did more than anything else to produce the disaster of World War II."[3]

From this broad security perspective, and mindful of the assumptions and caveats above, this chapter is divided into two parts. The first evaluates the EC's contribution to the management or resolution of the security, welfare, and legitimacy problems confronting its members in their relations with each other. At the end of World War II, these states confronted five systemic challenges: (1) the construction of a viable balance of power in Europe; (2) the reintegration of Germany into the European political system; (3) the transformation of nationalism from a source of conflict to a force for cooperation; (4) the advancement of the material welfare of the EC's populations; and (5) the promotion and extension of open, free, and democratic institutions and human rights.

This chapter argues that the EC's institutional development has contributed decisively to the creation of a security community in Western Europe that has not only overcome the hostility of some of the globe's bitterest and bloodiest rivalries, principally between the French and German peoples, but also created a structure of incentives that urge the EC's peoples and states to cooperate in pursuing their shared interest in economic growth, in the enhancement of their national and collective welfare and security, and in the maintenance of democratic government.

The achievements of the EC constitute a historic transformation of the security regime in Europe from one of real and chronically incipient armed conflict — a primitive anarchy — to a regime based on mutual confidence and consensual cooperation, replacing a regime of threats and military force in governing Europe. The gradual development of European economic and political union within the EC thus approaches the final rung of the conflict resolution ladder sketched in chapter 1. It also approximates what Karl Deutsch characterized as a "security-community . . . in which there is real assurance that the members of that community will not fight each other physically, but will settle their disputes in some other way."[4]

The evolution of Europe toward a Deutschian security community, in which former adversaries are able to resolve difference and pursue common aims, contrasts with other regions, such as the Middle East or South Asia; the latter are still at the bottom or middle rungs on the conflict-cooperation ladder.[5] The central point to be made is that the strengthening and expansion of the EC's competence and authority over the principal welfare and security concerns of its members is tantamount to a significant contribution to the amelioration, improved management, and eventual resolution of global conflict. The participation of the EC or its member states in out-of-region peacekeeping and peacemaking should thus be viewed as a bonus. Certainly such efforts as the dispatch of French and British troops to Yugoslavia or of French forces to Rwanda should be undertaken only if they are consistent with the imperatives of EC cohesion.

Of course the EC was not alone in contributing to this transformation process; nor can it be argued that its current levels of institutional development and policy coordination, either in economic or foreign policy, represent unconditional successes. There is no assurance that the EC will not erode or backslide in the future. In some sense, it is enough that the EC copes with its own problems and inner conflicts; by overcoming its own divisive and destructive past, it contributes to the resolution of international conflicts.

The second part of this chapter assesses how well the EC is coping with its current internal differences, especially in progressing toward economic and political union and a common defense and foreign policy, and contributing to coping with conflicts outside its borders.

▲ The European Community's Role in European Conflict Management and Resolution

Economic Welfare and Democratization

The EC's most notable contribution to European peace and prosperity stems from the creation of an integrated market, disciplined by common rules and regulations, to promote the free circulation of goods and services as well as the factors of production among the member states. This is no small achievement. The impetus, if not inspiration, for the creation of a single European market of 340 million people in the postwar period can be traced to the Marshall Plan. U.S. economic assistance was contingent on the development of a plan for investment that viewed Europe, or at least Western Europe, as a single economic unit.

The rationale for the Marshall Plan was as much political and strategic as economic. It identified chronic economic deprivation as a primary cause of armed conflict between states and of civil strife, detrimental to the maintenance of democratic regimes.[6] The Nazi, fascist, and communist movements were viewed as different species of the same genus of threats to peace. They were seen to have taken root in the failure of world capitalism and democratic regimes to meet the welfare demands of their populations. World markets and a liberal trading system—the open door—were advanced as an antidote to such radical political solutions to welfare imperatives. The EC's development and its openness to global markets was then conceived as a critical support for a liberal economic order on which the peace of the member states, their prosperity, and their enjoyment of democratic institutions would depend.

If the impetus to economic and political union may initially have come from Washington, the will and resources to create a European community necessarily had to come from the Europeans themselves. The slow, often crisis-marked road to a common market and to the growing possibility of political union can be sketched as the product of five stages of growth: the creation of the European Coal and Steel Community (ECSC) in the early 1950s; the signature of the Rome Treaty, creating the Common Market and Euratom, and the eventual merging of these authorities with the ECSC to form the EC; the enlargement of the EC to include Britain, Ireland, and Denmark in the 1970s and its later inclusion of Greece, Portugal, and Spain; the resurgence *(relance)* of the EC after years of economic stagnation in the Single European Act of 1986 (SEA), which led to the completion of the common market envisioned a generation earlier; and, finally, the signature and ratification of the Maastricht Treaty in the early 1990s.

The institutional seeds of the EC were first planted in the immediate postwar period. The ECSC responded to several conflicting imperatives at its formation in 1951. First was the need to ensure Europe's postwar economic recovery through the coordinated development of its coal and steel resources. The ECSC also provided multilateral controls over German energy and steel resources, affording Germany's partners a say over their possible military uses. The ECSC ensured increased German and European economic production while assuring Germany's neighbors that its economic regeneration would not be the prelude to the reemergence of German militarism and expansion.

The ECSC also served to contain Soviet power. An economically recovered and politically confident Western Europe, including West Germany, would not only weaken the Communist Party's influence at home (it was particularly strong in France and Italy) but also lay the basis for a final political solution to Franco-German rivalry, preconditions for meeting the Soviet political and military threat to democratic Europe. The ECSC responded not only to pressures from Washington for a coordinated approach but also to the vision of its founders, notably Robert Schuman and Jean Monnet, who were animated by the prospect of rebuilding Europe as a federal union to end the Continent's age-old national divisions and to make Europe again a major power in world politics, with its own political personality and views about how world order and welfare might be legitimately achieved.[7]

The failure of the European Defense Community, discussed below, spurred the search for an alternative route to European union. Building on the success of the ECSC, France, West Germany, Italy, and the Benelux countries signed the Rome Treaty, creating Euratom and the European Economic Community (EEC), in 1957. The EEC drew its authority directly from the treaty signed by the six states. Its decision-making institutions, primarily the Commission, the Council of Ministers, Parliament, and the European Court, exercised powers delegated to them by the member states.

The EC weathered several major crises in its early years. Challenges to its very design and legitimacy as an international body independent of the member states that created it were launched in successive waves by the French Fifth Republic and its first president, Charles de Gaulle. De Gaulle's conception of a Europe of nations *(Europe des Patries)* appeared incompatible with the EC, certainly in its federal expression. De Gaulle and German Chancellor Konrad Adenauer succeeded, nevertheless, in reconciling their otherwise divergent national interests and solutions to Europe's welfare and security problems. In the bargain, the EC was underwritten by a web of Franco-German commitments based on traditional nation-state understandings.

For Adenauer's Germany, the EC had several compelling attractions: Germany's political and moral rehabilitation as a nation; its subordination to a multilateral organization to monitor and check any future nationalist revival; acceleration of economic growth through open markets and increased EC trade; the strengthening of the U.S. security guarantee in return for Europe's response to Washington's preference for a united Europe as a counterpoise to Soviet power; and, not least of all, reconciliation of the French and German peoples.

For de Gaulle, France's commitment to the EC and the Common Market depended on different but complementary considerations. The EC adopted the Common Agricultural Policy (CAP) to underwrite French agriculture, lowered tariffs gradually to afford French industry time to adjust to world market competition, and eased the burden of French overseas commitments by creating a common developmental fund—again fueled by German capital. If Germany preferred a federalist Europe, in which it would participate as an equal, Gaullist France opted for a community in which France's political autonomy and economic interests would be maximized and its claimed special political status as a great power, free of EC restraint, would be preserved, allowing it to enjoy its war-won rights to define Germany's political future and represent German interests in East-West negotiations. By restricting the EC to economic policy, Gaullist France would be free to pursue an independent military strategic policy, based on nuclear weapons and on resistance to the bloc politics of NATO and the Warsaw Pact under U.S. and Soviet leadership.

Having survived a hazardous birth, the EC faced the next challenge issuing from France, which centered on de Gaulle's rejection of Britain's application for entry into the Common Market. British entry was incompatible with almost every foreign, military, and economic policy tenet of the Gaullist Fifth Republic. Britain's special relation with the United States, solidified by the Polaris accord of December 1962, which assured Britain's status as a nuclear power, was viewed by de Gaulle as an insuperable obstacle to European union and common foreign and defense policy. The impediments to Britain's entry on economic grounds were also formidable: its privileged ties to the Commonwealth; the incompatibility of its monetary and agricultural policies with those of the EC regime; and its historic preference for free trade rather than a Continental preferential system.[8]

De Gaulle also assaulted the EC Commission and, indirectly, Germany for its support of the Commission's plan proposing full EC responsibility for CAP and parliamentary approval of EC levies raised to support CAP. The Commission's proposal would have tilted the EC's internal balance of power toward a federal principle. The powers of the Commission and the Parliament would have been bolstered at the expense of the legislative authority of the Council of Ministers, which was dependent on the member governments. Gaullist France boycotted the EC until a compromise between Paris and its partners was reached at Luxembourg. The Luxembourg accord acknowledged that no EC rule or regulation could be approved if it violated the vital interests of a member state. This compromise had no standing under the Rome Treaty, but the treaty could not be implemented if it did not abide by this implicit principle in EC deliberations and decision making.[9] In 1967 the ECSC, the Common Market, and Euratom were merged into a single European Community with a common commission and council.

De Gaulle's resignation in 1969 paved the way for the admission of Britain, along with Denmark and Ireland, into the EC. The adaptation of these countries to the EC discipline proved more difficult than had been anticipated. Not without irony, Britain resisted EC regulation as much as Gaullist France had before it. Gaullist and Thatcherite conceptions of national independence and the maximal autonomy of the state to define its economic policies were hardly distinguishable. During the 1970s the EC made little progress toward internal political integration. The most notable breakthrough was the formation of the European Council, composed of the heads of state and government of the member states. Although it had no formal standing within the EC, the decisions of the intergovernmental body essentially determined EC progress toward union.

So matters stood for twenty years until the *relance* of the EC in the SEA in 1986. In the 1980s, a convergence of economic and geopolitical interests among the major states of the EC, principally Germany, Britain, and France, prompted both a dramatic liberalization of the EC's economy, well beyond trade and tariff reform, and a relaxation, if not formal renunciation, of the Luxembourg veto. Enhanced as a consequence was EC authority, centered in the Commission to ensure the implementation of the SEA.

All of the European states shared the assumption that nationally based Keynesian fiscal policies could not spur European economic growth, which had been slowed since the 1970s by a series of oil shocks and global inflation, high interest rates, continued burdensome military spending, and widespread governmental mismanagement of national economies. In France the socialist government's unilateral efforts to reflate the economy dismally failed in the early 1980s; in Britain long-term economic decline, financial and monetary instability, and chronic labor-management disputes and debilitating strikes hindered economic growth. Liberalizing the internal market was viewed as a stimulus to a lagging EC economy as well as a response to the growing economic and welfare problems confronting the member states.

There was also the broader geopolitical concern, centered in Paris and Bonn, that EC drift weakened the Franco-German axis and Bonn's commitment to define its economic future within the context of overall EC development and strengthening. Stagnation also risked the renationalization of European economic policies. Such trends served neither French postwar policy to check and channel German power nor Germany's continued dependence on its Western allies in order to pursue long-term unification on the basis of close and confident political and security ties within the EC and the Atlantic Alliance.[10]

Discord centered on the extent of member states' coordination of their economies through the EC and the scope of EC powers to effect market liberalization. French and German differences over qualified voting narrowed, with Britain holding out for retaining as much of the Luxembourg accord as its bargaining leverage might permit. The Commission, under Jacques Delors, successfully pressed the point that liberalization depended on internal procedural reform. A Bonn-Paris strategy of carrots and sticks overcame British reservations and small-state opposition to the SEA. Britain's share of the EC budget was reduced by increasing Germany's contribution, while threats of proceeding forward along a two-track system without Britain prompted London's compromise on expanding EC power out of fear that Britain would again be excluded from shaping Europe's future. Side payments to Spain, Portugal, and Greece, which had entered the EC on the condition of their adoption of democratic rule, quelled their objections.

The implications of the SEA for EC development were both impressive and circumscribed. Qualified voting was essentially accepted over the Thatcher government's vigorous objections; in counterpoint, the EC's authority was confined to procedural and substantive matters directly linked to liberalization. If the Luxembourg accord was not formally renounced, the SEA loosened the member states' hold over the EC.[11] The Commission and the Court were granted greater latitude to enforce member state compliance with the 1992 program. EC law took precedence over national law in these domains, and national courts were obliged to apply European rules in reaching their decisions.[12] These enforcement mechanisms were balanced by concessions to member states of significant exemptions and escape clauses where their special interests applied. Efforts of the Commission, bolstered by France, to convince Britain and Germany to include monetary union in the SEA were to no avail. The SEA placed the European Monetary System under the unanimity rule of Article 236. Britain was implicitly granted a veto over a system to which it did not then belong. Extension of EC authority to social and fiscal policy was also blocked.

The latest step toward European unity, the Maastricht Treaty, must be viewed not only against the success of the SEA but also, and more decisively, as a response to the crises besetting the EC and, more broadly, all of Europe in the post–Cold War environment. The end of the Cold War, the collapse of the Soviet state and empire, and the rapid unification of Germany fundamentally altered the assumptions on which European economic development and prospects for a common foreign and security policy had been based since World War II. The very success of SEA liberalization and the globalization of European monetary, financial, service, and merchandise markets also had the unanticipated effect of weakening the ability of both the EC and its member states to define and control the conditions of their economic and political development. The explosive emergence of a host of states—the Slavic states of the former Warsaw pact and the fifteen states of the former Soviet Union—introduced new volatilities and uncertainties into European politics that the EC had not anticipated and was ill-prepared to address. An integrated German economy with 80 million people also upset the economic and political balance within the Community.

On its face, the Maastricht Treaty dramatically enlarges the scope of the EC's competence and invests EC institutions with new and enlarged powers to advance toward European economic union and a common foreign and defense policy.[13] The European union formed by Maastricht covers monetary union, enforcement mechanisms to strengthen EC oversight of economic policy and budgetary management, safeguards for a single market, the maintenance of equity between rich and poor states, the extension of civil rights, and the creation of a framework for a common foreign and defense policy.

EC business is to be "served by a single institutional framework." The European Council is charged to "provide the Union with the necessary impetus for its development."[14] Thus, the institutional development of a European Political Cooperation (EPC), based on intergovernmental accord, is brought squarely within the EC. This step went further than the SEA to synchronize the evolution of EC institutions and those of the EPC.[15] The initial gainer in this process is the Council of Ministers. Its autonomy, authority, and efficiency are strengthened to give institutional effect to the will of the "High Contracting Powers." Toward that end, the Committee of Permanent Representatives (COREPER) is furnished greater resources to improve its responsiveness to Council needs.

The treaty establishes a three-step process and a timetable for the realization of a monetary union, a single currency, and the creation of a European central bank and banking system. Monetary union can be instituted by 1997 only if a simple majority of the EC's member meet the treaty's conditions. In 1999 only a minority will be required to establish a monetary union, although how one might square such an arrangement with EC union is not explained. Conditions for joining include a high degree of price stability, sustainable national financial policies, adherence to currency fluctuations within a fixed band, and long-term convergence of interest rates.[16] The aim of monetary union is ambitious and the criteria for its realization are appropriately rigorous. Whether these stiff political and economic conditions can be met in the strict timetable set by the treaty is problematic, as the analysis below suggests.

Toward a Common Defense and Foreign Policy

Economic integration has been the preferred solution to European political union, which implies a common defense and foreign policy. The failure of the European Defense Community (EDC) Treaty in 1954 provided clear evidence that the states and peoples of Europe were unwilling to meld their national identities into a political union along the model of the United States. Europe's defense was essentially assumed by the Atlantic Alliance and NATO. The WEU, formed in the wake of the EDC's defeat to retain control over Germany's armament, was rendered moribund almost immediately. Meanwhile, the Fouchet Plan, designed by French President de Gaulle in the early 1960s to redefine the EC as a confederation of states and the basis for a common defense and foreign policy, also proved unacceptable to France's partners. They insisted on preserving the independence of the EC within its sphere of authority and ensuring that the plan did not weaken the U.S. defense commitment to Europe.

So matters stood until the 1980s. The impulses that prompted the *relance* of the EC in the 1980s and the signature of the SEA also propelled the EC to extend its purview to foreign and security policy. As Juliet Lodge observes, "The [SEA] Act was to break the taboo about the legitimacy of the EC discussing, and more importantly acting in, security matters broadly conceived. . . . On the one hand, articles explicitly condoned such developments. On the other hand, European Political Cooperation (EPC), which had run parallel to the EC but which had not been fully integrated into the supranational decision-making structure, was brought into the EC treaties system." [17]

Under Article 30, "The High Contracting Parties," that is, the members of the European Council, are supposed "to formulate and implement a European foreign policy." [18] Under other articles, the ministers for foreign affairs and the Commission are charged to meet at least four times a year to discuss foreign policy matters within the framework of the EPC. The member states also pledge their commitment to the aim "that closer cooperation on questions of European security would contribute in an essential way to the development of a European identity in external policy matters [and that] . . . they are ready to coordinate their positions more closely on the political and economic aspects of security." [19] The EC was obliged, however, to coordinate its work with the WEU and the Atlantic Alliance in order to ensure that nothing under Title III of the SEA "shall impede closer cooperation in the field of security" between the EC and these security organizations. [20]

Internal bargaining within the EC limited the import of these articles. Military policy was excluded from consideration. Moreover, neither the Parliament nor the Court of Justice was granted rights to oversee foreign policy questions similar to the extension of their oversight over economic issues affecting EC business. In foreign and security policy, the SEA placed the emphasis on the sovereign status of the "High Contracting Powers" and continued to center the EPC more on the states than on the Community as such.

On the other hand, the SEA opened the way for formal development of EC and WEU foreign and security relations. A natural division of labor was gradually recognized between the EC, as a civil and economic agency, and the WEU, as the principal vehicle for extending the EC's reach over security and defense issues. The WEU had several advantages. Member states did not suffer from a reflex opposition to the WEU's treatment of security questions, as they did when they were acting within the EC process. Changing hats made a difference. The internal organization and powers of the WEU did not raise the issue of an integrated or federal body as EC processes did. The WEU, unlike the EC, was also a useful bridge between France's refusal to participate in NATO and the interest of France's EC partners, also members of the WEU, to draw a willing Paris into consultations on European defense.[21] EC members that were not members of the WEU — Ireland, Denmark, and Greece — were also a lesser drag on progress by their absence. Perhaps most important of all, the experience garnered by the EC in more closely associating the EC and WEU processes with foreign policy and security questions under the SEA paved the way for a more ambitious enlargement of these relations in the Maastricht Treaty.

As a House of Commons research paper observes, the "Common Foreign and Security Policy" (CFSP) of the Maastricht Treaty "inherited the mechanisms and procedures utilized by EPC."[22] In a declaration attached to the treaty, the European Council invites the foreign ministers to reach an EC policy on the CSCE process, disarmament and arms control in Europe, nuclear nonproliferation, and the economic aspects of security, particularly the transfer of military technology. For the first time, the principle of qualified majority voting is also introduced to cover decisions on implementing a previously adopted policy, although what constitutes a joint policy, agreed to unanimously, and the execution of that policy may well be difficult to distinguish in practice.[23]

The treaty also codifies the informal arrangements developed by the EPC and the WEU on behalf of the EC. Article J.4 identifies the WEU as "an integral part of the development of the Union." The WEU is at once charged "to elaborate and implement decisions and actions of the union that have defense implications" and to harmonize those initiatives with the obligations of the member states under the Atlantic Alliance.[24] The ambiguity of the EC's role as the European pillar within NATO or the basis for a separate EC defense policy is deliberately introduced into the treaty and into the EC process for resolution through member bargaining and compromise.

What is significant is that the debate and bargaining over a common European foreign and defense policy, including the roles of the EC and the WEU, is made a part of the EC process and not consigned to the EPC outside of EC institutions. The Council of Europe and the Council of Ministers and its subordinate bodies are assigned primary responsibility for developing policies within the framework of the CFSP. The CFSP secretariat remains independent of the Commission. The Parliament is restricted to a consultative role, although it is supposed to be kept informed about the development of foreign and security policy through the EPC and the European Council president.[25]

▲ Coping Roles in the Post–Cold War Environment

Focusing narrowly on the text of the Maastricht Treaty distorts the true measure of the EC's current and future role in coping with security problems. Those roles, as the analysis below of EC economic and monetary policy suggests, are more plausibly and realistically assessed as a function of challenges to be addressed. Viewed from a systemic perspective (from the top down) as well as from the perspective of the popular, bureaucratic, and governmental support needed to underwrite an expansion of the EC's foreign and security roles (from the bottom up), some proportion of these roles can be introduced in defining the Community's past success (or failures) and the likely future roles that it can feasibly assume. Such a dual perspective guards against discounting the progress that has been made in coping with regional conflict, especially by the European EC,[26] or expecting too much of the EC as a coping mechanism.

In this broader context, as argued above, the EC has been a necessary, if not sufficient, organizational response to Europe's order and welfare problems since World War II. If it did not exist, it would have had to be invented. On this not negligible score, it is a model that might well be adapted to other regions. On the other hand, the EC has been less than equal to the security and welfare challenges of the post–Cold War world in at least four realms: monetary union as a precondition for political union; out-of-area threats to European security; virulent and deadly national and ethnic conflict in Europe, most pointedly in the former Yugoslavia; and political and economic assistance to the peoples and states of the former Warsaw Pact and the Soviet Union, leading to the incorporation of at least some of these states into the EC. Cutting across these four challenges is the EC's long-term ability to accommodate and channel German power into the new Europe.

Prospects of Monetary Union and the Challenge of Enlargement

Economic unity is threatened by the very liberalization and globalization of Europe's markets that were supposed to foster union. National governments are tempted to employ their differential leverage to use these markets for their advantage at the expense, whether intended or not, of their EC partners. These powerful economic and political forces seriously question Maastricht's prospects as the blueprint for European union. The ambiguities and hedges within the treaty itself also register fundamental divisions among the member states about the kind of union they want and about their ability to achieve those elements of union on which they may agree. Britain is permitted to opt out of monetary union if it is unwilling to accept a common currency or a European bank.[27] Some states, like Greece, have been all but written off as ever being able to accept the regime of a monetary union.[28]

The disruption of European currency markets just before the French referendum on the Maastricht Treaty revealed compelling forces, deep within the Community, opposed to the regime that monetary union imposed. Private, nongovernmental actors, as a group holding monetary assets greater than those of any member state, proved more powerful than the European states in forcing a devaluation of pound and lira. Frantic moves by the British to double interest rates could not arrest the attack. Interventions into the market by European central banks—the German Bundesbank reportedly spent $40 billion to maintain exchange rate fluctuations within agreed limits—were similarly impotent to stem the tide.[29] On a regular trading day, more than $1 trillion in currency transactions are recorded, well beyond the limit of central national banks to control or decisively affect exchange rates. The expectations underlying the Maastricht Treaty that the EC's biggest and most powerful economic national economies could soon meet its criteria for monetary union were obviously unrealistically optimistic, at least in the short run.[30]

If global currency markets, driven by private, speculative interests, and popular national sentiment obstructed monetary union, the underlying structure of national interests and governmental advantage also impeded progress. The heavy and largely unanticipated costs of German unification induced the Kohl government to pay for the country's economic and political integration partly through borrowing and higher interest rates. Sole reliance on taxation was ruled out not only because it was an unpopular option but also because the German people, particularly those in the West, were already disgruntled over the economic burdens of unification associated with equalizing the living standards of the eastern states (Länder).

The independent Bundesbank's reluctant and conditional support of the German government's policies inevitably favored the mark over other European currencies, particularly the pound and the lira. High German interest rates attracted foreign capital seeking greater return on investment. The fillip of a strong currency speeded the flight of capital to the mark for profit and safe haven. The efforts of other European capitals, particularly London, Rome, and Paris, to maintain the stability of their currencies and to stimulate their economies by attracting foreign capital were hostage to German interest rates in implicit collusion with global market forces.

The political imperative of German unification and the constraints confronted by Bonn in its efforts to find a domestically palatable solution for its financing proved too powerful for the Kohl government—and the Bundesbank—to resist. The course of least resistance was to transfer the political and economic costs of unification to the market in the form of higher German interest rates and a strong German mark. These policies inevitably fell with unequal burden and economic effect on the members of the European Exchange Rate Mechanism (ERM).[31] Other European states and the United States experienced greater difficulty in attracting investment capital to pull their sagging economies out of recession. Their efforts to maintain the price stability of their currencies was no less a failure in the face of external market pressures and German refusal to substantially lower interest rates. The small, .25% drop in the interest rate announced by the Bundesbank in September 1992 signaled to the market that Berlin and the Bundesbank were not ready to stabilize European currency rates at the expense of German economic and political interests. The weak currencies of the EC were exposed, and the monetary crisis overwhelmed Community resources and will to limit the blow to the ERM.

Even before the September crisis there was accumulating evidence that neither the Bundesbank, jealous of its legal and economic independence, nor the German people were keen on pressing forward on European monetary union. The Bundesbank was locked in battle with the Kohl government over the financing of the eastern provinces. There was little or no incentive for its leadership to accede to a European central bank in which the Bundesbank would be checked by the banking interests or governments of the EC. The Bundesbank had all of the advantages of being able to act as a central bank for Europe without the inconveniences of having to negotiate with weaker national units over its policies, including setting interest rates and maintaining the mark within EC-stipulated exchange rates. The German people were also increasingly reluctant to trade a strong mark for the purported benefits of a European currency and monetary union. The high costs of rehabilitating the eastern *Länder* by inflating the value of the East German mark suggested that they would also have to support the lame economies of their EC partners if monetary union went forward.

If German unification raised serious obstacles to EC economic and monetary coordination, the prospect of EC enlargement by extending Community membership to the former Eastern European members of the Warsaw Pact, particularly the Czech Republic, Hungary, and Poland, would appear to preclude the creation of a single European currency and central bank for all member states anytime soon. These states have little chance of meeting the stiff criteria for membership in the monetary union unless they receive extensive assistance. Until now, EC aid has fallen well short of these standards. The EC has been slow to make trade concessions to the East, particularly on farm products or immigration, although trade and wage transfers are among the few means for these states to earn hard currency to stabilize their failing economies as they attempt to introduce market reforms. By the end of 1993, EC aid to these states was estimated at approximately 6 billion European Currency Units (ECUs). Developmental assistance to Spain, Portugal, and Greece was almost six times that amount. The latter states, moreover, resisted increased assistance to the Eastern European peoples, fearing, and not without reason, that they will receive less, an expectation that has already been confirmed in the costs and in the forgone aid that they perceived to be the consequence of rapid German unification. Half of all aid, grants, and loans that have been extended to Eastern Europe and to the former republics of the Soviet Union, especially the Russia Federation, have come from Germany, not the EC or the United States.[37] While the EC has formal responsibility for the extension of EC assistance to Eastern Europe, in reality Germany predominates in this domain.

Extension of EC membership to the neutral states of Sweden, Finland, and Austria poses a no less serious problem for economic and monetary union, but for reasons just the opposite of those at play in Eastern Europe. They may be *too* well positioned to enter a European monetary union. The European neutrals are rich states with a long history of successful experience in global markets. Although they were also buffeted by the EC monetary crisis — Sweden raised interests rates severalfold, and Finland devalued its currency — some of them are likely to meet the EC's criteria for membership in the monetary union sooner than Britain or Italy, and certainly at a faster pace than the EC's other southern members. In addition, the populations of some neutral states appear to be less reluctant than the British to accept a common European currency and a central European bank.

The actual rate of national adaptation to the EC regime will inevitably be different for each state of the Community. These hard economic realities dictate variable rates of advance toward monetary union for the swift and for those less surefooted. Some will quite likely never make the mark. Maastricht's legitimation of variable-speed monetary union, with some states, even a majority, written off at the start, affirms the aim of European monetary union as a precondition for a common foreign and defense policy, while permitting the EC, ironically, to opt out from pursuit of its own stated goal. Protestations that the EC rejects a two-track, or Franco-German, monetary axis at the expense of some partners is belied by harsh economic constraints and the Maastricht compromise, which passes for a solemn commitment to union.[33]

Prospects of a Common Foreign and Security Policy

The problems confronted by the EC in overcoming member states' resistance to expanding the scope of its competence and powers over a broad range of economic, financial, and monetary policy areas and to strengthening its institutional mechanisms to pursue EC missions in these domains are obviously formidable. Those associated with developing an EC foreign and security policy have proved to be even more daunting and intractable, and not surprisingly, EC solutions have been more elusive, and the results ambiguous and circumscribed. The EC's origins, treaty obligations, and institutional competence have essentially confined its policy focus and resources to nonmilitary affairs.

The member states of the EC, especially Britain and France, have jealously preserved the domains of security and foreign policy for themselves. London and Paris insist on maintaining independent nuclear forces. Britain's forces are nominally assigned to NATO but essentially remain under national control. France has never acceded to external control or influence over its nuclear forces.[34] Except for France, and then not always consistently, the member states of the EC have usually opted for institutional devices other than the EC as the preferred solution to a security problem when a multilateral response was sought. Central to this policy has been European dependence on the Atlantic Alliance and NATO and on the U.S. guarantee. Except for Gaullist France, there appeared to be no need for a separate European defense effort outside of the Atlantic Alliance and NATO during the Cold War. Some even applauded the EC's distance from these issues and hailed its success as a "civilian" power.[35] As noted earlier, the WEU has been upgraded, and its formal authority enhanced, by Maastricht, but operationally it is no substitute for NATO, the United Nations, or even the sprawling and ill-defined CSCE. The latter has served as an important framework for the conventional disarmament of Europe and as a forum, along with the North Atlantic Consultative Council (NACC), for closer consultation between East and West. NATO is the chosen vehicle for the gradual extension of collective security guarantees to the Eastern European states through the Partnership for Peace. NATO is also the designated framework within which to incorporate Russia, as a distant goal, into a Northern Hemispheric security system, including North America and Europe, to replace the bipolar Cold War confrontation. Meanwhile, the United Nations has served as the international organization of preference in responding to out-of-Europe security issues.

The end of the Cold War, the collapse of the Soviet state and empire, the resulting prospect of growing political and economic instability as well as national and ethnic conflict in Eastern Europe, Germany unification, and continued domestic demands for greater economic growth and social welfare have reinforced pressures for greater EC-wide foreign and defense cooperation.[36] Called into question are the viability and responsiveness of the EC to meet these new challenges in Europe and its adaptability in addressing out-of-region threats. These include rising Muslim fundamentalism, regional conflicts on Europe's frontiers, terrorism, immigration waves disruptive to social harmony and economic development, or territorial grabs, like the Iraqi takeover of Kuwait, that hold Europe's security and welfare interests prey to foreign predators.

The member states are fundamentally split over what foreign and security roles they should assign to the EC to meet these diffuse threats. While most Community members espouse continued security ties with the United States and greater European defense cooperation—critical points of agreement often overlooked in pessimistic appraisals of European progress toward a common foreign and security policy—they are divided into several camps with regard to how to pursue these aims, most notably between Atlanticist and European-leaning groups.[37] Led by Britain, the Atlanticist wing of the EC resists any form of European defense cooperation that might weaken the U.S. commitment to European security or hasten the complete departure of U.S. troops. A separate European defense community is viewed as incapable of substituting for the degree of political and military cooperation that has been achieved in NATO. The Atlantic Alliance was seen as the principal mechanism in meeting the Soviet threat. U.S. presence and a strong Atlantic Alliance are also conceived as insurance against future threats to European security. Why, ask Atlanticists, should the EC increase expenditures on defense to recreate assets already available within the Atlantic Alliance?

France, joined by former Commission president Jacques Delors, pressed for a greater role for the EC in foreign and defense policy. Since de Gaulle's decision to withdraw from NATO, Paris remains openly skeptical about the long-term reliability of the U.S. security guarantee and the presence of U.S. troops. Preparing for an anticipated withdrawal or the continued reduction of the U.S. commitment, not only does Paris want a European defense policy and system in place but it is determined to strengthen Germany's ties to the EC in response to the seismic shocks that have fundamentally altered Europe's political and security landscape in the wake of the collapse of the Cold War system. Paris's nightmare is a Germany once again pursuing foreign and military policies independently of the multilateral controls and the expectations of mutual cooperation that have been created among EC members since World War II. The growing economic power of Germany and the speed with which the Kohl government ended Four Power control over Germany and reintegrated the country has only served to strengthen these concerns. These traditional geopolitical considerations underlie more diplomatically palatable arguments that advise the enhancement of the EC's political and security powers as a logical extension of its important economic role in world affairs, much the aim of the founders of the original federalist movement[38] and a view shared by the Kohl government.

Not surprisingly, the Maastricht Treaty did not resolve the differences among the major states over the roles of the EC and the WEU in developing a common foreign and defense policy. On the surface, the British position, which placed limits on the EC's reliance on the WEU, appeared to have won the battle of the treaty text. The treaty did not subordinate the WEU to the union as the French might have hoped; rather, it favored the British position of making the WEU a bridge between NATO and European union. On the other hand, the Franco-German decision to transform their brigade into a corps of approximately thirty thousand to thirty-five thousand men, with its own command structure, appeared to contradict British views that such a force would not only weaken NATO's integrated command structure and draw units away from the alliance but also weaken the U.S. security commitment to Europe. On paper the corps would also be the WEU's principal military arm, implicitly extending to the WEU a parallel and equal status with NATO.

The dimensions of British-French differences over the WEU and the EC's role in European military security can be exaggerated.[39] The Eurocorps will have limited capability, being composed largely of conscripts hindered by differences in language, training, doctrine, and equipment. Early on, French President François Mitterrand signaled France's interest in greater cooperation with the United States as long as Gaullist strictures against France's return to NATO's integrated structure were not violated (witness his 1982 speech to the Bundestag, in which he called for German acceptance of NATO missiles and nuclear weapons). U.S.-French cooperation, while never straight or smooth, continues today.[40] The Eurocorps also represents a major concession of French sovereignty within the WEU. Meanwhile, the German and French governments affirm their commitment to NATO and the subordination of the projected corps to Alliance command in times of crisis.

The Gulf War represented the first out-of-region threat to Europe's security in the post–Cold War environment. The disarray among Europe's major powers was evident from the start. Strong U.S. leadership was needed to discipline the EC and its members to assume a common position in support of the U.N. action. Britain responded early with battle-ready ground and air forces. Although it possessed larger ground and air forces, France was slower to react, and its military contribution proved less effective throughout the Desert Storm campaign.[41] The French government temporized about the role it would assume in the early stages of the war, and its internal incoherence was not reduced until a defense minister sympathetic to the Iraqi cause was replaced. The German constitution hampered Bonn from sending troops out of the NATO region, and sharp political division precluded a prompt or decisive response to the Gulf crisis.

Eventually the EC and its principal members harmonized these differences. The Community agreed, with little rancor, to impose an economic embargo on Iraq. The WEU played a useful, if ancillary, role in coordinating naval operations.[42] The German government contributed a notable share of the financing of the war, and German fighter aircraft were sent to Turkey, a NATO ally. With evident lapses, the French and British governments eventually coordinated their policies with the United States to ensure U.N. Security Council support for the intervention. What became apparent, however, was that the EC was ill-prepared politically—and ill-equipped militarily—to cope with the Iraqi problem. These shortcomings exposed the need for closer EC cooperation and preparation in responding to out-of-region threats.

Similarly, the EC has been less than decisive in meeting the threats posed by national and ethnic rivalry in Europe. EC mediation efforts failed to arrest the civil war or to arrest the practice of "ethnic cleansing" that condemned thousands to death and that essentially confirmed the territorial expansion of Croatia and Serbia at the expense of the Muslim populations in Bosnia-Herzegovina. When Germany unilaterally recognized the independence of Croatia and Slovenia in early 1992, the stage was set for the declaration of Bosnian independence, which had the unwitting effect of widening the civil war. In forcing the hand of its EC partners and the United States, Germany exposed the deep divisions within the EC toward addressing the reemergence of virulent and expansive nationalism in Europe. It also revealed the new diplomatic status of a united Germany willing to exercise its power in pursuit of its conception of its national interests. That the EC closed ranks behind Germany evidences more its impotence in the face of Bonn's initiative rather than a lately discovered unity and cohesion.

As suggested earlier, the EC has also been less than responsive to the challenge of political and economic reform in Eastern Europe and among the peoples of the former Soviet Union. Its assistance toward the development of its own members dwarfs its contribution to its Eastern European neighbors. Germany again has been largely left to cope with the problem. It also effectively, if not always efficiently, used economic assistance to press rapid Soviet and allied Big Three acquiescence in German unification. Germany's massive assistance to its eastern neighbors and the ambitious program of rapid and costly integration of the eastern *Länder,* assumed by Bonn at a cost exceeding $100 billion, raise serious questions about the EC's ability to confront the Eastern European challenge and growing German power. The magnitude of the German effort suggests that the significance of the formal authorization of the Group of Seven Industrialized Democracies (G-7) to rely on the EC to coordinate assistance to Eastern Europe is less than meets the eye. The determination, moreover, of the United States to work alone or through the IMF equally casts doubt on the significance of the EC's role in this policy domain.

One implication of these German initiatives and the accumulating investments in political and economic capital that Germany has made in Eastern Europe and in the former Soviet Union is that it has a major stake in the reform movement in this vast region quite separate and distinct from those of its European and NATO partners. The U.S.-led effort to provide IMF funds for Russia through a multilateral consortium only slightly rebalances the distribution of stakes and leverage among the Western states. These new and growing networks of ties between Germany and Eastern Europe urge, as some analysts have argued, a faster pace in the EC's movement toward enlargement.[43] It faces the task of somehow getting ahead of the onrush of decisions and actions taken elsewhere—by Washington, by nationalist extremists, and most notably by Germany outside and despite the EC—that compromise its integrity as an international body. But as the EC moves toward enlargement, its internal discipline and coherence in foreign and security policy is likely to weaken, and its ability to contribute to coping initiatives outside Europe will be correspondingly limited. The extension of Community membership to Austria, Finland, and Sweden adds three traditionally neutral states to the EC whose foreign and security policies diverge from those of most of their new partners.

▲ Conclusions

The EC's efforts to cope with its economic, political, and military security problems appear woefully inadequate, often late, and even beside the point. However, such a pessimistic assessment overlooks several critical elements essential to any evaluation of the EC's past, present roles, and future prospects as a coping mechanism. First, it unduly depreciates the critical importance of the EC in overcoming the past failures of the European peoples in coping with their own conflicts over four centuries since the emergence of the nation-state. The movement to political union and to an integrated economy are animated by the shadow of a bleak past. The EC is testimony to the shared view of its member states and peoples that Europe's security and welfare problems cannot be resolved either through war or through narrow protectionist policies. Even a casual tracing of the evolution of the EC as an agent working on behalf of its members' security and welfare interests indicates that it has progressed further than its most ardent detractors and even some of its supporters could envision.

Second, a pessimistic appraisal of the EC's coping mechanisms ignores the importance of the dense political and economic, not to say security, understandings that constitute what Karl Deutsch has defined as a security community. These understandings are given life in the habits of cooperation, internalization of common norms, and mutual regard for the interests and aims of member peoples and states that animate EC processes and institutions. Contrast the EC's acceptance of German unification and its decision to accept the challenge—yet to be met—of accommodating German national power within the delicate balances of the Community with the failure of the Eastern European states and the former republics of the Soviet Union to cope with the reemergence of egoistic nationalism and ethnic strife in their midst.

Third, the EC should also be assessed from the perspective of the shadow it casts into the future.[44] The Rome and Maastricht treaties and the SEA represent not only temporary, conjunctural accords of momentary convenience. They are a commitment of the member states to a process of future development leading to economic and political union. It is not at all certain how that process will turn out. The EC may well dissolve under the pressures of global markets, national and ethnic rivalries, and a failure of vision, leadership, and popular will to pool sovereignty and national power for the sake of collective security and welfare gains. The persistent appearance of a visionary union throughout the EC's history has itself inspired the cooperation needed to surmount obstacles to its achievement. Despite the defeat of the Maastricht Treaty in the first Danish referendum, the slim 51 percent victory in France, and the British government's resistance to bringing the treaty to a vote pending the outcome of the successful second referendum in Denmark, the fact remains that the treaty was eventually passed by all of the Twelve. As Mark Twain might have observed, news of Europe's death appears premature.

Fourth, it would be a mistake to assume that the EC is capable of meeting the security problems confronting Europe and the world community on its own. It is one, indispensable institution in an environment populated by others that have emerged and evolved to cope with the complex interdependencies generated by more than 180 states and a world population divided against itself of more than 5 billion people—and counting. The EC can perhaps best be evaluated in terms of its ability to join its resources and will with those of other agencies. The United Nations as well as U.S. leadership and arms proved critical in defeating Iraq and in forcing the Hussein regime to abide by the terms of the peace accord. The United Nations, the Atlantic Alliance, the WEU, the CSCE, the World Bank, and the IMF—as well as U.S. power and German and Japanese financial support—will be needed to cope with Eastern European and Russian reform efforts. These institutions and those that will have to be created, as envisioned in the Maastricht Treaty, are also positive responses to the need for accommodating German power and genius in ways that are both effective and legitimate in the eyes of the German people. Specifically, Germany's status of equality in NATO and its future accorded status as a permanent member of the United Nations would appear to be indispensable for bolstering its position and commitment to European union.

Finally, the EC's capacity to cope with Europe's welfare and security problems should not be conceived as a straight-line projection of the past. Movement forward should be expected to occur on several fronts simultaneously, with retreats along the way, much as the blockage of the EDC eventually led to the formation of the EEC. Rather than "spillover" being both explanation and prescription for the Community's development, it would appear that continued tension between EC claims for the expansion of its competence, powers, and membership and the strengthening of its institutions vis-à-vis member states and national electorates is needed to define both the limits *and* the opportunities of pooled sovereignty in the EC's pursuit of common policies. That the EC could be abolished now is as inconceivable as the prospect of war among the major European states. But the EC's utility as a coping mechanism, especially outside Europe, will depend, ironically, on how well it is able to challenge the states on which it depends for support to enlarge its competence as a precondition for the realization of their diverse national needs.

The external and internal limits constraining the Community's development as a coping instrument should not be underestimated. These limits arise from differences deep within the nation-state structure and the national and ethnic groupings of Europe. These are crystallized in the post–Cold War era by the reemergence of a united Germany and more than twenty newly independent states in Eastern Europe, the Balkans, and among the republics of the former Soviet Union. The renationalization of European politics, economic reform and development, and military security concerns, those inside and especially those outside the EC, also have to be reconciled with the workings of global markets, which neither the states of the EC nor the EC itself can control for their own purposes but with which they cannot do without.

In the immediate future, the kinds of coping activities and resources needed to address security problems will depend more on the decision of the member states of the Community than on EC restrictions. This has been the case in a succession of crises, including Yugoslavia, the Gulf War, Somalia, and Rwanda. The major powers within the EC are reluctant to relinquish their autonomy over the use of their military forces abroad or their final say over what support they might lend to coping activities to manage or resolve armed conflict outside of Europe.

These limitations should not obscure, however, the success of the European peoples in addressing and surmounting their own seemingly intractable rivalries. A realist paradigm of perpetual state conflict fits the past more than it does the present or the future. A pessimistic reading of the past can also be exaggerated, serving as a misleading guide for future European state conduct.[45]

In responding to Europe's systemic needs for order, welfare, and legitimacy in rebuilding postwar Europe, in fighting the Cold War, and in constructing post–Cold War Europe, the EC represents a unique human achievement for coping with the contradictions that are inherent in the solutions—the nation-state, global markets, and democratic rule—devised over the past several centuries to address these global imperatives. Stanley Hoffmann's characterization of "the New Europe" might be amended to capture the EC's hybrid status and its future prospects as a coping mechanism within and outside of Europe.[46] The EC cannot be reduced to a balance-of-power system, as some might prefer, because the development of a European security community in the Deutschian sense of that term would have to be denied. It should also not be portrayed as a concert, and even less so as a collective security body. Nor should it be viewed simply as just another form of anarchical order,[47] a reductionist convenience that obfuscates the critical differences between different regional security communities in its effort to simply and clarify.[48] The EC is "all of the above," and Europe, or at least a large part of Europe, is safer and more prosperous as a consequence.

NOTES

I use the terms *European Community,* or *EC,* and *Community* as synonymous with each other and with *European Economic Community (EEC)* and *European Union (EU).* I use *EC* or *Community* in the broadest sense to refer to the member states as capable of acting together as a body in security, foreign, and economic policy either through the institutions of what is now the European Union, through the coordination of their policies within other multilateral organizations, like NATO, or through traditional diplomatic channels.

1. Compare the contrasting analyses of Ernst Haas, *Beyond the Nation-State: Functionalism and International Organization* (Stanford: Stanford University Press, 1964), and Leon Lindberg, *The Political Dynamics of European Economic Integration* (Stanford: Stanford University Press, 1965), vis-à-vis Stanley Hoffmann, "Obstinate or Obsolete? The Fate of the Nation-State and the Case of Western Europe," *World Politics* 13 (Oct. 1968): 140–54.

2. See Edward A. Kolodziej, "What Is Security and Security Studies? Lessons from the Cold War," *Arms Control* 13 (Apr. 1992): 1–31.

3. Robert E. Hunter, "The Future of European Security," in *The European Community after 1992,* ed. Armond Cleese and Raymond Vernon (Baden-Baden: Nomos, 1991), 170.

4. Karl Deutsch et al., *Political Community and the North Atlantic Area* (Princeton: Princeton University Press, 1957), 5.

5. For additional analysis of the concept of a mature anarchy and its dependence on stable nation-states, see Barry Buzan, *People, States, and Fear,* 2d ed. (Boulder, Colo.: Lynne Reinner, 1991), esp. 175–81, 261–65.

6. For an exposition of the rationale underlying the Marshall Plan, see Michael J. Hogan, *The Marshall Plan: America, Britain, and the Reconstruction of Western Europe, 1947–1952* (New York: Cambridge University Press, 1987).

7. See Jean Monnet, *Memoirs,* trans. Richard J. Mayne (Garden City, N.J.: Doubleday, 1978).

8. Charles de Gaulle, *Discours et messages,* vol. 4 (Paris: Plon, 1970), 66–79.

9. See Edward A. Kolodziej, *French International Policy under De Gaulle and Pompidou: The Politics of Grandeur* (Ithaca: Cornell University Press, 1974), 292–340; and John Newhouse, *Collision in Brussels* (New York: W. W. Norton, 1967).

10. Andrew Moravcsik, "Negotiating the Single European Act: National Interests and Conventional Statecraft in the European Community," *International Organization* 55 (winter 1991): 50. My analysis of SEA owes much to Moravcsik's review in ibid., 19–56. See also Wayne Sandholtz and John Zysman, "1992: Recasting the European Bargain," *World Politics* 42 (Oct. 1989): 95–128; and Geoffrey Garrett, "International

Cooperation and Institutional Choice: The European Community's Internal Market," *International Organization* 56 (spring 1992): 533–60.

11. Peter Ludlow's conclusion that the most important achievement of the SEA was its "liberation of the Council machinery from excessive control by individual member states" appears somewhat exaggerated in light of the restrictive clauses inserted in the SEA to confine the EC to the 1992 program (see Peter Ludlow, "The Maastricht Treaty and the Future of Europe," *Washington Quarterly* 15, no. 4 [1992]: 119–40).

12. Martin Shapiro, "The European Court of Justice," in *Europolitics,* ed. Alberta M. Sbragia (Washington, D.C.: Brookings Institution, 1992), 123–56.

13. This analysis of the Maastricht's complex provisions is based on a reading of the text, guided by Peter Ludlow's useful summary in "The Maastricht Treaty and the Future of Europe." For the text of the treaty, see European Information Service, *Supplement to European Report: Treaty on European Union,* No. 1746 (Washington, D.C., Feb. 22, 1992).

14. Ibid., 2 (Article C).

15. Juliet Lodge analyzes European Political Cooperation with particular reference to the SEA in "European Community Security Policy: Rhetoric or Reality?" in *European Security—Towards 2000,* ed. Michael C. Pugh (Manchester, England: Manchester University Press, 1992), 49–66. Also useful is Alfred Pijpers et al., eds., *European Political Cooperation in the 1980s: A Common Foreign Policy for Western Europe?* (Dordrecht: Nijhoff, 1988).

16. Ludlow, "The Maastricht Treaty and the Future of Europe," 133–34.

17. Lodge, "European Community Security Policy," 50–51.

18. *Single European Act,* Title III.

19. Ibid., Article 6(a).

20. Ibid., Article 6(c).

21. Lodge, "European Community Security Policy," 62–63.

22. United Kingdom, House of Commons, International Affairs and Defense Section, *Research Note: Europe the Next Phase: New European Community Structures for Foreign Affairs and Defence,* May 15, 1992, 3.

23. Ibid., 3–5.

24. European Information Service, *Supplement to European Report: Treaty on European Union,* Article J.4.

25. House of Commons, *Research Note,* 6–8.

26. Buzan, *People, States, and Fear,* cautions against this error in distinguishing between mature and immature anarchies, a critical task for any sensible understanding of why some regional and state security systems survive and others fail.

27. For a summary of the British government's reservations about Maastricht, see British Information Services, Policy Statement: *Agreement at Maastricht,* 82/91 (Washington, D.C.: Embassy of Britain, 1991).

28. Ludlow, "The Maastricht Treaty and the Future of Europe," 135.

29. *New York Times,* Sept. 23, 1992.

30. Ludlow's analysis reflects this optimism ("The Maastricht Treaty and the Future of Europe," 133–37).

31. The British prefer to call it by the name European Exchange Rate Mechanism, or ERM, rather than European Monetary System (EMS).

32. *New York Times,* Jan. 23, 1992.

33. Ibid., Oct. 1, 1992.

34. Periodically, the French government or its spokespersons have suggested that French nuclear forces could become the basis for a European deterrent. President Mitterrand's restatement of this possibility in January 1992 is the most recent example of this visionary possibility, which has not progressed beyond a rhetorical level since the creation of French nuclear forces in the 1960s. Current French nuclear policy is discussed in Edward A. Kolodziej, "French Nuclear Policy: Adapting the Gaullist Legacy to the Post–Cold War World," in *Toward Nuclear Peace*, ed. Michael Mazarr and Alexander Lennon (New York: St. Martin's Press, 1995), 165–204.

35. Panos Tsakaloyannis traces this evolution of the EC's fixed concern from economic policy to military and defense questions in "The EC: from Civilian Power to Military Integration," in *The European Community and the Challenge of the Future*, ed. Juliet Lodge (New York: St. Martin's Press, 1989), 241–55.

36. Recent useful assessments of EC development toward a common foreign and defense policy may be found in Walter Carlsnaes and Steven Smith, eds., *European Foreign Policy: The EC and Changing Perspectives in Europe* (London: Sage, 1994).

37. The range and subtlety of these positions cannot be restated here. The major outlines of these schools of thought are perceptively reviewed in Adrian Hyde-Price, *European Security beyond the Cold War: Four Scenarios for the Year 2000* (London: Sage, 1991), esp. 187–262. Excluded from discussion is the option of a *Europe des Etats*, characterized as a return by and large to pre–World War II balance-of-power arrangements. Europe may well degenerate to this condition, reminiscent of the anarchy of the interwar period, but that is not the question before us here, namely, the role of the EC in foreign and security affairs. For an analysis of the possibility of European reversion to past national habits, see Jack Snyder, "Averting Anarchy in the New Europe," *International Security* 14 (spring 1990): 5–41.

38. Jacques Delors, the former president of the Commission, develops this argument in "European Integration and Security," *Survival* 23 (Mar.–Apr. 1991): 99–109.

39. This is the balanced view of House of Commons, *Research Note*, 8–10.

40. At a September strategic studies meeting, French Defense Minister Pierre Joxe reportedly allowed that in the future France would participate more in defining NATO military and political roles in Europe (*New York Times*, Sept. 30, 1992). The victory of the Right in the March 1993 elections has not thrown policies favoring greater cooperation with the United States into question.

41. For a critical assessment of the European contribution, see François Heisbourg, "Quelles leçons stratégiques de la guerre du Golfe?" *Politique etrangère* 56, no. 2 (1991): 411–22. The French publicly conceded some of the shortcomings of their preparation for the war (*New York Times*, May 8, 1991).

42. Hyde-Price, *European Security beyond the Cold War*, 245.

43. Hyde-Price evaluates several multilateral frameworks within which to integrate members of the former Warsaw Pact into a European security system; see ibid, 193–262.

44. Robert Axelrod's otherwise insightful exposition of the determinants of consensual cooperation fails to place enough emphasis on the role of the "shadow of the past" in inducing cooperation (Robert Axelrod, *The Evolution of Cooperation* [New York: Basic Books, 1984]). His view is echoed in Kenneth A. Oye., ed., *Cooperation under Anarchy* (Princeton: Princeton University Press, 1986). Barry Buzan, *People*,

States, and Fear, and Hedley Bull, *The Anarchical Society* (London: Macmillan, 1977), more prudently emphasize what social and political organization has been accomplished to overcome the deficiencies of immature anarchies.

45. Thomas Risse-Kappen, "The Long-Term Future of European Security," in Carlsnaes and Smith, *European Foreign Policy,* 45–60.

46. Stanley Hoffmann, "Balance, Concert, Anarchy, or None of the Above," in *The Shape of the New Europe,* ed. Gregory F. Treverton (New York: Council on Foreign Relations, 1991), 191–220.

47. A minimalist reply to this view is offered by Buzan in his useful distinction between mature and immature anarchies *(People, States, and Fear).* A more thorough response is Deutsch's notion of a security community (Deutsch et al., *Political Community and the North Atlantic Area).*

48. The behavior and habitats of elephants and whales might as well be treated alike because they are both mammals.

MOHAMMED AYOOB

9 Subnational and Transnational Actors

This chapter seeks to achieve four interrelated objectives. First, it attempts to build on the thesis that most conflicts in the Third World are rooted primarily in the domestic political arena although many of them also take on the character of interstate conflicts and acquire other international dimensions. Second, it strives to show that while most original actors involved in these conflicts are internal to states, they are crucially dependent upon external sources for support, and the policies of external powers are often critical for the success or failure of internal actors in terms of achieving their goals. Third, it attempts to demonstrate that pan-movements such as Arab nationalism and militant Islam, although they appear to be transnational in character, are for the most part used by domestic actors in the furtherance of their own goals and are therefore operationalized in subnational rather than transnational terms. One can, in fact, argue that the proponents of such ideologies in discrete countries form a subcategory of subnational actors. Fourth, it concludes that any attempt to find mechanisms that can cope with conflict in the Third World must therefore concentrate on subnational sources of conflict and on the linkages between internal and external actors, which often transform intrastate conflicts into interstate ones. Such an approach to conflict management is necessary, since in the absence of a clear understanding of the domestic roots of conflict in the developing countries and their linkages with external sources of support it will be impossible to alleviate, let alone resolve, conflicts in the Third World.

▲ Domestic Roots of Third World Conflict

That most conflicts in the Third World have their roots in the domestic or intrastate arena has by now been amply demonstrated. Just to quote one source, the Stockholm International Peace Research Institute (SIPRI), of the thirty-one major conflicts in the world in 1990, almost all of them in the Third World, only one was of an interstate character.[1] The remainder were divided almost equally between those for the control of government, where the legitimacy of regimes was challenged, and state-formation conflicts, where the legitimacy of existing states was challenged. These data bear out the conclusion reached elsewhere by me regarding the centrality of the process of state making, especially the stage at which most Third World states currently find themselves, to the security problem of developing countries.[2]

This does not mean that the regional dimension of security, such as the element of conflict between neighboring, usually contiguous, states over disputed territories and populations, should be ignored. Regional dynamics also affect the security of developing states and regions and are related to, among other things, regional balances of power. However, this regional dimension of conflict most often comes to the fore in the Third World when contiguous states concurrently undertake the process of state making. It is the simultaneity of this process, which frequently includes the assertion of political and military control over demographic and territorial space contested by neighboring states, that underlies many of the conflicts among developing countries that appear to the outside observer as instances of regional conflict tied to regional balance-of-power issues. The link of the state-making process to the regional balance is obvious: the more that balance is tilted in a particular state's favor, the easier it will be for that state to enhance its state-making goals by successfully asserting its control over contested territories and populations at the expense of neighboring states.

Such an analysis also does not ignore the role of the great powers in conflicts in the Third World. Since the beginning of the decolonization process, major external powers have demonstrated a strong tendency to get involved in both intrastate and interstate conflicts in the Third World in order to promote their own global and regional objectives, to support client states and regimes, to sell weapons for economic and political profit, and to test sophisticated military hardware in battlefields far removed from the global industrial and strategic heartland. Such interventionist proclivities on the part of major powers does not, however, detract from the fact that although they and their actions may be crucial to the exacerbation or mitigation of conflict in the Third World, they usually are not the prime originators of such conflicts. This holds true even for such dramatic Third World conflicts as those in Vietnam, Afghanistan, and the Persian Gulf in 1990–91. In all these cases the primary moving spirits were local in character, whether they were subnational actors, states, or a combination of the two. Moreover, the primary motivations of these local protagonists were the products of the interrelated processes of state making, state breaking, and state expansion.

▲ The Linkage between Internal and External Factors

If we accept the argument that most regional conflicts are related to issues of state making and state breaking as well as those of regime legitimacy (an argument augmented by the events of the last several years in the Balkans and in the republics of the former Soviet Union), a logical conclusion would be that domestic factors play a much more important role than interstate ones as far as the origins of these conflicts are concerned. This conclusion would help us to compare the contribution of domestic factors with that of external or international factors to conflicts in the Third World. It would also help us to clarify the confusion regarding the importance of various actors in particular conflicts. For example, it would permit us to give relatively realistic weight to the importance of the Kashmiri militants in comparison with the Pakistan factor in the continuing insurgency in the Indian state of Jammu and Kashmir; or, to give another example, the importance of Tamil secessionists vis-à-vis Indian involvement in the Tamil insurgency in Sri Lanka.

This relatively simple conclusion about the basic domestic roots of much of the conflict in the Third World becomes difficult to verify clearly in many instances. In probably the majority of conflicts that originated as intrastate conflicts, the relationship between internal and external factors is symbiotic in that one set of factors cannot thrive without the presence of the other, and vice versa. Donald Horowitz's conclusion regarding secessionism, which is the most dramatic manifestation of intrastate conflict, has a relevance that goes beyond the issue of secessionism itself. According to Horowitz, "Whether and when a secessionist movement will emerge is determined mainly by domestic politics, by the relations of groups and regions within the state. Whether a secessionist movement will achieve its aims, however, is determined largely by international politics, by the balance of interests and forces that extend beyond the state. . . . Secession lies squarely at the juncture of internal and international politics."[3] It would not be wrong to assert that, like secessionism, conflict in the Third World in general lies squarely at this same juncture.

Such a conclusion leads to two logical corollaries: (1) that subnational actors are extremely important in regional conflicts because they are often the primary, in the sense of original, participants in such conflicts; and (2) that the role subnational actors play in such conflicts is often substantially determined by their linkages with external actors and cannot be adequately analyzed in isolation from those linkages. Quite often external linkages are crucial to the attainment of the objectives subnational actors set for themselves and demarcate the difference between success and failure. After studying and comparing seven cases of attempted secessionism, Alexis Heraclides concluded that

in armed struggles for separatism, the posture of the international system (primarily states and IGOs [international governmental organizations]) is salient to conflict resolution. The role of states is the crucial intermediate variable for the conflict's violent or peaceful resolution or nonresolution. If a secessionist movement is unable to win a military victory and is not prepared to compromise on independence, it can only be "saved" if there is high level external state intervention and diplomatic recognition. If a movement is willing to settle for less than complete independence, external state involvement can be crucial for raising the costs of the conflict and creating a stalemate, thereby "convincing" the incumbent government and secessionists to negotiate and agree on some form of meaningful devolution. Alternatively, lack of external state support can lead either to the defeat and abandonment of the separatist bid or to the lengthy continuation of the armed conflict.[4]

It is therefore not surprising that in many cases the very formulation of the subnational actors' objectives is subject to, and sometimes determined by, the nature and strength of their linkages with external actors and their perception of the degree of support and/or opposition to their demands from foreign actors, be they states or international organizations, that are crucial to their cause. The best example of this phenomenon is the persistent refusal on the part of the major Kurdish nationalist movements to openly couch Kurdish demands in the vocabulary of independent statehood. This was especially evident in the wake of the Iraqi defeat in the Gulf War, when the prospects for an independent Kurdish state in Iraqi Kurdistan appeared to the brightest they had ever been since the Ottoman defeat in World War I. However, given the Iraqi Kurds' dependence on several foreign backers, especially Turkey and

Iran, which are faced with their own Kurdish problems, the Iraqi Kurdish leadership, itself divided into competing factions, steadfastly stuck to its demand, at least in public, for autonomy within, rather than secession from, the Iraqi state in order not to alienate these crucial foreign supporters.

In fact, one can argue that in order to be successful a secessionist movement needs strong external military support, preferably from the preeminent regional military power. In this context, three things seem to be crucial: *(a)* the external supporter must be willing to fight, and be capable of winning, a war against the state from which the secessionist movement wants to separate; *(b)* the external supporter's military capabilities in the region and its political influence internationally should be sufficient to deter other external powers, whether regional or extraregional, from intervening militarily on behalf of the parent state to prevent successful secession; and *(c)* the external supporter's objectives must coincide with those of the secessionist movement in terms of breaking the parent state, for otherwise the former could come to a compromise settlement with the parent state even in the midst of a war, leaving the secessionist movement out in the cold and probably much worse off than if it had not attempted a secessionist war in the first place.

The two major cases of successful attempts at secession from postcolonial states, Bangladesh and Northern Cyprus, attest to the validity of the above propositions. In both cases the external supporters, India and Turkey, respectively, were preeminent regional military powers that could deter counterintervention by external powers. The objectives of both India in 1971 and Turkey in 1974 coincided with those of the separatist movements in East Pakistan and Northern Cyprus in terms of breaking up Pakistan and Cyprus. In both cases, the parent state was unable to offer the external supporter of the separatist movement a blueprint for a compromise settlement that was acceptable to the latter and that therefore could convince the latter to scale down its support to the secessionist forces.

That such a combination of circumstances is extremely difficult to replicate is borne out by the fact that although there have been a plethora of secessionist attempts in the Third World, only these two have been successful. Eritrea, which has always been a special case in the sense that it was trying to reestablish its colonial borders, can be added now. The failure of the Biafran attempt to secede from Nigeria in the civil war from 1967 to 1970 and the repeated failure of Iraqi Kurdish attempts at autonomy and secession, despite the support of diverse external sources ranging from the United States to Iran, testifies to the importance of the three conditions mentioned earlier that are crucial to the success of a secessionist movement.

▲ Strategies for Conflict Management

Given the intimate linkage between domestic and external factors in secessionist and other types of Third World conflict (e.g.,those involving a change in regime, as in Afghanistan and Lebanon), any realistic analysis of regional conflict in the Third World, particularly if it is interested in prescribing strategies for coping with such conflicts, must start by critically appraising the linkage in each case between subnational and external actors, both of which are inexorably present in almost every Third World conflict. Conflict resolution strategies that do not adequately take into account the importance of such linkages and, therefore, try to find ways of resolving conflicts by limiting their scope either to the interstate or the intrastate level, attempting to satisfy actor demands at one of these levels only, will not succeed and may even be counterproductive in the long run.

For example, attempts to resolve the Lebanese conflict by finding a formula acceptable to major Lebanese factions without taking into consideration Syrian and Israeli stakes in Lebanon are as likely to fail as strategies that attempt to satisfy Syrian and Israeli objectives vis-à-vis Lebanon without taking into account the political and security goals of the major Lebanese factions that harbor objectives autonomous of their external supporters.

Analysts interested in prescribing conflict resolution strategies for regional conflicts in the Third World will therefore have to evolve much more complex matrixes than are presently available. Many of these will have to be constructed to suit discrete contexts and situations and will not fit other superficially similar cases. For example, a strategy that might be suitable in addressing the Syria-Israel-Lebanon case may be totally inapplicable to the case of India, Pakistan, and Kashmir or that of India, Sri Lanka, and Tamil secessionists because the actor objectives, historical circumstances, and geopolitical contexts are so different.

Furthermore, although India is involved in both the second and the third case mentioned above, the formula evolved for the satisfaction of Indian objectives vis-à-vis the Sri Lanka–Tamil case is bound to be totally inapplicable to the Pakistan-Kashmir case for the simple reason that India's objectives in the former are much more limited than its goals in the latter. This difference results from the fact that in the latter instance the continued accession of Kashmir to the Indian Union is seen by the Indian political elite as being vital to the success of its state-making and nation-building endeavors. Although the Tamil insurrection in Sri Lanka encompasses both domestic concerns (because of the presence of 60 million Indian Tamils in the Indian Union) and strategic considerations (the prevention of anti-Indian foreign presences in Sri Lanka), for India it is not central to requirements of state making and regime legitimacy in the country. New Delhi can therefore afford to be more relaxed, and to make greater concessions, in the Tamil–Sri Lanka case than it can in the Kashmir-Pakistan issue.

▲ Transnational Actors and Pan Ideologies

If subnational actors and especially their linkages with external parties are critical to the analysis and resolution of regional conflicts in the Third World, transnational actors, especially adherents of pan ideologies that transcend state boundaries, may be of equal importance. State boundaries, state institutions, and regimes in the Third World lack the unconditional legitimacy that has become a hallmark of developed industrialized states. Therefore, Third World states and regimes are open to challenges both from inside and from outside, that is, from both subnational and transnational forces and actors.

This perception equating the importance of transnational actors with that of subnational ones is buttressed by the experience of one critical region in the Third World—the Middle East—where since the 1950s first Arab nationalism (pan-Arabism) and then militant (or radical) Islam has posed a major threat to the legitimacy of several Middle Eastern, especially Arab, states and/or to the security of their regimes. However, these transnational forces and actors differ in subtle but very important ways from their subnational counterparts in terms of their operation and the way they impinge on regime and state security. These differences need to be analyzed carefully in order to realistically assess the impact of transnational forces on state and regime security in the Third World and their contribution to regional conflicts.

▲ Arab Nationalism

To begin with, one must distinguish the pan ideologies, whether pan-Arabism or pan-Islam, from actors who have adopted them to achieve objectives that may or may not be consistent with the internal logic of the ideologies themselves. In the case of Arab nationalism, while it is no doubt true that a pan-Arab identity, one of the many identities of peoples in the Arab Middle East, does exist in the Arab world—more strongly in the Fertile Crescent than in North Africa or in the sheikhdoms of the Gulf—it would be wrong to conclude that it has played a direct and significant role in the arenas of conflict and security even in the Fertile Crescent. At most, it has had considerable *instrumental* value in defining one of the major challenges to the legitimacy of Arab states and regimes. (I use the term *instrumental* deliberately, to denote the serviceability and therefore the malleability of this ideology, a malleability that has been taken advantage of by various actors within Arab states, whether those in power or those seeking power, to serve political ends that have had very little to do with the overriding political objective of the pan-Arab ideology, namely, the creation of a unified, strong Arab state at least encompassing the Fertile Crescent and Egypt.)

Even if one accepts the minimal definition of *pan-Arabism* — Arab unity on major regional and international issues within a single state if possible, outside it if necessary — one runs into major problems when one studies the various attempts that have been made in the recent past to make this ideal operational. There is clearly a difference between the political objectives of the major proponents of Arab nationalism and the objectives that one can deduce from the ideology. Analyses of the cases of former President Gamal Abdel Nasser of Egypt, President Hafez el-Assad of Syria, and President Saddam Hussein of Iraq, all of whom at one time or another professed to espouse the Arab nationalist cause, make very clear the discrepancy between theory and practice, or between the ideal and the reality.

Each of the three in his own way tried to use the Arab nationalist ideology to provide himself with sufficient political clout and legitimacy to build a pan-Arab constituency by appealing to the Arab masses over the heads of the rulers of individual Arab states, but for reasons that were far removed from the ideal of Arab unity except on limited issues and on terms beneficial to the individual promoter of the cause at a particular point in time. That each succeeded partially may be testimony to the relative lack of legitimacy of Arab states — and more particularly, of their regimes — but such success cannot be equated with the victory of pan-Arabism over state or regime considerations nor, certainly, over the state and regime interests represented by Nasser, Assad, and Saddam.

Nasser, who might be termed the reluctant Arab nationalist, was pushed into the role of pan-Arab hero by a conjunction of historical circumstances, above all by the importunity of Syrian politicians who implored him in 1957–58, after his political victory over the nationalization of the Suez Canal, to join Egypt in a union with Syria in order to prevent Western and Iraqi machinations that might lead to the Iraqi domination, if not annexation, of Syria and the creation of a pro-West, Hashemite-ruled Fertile Crescent, which was anathema to Arab nationalists of almost all hues. However, once he adopted the role of the pan-Arab hero, Nasser attempted to use his status for Egyptian ends, which thus led to Syrian disenchantment and the eventual abrogation of the Egyptian-Syrian Union in 1961. Even after the dissolution of the union, Nasser continued to don the mantle of the pan-Arab leader largely to preserve and promote Egypt's dominant role in inter-Arab politics.[5] But the strategy boomeranged in 1967 when Syrian adventurism pushed Egypt into a war with Israel that ended disastrously both for Egypt and for Nasser personally. What this episode makes clear is that Nasser viewed the Arab nationalist ideology primarily as an instrument, and he used it to serve Egypt's and his own interests rather than the interests of the Arab "nation" as a whole.

If Nasser's use of the pan-Arab ideology was largely opportunistic, the use that this ideology has been put to by Assad and Saddam has been both blatantly and vilely self-serving. Nasser at least carried some credibility both because of his initial reluctance to embrace the pan-Arab cause and because of his occasional genuine attempts to reconcile the conflicting demands of Arab nationalism with the interests of the Egyptian state. In fact, his decision to escalate the confrontation with Israel in May–June 1967, which ended so disastrously both for him and for Egypt, was the result of his inability to jettison a larger Arab cause even when it appeared to run directly contrary to Egyptian state interests and to the interests of his own regime.

Assad and Saddam, on the other hand, have not hesitated to jettison causes or embrace them when it has suited the interests of their regimes. In fact, by taking over the Syrian and the Iraqi Baath parties and making them handmaidens of their narrowly based regimes, Assad and Saddam have done incalculable harm to the Arab nationalist cause and the pan-Arab ideology, because the Baath, more than any other political organization in the Arab world, was responsible for a relatively clear formulation of the Arab nationalist ideology and had been its foremost proponent in the Fertile Crescent. By discrediting the Baath in the eyes of their own peoples, Assad and Saddam contributed greatly to discrediting the ideology the Baath had traditionally espoused. Their handling of the Palestine issue — *the* pan-Arab cause if there ever was one — and their treatment of Palestinian leaders and factions, who were wooed, used, and discarded depending upon what suited the needs of the Assad and Saddam regimes, are clear indications that they lacked commitment to the pan-Arab cause even while they continued to mouth Arab nationalist rhetoric.

Saddam's attempts to present himself as the great Arab hero during the Iran-Iraq War and then as the great defender of Islam during the Gulf War are examples of his opportunistic treatment of pan-Arabism and pan-Islam. Finally, the narrowly based, sectarian nature of the Syrian and Iraqi regimes — both of which draw their principal strength from minority regions and communities, the Alawites in Syria and certain segments of the Sunni Arabs in Iraq—attests to the fact that they view pan-Arabism as an instrument, and they use it principally to legitimize their unrepresentative and authoritarian rule in the eyes of their disgruntled populations.[6]

Thus, the foremost practitioners of pan-Arab politics have, in fact, subverted the cause, discredited the ideology, and behaved—especially Assad and Saddam—not merely as leaders of individual states with discrete interests but, what is worse, as sectional leaders within states desperately trying to preserve their regimes through any means, fair or foul, including the use of Arab nationalist symbols and rhetoric. They have, in fact, ended up acting as subnational rather than transnational actors even if they have used a transnational ideology to provide a veneer for their often bloody actions, inspired by no loftier ideal than the preservation of their regimes. Transnationalism, in the form of pan-Arabism, has been a failed God in the Arab world thanks to the total distortion of the ideology by the likes of Assad and Saddam. Genuine ideologues of pan-Arabism, such as Michel Aflaq or Salah-al-Din Bitar, the founding fathers of the Baath Party, have had little real effect on the course of Arab politics and have often ended up as tools of Arab leaders who have had their own axes to grind. One wonders whether with friends like Assad and Saddam, Arab nationalism has ever had any need for enemies.

▲ Political Islam

Political Islam, especially of the radical or militant variety, often incorrectly referred to as "Islamic fundamentalism," has had a history in the Middle East similar to that of Arab nationalism. There is one significant difference, however, in the fundamental tenets of political Islam and those of Arab nationalism. Political Islam never shared Arab nationalism's aspiration to unite the diverse peoples of the Muslim world, or even of the Middle East, into one political entity. The common theme of Islamic movements in the Middle East and in predominantly Muslim countries elsewhere is not unification but the transformation of existing Muslim states and societies into truly Islamic ones. They believe that this can be achieved by changing the framework of governance in Muslim states to conform to the rules of the *sharia* (Islamic law based on the Quran and the Prophet's traditions) and, more importantly, to the particular conceptions of an Islamic state that Islamic movements have evolved based on their often divergent interpretations of the golden age of Islam, during the time of the Prophet and his immediate political successors.

Even the earliest and one of the greatest political activists who worked on behalf of the pan-Islamic cause, Jamal-al-Din al-Afghani (1839–97), did not equate Islamic political resurgence with the political unity of the Islamic *umma* (the community of true believers). His main goal, and that of most of the ideological precursors of the current Islamic political resurgence, was to rid the Muslim world of Western colonial dominance, which he believed could not be done without reforming and strengthening Muslim societies. This reform and strengthening, he believed, could not be achieved without inculcating among Muslims—in predominantly Muslim countries as well as in those where they formed a large and politically very important minority—the idea of nationalism, even if it was at the expense of religious unity. To quote James Piscatori, "If there is irony in the idea of pan-Islam leading to the idea of nationalism, there is further irony in al-Afghani, the advocate of pan-Islam, arguing that religious unity was less important than national unity."[7] Afghani saw no contradiction between political Islam and nationalism, since both shared the objectives of anticolonialism, social reform, and national autonomy.

The history of Islamic political movements during the colonial period—from the Mahdi of the Sudan and the "Mad Mullah" of the Somali coast, through the Salafiya movement of North Africa and the followers of Abduh and Rida in Egypt, to the Sarekat Islam of Indonesia and the Jamiat-ul-Ulema-i-Hind of India—bears out this connection between political Islam, anticolonialism, and national autonomy. Most of the current manifestations of political Islam are heirs to this tradition. The difference is that Western "neocolonialism"—economic, military, and cultural—has been substituted for colonialism, and autocratic, often illegitimate, regimes have been substituted for colonial authority. Since in many instances, as in the case of Iran under the Shah, neocolonial dominance and unrepresentative, autocratic regimes work hand in glove with each other, the distinction between the two is often blurred, and an attack on the one becomes an attack on the other as well.

The critical variable in this set of relationships is the nature of the regime rather than the opposition to Western dominance. First of all, Western domination is no longer a matter of direct colonial subjugation; where it does operate, in either economic or political terms, or both, it is filtered through indigenous regimes and elites that are perceived to be acting as the agents of the West. In addition, Islamic movements are not alone in opposing Western domination. Various secular movements within predominantly Muslim countries also subscribe to this objective.

The autocratic and repressive nature of most regimes in the Muslim world, however, affects the importance or saliency of Islamic, as opposed to secular, avenues for the expression of dissent. The stifling of dissent and the violent and brutal suppression of political opposition by unrepresentative regimes usually leads to the virtual decimation of secular opposition movements. However, there are limits to governments' control of religious activity, whether undertaken within the mosque or outside it, even when such activity takes on a political character. Religious idioms, literature, observances, and institutions become both sources and conduits for the generation and spread of antiregime views and activities and play an unduly prominent role in the political arena of many Muslim countries. This is what happened in Iran in the 1970s and in Syria in the 1980s, and this is what is happening in Algeria, Tunisia, and Egypt today.[8]

Political Islam manages to become the focal point of opposition activities particularly in those parts of the Muslim world where autocratic regimes have been most successful in eliminating all political alternatives to Islamic militancy as avenues for the expression of popular dissent. As Ghassan Salame has put it, "In most Muslim countries, decades of repression of nationalist, liberal, and Marxist trends left a wide-open, depoliticized society, a political and intellectual vacuum, that is now filled mostly by Islamic militants."[9]

Given these movements' similar political vocabularies and their culturally hostile attitude toward the West—which is at least partially related to the fact that indigenous regimes and political and economic elites who are their immediate targets are often Westernized, if only superficially—it is easy to misrepresent them as parts of a unified fundamentalist movement bent on undermining, indeed destroying, Western interests throughout the Muslim world. Even eminent Western historians of the Muslim world such as Bernard Lewis have at times fallen prey to this fallacy.[10]

A more accurate explanation of Islamic political activism can be arrived at by viewing instances of Islamic militancy within their discrete social and political contexts and in terms of the nature of the regimes and the strategies these regimes employ to stifle dissent. That these movements share a common religious vocabulary tends to hide the fact that there are multifarious differences among them, determined by their specific contexts. Bernard Lewis, who, as stated above, has not been averse to demonizing political Islam as a monolithic force threatening Judeo—Christian values, has himself recently been forced to admit that "Islamic fundamentalism is a loose and inaccurate term that designates a number of different, and sometimes contrasting, forms of Islamic religious militancy. . . . The more oppressive the regime, the greater help it gives to the fundamentalists by eliminating competing oppositions."[11] When political Islam is interpreted in this way, it becomes clear that it is very much a subnational rather than a transnational phenomenon, although it does possess a transnational vocabulary and can on occasion produce sympathetic vibrations across state boundaries.

Furthermore, although political Islam has in several recent instances been a major force opposing established regimes and challenging their legitimacy, in a number of cases it has been used as an instrument to legitimize existing political orders and ruling elites. In Iran, political Islam was used in quick succession to serve both purposes. In 1978–79 it was used as the major instrument for the overthrow of the Shah's regime. With the victory of the revolution, Islam was adopted as the premier agent for the legitimization of the revolutionary regime. It is instructive to note that even within the coalition of revolutionary forces that overthrew the Shah there were several different interpretations of what political Islam was supposed to signify. The Khomeini-clerical variety had to contend with and overcome, sometimes with the use of brute force, other strands of political Islam—for example, the liberal Islamic strand symbolized by Mehdi Bazargan and the socially revolutionary variety represented by the Mojahedin-e-Khalq—before it could consolidate its power within the country and its control over the entire political process.

In Saudi Arabia, Egypt, and Pakistan, the Islamic establishment has often been used to provide legitimacy to the regime in power. In some cases this has led to a division in the political realm between establishment and counter-establishment Islam, or between Islam from above and Islam from below. The takeover of the Grand Mosque in Mecca by Islamic radicals in 1979 and the assassination of Egyptian president Anwar Sadat by Muslim militants in 1981 were as much a challenge to the Wahabi religious establishment in the first case and to the official Islam represented by Al-Azhar in the second as they were to the Saudi monarchy and the Egyptian government.

It would not be wrong to conclude that political Islam presents a very fractured picture whose pieces do not fit together because they are determined not so much by an abstract ideology—assuming that one can get a consensus about the ideology itself—as by their discrete social and political contexts and their specific historical circumstances. It follows, therefore, that attempts to project such a fragmented and context-specific phenomenon as a monolithic threat to Western civilization and to international order are exercises in an extreme form of sophistry.[12]

▲ The Paradox of Transnational Ideologies as Subnational Actors

It also follows—and this is more important from the point of view of this volume—that political Islam, far from being a transnational actor, is, like Arab nationalism (in its operationalized form), a subnational actor, although sometimes an exceptionally forceful one that can and does have major consequences, often negative but sometimes positive, for the legitimacy of established regimes in predominantly Muslim countries. In the final analysis, however, such consequences are directly related to the nature of the regimes themselves rather than to some abstract politico-religious ideology that has been presented under the misnomer "Islamic fundamentalism."

Challenges to unrepresentative and autocratic regimes in the Third World have emerged in the guise of several militant and messianic ideologies, ranging from Marxism-Leninism to Catholic liberation theology. Political Islam is one such challenge. However, to trace these challenges solely, or even primarily, to the ideologies mentioned above while disregarding the character of regimes and the nature of the socioeconomic and political order over which they preside is likely to thoroughly distort all subsequent analysis that flows from this fundamentally flawed premise.

For our purpose it is better to treat both Arab nationalism and political Islam, or rather the movements and personalities that arrogate to themselves the right to speak and act on behalf of these ideologies, as subnational rather than transnational actors. These are actors who certainly contribute substantially to the dynamics of conflict in the Third World, above all by either challenging or supporting vulnerable regimes, but do so within specific states and in contextually determined situations. One cannot deny that many intrastate conflicts related to the Arab nationalist or the Islamic challenge have the potential to become interstate ones; but as noted above, this is also true of many ethnic and secessionist conflicts in the Third World that are unrelated to either political Islam or Arab nationalism.

The primary blame for such conflicts therefore cannot be laid at the door of the ideologies discussed above. It rests squarely with the states and regimes in the Third World, many of which lack the required degree of legitimacy as well as the sagacity essential for the containment, if not the total elimination, by political and accommodationist means of internal challenges to their existence and rule. The secondary blame rests with those foreign powers, especially the major ones among them, who for geostrategic or geoeconomic reasons, or a combination of the two, provide aid and succor to the governments or insurgents involved in intrastate conflicts in the Third World. For analysts interested in coping with regional conflict, a clear appreciation of this two-dimensional reality that is at the root of much Third World conflict is absolutely necessary.

▲ Summary and Conclusions

A clear understanding of the importance and the essential nature of the involvement of subnational and transnational actors in regional conflicts in the Third World makes it possible to some degree to make general prescriptions that could help further the objectives of conflict management, conflict reduction, and conflict resolution, which the editors of this volume have posited as inherently desirable. The first of these prescriptions can only be couched in the nature of a general warning: do not overlook the unique and specific nature of historical, social, economic, and, above all, political contexts that give rise to each discrete conflict. Superficial similarities between attempts at secession or between irredentist claims may hide fundamental differences between actors' goals and strategies as well as between the regional and international environments that would render the optimum solution in one case totally irrelevant in another.

Second, this does not mean, however, that no general guidelines can be developed to help analysts and policymakers map out the contours of strategies that can move regional conflicts toward desirable conclusions. It only means that analysts and policymakers alike must be fully aware both of the forest and of the trees when they design such strategies.

Third, in most, if not all, conflicts in the Third World the goals of order, welfare, and legitimacy (OWL) cannot be enhanced without primary emphasis on the domestic dimension of such conflicts and on the goals espoused by *internal, therefore subnational,* actors, including governments, insurgent groups, ideological movements, and sympathetic populations. Even when some of these actors take recourse to transnational ideologies to justify their positions, they act basically as subnational rather than transnational protagonists. Attempts to impose solutions that cater primarily to the interstate dimension of conflicts in the Third World in most cases will not address the root causes that triggered these conflicts in the first place. This means that the often contradictory demands of ethno-nationalism and state making and of regime change and regime preservation will have to be carefully balanced while attempts are made to find solutions that may be acceptable to all the domestic parties concerned.

Optimally, reconciliation between these apparently contradictory sets of demands is feasible only through a liberal-constitutional and democratic framework, within which solutions can be negotiated on the basis of the give-and-take that undergirds all open, participatory political systems. But given the fragility of many Third World states' structures, the weakness of their political institutions, and the unrepresentative character of their regimes, it is unrealistic to expect to transform them overnight into representative polities and cohesive societies. Nonetheless, any inducements, including conditions imposed on external assistance, that can move such states along the road to greater participation and less coercion may be useful in the long run, even if only marginally, in creating the necessary conditions for the management and reduction of internal conflicts.

Fourth, it would be naive, however, to assume that the democratization of Third World polities will by itself provide conditions sufficient for the elimination or resolution of internal conflicts. State making, even if carried out primarily by persuasive means, inevitably entails some degree of violence on the part of the state and counterviolence on the part of recalcitrant segments of the population.[13] This is borne out by the case of present-day India, where the relatively successful functioning of a democratic system has not prevented the emergence of major challenges to the Indian state from disgruntled ethnic and religious groups in the northeast, as well as in Punjab and Kashmir. In the final analysis, when the values associated with order, as interpreted by state elites, come into headlong confrontation with those associated with welfare or legitimacy, the state considers itself duty-bound to see that the former triumph over the latter, even if it means using brute force. That the state may not be successful in imposing order in many instances is a different matter. In fact, the less successful the state is in imposing order quickly, as in Lebanon during the fifteen years of civil war, the greater the intensity of violence and the more extensive the arena of conflict.

Fifth, conflicts in the Third World, even when they are primarily internal, do not take place in an international vacuum. The major protagonists in Third World conflicts usually attempt to manipulate the international environment in order to further their objectives. Given this dependence of the principal actors on the international environment for political support, weapons supply, economic aid, and so forth, external parties, especially the great powers and international organizations, can play a role in controlling and managing conflict in the Third World if they act "responsibly." With the end of bipolarity and of the Cold War, there are greater opportunities for international institutions like the United Nations and for a concert of great powers to act in such "responsible" fashion in the arena of Third World regional conflicts.

There are, however, inherent limits to such international involvement, especially in the arena of conflict and security, in a system composed primarily of sovereign states.[14] Moreover, if "responsible" action is simply equated with the maintenance of a status quo that is unacceptable to one of the principal parties to a conflict (as in the conflict between Israel and the Palestinians) or with rewarding the aggressor because it appears too costly to force the latter to vacate its aggression (as in Bosnia), it can very easily delegitimize international involvement in the eyes of substantial segments of the world's population. Again, if the collective security mechanism is applied selectively to suit great-power ends (as in the Gulf War) rather than as an automatic mechanism that is designed to become operational in any and all instances where certain fundamental rules of international law are violated, it will delegitimize such external intervention.

Furthermore, institutional mechanisms are difficult to implement when, as is the case in many Third World conflicts, at least one of the main protagonists is not a state but a subnational entity. The state-centric bias of the international system makes it virtually impossible to use formal, institutional mechanisms to pressure established states to come to terms with dissident or secessionist elements within their populations. Also, subnational groups are relatively immune to such institutional pressures because they are not formal participants in the system and thus have to routinely work around the systemic constraints imposed on them in times of conflict.

Informal pressures relating to weapons transfers, economic assistance, human rights monitoring, and so forth, may be somewhat more effective in the management and containment of Third World conflicts, whether they are of an interstate or intrastate character or a mixture of the two. However, even then, both policymakers and analysts must be aware that international pressures, while they may have a major impact on the outcome of conflicts in the short run, are only marginally effective as far as the outbreaks and the continuous festering of such conflicts are concerned. This is because most of the conflicts in this category are fundamentally rooted in the domestic and regional dynamics of Third World politics, which are largely autonomous of international control. This relative autonomy is, in turn, associated with the fact that most Third World conflicts are essentially related to, if not the direct consequence of, the primary political enterprise in the Third World, namely, that of state making and nation building. This enterprise inevitably pits not only the state-defined concept of nationalism against ethno-nationalism but also contiguous states against one another as the latter simultaneously try to impose order and extend control over contested territorial and demographic space. Such conflicts of state making and nation building, as the Western European experience of a bygone age, not to mention the current situation in the Balkans, testifies,[15] are the most intractable of all political contestations. The presence of highly emotive transnational ideologies, like pan-Arabism and political Islam, that can be used to challenge state structures and regimes in strategically important parts of the Third World adds both to the conflict potential in these regions and to the difficulty of finding modes of conflict management and reduction.

Coping with regional conflicts in the Third World is a very difficult, if not impossible, exercise because even the most favorable international environment and the most cooperative international venture cannot deal, except marginally, with the fundamental roots of these conflicts and the visceral desires that motivate the protagonists. The best one can do is to fully inform oneself of all the complexities involved in such conflicts in order not to approach them with abstract paradigms that may be totally alien to the reality.

NOTES

1. Karin Lindgren, Birger Heldt, Kjell-Ake Nordquist, and Peter Wallensteen, "Major Armed Conflicts in 1990," *SIPRI Yearbook 1991: World Armaments and Disarmament* (Oxford: Oxford University Press, 1991), 345.

2. For the argument that state-making and societal responses to it form the fundamental basis of the Third World states' security problems, see Mohammed Ayoob, "The Security Predicament of the Third World State: Reflections on State-Making in a Comparative Perspective," in *The Insecurity Dilemma: National Security of Third World States,* ed. Brian Job (Boulder, Colo.: Lynne Reinner, 1992), 63–80.

3. Donald L. Horowitz, *Ethnic Groups in Conflict* (Berkeley: University of California Press, 1985), 230.

4. Alexis Heraclides, "Secessionist Minorities and External Involvement," *International Organization* 44 (summer 1990): 378.

5. For details of Nasser's preeminent role in inter-Arab politics, see Malcolm H. Kerr, *The Arab Cold War: Gamal 'Abd al-Nasir and His Rivals, 1958–1970,* 3d ed. (New York: Oxford University Press, 1971).

6. For the best available and relatively up-to-date accounts of the Assad and Saddam regimes, see Patrick Seale, *Asad: The Struggle for the Middle East* (Berkeley: University of California Press, 1988); and Efraim Karsh and Inari Rautsi, *Saddam Hussein: A Political Biography* (New York: Free Press, 1991).

7. James P. Piscatori, *Islam in a World of Nation-States* (Cambridge: Cambridge University Press, 1986), 78.

8. For North Africa, see Claire Spencer, *The Maghreb in the 1990s,* Adelphi Papers No. 274 (London: International Institute for Strategic Studies, Feb. 1993). Spencer concludes that "although Islamism may be seen as a cause of current unrest, it is more properly a symptom. More than any other force in the region, it has articulated the

deep-rooted malaise of repressed populations and proffered alternative visions of a more moral society" (57). For a journalistic account of the recent upsurge in Islamic militancy in Egypt, see Chris Hedges, "As Islamic Militants Thunder, Egypt Grows More Nervous," *New York Times*, Nov. 12, 1992, A1, A7.

9. Ghassan Salame, "Islam and the West," *Foreign Policy* 90 (spring 1993): 30. Salame goes on to argue that "In retrospect, it seems the real moment to democratize was a decade or two ago, when a secular alternative to the ruling regimes remained. Then, Islamists were still politically marginal, the political discourse was predominantly secular, most elites were Western-educated, governments were still able to control societies, the demographic bomb had not yet exploded, urbanization was still manageable, and secular parties had not yet been discredited" (30).

10. See, for example, Bernard Lewis, "The Return of Islam," *Commentary* 61 (Jan. 1976): 39–49; and idem, "The Roots of Muslim Rage," *Atlantic Monthly*, Sept. 1990, 47–60. In the former article Lewis goes to the extent of asserting categorically that given the history of Islam's antagonistic relations with the West, and particularly that of Muslim subjugation by the West during the last century, "both the Saturday people [Jews] and the Sunday people [Christians] are now suffering the consequences" of the Islamic backlash in the Middle East, most specifically in Palestine-Israel and in Lebanon (49). This one-dimensional explanation of complex conflicts such as those between Zionists (later Israelis) and Palestinian Arabs (both Muslim and Christian) and among the various politico-religious factions in Lebanon (in which at one time or another have been pitted not only Muslims against Christians but Sunnis against Shias, Shias against Shias, Maronites against Maronites, and each one of these factions against the Palestinians) is a classic example of the reductionist "orientalist" explanations of political phenomena in the Muslim world so forcefully castigated by Edward W. Said in his book *Orientalism* (London: Routledge & Kegan Paul, 1978).

11. Bernard Lewis, "Rethinking the Middle East," *Foreign Affairs* 71 (fall 1992): 115–16.

12. For an excellent refutation of the "Islamic threat" thesis, see John L. Esposito, *The Islamic Threat: Myth or Reality?* (New York: Oxford University Press, 1992).

13. For a very persuasive argument that leads to this conclusion, see Youssef Cohen, Brian R. Brown, and A. F. K. Organski, "The Paradoxical Nature of State-Making: The Violent Creation of Order," *American Political Science Review* 75, no. 4 (1981): 901–10.

14. For a more detailed argument, see Mohammed Ayoob, "Squaring the Circle: Collective Security in a System of States," in *Collective Security in a Changing World*, ed. Thomas G. Weiss (Boulder, Colo.: Lynne Reinner, 1993), 45–62.

15. For details, in addition to the standard history books on modern Europe, see Charles Tilly, ed., *The Formation of National States in Western Europe* (Princeton: Princeton University Press, 1975).

THREE | Capabilities, Roles,
and Strategies

JANICE GROSS STEIN

10 Communications, Signaling, and Intelligence

Embedded enemy images are a serious obstacle to conflict management, routinization, reduction, or resolution. Once formed, enemy images tend to become deeply rooted and resistant to change, even when one adversary attempts to signal a change in intent. The images themselves then contribute autonomously to the perpetuation and the intensification of conflict.

Structural explanations of conflict generally give little attention to the processes that mediate between attributes of the environment and behavior. These kinds of explanations assume that conflict can be explained independently of the images of its participants. Yet, modern psychology has demonstrated repeatedly that stimulus-response models are inaccurate representations of human behavior. Insofar as the same stimulus is interpreted differently by different individuals, individual beliefs matter. The way people see the world shapes how they formulate their goals, assess the constraints, process information, and choose strategies. Individuals are not passive receptors of environmental stimuli; they actively construct representations of their environment. The extent of individual variation in interpretation suggests that structural explanations of political behavior are rarely determining.

247

Images of an enemy can form as a response to the persistently aggressive actions of another state or group. These kinds of images are not the subject of this chapter. A conflict generated by an aggressive Hitler or militant leaders with vested interests in escalating conflict is generally not amenable to reduction unless intentions change. Rather, I focus on conflict generated by images that form when the intent of the other is not hostile but action is ambiguous in an unstructured environment; and conflict generated by images that were once accurate but no longer reflect the intentions of one or more parties. Under these conditions, social-psychological analysis is important both in the explanation of conflict and in generating prescriptions to reduce its intensity.

My analysis focuses on the images of paramount leaders, but I also examine the roles of elites and publics to analyze the still ill-understood social-psychological processes of the creation, retention, and revision of enemy images. First I examine the psychological, social, and political processes that create and reinforce hostile images. Nevertheless, at times leaders have changed their images. Drawing on historical cases, I explore the conditions under which adversarial images are modified and look particularly at the strategies of reassurance one adversary can use to promote change of image by another.

▲ The Creation of Enemy Images

An image is a set of beliefs or hypotheses and theories that an individual is convinced are valid. An image includes both experience-based knowledge and values or beliefs about desirable behavior.[1] A stereotyped image is a simplistic, unsophisticated belief about another individual, group, or state that can include both descriptive and normative components. Most enemy images are simple in structure and stereotypical in content. Converging streams of evidence from motivational psychology, social psychology, cultural anthropology, international relations, and comparative politics suggest that people are motivated to form and maintain images of an enemy even in the absence of solid, confirming evidence of hostile intentions.

Several fundamental human needs can interact together to promote and reinforce enemy images. Motivational psychologists suggest that the innate human need for security is closely connected to the emotion of fear.[2] In part because the need for security, like all other human needs, is difficult to satisfy permanently and completely, people tend to fear that their security is threatened. Other things being equal, this fear can generate hostile images.

Social psychologists have also identified a fundamental human need for social identity and group belonging.[3] Intergroup behavior is generally defined as individuals interacting in terms of their group identifications.[4] This need for collective as well as individual identity leads to a differentiation between "we" and "they," a distinction between "insiders" and "outsiders." These distinctions can promote the creation of enemy images when environmental conditions are conducive. In the effort to establish or defend group identity, groups and their leaders can identify their distinctive attributes as virtues and label those of others as vices. This kind of *labeling* responds to deep social-psychological needs and can easily lead to the creation of enemy stereotypes.[5]

An examination of massive state repression leading to group extinction concludes that genocides and politicides are extreme attempts to maintain the security of one's identity group at the expense of other groups.[6] The evidence from cultural anthropology is generally supportive of the impact of group identity on stereotyping and intergroup conflict. Primordial attachments to language, culture, and group identity grow, rather than diminish, as processes of social mobilization intensify in modern societies.[7] Ethnocentrism, or strong feelings of self-group centrality and superiority, often draw on myths that are central to national culture. Ethnocentrism breeds stereotyping and a misplaced suspicion of others' intentions.[8]

Conflicts of identity are particularly acute when group members think that recognition of another's identity can compromise their own, when they perceive granting rights to the other as an abdication of their own identity. The Israeli-Palestinian conflict has been this kind of existential conflict; because both identities are tied to the same territory, leaders on both sides have long felt that acknowledgment of the other's identity would fundamentally compromise their own.[9] In these kinds of existential conflicts over identity, enemy images are easily formed and resistant to change.

Common cognitive biases also can contribute to the creation of enemy images. The egocentric bias leads people to overestimate the extent to which they are the target of others' actions. Leaders are then likely to see their group or state as the target of the hostility of others even when it are not. The fundamental attribution error leads people to exaggerate the importance of dispositional over situational factors in explaining the undesired behavior of others. Leaders are therefore likely to attribute undesirable behavior to the disposition of their adversary rather than to the environment their adversary faces.[10] Finally, the self-serving bias, or attribution of positive events to oneself and negative events to others, can contribute directly to the creation of an enemy image.

Fundamental human needs and cognitive biases do not always contribute to stereotyping and conflict. These are necessary but insufficient explanations of the formation of enemy images. If they were sufficient, individuals, groups, and states would have strong enemy images all the time. This is clearly not the case. The critical variables are the kinds of environments in which individuals and groups seek to satisfy their needs. Certain kinds of international and domestic conditions facilitate the formation of enemy images.[11]

The international environment of states can promote the creation of enemy images even in the absence of aggressive behavior by others. The distinguishing characteristic of a *security dilemma* is that behavior perceived by adversaries as threatening and aggressive is a defensive response to an inhospitable strategic environment. To enhance their security, leaders take measures that simultaneously diminish the security of others. They are likely to do so when geography is harsh and provides no buffer zone or margin for error; when offensive and defensive technologies are difficult to distinguish; and when the relative power balance between adversaries is changing, so that for at least one of the two the advantages of striking first are substantial.[12] When defensive action by one is interpreted as offensive by another, this can feed and fuel an image of an enemy that is then reinforced over time in a spiraling process of interaction.

The formation of enemy images can also be triggered by domestic factors. Lower levels of modernization, for example, are correlated with stronger nationalism and distrust of others.[13] Groups and coalitions whose interests are served by conflict abroad or ongoing hostility can capture the political process and propagate enemy images designed to intensify hostility. To gain public support, parochial interest groups that benefit from militarist or imperialist policies create strategic rationalizations or "myths." Especially in controlled political regimes, leaders and elites who dominate the instruments of communication can manipulate mass images. Over time, some elites come to believe the myths that they have created, making these images extraordinarily resistant to change. This process of national mythmaking that perpetuates militaristic behavior is most likely in countries with concentrated interest groups who trade and logroll.[14]

▲ The Persistence of Enemy Images

Once enemy images are in place, they are extraordinarily difficult to change. In the first instance, because enemy images generate behavior that is hostile and confrontational, an adversary will respond with hostile action. A cycle of reciprocal behavior then reinforces adversary images by providing allegedly confirming evidence of hostile intentions. Enemy images tend to become self-fulfilling and self-reinforcing.[15]

Enemy images are also the product of deeply rooted social and psychological needs and frequently serve the interests of important groups and elites. Consequently, they become central and well embedded within larger belief systems. Theories of cognitive consistency postulate that individuals possess *belief systems,* or sets of internally consistent and hierarchically organized beliefs.[16] Theories of cognitive consistency expect that the least central parts of a belief system, that is, those with the fewest interdependent cognitions, will change first. Central beliefs are generally most resistant to change. People tend to modify at the margin and to change peripheral beliefs first.

Closely related, cognitive theories predict that in the process of making inferences, people seek to maintain their beliefs by reducing the challenge of discrepant information. The well-established tendency to discount inconsistent information contributes significantly to the persistence of beliefs.[17] When people receive discrepant information, they generally make the smallest possible change in their beliefs; they will change their beliefs incrementally, allow a large number of exceptions and special cases, and make superficial alterations rather than change their central beliefs. Indeed, exposure to contradictory information frequently strengthens beliefs.[18] In addition, people tend actively to seek and interpret information that confirms the negative image.[19]

Cognitive psychology has identified a number of heuristics that can make enemy images resistant to change even in the face of discrepant information.[20] Heuristics are the rules leaders use to test the propositions embedded in their beliefs. They describe how individuals process information, using convenient shortcuts or rules of thumb. Three of the best-documented heuristics are availability, representativeness, and anchoring. The heuristic *availability* refers to people's tendency to interpret present information in terms of what is most easily available in their cognitive repertoire.[21] An enemy image is usually easily available and salient. The heuristic *representativeness* refers to people's proclivity to exaggerate similarities between one event and a prior class of events.[22] When action is ambiguous, people tend to classify it as representative of earlier hostile behavior. The heuristic *anchoring* refers to the estimation of the magnitude or degree of the same phenomenon by picking an *available* initial value as a reference point and making a comparison.[23] Again, enemy images often provide the *available* reference point and drive the interpretation of the data.

▲ Image Change

Stability in enemy images is the default, and change is the exception. Yet conservatism does not hold unconditionally. Belief systems and schemata, the active reconstruction of experience at a higher level of abstraction, also change, at times dramatically. Psychological, social, and political variables affect the propensity of change in enemy images.

Change in images is in part a function of the rate at which discrepant information occurs. Cognitive psychologists identify several factors that facilitate change.[24] They suggest that important beliefs can change dramatically when there is no other way to account for "large" amounts of contradictory data, but they do not specify thresholds.[25] Greater change will occur when information arrives in large batches rather than bit by bit. Significant change in beliefs about another also occurs when subjects are exposed to incongruent information and are persuaded that the behavior is not arbitrary, but reflects the nature of the target, when inconsistent information is attributed to dispositional rather than situational factors.[26] However, the social and political conditions that promote such uncharacteristic attributions to dispositional factors have not been satisfactorily identified.[27]

Images can also change incrementally over time. As people consider information about an adversary that is inconsistent with their previous knowledge, they incorporate into their belief the conditions under which the image does not hold. This kind of process permits gradual change and adjustment.[28] When permeability grows in controlled political systems, or as leaders and elites receive new information about their rival, their image of their adversary can change incrementally.

Change is also a function of cognitive complexity, or the complexity of the cognitive rules used to process information about objects and situations. *Cognitive complexity* refers to the structure or the organization of cognition, rather than to the content of thought. Complexity has a somewhat contradictory impact on image change.

The more complex the cognitive system, the more capable the decision maker is of making new or subtle distinctions when confronted with new information.[29] Experts with highly complex cognitive schemata are more sensitive to new information than novices with low cognitive complexity, whose schemata are likely to be fixed and rigid.[30] On the other hand, because experts have more relevant information, they can more easily incorporate inconsistent information as exceptions and special cases; therefore, incongruent data have less impact on their schemata than they would have on those of novices.[31]

When experts are confronted with inconsistent information over time, they are more likely to change their images than are novices. Experts located in politically relevant institutions are likely leaders in the social and political process of image change. An individual's level of cognitive complexity is not unchanging, but responds to situational and socializing factors. Crisis-induced stress decreases cognitive complexity, while pluralistic values socialize people to the need to balance competing images.[32]

Cognitive complexity does not provide an entirely satisfactory explanation of the cognitive dynamics of image change. The content of images can change in the absence of structural change; cognitive content and structure can change simultaneously; or changes in cognitive structure can lead to changes in cognitive content. Analysts of cognitive complexity do not explain how and why complexity increases and whether it precedes or accompanies change in the content of images.

Cognitive explanations of image change also pay insufficient attention to the emotional factors that can motivate — or inhibit — change. Not only "cold" cognition but "hot" emotions also affect the likelihood of image change. The less the intensity of an emotional commitment to an image, the less resistant it is to change in the face of disconfirming information.[33]

Finally, theories of social cognition do not specify the external conditions or mediating causes of any of these changes.[34] Critics rightly contend that the neglect of context is disturbing; the social in social cognition research is largely absent.[35] Theories of social cognition do not model explicitly the processes that link environmental stimuli to cognitive constructs and explain how images change. They do not examine the political and social interests that have a stake in change, nor do they explore the social configurations that promote change in group images. Until they do, theories of social cognition will remain incomplete as a theoretical tool in the analysis of change in enemy images.

▲ Political Learning

To explain the changes in enemy images that facilitate conflict management, routinization, reduction, and resolution, I draw on propositions from social psychology to develop a concept of "trial-and-error learning" from failure. Learning is a subset of cognitive change; not all change is learning, but all learning is change. Theories of learning are inherently dynamic. Learning is also an explicitly normative concept; it measures cognitive change against some set of explicit criteria.

There is as yet no unified theory of learning, and psychology has not identified the conditions or thresholds at which different forms of learning are likely to occur. Most psychological theories of learning are not very useful in specifying the dynamics of learning, in large part because they analyze learning within highly structured environments. Learning theorists in educational and experimental psychology are associationist. They treat learning as a change in the probability of a specified response in the face of changing reward contingencies.[36] This concept of learning is not helpful in those social and political environments where appropriate responses are unknown or disputed.

Political psychologists distinguish between simple and complex learning. Learning is simple when means are better adjusted to ends. Complex learning occurs when people develop more differentiated images and when these images are integrated into higher-order structures that highlight difficult trade-offs.[37] Learning can be causal, an analysis of causal paths, or diagnostic, an examination of the conditions under which causal generalizations apply.[38] At its highest level, complex learning may lead to a reordering or a redefinition of goals. From this perspective, learning must include the development of more complex structures as well as changes in content.[39]

These concepts of learning are a useful first cut at explaining changes in leaders' images of their adversaries that then shape new directions in policy, but they fail to distinguish change from learning. Without some evaluative criteria, any cognitive change can be considered learning, and the concept of learning becomes redundant. Change in cognitive content or structure does not always constitute the "learning" that is necessary for conflict reduction. Saddam Hussein, for example, in the year preceding his decision to invade Kuwait, extended his schema and developed a differentiated analysis of a changing international system. He then concluded that the United States was engaged in a conspiracy to undermine his regime. Since the United States had no intention whatsoever of undermining his regime and took no action to do so, this cognitive change is accurately characterized as paranoid thinking that led to escalation of conflict.[40] These changes in Saddam's schema do provide a powerful explanation of his foreign policy behavior.[41] They cannot, however, be considered learning. Inescapably built into the concept of political learning is an evaluation of the structure and content of cognitive change.[42] These kinds of evaluative judgments inevitably are and will be essentially contested.

More helpful are several strands of social-psychological theory and research that examine the liabilities of success and the benefits of failure in promoting organizational learning.[43] When failure challenges the status quo, it can draw attention to problems and stimulate the search for solutions. Only certain kinds of failure promote learning; highly predictable failures provide no new information, but unanticipated failures that challenge old ways of representing problems are more likely to stimulate new formulations. Responding to failure, leaders can "learn through experimentation" rather than through more traditional patterns of avoidance.[44]

Learning through failure can provoke a series of sequential experiments that generate quick feedback and allow for a new round of trial-and-error experimentation.[45] This trial-and-error model of learning captures the dynamics of social cognition far more effectively than do cognitive theories in which the perceiver is a "passive onlooker, who . . . doesn't *do* anything—doesn't mix it up with the folks he's watching, never tests his judgments in action or interaction."[46] It does not represent learning as a neat linear process with clear causal antecedents, but as a messy, dynamic, interactive social, organizational, and political process.

In my analysis I first examine the internal conditions that can promote learning by one adversary. For purposes of this chapter, I define learning as changes in enemy images that promote conflict management, routinization, reduction, and resolution. I then explore the strategies that leaders can use to promote the kinds of changes in their adversary's image of them that can lead to a reduction in conflict. The distinction between internal and external stimuli to learning and change in enemy image is artificial, since the process is usually highly interactive, but it is convenient for analytic purposes.

Former Presidents Anwar el-Sadat of Egypt and Mikhail Sergeevich Gorbachev of the Soviet Union are two outstanding examples of political learning. Both developed far more complex and differentiated images of their adversary and initiated a series of actions that triggered a process of image change by their adversaries and, consequently, of conflict reduction.[47] Changes in the images of their adversary led to changes in behavior that in turn provoked further changes in their enemy images. Learning accelerated in the doing.

From 1986 to 1988, Gorbachev and some of his colleagues did not reject the earlier Soviet image of the imperialist intentions of the United States. Rather, they located this belief within a broad set of situational constraints that created new imperatives for the United States and the Soviet Union. Gorbachev acknowledged the mutuality of security in the nuclear age, the interdependence of states in an integrated system, the danger of inadvertent war and the risks inherent in the security dilemma, the importance of "defensive defense" in ameliorating the security dilemma, and some of the difficult trade-offs inherent in this representation of the problem of security. These changes reflected to a far greater degree than earlier Soviet concepts did the consensus of experts, within the Soviet Union and abroad, on the representation of the problem of security in the nuclear age.[48]

Political psychologists have noted that turning-point decisions, or decisions that deviate significantly from the pattern of prior decisions, depend on resolving the contradiction between the attitude toward the object and the attitude toward the situation in favor of the latter.[49] Gorbachev did just that and began the process of change in his image of the enemy and definition of the situation that were critical to the process of conflict reduction.

Sadat acknowledged Israel's deep-seated need for recognition and legitimacy and recognized the psychological obstacles, the fear and distrust, and the stereotypical images that impeded learning and change. In both cases, leaders located their image of their adversary within a more complex cognitive structure that acknowledged some of the difficult trade-offs. This nesting of an enemy image within a broad set of situational constraints was the first critical step in the modification of their images.

To develop a satisfactory explanation of image change through political learning, it is necessary to identify the conditions and strategies that promote learning. One obvious explanation is the changes in the international distribution of capabilities, the relative decline in Soviet and Egyptian capabilities in relation to those of the United States and Israel, respectively. If changes in Soviet and Egyptian enemy images are a straightforward response to structural changes in the international system, then the analysis of political dynamics and image change is epiphenomenal and unnecessary. If, on the other hand, there were important divisions within the Soviet and Egyptian leadership, and interpretations of the environment were contested, then structural factors alone cannot provide a sufficient explanation of the change in Soviet and Egyptian concepts. In both the Soviet Union in the mid-1980s and in Egypt in the mid-1970s there were deep divisions within the leadership. New interpretations were bitterly contested. It is therefore unsatisfying to explain the changes in Soviet and Egyptian images of their adversaries as rational adaptation to unambiguous feedback from their environments.[50]

Broad social and political factors have also been suggested as conditions of image change and political learning.[51] Shifting political coalitions can be a powerful explanation of image change if leaders are chosen primarily because of the content of their beliefs. Both Gorbachev and Sadat, however, struggled to shape coalitions to support policies that flowed from their changed images; in both cases, new coalitions did not demand changes toward their adversary from their leader.

Generational change and political succession can also explain a fundamental change in leaders' images; the source of change is not individual learning but a change in elites. Generational change, however, is helpful, but not entirely satisfactory, as an explanation of image change in the Soviet Union, but it is irrelevant in Egypt. Gorbachev was a generation younger than Brezhnev and many of his colleagues, but many in Gorbachev's generation did not change.[52] In Egypt, Sadat was of the same generation as Gamal Abdel al-Nasser, and he learned after he had been president for several years.

Political succession and domestic politics are helpful in explaining whose images prevail under what set of political conditions. Shifts in social structure and political power determine whether leaders can implement policies based on changed images. They do not and cannot address the important questions of why Gorbachev and Sadat began to "think" differently about security and how and why they changed their images and developed new concepts to organize their thinking about foreign and defense policy.

▲ Why Leaders Learn

The changes in Gorbachev's and Sadat's images of their adversary are suggestive of two conditions that motivated political learning.[53] The first condition was the importance of domestic reform to both men. Gorbachev came to office committed to domestic restructuring of a largely stalemated economic and political system. He quickly learned that future resource commitments implicit in the standing threat assessments of the Soviet military would seriously constrain economic restructuring at home.[54]

Anwar el-Sadat similarly was motivated by his domestic agenda. After the Ramadan War in October 1973, Sadat gave new importance to the roles of the private and the foreign sector, which were expected to provide both finance and technology. The new economic strategy of quasi-liberal experimentation, *al-infitah al-iqtisadi*, was consistent with Sadat's strategy of conflict reduction; stabilization of Egypt's security environment was essential if the capital and investment necessary to push the economy forward were to flow into Egypt.

A second factor common to both leaders was their prior experience of the failure of alternatives to accommodation. Even before he became general secretary, Gorbachev invited experts from the Foreign Ministry and the academic institutes of the Academy of Sciences to private discussions of Soviet policy in Afghanistan. He was told of the growing costs of the Soviet intervention and its poor prospects; Afghanistan was the Soviet "Vietnam."[55] Many argued as well that NATO's deployment of Pershing-II missiles had been provoked by Moscow's deployment of highly accurate intermediate-range nuclear systems.[56] Stimulated by the failures in the Soviet economy, in policy in Afghanistan, and in arms control, Gorbachev learned through extensive consultation with specialists and experts and trial-and-error experimentation.[57]

Sadat also learned from failure. He, as well as Egyptian generals, recognized that Egypt had fought the war in 1973 under optimal conditions; a military alliance with Syria had permitted a coordinated two-front attack for the first time, Arab oil producers had joined in the accompanying diplomatic offensive, and Egypt had had the strategic advantage of surprise. Yet, even under those conditions Egypt had come perilously close to a serious military defeat after important initial military successes in crossing the Suez Canal. In the years following the October War, Sadat expanded the gains he had made through a process of phased disengagement with Israel. In this context, he was reluctant to risk the limited gains he had achieved in renewed warfare. In both cases, failure of earlier policies underlined asymmetric capabilities and unfavorable trends.

The evidence suggests that both leaders were motivated to learn and to change their images of their adversary. Both searched for new information, Gorbachev from experts in academic institutes and in government and from American interlocutors, and Sadat through intermediaries and then through secret meetings between high-level Egyptian and Israeli leaders. They were receptive to the information they received in large part because they were motivated to change existing images and policies. Both began with a small change in image, moved tentatively to small actions, were receptive to feedback, learned, and initiated a new series of actions that generated further feedback and change.[58] Gorbachev and Sadat ultimately developed confidence that their acts of reassurance would be reciprocated by their adversaries. Learning was not orderly and linear but experimental, through trial and error. In both cases, enemy images changed as a result of a complex interactive relationship between political learning and action that provided quick feedback.

Some analysts have suggested that Gorbachev's "new thinking" was more a product of "instrumental necessity than of military-strategic enlightenment."[59] This is a false dichotomy. Learning is the product not only of "cold" cognitive processes but also of "hot" emotional factors. Learning theorists in educational and behavioral psychology model enlightenment as a response to incentives. That both Gorbachev and Sadat were motivated to change their image of their adversary by their interest in freeing resources for domestic reform and the earlier failure of alternatives to accommodation is not at all inconsistent with the proposition that they learned.

These two stimuli to learning are not easily manipulated from the outside by others. They were the cumulative result of longstanding trends in Soviet and Egyptian domestic and foreign policy. Although this kind of fundamental learning is not necessary for crisis management or the routinization of conflict, it was an essential precondition of conflict reduction and resolution. Once they began to learn, both Gorbachev and Sadat used a strategy of reassurance to initiate a process of conflict reduction.

▲ Reassurance and Crisis Management and Routinization

A strategy of reassurance presumes ongoing hostility but roots the source of that hostility not in an adversary's search for opportunity but in its needs and weaknesses.[60] Reassurance does not require fundamental change in the image of an adversary in the first two phases of regional conflict management—crisis management and routinization—but enemy images must change if a conflict is to be reduced and resolved. I look briefly at strategies that are appropriate in these two phases before turning to the more demanding stages of conflict reduction and resolution.

The exercise of restraint, both in the language leaders use and in the deployment of military forces, can reduce the risk of provocation in crisis prevention and management. Leaders can also attempt to reduce the difficulties of interpreting their own and their adversary's intentions by providing more valid, consistent, and reliable information. They may seek to reassure each other, for example, by communicating through third parties who are credible to both sides. Syria and Israel have communicated successfully through the United States repeatedly in the last decade in an attempt to reassure each other of the limits of their intentions.

To routinize and contain a conflict, a strategy of reassurance can also attempt to reduce the uncertainty that is endemic to adversarial relationships by clarifying the acceptable limits of conflict and developing shared norms of competition.[61] Informal, shared norms among adversaries may delegitimate certain kinds of mutually unacceptable action and, consequently, reduce the need to manipulate the risk of war. They may also establish mutually acceptable boundaries of behavior and reduce some of the uncertainty that can at times lead a would-be challenger to miscalculate.[62]

Leaders can also attempt to put in place limited security regimes designed to routinize a conflict. In an effort to reduce the likelihood of an unintended and unwanted war, adversaries have agreed, at times informally, on principles and put in place procedures to reduce the likelihood of accidental or miscalculated war. Technically, these arrangements are referred to as *limited security regimes*.[63] The principles and procedures of the regime may be formal or informal, tacit or explicit, but because some norms are shared, the behavior of leaders is constrained.

The creation of limited security regimes is most likely when leaders share a common aversion to war and to its consequences.[64] A shared fear of war is not restricted only to the nuclear powers; it occurs among regional states as conventional military technology threatens ever greater destruction. Insofar as limited security regimes provide reliable, low-cost information about members' activities, they make action less opaque and estimation less difficult and reduce the likelihood of miscalculation. They reduce uncertainty both about the behavior of adversaries and about the boundaries of the conflict. Limited security regimes also link issues together, lengthen the "shadow of the future," and increase the incentives to sacrifice immediate for future gain.[65]

Reassurance through the creation of limited and focused security regimes can be of considerable help in reducing fear, uncertainty, and misunderstanding between adversaries. At a minimum, adversaries gain access to more reliable and less expensive information about each other's activities that can reduce uncertainty, the incidence of miscalculation, and an inappropriate manipulation of the risk of war. In a complex international environment that is often information-poor and technologically driven, lower cost and more valid information can be considerable advantages in the institutionalization and routinization of conflict. The Soviet Union and the United States, and Egypt and Israel, built limited security regimes to manage and routinize their conflict. Gorbachev and Sadat drew on their experience in these regimes when they began to consider an attempt to reduce their conflict with their adversary.

These kinds of strategies can be helpful in containing a conflict, but more is required if the conflict is to be reduced. I have argued that fundamental change in images is a prerequisite to conflict reduction. Once leaders have begun to change their image of their adversary and are interested in moving beyond routinization to conflict resolution, they must change the image their adversary has of them before conflict reduction can seriously begin.

▲ Reassurance and Conflict Reduction and Resolution

When leaders recognize that misperception and stereotyping govern their adversary's judgments as well as their own, they can try, by making an irrevocable commitment, to reassure their adversary of their benign intentions and to create incentives for conflict reduction.[66] This is precisely the strategy that President Anwar el-Sadat adopted in 1977.[67]

Dissatisfied with the progress of negotiations in the autumn of 1977 yet unprepared to accept the status quo, Sadat began again to consider seriously a use of force and simultaneously searched for a dramatic move that would both reduce the tension and distrust between Egypt and Israel and induce Israel to make major concessions to reduce the conflict. It was the distrust built up over decades, he argued, that constrained the attempt to negotiate the issues at stake and fueled the cycle of wars. Sadat began with secret negotiations between Egypt's deputy prime minister and Israel's foreign minister in Morocco, where each agreed to make a critical concession: Israel indicated its willingness to return most of the Sinai peninsula to Egyptian sovereignty, and Egypt agreed to peace and the establishment of diplomatic relations with Israel.[68] Although these proposals were not fully satisfactory to either party, both sides were assured that their concessions would be reciprocated rather than exploited.

Shortly thereafter, in a speech to the People's Assembly in Cairo, Sadat offered to travel to Jerusalem to personally address Israel's parliament in an effort to persuade its members of the sincerity of Egyptian intentions. The reaction was outrage in the Arab world, incredulity among the Israeli public, and alarm among some of the senior military in Israel, who considered the proposed visit a ruse to provide cover for a renewed attack. Within days, however, Sadat went to Jerusalem and spoke to the Knesset of the Egyptian terms for peace. Egyptian demands were unchanged, but Israel's leaders and public paid attention to the deed rather than to the words. In large part through this single, dramatic act of reassurance, Sadat changed the trajectory of the conflict by changing Israel's incentives to negotiate.

Why did reassurance through irrevocable commitment succeed? Several factors were at play, some general and some specific to the historical context. First, the initiative was irreversible; once the president of Egypt had traveled to Jerusalem, he could not undo the deed. Because it could not be reversed, the action was treated as a valid indicator of Egyptian intentions rather than as a signal that could be manipulated. Israel's leadership and public recognized the irreversibility of the action and consequently gave it great weight.

Second, the substantial political cost to President Sadat of breaking the longstanding Arab taboo against dealing directly with Israel was also apparent to Israel's leaders. Dissension within the Egyptian government was pronounced; the Egyptian foreign minister resigned in protest. A tidal wave of criticism from the Arab world engulfed the Egyptian leader, and Arab states moved in near unison to sever diplomatic relations with Egypt. Experimental studies suggest that people determine the motives of a donor by how much the gift cost the giver in utility: the greater the relative cost to the donor, the less likely are ulterior motives.[69] These studies in attribution are consistent with evidence of the impact of the cognitive heuristic *proportionality;*[70] Israel's leaders reasoned that Egypt's president would not incur such heavy costs were he not sincere.

Third, Sadat's arrival in Jerusalem challenged the most important set of beliefs about Arab goals among Israel's leadership and public. His visit provided the dramatic evidence that was needed to overcome deeply entrenched enemy images. A broad cross section of Israelis had assumed that Arab leaders were unrelentingly hostile, so much so that they were unprepared to meet Israel's leaders face to face. Once these core beliefs were shaken, it became easier for Israelis, as cognitive psychologists predict, to revise associated assumptions and expectations.

Fourth, President Sadat spoke over the heads of Israel's leadership directly to Israel's public. With his flair for the dramatic, he created the psychological and political symbols that would mobilize public opinion to press their more cautious and restrained leaders. In so doing, he removed a constraint on Israel's leaders and created a political inducement to action. The strategy of reassurance had multiple audiences and multiple constituencies.

Under this very special set of conditions, reassurance through irrevocable commitment succeeded brilliantly. The two critical components that make an irrevocable commitment reassuring to an adversary are its obviously high cost to the leaders who issue the commitment and its irreversibility. The strategy has been used so infrequently in part because it is often very difficult and very risky to design a commitment that is both high in cost and irreversible.[71] Leaders frequently have neither the resources nor the information necessary to make irrevocable commitments. A simulation of tacit bargaining in arms control finds that leaders are rarely certain enough about an opponent's response to make a large gesture, while the opponent is rarely trusting enough to respond enthusiastically to a small one.[72] In attempting to change an adversary's image through a self-binding commitment, leaders face a difficult trade-off; they are more likely to make offers that are reversible and less costly, but reversible low-cost offers are far less likely to provoke fundamental change in an adversary's image.

Reassurance through irrevocable commitment also requires a degree of freedom from domestic political and bureaucratic constraints. In Egypt after the October War, Sadat had great autonomy in decision making and, indeed, could withstand the resignation of his foreign minister. Even then, the making of an irrevocable commitment to leaders long identified as antagonists can be difficult to justify to the public. Yet it is the public nature of the commitment that contributes to its irreversibility and credibility.[73] For all these reasons, the making of self-binding commitments to jolt an adversary to change its image and learn is likely to be difficult.

When self-binding commitments are difficult, leaders can attempt to change their adversary's image and reduce their conflict through actions that they hope their adversary will reciprocate. These actions are smaller in scope than irrevocable commitments and can be reversed. Reciprocal behavior is most usefully conceived as a pattern of contingent, sequential, and diffuse exchange.[74] Different streams of evidence from experimental studies, computer simulation, analyses of international interaction, and historical case studies converge to suggest that at times a strategy of reciprocity can be effective in eliciting cooperation.[75]

In a series of computer tournaments, a variant of a reciprocal strategy, tit for tat, proved most effective in inducing cooperation among egoistic players in an anarchic environment. Tit for tat succeeded because of its special attributes; it cooperates on the first move and thereafter replicates what the previous player has just done. It is therefore "nice," "forgiving," but "firm": nice because it begins cooperatively in an effort to promote reciprocal concession; forgiving because although it retaliates for one defection, thereafter it forgives an isolated defection after a single response; but firm because it reciprocates defection with defection and thereby reduces the risk of exploitation for those who use the strategy.[76] It is even more effective if retaliation is marginally less than provocation.

It is not at all clear that reciprocal exchange of this kind can provoke fundamental learning. On the contrary, analysts of tit-for-tat strategies explicitly assume evolutionary adaptation premised on behavioral conditioning.[77] Tit for tat pays no attention to the beliefs of the players. Experimental studies show, however, that people learn to reciprocate by reasoning and making inferences about the other side's motives and future action.[78] A cooperative move is unlikely to be reciprocated if an adversary has longstanding and deeply held negative images that have been reinforced over time. U.S. Secretary of State John Foster Dulles held such a "bad-faith" image of the Soviet Union. Consequently, he dismissed almost every conciliatory Soviet action as designed to deceive the United States and create an illusory and dangerous sense of complacency.[79]

Theories of social exchange suggest that the way a target interprets the initiator's motives is crucial to the success of reciprocity. Particularly important is the attribution that an adversary made the concession freely and voluntarily rather than accidentally or through compulsion.[80] People are also more inclined to be receptive if they consider their opponent's motives to be benign. If they estimate that their opponent is engaged in deceit or has ulterior motives, they do not feel obliged to reciprocate.[81] Whether leaders interpret an action as conciliatory or aggressive is often a function of their image of their adversary and their perception of the goals and strategy that motivate the action.

A somewhat more promising strategy that builds in some opportunity for learning is an adapted version of graduated reduction in international tension (GRIT).[82] The initiator announces in advance that it is beginning a series of conciliatory actions designed to reduce conflict and then implements these actions whether or not the other side reciprocates. The actions, moreover, should be easily verifiable. As each step is implemented, the initiator invites its adversary to reciprocate but does not specify the appropriate response. Further, a reciprocal response by an adversary should be rewarded by a somewhat more conciliatory action. These actions, however, should not impair the defensive capacity of the initiator. If the other side attempts to exploit the concession, the initiator should respond with an appropriate action, but only to the degree necessary to restore the status quo.

Experimental studies concur that strategies like GRIT, which build in a series of conciliatory initiatives taken independently of the other's actions, are more effective than tit for tat in eliciting a reciprocal response.[83] Moreover, they were as effective among players who were judged generally competitive by their previous play as they were among those who were generally cooperative. A second variant that is also effective is a reciprocal strategy that is slow to retaliate and slow to return to conciliation; this variant of reciprocity allows for initial misperception and modest learning.[84]

The experimental evidence may be overoptimistic when action occurs outside the laboratory. Gorbachev went far beyond a graduated strategy of reciprocity as he attempted to change American images of the Soviet Union. He initiated and persisted with a series of unilateral conciliatory actions even when they were not reciprocated. In 1985 Gorbachev announced the suspension of Soviet countermeasures in response to the deployment of intermediate-range nuclear forces (INF) by NATO and a moratorium on further deployments of SS-20s. That same year, he proclaimed a unilateral moratorium on nuclear testing. The Soviet Union also paid its back dues to the United Nations for peacekeeping, began to cooperate with the International Atomic Energy Agency, and reworked its position in the Strategic Arms Reduction Talks

(START) in October 1985. In January 1986 Gorbachev urged a program of complete nuclear disarmament to be achieved in three stages by the year 2000. In 1987 the Soviet Union agreed to intrusive on-site verification inspections as part of the INF agreement and announced its decision to withdraw from Afghanistan. In December 1988, at the U.N. General Assembly, Gorbachev also announced the unilateral reduction of active Soviet military forces by 15 percent and the withdrawal from Eastern Europe of more than 40 percent of Soviet tank divisions, together with 50 percent of Soviet tanks.

Despite this series of unilateral Soviet actions, many in Washington resisted change in their image of the Soviet Union and remained skeptical of Gorbachev's intentions.[85] Paradoxically, it was Gorbachev who "learnt by doing" in a complex interactive relationship between beliefs and behavior; action led to further change in his beliefs as he made inferences from his behavior about his convictions.[86] Large and significant amounts of discrepant information were necessary before American leaders changed their image of the Soviet Union. It took Soviet tolerance of the destruction of the Berlin Wall, a dramatic and irreversible signal, to change American images and provoke fundamental learning.

▲ Conclusion

This analysis of enemy images and conflict management, routinization, reduction, and resolution is sobering. It argues that enemy images respond to fundamental human needs and, consequently, that they are easily formed under certain kinds of domestic and international conditions. Once formed, cognitive and motivational processes reinforce existing images and make them resistant to change. Only learning, a specific kind of cognitive change, permits conflict reduction. Small-scale, incremental adjustment of enemy images may be sufficient for crisis prevention and management and for the routinization and institutionalization of conflict but not for conflict reduction and resolution. The two political prerequisites of learning that I have identified are demanding and not easily manipulable from the outside.

My review of strategies of reassurance that can provoke learning by one adversary once the other has changed its image finds that they are either difficult to implement or insufficient to provoke fundamental change. The record is not as bleak with respect to the institutionalization and routinization of conflict. It may well be that many regional conflicts, where fundamental conflicts of identity are at issue, may have to be managed until conditions permit leaders to learn or outsiders to teach.

NOTES

1. Milton Rokeach, *The Nature of Human Values* (New York: Free Press, 1973), 5; Yaacov Vertzberger, *The World in Their Minds: Information Processing, Cognition, and Perception in Foreign Policy Decisionmaking* (Stanford: Stanford University Press, 1990), 114–27.

2. Paul Sites, "Needs as Analogues of Emotion," in *Conflict: Human Needs Theory*, ed. John Burton (New York: Macmillan, 1990), 16.

3. Jonathan H. Turner, *A Theory of Social Interaction* (Stanford: Stanford University Press, 1988).

4. M. Sherif, *In Common Predicament: Social Psychology, Intergroup Conflict, and Cooperation* (Boston: Houghton Mifflin, 1966).

5. Vamik Volkan, "Ethnonationalistic Rituals: An Introduction," *Mind and Human Interaction* 4 (Dec. 1992): 3–19.

6. Barbara Harff and Ted Robert Gurr, "Toward Empirical Theory of Genocides and Politicides: Identification and Measurement of Cases since 1945," *International Studies Quarterly* 32, no. 3 (1988): 359–71.

7. Clifford Geertz, *The Interpretation of Cultures* (New York: Basic Books, 1973).

8. K. Booth, *Strategy and Ethnocentrism* (London: Croom Helm, 1979).

9. Herbert C. Kelman, "Creating the Conditions for Israeli-Palestinian Negotiations," *Journal of Conflict Resolution* 26 (1982): 39–76, 61.

10. Richard Nisbett and Lee Ross, *Human Inference: Strategies and Shortcomings of Social Judgment* (Englewood Cliffs, N.J.: Prentice-Hall, 1980); Daniel Kahneman, Paul Slovic, and Amos Tversky, *Judgment under Uncertainty: Heuristics and Biases* (New York: Cambridge University Press, 1982); Susan T. Fiske and Shelley E. Taylor, *Social Cognition* (Reading, Mass.: Addison-Wesley, 1984), 72–99.

11. D. M. Taylor and F. M. Moghaddam, *Theories of Intergroup Relations: International and Social Psychological Perspectives* (New York: Praeger, 1987).

12. Robert Jervis, "Cooperation under the Security Dilemma," *World Politics* 30 (Jan. 1978): 167–214.

13. Margaret G. Hermann, "Who Becomes a Political Leader? Some Societal and Regime Influences on the Selection of Head of State," in *Psychological Models in International Politics*, ed. L. S. Falkowski (Boulder, Colo.: Westview Press, 1979): 15–48, 39.

14. Jack Snyder, *Myths of Empire: Domestic Politics and International Ambition* (Ithaca: Cornell University Press, 1991), 2–6, 31–49.

15. Dean G. Pruitt and Jeffrey Z. Rubin, *Social Conflict* (New York: McGraw Hill, 1986), 117–18.

16. J. R. Anderson, *The Architecture of Cognition* (Cambridge: Harvard University Press, 1982).

17. L. Ross, M. R. Lepper, and M. Hubbard, "Perseverance in Self Perception and Social Perception: Biased Attributional Processes in the Debriefing Paradigm," *Journal of Personality and Social Psychology* 32 (1975): 880–92.

18. E. R. Hirt and S. J. Sherman, "The Role of Prior Knowledge in Explaining Hypothetical Events," *Journal of Experimental and Social Psychology* 21 (1985): 519–43.

19. Pruitt and Rubin, *Social Conflict*, 112–19.

20. D. von Winterfeldt and E. Edwards, *Decision Analysis and Behavioral Research* (New York: Cambridge University Press, 1986), 126–59.

21. Amos Tversky and Daniel Kahneman, "Availability: A Heuristic for Judging Frequency and Probability," *Cognitive Psychology* 5 (1973): 207–32; J. B. Pryor and N. Kriss, "The Cognitive Dynamics of Salience in the Attribution Process," *Journal of Personality and Social Psychology* 35 (1977): 49–55; Michael Ross and Fiore Sicoly, "Egocentric Biases in Availability and Attribution," ibid. 37 (1979): 322–36; Shelley E. Taylor, "The Availability Bias in Social Perception and Interaction," in Kahneman, Slovic, and Tversky, *Judgment under Uncertainty*, 190–200.

22. Daniel Kahneman and Amos Tversky, "Subjective Probability: A Judgment of Representativeness," *Cognitive Psychology* 3 (1972): 430–54; idem, "On the Psychology of Prediction," *Psychological Review* 80 (1973): 237–51; Amos Tversky and Daniel Kahneman, "Judgments of and by Representativeness," in Kahneman, Slovic, and Tversky, *Judgment under Uncertainty*, 84–98.

23. Fiske and Taylor, *Social Cognition*, 250–56, 268–75.

24. Robert E. Lane and David O. Sears, *Public Opinion* (Englewood Cliffs, N.J.: Prentice-Hall, 1964); Ole R. Holsti and James N. Rosenau, *American Leadership in World Affairs: Vietnam and the Breakdown of Consensus* (Boston: Allen & Unwin, 1984).

25. Robert Jervis, *Perception and Misperception in International Politics* (Princeton: Princeton University Press, 1976), 288–318.

26. Jennifer Crocker, Darlene B. Hannah, and Renee Weber, "Person Memory and Causal Attributions," *Journal of Personality and Social Psychology* 44 (1983): 55–66, 65.

27. Lee Ross, "The Intuitive Psychologist and His Shortcomings: Distortions in the Attribution Process," in *Advances in Experimental and Social Psychology*, vol. 10, ed. L. Berkowitz (New York: Academic Press, 1977).

28. E. T. Higgins and J. A. Bargh, "Social Cognition and Social Perception," in *Annual Review of Psychology*, vol. 38, ed. M. R. Rosenzweig and L. W. Porter (Palo Alto, Calif.: Annual Reviews, 1987), 386.

29. P. Tetlock, "Integrative Complexity of American and Soviet Foreign Policy Rhetorics: A Time-Series Analysis," *Journal of Personality and Social Psychology* 49 (1985): 1565–85.

30. Vertzberger, *The World in Their Minds*, 134–37.

31. Higgins and Bargh, "Social Cognition and Social Perception," 369–425.

32. P. Tetlock, "Cognitive Style and Political Ideology," *Journal of Personality and Social Psychology* 45 (1983): 118–26.

33. Vertzberger, *The World in Their Minds*, 136.

34. An exception is Ralph Erber and Susan T. Fiske, "Outcome Dependency and Attention to Inconsistent Information," *Journal of Personality and Social Psychology* 47 (1984): 709–26.

35. James H. Kuklinski, Robert C. Luskin, and John Bolland, "Where Is the Schema? Going Beyond the 'S' Word in Political Psychology," *American Political Science Review* 85, no. 2 (1991): 1346.

36. T. L. Good and J. E. Brophy, *Educational Psychology: A Realistic Approach* (New York: Longman, 1990).

37. Ernest Haas, *When Knowledge Is Power* (Berkeley: University of California Press, 1990), 84.

38. Jack Levy, "Learning and Foreign Policy: Exploring a Conceptual Minefield," *International Organization* 48 (spring 1994): 279–312.

39. See, e.g., Haas, *When Knowledge Is Power*.

40. In an effort to deal with the problem of evaluation, analysts refer to pathological learning, or changes that impede future cognitive growth. See James Clay Moltz, "Divergent Learning and the Failed Politics of Soviet Economic Reform," *World Politics* 45 (Jan. 1993): 301–25, 303.

41. See Janice Gross Stein, "Deterrence and Compellence in the Gulf: A Failed or Impossible Task?" *International Security* 17 (fall 1992): 147–79.

42. For a similar argument, see George W. Breslauer, "What Have We Learned about Learning?" in *Learning in U.S. and Soviet Foreign Policy*, ed. George W. Breslauer and Philip E. Tetlock (Boulder, Colo.: Westview Press, 1991), 825–56.

43. Sim B. Sitkin, "Learning through Failure: The Strategy of Small Losses," *Research in Organizational Behavior* 14 (1992): 231–66.

44. D. T. Campbell, "Reform as Experiments," *American Psychologist* 24 (1969): 409–29.

45. See C. Argyris and D. A. Schon, *Organizational Learning* (Reading, Mass.: Addison-Wesley, 1978), for a discussion of the importance of "theory in action"; and T. Peters and R. H. Waterman, *In Search of Excellence* (New York: Harper & Row, 1982), for an analysis of "action bias."

46. Ulric Neisser, "On 'Social Knowing,'" *Personality and Social Psychology Bulletin* 6 (1980): 601–5, 603–4, cited in Kuklinski, Luskin, and Bolland, "Where Is the Schema?" 1346.

47. The scope of their learning is detailed in Janice Gross Stein, "Political Learning by Doing: Gorbachev as an Uncommitted Thinker and Motivated Learner," *International Organization* 48 (spring 1994): 155–84; and idem, "The Political Economy of Strategic Agreements: The Linked Costs of Failure at Camp David," in *Double-Edged Diplomacy: International Bargaining and Domestic Politics*, ed. Peter Evans, Harold Jacobsen, and Robert Putnam (Berkeley: University of California Press, 1993), 77–103.

48. If a more demanding and problematic criterion of learning is used, namely, movement toward accuracy in cognitive content, the evidence suggests that Gorbachev learned.

49. Yudit Auerbach, "Turning-Point Decisions: A Cognitive-Dissonance Analysis of Conflict Resolution in Israel–West German Relations," *Political Psychology* 7 (1986): 533–50.

50. Steven Weber, "Interactive Learning in U.S.-Soviet Arms Control," in Breslauer and Tetlock, *Learning in U.S. and Soviet Foreign Policy*, 784–824.

51. Haas, *When Knowledge Is Power*.

52. For evidence of how politically contested much of Gorbachev's "new thinking" was, see Stephen M. Meyer, "The Sources and Prospects of Gorbachev's New Political Thinking on Security," *International Security* 13 (fall 1988): 124–63.

53. Richard Ned Lebow, "When Does Conciliation Succeed?" in *International Relations Theory and the Transformation of the International System*, ed. Richard Ned Lebow and Thomas Risse-Kappen (New York: Columbia University Press, 1995).

54. Meyer, "Sources and Prospects."

55. Vadim Zagladin, interview by the author, Moscow, May 18, 1989, and Anatoliy Gromyko, Moscow, May 19, 1989.

56. See Robert Herman, "Soviet New Thinking: Ideas, Interests, and the Definition of Security" (Ph.D diss., Cornell University, 1995).

57. For a detailed examination of the political context of learning and the importance of experts in the process, see Sarah Mendelson, "International Battles and External Wars: Politics, Learning, and the Soviet Withdrawal from Afghanistan," *World Politics* 45 (Apr. 1993): 327–60; Jeff Checkel, "Ideas, Institutions, and the Gorbachev Foreign Policy Revolution," ibid. 45 (Jan. 1993): 242–70; and Stein, "Political Learning by Doing."

58. See Stein, "The Political Economy of Strategic Agreements"; and idem, "Political Learning by Doing."

59. See Meyer, "Sources and Prospects," 129.

60. Janice Gross Stein, "Deterrence and Reassurance," in *Behavior, Society, and Nuclear War II*, ed. Philip E. Tetlock, J. L. Husbands, Robert Jervis, Paul C. Stern, and Charles Tilly (New York: Oxford University Press, 1991), 8–72.

61. Philip Bonacich, "Norms and Cohesion as Adaptive Responses to Potential Conflict: An Experimental Study," *Sociometry* 35 (Mar. 1972): 357–75.

62. Janice Gross Stein, "The Managers and the Managed: Crisis Prevention in the Middle East," in *New Issues in Crisis Management*, ed. Gilbert Winham (Boulder, Colo.: Westview Press, 1987), 171–98.

63. The concept of regime was borrowed from international law and broadened to incorporate the range of shared norms, principles, rules, and procedures around which leaders' expectations converge. See S. Krasner, "International Régimes," *International Organization*, special Issue, 39 (spring 1982). For a discussion of limited security regimes, see C. Lipson, "International Cooperation in Economic and Security Affairs," *World Politics* 37 (Oct. 1984): 1–23; Janice Gross Stein, "Detection and Defection: Security Regimes and the Management of International Conflict," *International Journal* 101 (1985): 599–627; J. S. Nye, "Nuclear Learning and U.S.-Soviet Security Régimes," *International Organization* 41 (summer 1987): 371–402; and R. K. Smith, "The Non-Proliferation Régime and International Relations," ibid. 41 (spring 1987): 253–81.

64. Arthur Stein, *Why Nations Cooperate: Circumstance and Choice in International Relations* (Ithaca: Cornell University Press, 1990).

65. Robert O. Keohane, *After Hegemony: Cooperation and Discord in the World Political Economy* (Princeton: Princeton University Press, 1984), 88.

66. Dean G. Pruitt and Peter J. Carnevale, *Negotiation in Social Conflict* (London: Open University Press, 1992), 146, term this kind of strategy "unilateral conciliatory initiatives."

67. Z. Maoz and D. S. Felsenthal, "Self-Binding Commitments, the Inducement of Trust, Social Choice, and the Theory of International Cooperation," *International Studies Quarterly* 31, no. 3 (1987): 177–200.

68. Moshe Dayan, *Breakthrough: A Personal Account of the Egypt-Israel Peace Negotiations* (New York: Knopf, 1981), 44–52.

69. Dean G. Pruitt, *Negotiation Behavior* (New York: Academic Press, 1981), 124–25.

70. Richard Ned Lebow and Janice Gross Stein, "The Limits of Cognitive Models:

Carter, Afghanistan, and Foreign Policy Change," in *Diplomacy, Force, and Leadership: Essays in Honor of Alexander L. George,* ed. Timothy McKeown and Dan Caldwell (Boulder, Colo.: Westview Press, 1993).

71. Maoz and Felsenthal, "Self-Binding Commitments," 198.

72. G. W. Downs and D. M. Rocke, "Tacit Bargaining and Arms Control," *World Politics* 39 (Apr. 1987): 297–325.

73. Maoz and Felsenthal, "Self-Binding Commitments," 191–92.

74. D. W. Larson, "The Psychology of Reciprocity in International Negotiation," in "International Negotiation: A Multidisciplinary Perspective," ed. Janice Gross Stein, *Negotiation Journal,* special issue, 4 (1988): 281–302.

75. G. H. Shure, R. J. Meeker, and E. A. Hansford, "The Effectiveness of Pacifist Strategies in Bargaining Games," *Journal of Conflict Resolution* 9 (1965): 106–16; M. Deutsch, Y. Epstein, Y. D. Canavan, and P. Gumpert, "Strategies of Inducing Cooperation: An Experimental Study," ibid. 11 (1967): 345–60; V. Sermat, "The Effect of an Initial Cooperative or Competitive Treatment upon a Subject's Response to Conditional Cooperation," *Behavioral Science* 12 (1967): 301–13.

76. Robert Axelrod, *The Evolution of Cooperation* (New York: Basic Books, 1984), 54.

77. Robert Axelrod argues that as long as the participants value their future relationship, as long as the "shadow of the future" is long, players will learn to cooperate through trial and error (ibid., 125–26, 173–74).

78. S. Oskamp, "Effects of Programmed Strategies on Cooperation in the Prisoner's Dilemma and Other Mixed-Motive Games," *Journal of Conflict Resolution* 15 (1971): 225–59, 243, 256.

79. D. W. Larson, *Origins of Containment: A Psychological Explanation* (Princeton: Princeton University Press, 1985), 29–34.

80. H. H. Kelley and J. W. Thibaut, *Interpersonal Relations: A Theory of Interdependence* (New York: Wiley, 1978).

81. C. Nemeth, "Bargaining and Reciprocity," *Psychological Bulletin* 74 (1970): 297–308.

82. Charles Osgood, *An Alternative to War or Surrender* (Urbana: University of Illinois Press, 1962).

83. S. Lindskold, P. S. Walters, and H. Koutsourais, "Cooperators, Competitors, and Response to GRIT," *Journal of Conflict Resolution* 27 (1983): 521–32.

84. Dean G. Pruitt and M. J. Kimmel, "Twenty Years of Experimental Gaming," *Annual Review of Psychology* 8 (1977): 363–92.

85. Policy Planning Staff and National Security Council staff, interviews by author, Washington, D.C., Feb. 1989.

86. M. P. Zanna, J. M. Olson, and R. H. Fazio, "Attitude-Behavior Consistency: An Individual Difference Perspective," *Journal of Personality and Social Psychology* 38 (1980): 432–40.

I. WILLIAM ZARTMAN

11 | Bargaining and
Conflict Reduction

Scarcely any violent conflict in the post–World War II world
has been resolved or even managed by direct negotiations by the parties themselves. As a result there are few positive lessons to draw from the historical
record, and the negative lessons—lessons of failure—are so overdetermined
that they do not yield much insight. Yet some conflicts have been managed,
and a few have been resolved. What is the key? The crucial phrase in the initial
judgment is "on their own," and the crucial ingredient is *third-party mediation,* a term used to cover the whole range of good offices and positive foreign
interventions.[1] Indeed, for a better understanding and analysis, the situation of
regional conflict should be recast into the framework of a relationship among
conflicting regional parties in which they cannot proceed to the strategies and
tactics of bargaining without first and simultaneously changing the conflictual context into one that supports cooperative moves. Within this context,
particular types of conflict require certain political and bargaining strategies.

The most important lesson to be drawn from the review of regional conflict
with which this book begins is that negotiations in any type of conflict must
be seen as part of the regional relationships. They are central acts, perhaps,
but understandable only after the prologue and meaningful only as prepara-

tion for the epilogue, rather than as single events that resolve a momentary issue. Thus, negotiations cannot simply be declared and conducted as a new policy; but can only be fruitful after they have been prepared for. The discussion thus turns to prenegotiation functions. It should be emphasized that this preparatory phase in no way implies the prior end of conflict. Conflict, even armed conflict, continues during prenegotiations and often struggles with it as a theme for government attention. Indeed, as already intimated, conflict continues after conflict management, although politics gradually replaces violence, and conflict may even exist, dominated and overridden but still subjacent, once resolution supposedly has taken place.

▲ Prenegotiation

A number of functions must be accomplished before actual negotiation — the joint establishment of a formula for managing the conflict and the collective decision on implementing details — can be undertaken. Unless these functions are performed, negotiation will be difficult if not impossible; unless they are accomplished before the parties actually begin to negotiate, they will have to be worked out during the negotiating process, delaying or undermining the process of arriving at a jointly decided outcome. These functions are six: cost and risk, requitement, support, bridges, parties, and agenda.[2] They differ from negotiation in that they are not necessarily performed by cooperation and direct communication among the conflicting parties; rather, they are conducted internally by each side and communicated indirectly to the other. Prenegotiation, therefore, contains many of the characteristics of tacit negotiation, with information being generated unilaterally and then exposed publicly or by channels, but rarely by direct bilateral decision making. Rather than a true joint decision-making process, a characterization reserved for the "real negotiations" later on, prenegotiation is a matter of arriving at parallel understandings. It is also a matter of removing important uncertainties surrounding the prospects of agreement that stand in the way of a cooperative policy track.

In order to enter into negotiations, parties must come to an understanding about the *costs and risks* involved in an agreement concerning their conflict. Conflicts continue beyond their usefulness because of uncertainty about the dangers of negotiating and the costs of settling. While full certainty only comes with implemented agreements, the circle of uncertainty that surrounds negotiation must be reduced. Parties to an intrastate secessionist or centralist conflict are concerned lest negotiation imply recognition — of the legitimate government by one side and of the rebels by the other — meaning that each will walk out of the talks carrying the legitimization that arms alone could not secure and that each will have thrown away on process the one card of recognition that could buy a lot of substance. They are also concerned lest concessions be a camel's nose, that is, an opening to ever larger surrenders on vital territorial and security matters as well as on more subtle intangibles, such as the right to interfere or the possibility of dominance.

One of the major subjects of cost and risk in regional conflict is the mutual assurance that negotiation does not mean destruction and surrender. For example, in preparations for negotiations between Israel and Palestinians, each side has long been afraid that talks would mean recognition, which would mean letting go of the one thing the other side wanted and, therefore, the one thing that could have bought some important concessions. In negotiations in South Africa, the National Party government was long afraid that negotiating with the African National Congress (ANC) was simply surrender to communist terrorism and the domination of the majority, whereas the ANC was afraid that negotiating with the government was simply surrender to the legal system of apartheid; thus, both were blocking the possibility of finding a creative middle ground.[3] In the two Gulf wars, Iraq and Iran and then Iraq, Kuwait, and the United States were all afraid that in negotiations the other side would require them to give up their military preparations and then would walk away, so that a signal of willingness to negotiate would cost them their current advantage and risk them total defeat. While the fears of uncertainty over the cost and risk of beginning negotiations were overcome in the Palestinian and South African cases, they were never overcome in the second Gulf war, and they were only surmounted after years of stalemate in the first.

Once the concern over costs and risks has been allayed, the parties need to establish *requitement,* the understanding that concessions will be reciprocated rather than banked. Negotiation is based on conventions of reciprocation in which free signs of disarmament—like handshakes, bows, tipped hats, and waves—are answered with similar gestures. No party will make such a gesture without the knowledge that it will be reciprocated in some measure. In regional conflicts, the concern of both sides, beginning with the recognition issue, is that concessions will be used as a stepping stone for demands for further concessions rather than reciprocated. Since reciprocation is the essence of negotiations in the prenegotiations stage, the rules on requitement need to be set.

During 1992, in the Syrian-Israeli "basket" of the Madrid peace process, the two parties came to the realization that they would have to trade territory—the Golan Heights—for peace, or normal relations, in some measure, and they conveyed that sense to each other. Hitherto, each side had only expected concessions from the other on its own terms, without having to pay for them on the other's terms. The establishment of requitement allowed them to proceed to a discussion of how much peace was worth how much territory, and vice versa. During the first decade of the Namibian negotiations, 1977–86, South Africa never felt that requitement was understood: there were only continual concessions with nothing in return. In the second half of that decade, under the Reagan administration, South Africa expected the reverse: it expected concessions and sweeteners from the U.S. mediator without having to make concessions of its own. Once the notion of requitement sank in on both sides, the talks moved rapidly in 1987 to active negotiations and then agreement.[4] In the second Gulf war, Washington and Baghdad obdurately made it clear that there would be no requitement and that each side's demands must be totally accepted by the other side. Predictably, the negotiation track was a dead end.

Once a better understanding of costs, risks, and requitement has been established, the parties can begin building *support* at home for their engagement in the negotiation process. Previously, the parties presumably enjoyed support for their engagement in the conflict. If the parties are to embark on the cooperation track, they must be assured that their clientele will support them. That much is obvious. It then follows, but is less widely recognized, that each party will have to spend some effort convincing the other's supporters of its own bona fides and of the correctness of the cooperative path for the other, while not weakening the support of its own followers for the same policy. Since parties negotiate for concessions from the other side and downplay the need to make concessions of their own, building up the other party's support is a delicate job.

President F. W. de Klerk and ANC President Nelson Mandela deployed considerable effort, especially in 1990 and early 1991, to reinforce the negotiation option by assuring the acceptability of the outcome to each other's followers. They did not seize on occasions when the other was seeking to gather support for negotiations—such as the March 17, 1992, "white referendum"—to attack the other party, and they moderated their own demands, even at some danger of losing their own followers, to help the other side bring along its own followers while make corresponding concessions. The king of Morocco has played a delicate and complex game of consolidating support behind his claims over the Western Sahara while at the same time allowing the possibility of meeting with the Polisario Front, which he did on January 15, 1990, to satisfy international pressures for negotiation. The Polisario still has not prepared its followers for any concessions in response, and so negotiations are stuck.

The other side of the same task is the building of *bridges* between the two parties. In order to be able to communicate effectively when they finally meet to negotiate, the two parties must start communicating beforehand and must begin to learn to know each other. Practice in communication is necessary so that messages can come across clearly and intelligibly and so that enough trust and confidence is created to enable the process to move ahead. Trust is not a precondition to negotiation, contrary to frequent claims, but some trust must be built as negotiations proceed. Egyptian President Anwar al-Sadat's visit to Jerusalem in 1977, discussed in chapter 10 of this volume, was an unusual exercise in building bridges in the Middle East conflict. The personal relations that quickly developed between de Klerk and Mandela were crucial to the preparation of negotiations between the two sides in South Africa; they also show how personal bonds can be shaken by disillusion and need institutional or collective reinforcement to tide over personal moods. The role of private mediators in preparing the ground for official negotiations has been shown to be crucial on many occasions.[5]

Finally, as the sides test cooperative waters and prepare to move toward negotiation, they must agree on the ingredients of the negotiation in terms of *parties* and *agenda*. Like the other functions of prenegotiation — costs and risks, requitement, support, and bridges — both parties and agenda are matters of uncertainty that can ensure or derail the negotiations. When are Jerusalem and statehood to be discussed in the Middle East? When does the Palestine Liberation Organization (PLO) become one of the parties? Indeed, will independence be discussed in any secessionist conflict, and which organization will speak for the rebels? Usually the spectrum of the conflict contains parties and issues that are not amenable to agreement on any terms; negotiation in part involves isolating the negotiable from the nonnegotiable parties and issues. The only rule for separation is that the included items must outweigh the excluded; the resolved issues must contain enough gain for both sides to make the unresolved secondary, and the agreeing parties must comprise enough players to keep the remaining disagreeing ones from upsetting the agreement. Uncertainty on both these issues must be reduced before invitations can be issued and the menu presented.

Unless the uncertainties covered by these six functions of prenegotiation are reduced, negotiations on regional conflict cannot begin and cannot come to a conclusion. But to initiate or undertake these activities takes an unusually firm and dedicated leadership, particularly for a party involved in pursuing conflict. Such a shift involves changing horses in the middle of the race, which is not accomplished easily. The party seeking to do so needs assistance, and the situation has to be conducive or propitious for such a shift.

▲ Ripeness

Whether conducted between the conflicting parties directly or with the help of a third party, negotiations to manage and resolve conflict are unlikely to be successful at just any point in the conflict. Beyond the processual timing, involving preparation, is the situational or structural timing, the perceived ripeness of the conflict for negotiation.[6] Ripeness is a perceptional matter, but like all matters of perception, it is related to objective reality. While the margin of interpretation is great, it is unlikely that parties will negotiate a compromise when one side is on the verge of victory and the other on the edge of defeat, as in the last years of the Eritrean war.[7] More significantly, resolution is unlikely when both sides face no prospects of either victory or defeat and the conflict is not costly to either of them, as in Cyprus.[8] Finally, it is unlikely when the deadlock is painful but the pain has been internalized into national myths and purposes, as in the Arab-Israeli conflict.[9]

Conflicting parties seek to win, which leads to a stalemate as they check each other's efforts. In an attempt to break that stalemate, both parties seek to escalate their way out and overcome the other party.[10] Since these efforts, like the initial level of conflict, are pursued by both sides, the result is the escalation of conflict and the reinforcement of stalemate. When both parties reach the point where they can no longer escalate their way to victory and the sunk costs plus the countering efforts of the other side make for a costly deadlock, the point of a *mutually hurting stalemate* has arrived. When this realization has taken hold, the situation is ripe for resolution. Since this realization is often slow in coming and ripeness can be a fleeting moment, the presence of a deadline with the same characteristics — a recently avoided or impending catastrophe that would sharply augment the pain and cost — can serve to lock in the perception of propitiousness. Additional elements are also required for the ripe moment: the perception that there is a way out and the presence of valid spokesmen for both sides.

Ripe moments based on mutually hurting stalemates, impending catastrophes, and a way out have been nearly universal elements in the management and resolution of regional conflicts. The classical case was the mutual encirclement of the Egyptian and Israeli armies on the east bank of the Suez

Canal at the end of the quick but exhausting October War in 1973, which set the stage for the disengagement agreements of 1974 and 1976.[11] Agreement on the withdrawal of Cuban troops from Angola and South African troops (and administration) from Namibia was the formula, or "way out," agreed to in 1988 after sanctions, troop costs and losses, and the battle of Cuito Carnavale combined to produce a hurting stalemate for both sides.[12] Two years later, another deadlock at Mavinga produced another mutually hurting stalemate for the National Union for the Total Independence of Angola (UNITA) and the Peoples Movement for the Liberation of Angola (MPLA) and resulted in the Estoril agreement.[13] In 1992 it was the drought that capped the grinding costs of an endless war between RENAMO (the National Resistance Movement) and the Mozambican government of FRELIMO (Front for the Liberation of Mozambique) that finally made both parties aware of their mutually hurting stalemate and brought them to sign a ceasefire agreement.[14] The list could go on.

The weakness in the concept of mutually hurting stalemate is not its perceptional quality, which merely confirms that it is a social phenomenon, involving choice and decision rather than objective physical effects, but the fact that it invites escalation. Recognizing that there is no conflict resolution without conflict, it teaches parties to escalate to block their opponent's escalation and therefore confirms that conflict management moves, which lower the cost and means of conflict without resolving its basic issues, are actually counterproductive. To be sure, the record shows that a special type of escalation is required. Rather than an escalation to raise, that is, to overcome the other party by breaking the stalemate, one of the parties usually makes an escalation to call, merely matching and checking the other, thereby signaling its willingness to shift to cooperation on equal terms. But this move nonetheless involves increased conflict. There is a need for a positive equivalent to the hurting stalemate to produce a ripe moment.

The positive side of ripeness is much more rare, if only because, inescapably, the name of the game is conflict. It exists, however, and can be called a *mutually enticing opportunity*, until a catchier label is found. In positive terms, a conflict is ripe for resolution when the parties perceive an opportunity in the ambient conditions to gain a favorable outcome. The emphasis is the reverse of that of the negative ripe moment, but it is not merely a restatement with a different accent. While the mutually hurting stalemate also requires the perception of a way out, in the mutually enticing opportunity it is that way out that leads the movement, rather than complementing it; the inability of the parties to escalate their way out is merely the background condition. At the time of the mutually enticing moment, parties are likely to find themselves in an ongoing deadlock of no particular cost rather than a hurting stalemate, a drag rather than a pain. Valid spokesmen are also required.

As suggested, examples of mutually enticing opportunities are fewer, a point that constructive practice might overcome. The 1990s phase of the Middle East peace process can hardly be attributed to a negative ripe moment, however. Instead, an opportunity appeared, in the window opened by the second Gulf War. But it is significant that the opportunity existed as much in terms of relations with the convener, the United States, now the only superpower left whose good graces both sides want to cultivate, as it did in terms of the bilateral possibilities of settlement. Indeed, the United States had to use unusual amounts of leverage as well as persuasion to bring and hold the parties together in the talks. However, the stalemate that developed in this process, compounded by the rising Islamic movement in Palestine, did create a ripe moment that Norway was able to seize in 1993 to bring about the Oslo autonomy agreements. A similar mutually enticing opportunity was thought to exist, along the same lines, for Cyprus in the first few years of the 1990s, but its evanescence shows the delicate nature of such opportunities. Other examples do not abound, but a few may be found.

As a final note, studies and experience show that negotiations reach a more satisfactory result most efficiently when there is a feeling of equality between the parties.[15] Equality in standing and in reciprocation are crucial both to the negotiation situation and the negotiation process. Parties need to remove barriers to perceptions of inequality on the part of their opponents if they are to negotiate effectively. Such actions may be purely verbal and symbolic, involving seating, venues, numbers, languages, and so on; or they may have substantive implications for the party perceived to be stronger, such as recognition and reciprocity; or they may require balancing behavior on the part of the party perceived to be weaker, such as exaggerated demands, hardline bargaining, and unconventional behavior. It may be objected that equality is empowering and therefore contrary to the stronger side's interests, but parties need empowerment to reach and hold an agreement.

Thus, negotiations for the management and settlement of conflict depend on the situational context, in negative or positive terms. Ripe moments exist and become operational when their objective existence is perceived, although that perception is not automatic. Since they exist and are perceived, they can be created, and their perception can be aided and encouraged. These helping efforts may well come from doves in the ruling coalitions of the conflicting parties, but they are likely to need some major assistance, through leverage and persuasion, from the outside.

▲ Mediation

Third parties, including superpowers and great powers but also the organs of the United Nations, may be external mediators. Or they may be agencies of a regional security regime, either regional organizations or more informal concerts of leading friends and neighbors.[16] Either type may be needed to bring conflicts to an end and watch over the final outcome, but their activities are more likely to be necessary in the prenegotiation stages, in varying degrees of ripeness. Since mediation helps parties find a way out of their conflict, a formula for its resolution, and may even be necessary to help create or consolidate the stalemate that is the core of ripeness, mediators cannot wait for moments to ripen on their own; their very role is part of the ripening or prenegotiation process, as well as part of the final resolution. Whatever the agency, its activities can be conceived along a continuum of roles derived from the parties' needs. Listed in order of the mediator's degree of involvement, they are mediation as communication, as formulation, and as manipulation.[17]

The *mediator as communicator* addresses the conflict as a breakdown in the ability of the parties to communicate with each other. The conflict may make direct contacts impossible. It may prohibit the flexibility required for concessions, which the parties cannot make unless they can find a way to convey them without appearing weak or losing face. In this situation, mediators may be needed to act simply as telephone wires, establishing contacts and carrying messages. Parties may also need mediation in order to hear clearly, or to see the meaning of messages through the dust of distortion thrown up by the conflict. They may be the target of communications when the parties cannot talk to each other and even the receiver of concessions when the parties cannot give in to each other. They may then pull the concessions together into a package to present to the parties. This role is completely procedural, with no substantive contribution by the mediator, and completely passive, only involving carrying out the parties' orders for the delivery of messages. Tact, trust, honesty, and sympathy are necessary character traits of the mediator as communicator, to be served in equal doses with accuracy and confidentiality.

Regional agencies are usually best suited to play the role of mediator as communicator. They have discreet and unobtrusive access to the conflicting parties, and they know the local nuances. By the same token, they tend to rely on persuasion, since they have few other sources of leverage, an aspect that also underscores their role as communicator. As a result, they are well placed to help conflicting parties deal with aspects of prenegotiation, particularly items such as cost and risk and requitement, and are able to convey other prenegotiation items from one party to the other, facilitating the eventual establishment of direct contacts between the parties to conclude the negotiations.

Within the framework of the Organization for African Unity (OAU), in 1963 Malian President Modibo Keita and Ethiopian Emperor Haile Selassie acted as communicators to mediate a ceasefire in the border war between Morocco and Algeria; and two decades later, in 1987, Saudi King Fahd mediated the beginnings of a reconciliation between the two countries that opened the way for an eventual U.N.-sponsored referendum in the second.[18] In the mid-1960s Presidents Ibrahim Abboud of Sudan, Julius Nyerere of Tanzania, and Kenneth Kaunda of Zambia communicated between Ethiopia and Somalia, mediating a ceasefire in their border war; and in the late 1980s the secretary-general of the Inter-Governmental Agency on Drought and Development (IGADD) arranged a conflict management meeting between the two.[19] In the early 1990s Presidents Daniel Arap Moi of Kenya, Robert Mugabe of Zimbabwe, Kamazu Banda of Malawi, and F. W. de Klerk of South Africa carried communications between the Mozambican government and its RENAMO insurgency, preparing for final mediated negotiations on a resolution process in Rome.[20]

The second mode of mediation requires the mediator to take a more substantive role. The conflict may not only prevent the parties from communicating with each other but so involve them that it prevents them from conceiving of ways out of the dispute. They need a *mediator as formulator*. Mediators should be capable of the innovative thinking that is blocked by the blinders worn by the parties to the conflict, and they should be capable of working out ways to get around the parties' constraining commitments. If the conflict prevents the parties from finding imaginative formulas for resolution on their own, it may also prevent them from seeing the value of the mediator's suggestions at first glance; thus, the mediator as formulator often needs not only to suggest but also to persuade. Persuasion is a form of power, requiring greater involvement from the mediator than does mere communication.

Since formulation helps the conflicting parties see a way out of their conflict, it also helps put into place the final elements of the ripe moment. It must be performed by a mediator who has the confidence of the parties and the imagination to see solutions that they cannot see. Regional friends and neighbors are well suited for this task, but external powers and personalities can also be useful as formulators. The mode takes more experience and creativity than mere communication, and therefore bodies set up for the purpose (such as the Group of Elders comprising former African heads of state, initially Julius Nyerere of Tanzania, Leopold Sedar Senghor of Senegal, Aristides Pereira of Cape Verde Islands, and Kenneth Kaunda of Zambia, and led by Olusegun Obasanjo of Nigeria) have a particularly important role to play.[21] Although little documentation is available on this mode, the role of President Felix Houphouet Boigny of the Côte d'Ivoire in resolving the Mali-Burkinabe conflict in 1988 appears to be an example.[22]

Yet this degree of involvement still may not be enough. In the third mode, the mediator acts as *manipulator,* with maximum involvement that makes him a party in the solution, if not in the dispute. The manipulator is required to use his power to bring the parties to an agreement, pushing and pulling them away from conflict and into resolution. Not only must the mediator promote his formula for a solution but he must also take measures to make that solution more attractive, enhancing its value by adding benefits to its outcome and distributing them in order to overcome imbalances that may have prevented one party or another from subscribing to it. Not only must the mediator help improve the absolute attractiveness of a solution but he may even have to do so relatively by increasing the unattractiveness of continued conflict, an involvement that may mean shoring up one side or condemning another and further straining the appearances of neutrality. This is the role of the "full participant," as the U.S. diplomatic position in the Middle East peace process in the 1970s and in the Namibian-Angolan negotiations in 1980s was described.

Since manipulation involves power, it is the mode of mediation that is more frequently open to external parties than to regional actors. It is also devoted more to the direct search for solutions than to the functions of prenegotiation. In addition, manipulation comes into play when third parties try to help conflicting parties into negotiation by working to ripen the moment. Sometimes manipulation is accomplished through tangible assets to sweeten the pot— U.S. promises of aid to Israel and Egypt in the Sinai withdrawal agreements and at Camp David—and sometimes it works through support for one side or the other to keep it in the contest and to preserve a balance—U.S. arms to Israel in the October War and to Morocco in the Saharan War. But other times, the means of manipulation is merely good relations with the party or parties: in the Madrid peace process or in the Angolan-Namibian negotiations, the prime source of power for the United States was the desire of all sides to maintain good relations with Washington.

Power or leverage is the ticket to mediation, yet the mediator is essentially rather powerless. Third parties are accepted as mediators only to the extent that they are likely to produce an agreement acceptable to both sides. Thus any power the mediator may have depends entirely on the parties. This somewhat circular dilemma plagues every mediation exercise. Contrary to a common notion, mediators are rarely "hired" by the parties; instead, they have to sell their services, entirely on the basis of the prospect of their usefulness and success. Because they have a greater interest in ending the conflict than do the parties, they often fear failure more than the parties do. Their leverage may be further weakened because their reputation for ending conflicts and their interest in a solution are at the mercy of the contestants. The parties have an interest in winning. To them mediation is meddling unless it can produce a favorable outcome. They welcome it only to the extent that the mediator has leverage over the other party, and they berate the mediator for trying to exert leverage over them.

A mediator has only four sources of leverage: the ability to portray an alternative future as more favorable than the continuing conflict; the ability to produce an attractive position from the other side; the availability of resources that the mediator can withhold from one side in the conflict or shift to the other; and the availability of resources that the mediator can add to the outcome. The first pair relate to formulation, the second to manipulation, further limiting the mediator's array of power.

The first source is persuasion. The mediator must be able to point out the attractiveness of conciliation on available terms and the unattractiveness of conflict, a purely communicative exercise independent of any resources. U.S. Secretary of State Henry Kissinger, whose country was not devoid of resources or the willingness to use them, nevertheless spent long hours painting verbal pictures of the future with and without an agreement for Egyptian, Syrian, and Israeli audiences.[23] President Jimmy Carter's mediation at Camp David and then in Jerusalem shows the same power and limitations of persuasion.[24]

The second source is the most circular of all, and yet it is the basis of all mediation. As already noted, mediation is unwelcome until it can provide the other party's agreement to a solution that is viewed favorably by the first party, and then vice versa. The crucial moment in many mediations comes when the mediator asks a party's permission to try for the other's agreement to a proposal, and this exchange is the heart of the mediation mode as formulation.

The last two sources carry mediation into manipulation, since they use the conflict and the proposed solution as the fulcrums for leverage. Leverage as shifting weight refers to the mediator's ability to tilt toward or away from a party in the conflict and thereby bring about a stalemate or reduce the possibility of escalating out of it. Such activity may be verbal, such as a statement or a vote of condemnation, or more tangible, such as visits, food aid, or even arms shipments. It is designed to stiffen the dilemma of parties rejecting mediation and to keep them in the search for a solution. Shifting weight may actually be used to prevent a loser from emerging, when either a particular winner or any winner in the conflict would produce a situation that would be less stable and hence less desirable in the mediator's eyes. The 1980 U.S. sales of arms to Morocco, which it had refused to arm in 1978, during the Western Saharan conflict; its willingness to condemn South Africa under Carter and then to withhold condemnation under Reagan during different rounds of the Namibian negotiations; and the 1991 refusal to guarantee loans to Israel until the Israeli government became more forthcoming on negotiations are examples of shifting weight for tactical purposes related to mediation. It is clear that such activity brings the mediator very close to being a party in the conflict, as the mode of manipulation suggests.

The fourth source of mediators' leverage is the side payment, the action to which the term *leverage* is usually applied. Side payments increase the value of the outcome to one or more parties and require considerable resources and engagement from the mediators. They are rarer than they are commonly thought to be, and they are certainly not the key to successful mediation. Yet there may be times when the outcome does not provide sufficient benefits for both parties and does outweigh the present or anticipated advantages of continued conflict. On such occasions, additional benefits are needed. Side payments may be attached to the outcomes themselves, such as third-party guarantees or financial aid to accomplish changes required by the agreement. Or they may be simply conditional benefits, unrelated to the outcome itself, that make agreement more attractive, such as U.S. development aid to Egypt and Israel or diplomatic recognition of the Angolan government. But side payments are also known as bribes and may therefore carry counterproductive connotations.

In the end, it is evident that in each case the source and effectiveness of leverage lie with the parties themselves, a characteristic that makes the mediator's power extremely limited. The overriding considerations in power are persuasion and need, on which depends the ability of the mediator to reorient the perceptions of the parties. Persuasion hangs on the more or less skillful employment of many different referents to make conciliation more attractive and continuing conflict less so. Need may refer to a solution that the parties cannot achieve by themselves, improved relations within the structure of regional or global interactions, or a larger package of payoffs to make a conciliatory outcome attractive. Perception of such need and susceptibility to persuasion can be enhanced by the mediator, but they cannot be created out of nothing. It is of such paradoxes and complexities that the job of peacemaker is made.

▲ Bargaining

It may appear that after the provision of prenegotiation functions, ripe moments, and third-party mediation, the matter of bargaining strategies is epiphenomenal. The reverse is true. Only after the preliminary elements are in place can actual bargaining be addressed; and since it too is conducted by fallible humans, it has all the possibilities of going awry, even after careful preparation, usually by others. After the elements of preparation and diagnosis are in place, conflicting parties should be at the point where they can address the possibilities of cooperation and reconciliation directly without abandoning their conflict policy track. Beyond the basic admonitions of successful negotiation—"find a relevant, flexible, coherent, irreplaceable, balanced and comprehensive formula," "implement it honestly in detail"—a few other specific guidelines are applicable to regional conflict. They stand out because of their particular importance in finding solutions to regional conflicts and because they are so frequently ignored.

Domestic regional and ethnic conflicts and demands should be handled early, by means of normal politics, while government legitimacy is still intact and grievances are manageable. If rebuffed and neglected, such demands cause the aggrieved community to turn inward, consolidate its political organization, challenge the legitimacy of the state, look for neighbors' support and sanctuary, and reject government efforts to meet their grievances as too little too late. In this "consolidation" phase, negotiations are out of the question, and an opportunity for low-cost resolution of the problem has been lost. Only in a later phase, when equality between government and rebellion has been established and a military stalemate has been achieved, is negotiation again possible, and then only on very different terms, or else the negotiation that is possible is only one involving surrender of one side to the other, following a prolonged escalating military confrontation. It takes a long and costly time for ripeness to be achieved in these cases. Neighboring governments, distant patrons, and regional organizations can all join to play a useful role in urging a government to handle its internal problems at an early stage, before these escalating costs and difficulties arise.[25]

The legitimacy of the other party and its concerns should be recognized, and it should be brought into a newly enlarged and cooperative political relationship. Negotiations take place because one party has been able to impose a problem and prevent the other from imposing its own solution, and they occur most fruitfully when they take place between parties that see themselves as equals. It is therefore not fruitful to seek to win at the negotiating table what has been out of reach on the battlefield, and attempts to do so will simple lead to renewed conflict, as events in Angola, Eritrea, and the Western Sahara show. Whether the issue is internal (secessionist or centralist) or regional (rank and relation), it is managed and led to resolution by an agreement that brings the parties into a new, expanded system of political interaction. Recognition of this fact has been the key to success in negotiations between the government and the various rebel groups in Colombia and in the long reconciliation process that included the Khmer Rouge in Cambodia; and it was the barrier to negotiations with the Shining Path in Peru, where the unassimilability of the rebel group shows the limits of the effectiveness of a recognition strategy. Regionally, the importance of mutual recognition between conflicting parties is the slow gradual lesson of a creeping settlement in the Middle East, and it was the barrier to negotiations in the two Gulf wars.

The maxim is particularly important in regard to negotiations over a mechanism of settlement that is definitive and has the potential to lead to the elimination of one party, such as a vote or referendum. In this case, the curious key to an agreement is the belief by both sides that they will win in the test. This was the key to the solution in Zimbabwe in 1979, in Namibia in 1989, and in Angola in 1992, and it was the purported key in the Western Sahara, Mozambique, and Cambodia in 1993–94. This illusion must be maintained, for it is the basis of any free vote; in most cases, without it people would not run. But the maxim also suggests that there must be a role for the loser after the vote and an assurance that political elimination does not mean physical elimination. Conflict-ending elections should determine the proportion of seats to allocate to the various parties, not the absolute winner in a winner-takes-all contest. The resulting power sharing will doubtless not be easy, and it is to be expected that the parties will continue maneuvering to best each other even as they are forced to cooperate. But the behavior of Robert Mugabe's winning ZANU Party in Zimbabwe in the early 1980s, as it tried to crush its opposition, and of Jonas Savimbi's losing UNITA Party in Angola in 1993, as it returned to rebellion after losing the elections, shows conclusively that parties to a long conflict have little idea of how to act as a loyal opposition, even less than they have of how to share power. Training in democracy takes a while; parties must be eased out of conflict and into management and resolution.

It is important to separate the internal conflict from its external support and to deal with the latter first, but negotiations with the former should seek an agree-

ment with the core of the rebellion rather than with an unrepresentative moderate fringe. When parties try to handle the external and internal manifestations of a conflict at the same time, they find it hard to play on both levels. Dealing with the external support first creates the context for successful management of the internal conflict and engages the domestic authority to deal with the rebellion fairly, lest its external supporters reenter the fray. This was Chester Crocker's lesson of the Namibian-Angolan conflict, as he mediated an agreement among the Cuban, Russian, Angolan, and South African governments before dealing with the internal Namibian and Angolan conflicts, and it holds broadly.[26] Again, an apparent exception may be the possibility of turning the hurtful stalemate against the external support of the rebellion, so that the host state becomes motivated to serve as the mediator between home state and rebellion and even to deliver the rebellion in the negotiations.[27] This is a fruitful possibility, as seen in the Addis Ababa agreement of 1972, but one that is rarer than theoretically possible. The other part of the same maxim is that negotiations with one's friends on the other side are merely a setup for escalating stakes. Against all sentiment, parties seeking agreement must jump over their friends and engage the core of the opponents forces if they are to find a truly valid spokesman with a chance of delivering compliance to an agreement.

Ceasefires should be created as testable signs of commitment, but parties should not use their temporary breach as an excuse to break off negotiations. Since a ceasefire removes the dynamic relationship between force and negotiation and the possibility of last-minute adjustments in power relations, it is more likely to conclude than to open negotiations. Temporary, unilateral, tacit, and informal ceasefires can be trial balloons that help negotiations get started and can even turn into longer-term, more formal arrangements. However, the conflict and the conflict resolution must have reached a point where the power structure is no longer in doubt and force is no longer necessary for a formal ceasefire to receive the parties' support. Beyond that point, refusal of a ceasefire is a sign of bad faith, but before that point it is not. However, identification of that point is a matter of such subjective interpretation that it is not always clear. Since the opening of direct talks can probably be considered a deescalation step, a conflict event—an attack, an arms delivery— during actual negotiations is almost certainly a clear negative signal, and so a ceasefire to accompany negotiations is a reasonable expectation. (One must still be careful to discriminate between central control and local initiative in such a case, where part of the job of negotiations may be to protect an accommodating central organization from local challenges, as well as from poor communications.) A ceasefire as a prelude to negotiations helps to create trust and to start the process of commitment; but it should not be a necessary pre-condition, and governments should not play into the hands of extremists by telling them that an incident will cause the talks to collapse.

Boundaries should be demarcated, but permeable, and they should be demarcated in a time of peace. All boundaries are artificial; any line that separates neighbors and tells them that they are basically different and foreign to each other disrupts human activity. New and young states need to "nationalize" their boundaries, making them part of their national life and history. If this is not done by diplomacy, it will be done by war. A large proportion of the Third World boundaries are not clearly and permanently marked on the ground, and only a small proportion of this number are currently in dispute. Left un-attended, the disputed boundaries are certain to erupt in conflict, either on their own over incidents that break out or as a result of deliberate policy deci-sions. Left unmarked, even the undisputed boundaries are tinder for conflict, accidentally or deliberately.

Two measures are needed to reduce the likelihood of such conflict. One is to make the demarcation of boundaries a deliberate national policy, remov-ing ambiguity from those boundaries already delimited and forcing agreement over those not yet resolved. If boundary settlements are carried out during times of good neighborliness, the weight of such relations works in their favor. The other measure is to make the established boundaries as permeable as pos-sible, consistent with each country's national security. Allowing border cross-ings and commerce with a minimum of difficulties helps reduce the potential for border incidents and larger conflicts that is inherent in artificial, disruptive barriers. As in many aspects of conflict reduction, a combination of precise and soft measures is the best recipe.

Conflict management is a more manageable goal than conflict resolution, but it raises expectations for, and must be followed by, conflict resolution measures. Resolution of conflicts is hard to negotiate cold, and it is even harder in the heat of violence. Management of conflict—the reduction or elimination of the means of carrying out the conflict—is easier to achieve and provides a cooling-off or winding-down period for the parties to the conflict. It is one of the great ironies of conflict management measures that in reducing the cost and pressure of conflict, they work to reduce the chances of a ripe moment. There may be no way around this problem, but it reinforces the need to turn conflict management moments to good use by pushing on to conflict resolution as the next step.

Both negative and positive examples are available.[28] After the Moroccan-Algerian war of 1963, which was mediated to a ceasefire by two African heads of state, an OAU committee studied the causes of the war for years, giving the parties time to back off from their war footing. At the end of the decade, the two neighbors began direct bilateral negotiation over a series of rapprochement agreements, ending in 1972 with a definitive border agreement covering an area where no border had previously existed; unfortunately, the Western Saharan issue arose two years later to destroy the progress that had been made. On the other hand, and on the other side of the continent, the Somali-Ethiopian war of 1964 was also mediated to a ceasefire by an African head of state. Further conflict management measures were mediated by two other African presidents in 1967. Somalia expected that a resolution of the disputed border issue would follow, but Ethiopia, with strong OAU support, resolutely denied that there was any dispute. In 1977, when the Ethiopian revolution appeared to sap the strength of the former empire, Somalia struck in an effort to resolve on the battlefield what could not be resolved diplomatically. Both sides were worse off when this attempt also failed.

Conflict resolution efforts should end by building cooperation, establishing mechanisms for handling further conflicts, and creating institutions for collaboration. If conflict reduction means a lessened propensity on the part of regional rivals to resort to threats or use of force to achieve their goals, then it is an ongoing matter of follow-through and prevention, not just a matter of ending a current dispute. Ending the conflict itself is not enough, for unless ongoing cooperative relationships are created, new conflicts will arise to undo the old resolutions and disrupt the new relations. Conflicting neighbors need to be engaged in continuing and institutionalized cooperation activities, with provisions for bodies and procedures to handle new or renewed problems as they arise. Former adversaries need to have their energies harnessed in building collaboration in other fields so that any new conflicts will have greater ties of interdependence to overcome before they can break out. Again, negative and positive examples abound. On the negative side, it is not surprising that states withdraw from regional organizations in order to pursue new paths of conflict, since organizational ties restrict the possibilities of engaging in conflict. On the positive side, Moroccan-Algerian reconciliation in 1988 was followed by the establishment in 1989 of the Arab Maghrib Union (UMA) to keep the neighbors in harmony; Somali-Ethiopian attempts at conflict management again in 1986–88 took place within IGADD. Conflicts are not just solved, as math problems are; like any kind of positive, living relationship, they need continual tending and monitoring.

NOTES

1. The South African internal conflict comes to mind as a rare, unmediated exception. Recent works in the extensive literature on mediation include C. R. Mitchell and K. Webb, eds., *New Approaches to International Mediation* (New York: Greenwood, 1988); Kenneth Kressell and Dean Pruitt, eds., *Mediation Research* (San Francisco: Jossey Bass, 1989); Jacob Berkovitch and Jeffrey Rubin, eds., *Mediation in International Relations* (New York: St. Martin's Press, 1992); and Saadia Touval and I. William Zartman, eds., *Theory and Reality in International Mediation* (Boulder, Colo.: Westview Press, 1987).

2. For a fuller discussion, see Janice Stein, ed., *Getting to the Table* (Baltimore: Johns Hopkins University Press, 1989); and esp. I. William Zartman, "Pre-Negotiation: Phases and Functions," in the same book.

3. See Timothy Sisk, *The Elusive Social Contract* (Princeton: Princeton University Press, 1994); and Stephen John Stedman, ed., *The New Is Not Yet Born: Conflict and Conflict Resolution in Southern Africa* (Washington, D.C.: Brookings Institution, 1994).

4. I. William Zartman, *Ripe for Resolution,* 2d ed. (New York: Oxford University Press, 1989), chap. 5.

5. Joseph Johnson and Maureen Berman, eds., *Unofficial Diplomats* (New York: Columbia University Press, 1977); Douglas Johnston and Cynthia Sampson, eds., *Religion: The Missing Dimension in Statecraft* (New York: Oxford University Press, 1994).

6. There is a growing literature on ripeness. See I. William Zartman, "The Strategy of Preventive Diplomacy in Third World Conflicts," in *Managing U.S.-Soviet Rivalry,* ed. Alexander George (Boulder, Colo.: Westview Press, 1983); idem, *Ripe for Resolution;* Richard Haass, *Conflicts Unending* (New Haven: Yale University Press, 1990); and Louis Kriesberg and Stuart Thorson, eds., *Timing the Deescalation of International Conflicts* (Syracuse: Syracuse University Press, 1991).

7. Marina Ottoway, "Eritrea: The Wrong Moment," in *Elusive Peace: Negotiating an End to Civil War,* ed. I. William Zartman (Washington, D.C.: Brookings Institution, 1995).

8. Norma Salim, ed., *Cyprus: A Regional Conflict* (London: Macmillan, 1992).

9. William B. Quandt, ed., *The Middle East Ten Years after Camp David* (Washington, D.C.: Brookings Institution, 1988).

10. For an excellent discussion of the escalation process, see Dean Pruitt, Jeffrey Rubin, and Song-Yoo Kim, *Social Conflict,* 2d ed. (New York: Random House, 1993).

11. Jeffrey Rubin, ed., *The Dynamics of Third Party Intervention* (New York: Praeger, 1981).

12. See Zartman, *Ripe for Resolution,* chap. 5.

13. Donald Rothchild and Carolyn Hartzell, "The Road to Estoril," in Zartman, *Elusive Peace.*

14. Ibrahim Msabaha, "The Mediation of Conflict in Mozambique," in Zartman, *Elusive Peace.*

15. Jeffrey Rubin and Bert Brown, *The Social Psychology of Bargaining and Negotiation* (New York: Academic Press, 1975), 213–33.

16. On agencies that may serve as third parties, see Berkovitch and Rubin, *Mediation in International Relations.*

17. See Stein, *Getting to the Table;* Zartman, "Pre-Negotiation"; and I. William Zartman and Saadia Touval, "Mediation: The Role of Third Party Diplomacy and Informal Peacemaking," in *Resolving Third World Conflict,* ed. Cheryl Brown and Kimber Schraub (Washington, D.C.: U.S. Institute of Peace, 1992).

18. See Zartman, *Ripe for Resolution,* chap. 2.

19. Saadia Touval, *The Boundary Politics of Independent Africa* (Boston: Harvard University Press, 1972); Zartman, *Ripe for Resolution,* chap. 2.

20. Msabaha, "The Mediation of Conflict in Mozambique."

21. Olesegun Obasanjo, *The Kampala Document* (New York: African Leadership Forum, 1991).

22. Jean Emmanuel Pondi, "Negotiations between Mali and Burkina Faso," in *Power and Asymmetry in Negotiation,* ed. Jeffrey Rubin and I. William Zartman (Laxenburg, Austria: International Institute of Applied Systems Analysis, in press). On African mediation and negotiation, see I. William Zartman, "Inter-African Negotiations," in *Africa in World Politics,* ed. John Harbeson and Donald Rothchild, 2d ed. (Boulder, Colo.: Westview Press, 1994).

23. Mati Golan, *The Secret Conversations of Henry Kissinger* (New York: Quadrangle, 1976).

24. William B. Quandt, *Camp David* (Washington, D.C.: Brookings Institution, 1986).

25. For further discussion of the life cycle of internal conflicts and its effect on negotiation, see Zartman, *Elusive Peace;* and idem, "Negotiation and Pre-Negotiation in Ethnic Conflict," in *Conflict and Peacekeeping in Multiethnic Societies,* ed. Joseph Montville (New York: Lexington Books, 1990).

26. Chester Crocker, *High Noon in Southern Africa* (New York: W. W. Norton, 1992).

27. For further discussion of the mediating role of host countries and neighbors, see I. William Zartman, "Internationalization of Communal Strife: Temptations and Opportunities for Triangulation," in *The Internationalization of Communal Strife,* ed. Manus Midlarsky (New York: Routledge, 1992).

28. Negative and positive examples are discussed in greater detail in Zartman, *Ripe for Resolution,* chaps. 2 and 3.

JACK SNYDER

12 | Military Force and Regional Order

The end of the Cold War has spurred much discussion of a new world order. Some contend that the liberal democratic "end of history" and the "obsolescence of major war" will be the defining features of the emerging international system.[1] But the millennium has not arrived yet. The first major issue of the new era was a million-soldier struggle in the Persian Gulf, justified in part by the need to uphold the peaceful principles of the new world order against the depredations of a regional aggressor. A second major issue has been the debate on the need for forceful "peacemaking," not just peacekeeping, to restore social order to hotbeds of interethnic strife.

Thus, the possible use of military force by the great powers will continue to cast a shadow over regional conflicts. However, decisions about the use of force will be taken against the backdrop of a dramatically changed international system. Indeed, the struggle to establish a new world order might itself be a stimulus to military interventions. Now that Cold War patterns of intervention are obsolete, what new pattern will emerge? And in a prescriptive mode, how should military intervention be used as a policy instrument in the new international environment?

To organize the discussion of these questions, I distinguish three patterns of great-power relations that shape the use of force in regional conflicts, that is, in conflicts involving smaller powers as key participants or targets. The first pattern posits competitive relations among the great powers. In this pattern, great powers' interventions in regional conflicts are driven by a concern to improve their power relative to that of their great-power competitors, to contain and deter them, or to gain mercantilist economic advantages over them. The second pattern posits the unilateral hegemony of a single great power, either globally or, more typically, within an exclusive sphere of influence. The third pattern is a multilateral hegemony in which all the great powers intervene in a concerted fashion to manage threats to regional order.

Real international systems have sometimes mirrored one or another of these ideal types closely, sometimes loosely. The future international order, like some past systems, may be a mixed type. Nonetheless, as a heuristic to uncover some of the patterns and pitfalls of possible future situations, it will be useful to think through the players' incentives and the typical outcomes in the ideal type cases.

In thinking through the typical motives and patterns in the three situations, I proceed from a highly modified version of realist political assumptions. That is, I assume that political actors, including states, are motivated by self-interest and above all by an interest in security. They are rational in the minimal sense that they are normally sensitive to cost, benefits, and the likelihood that their endeavors will succeed. Unlike a typical realist analysis, however, I assume that states' cost-benefit calculations are influenced by the relative power of domestic political groups and coalitions, which may have interests in different policies toward regional conflicts. I also assume that cost-benefit calculations are influenced by strategic myths and misperceptions that color debates on military intervention in regional questions.[2]

This is not a chapter on how to use force to cope with the problems of regional conflict, assuming the existence of will, wallet, and a benign intent on the part of the powerful. Rather it is mostly a commentary on how problematic the preconditions for such a policy are. Insofar as it is prescriptive, it points to the need to identify constructive policy instruments to fit that problematic reality.

▲ The Competitive Pattern

In the competitive pattern, states are driven by the fear that if they fail to maintain their relative power, they will become vulnerable to conquest or exploitation in the long run.[3] This pattern is the main one prevailing throughout recorded history; despite predictions of the end of history, it can hardly be written off. Even if great-power military competition might strike many observers as improbable in the short run, concern over relative gains in economic competition between rival trading blocs has a decidedly contemporary ring.[4] There are also signs that Russian nationalists' ideas about how to settle regional disputes along Russia's periphery differ markedly from the attitudes of the advanced democracies. Military or economic competition among the great powers may once again shape choices about military intervention in regional conflicts.

A great power adopting this competitive outlook faces a dilemma when responding to regional conflicts: military intervention may be necessary to protect strategic positions or resources on which one's relative power depends, yet the costs of fighting for those positions may at the same time sap one's power.[5] On one hand, there is an incentive to use military force to intervene unilaterally in weak or troubled regions in order to seize valuable resources, control strategic geographical positions, or defend regional allies. Such interventions may be spurred as much by the desire to keep such resources out of the hands of competitors as by the desire to control the resources for oneself. Especially because the future value of underdeveloped resources is unknown, there is often a strong tendency to seize the assets as a hedge against uncertainty.

On the other hand, intense military competition for control of uncertain regional assets can drain resources and divert investment from domestic productivity, on which the state's future relative power depends. Sometimes it will be prudent to let others exhaust themselves for little profit, improving one's relative position by doing nothing.[6] Thus, concern over long-run competitive position leads to a distinctive mode of calculation vis-à-vis regional turmoil, but it does not necessarily lead to favorable decisions on the use of military force.

An example is provided by the scramble for Africa in the 1890s and what Paul Kennedy calls the "crisis of the middle powers."[7] Earlier, Alexis de Tocqueville had predicted that Russia and the United States, by virtue of their continental size and resources, would be the superpowers of the future. At the end of the nineteenth century, the European states became increasingly convinced that to survive as great powers in a future system of larger entities, old nation-states would have to carve out continent-sized, potentially autarkic resource bases, whether in "Mitteleuropa," "Mittelafrika," or elsewhere. In the Darwinian struggle they envisioned, failing to compete aggressively was a sure way to lose. Likewise, the Japanese in 1941 worried that they would "miss the bus" if they failed to use Hitler's diversion as a chance to carve out their own autarkic empire, defensible even against their continent-sized foes.[8] No one was sure whether a place like Africa would turn out to be a geopolitically and economically crucial "second India," but the perceived pressure to achieve a continent-sized base made military competition there and elsewhere seem an unavoidable risk.[9]

However, the participants in the scramble also found that the costs of competition were high, in terms of both resources and diplomatic isolation. Because of the expense of the Boer War and the colonial enmity British policies had provoked among all the European powers, Britain found itself hard pressed to maintain its accustomed position as the arbiter of the European balance of power. Although it remained centrally concerned with the security consequences of shifts in relative power, Britain came to understand that selective conciliation, rather than indiscriminate military intervention, would best ensure its comparative position.[10]

Similarly, American debates on how to contain Soviet power often focused on the consequences for America's long-run power position of intervention in regional contests. Proponents of selective containment argued that only competition for the great industrialized powers mattered, because only they had the ability to affect the overall balance of power between the two superpowers. Fighting brushfire wars would only weaken the United States on the important fronts.[11]

Conversely, proponents of global containment argued that even small setbacks in the periphery could snowball into larger defeats at the core. They contended that the short-run costs of military intervention should be weighed against the allegedly greater long-run costs of passivity. Like Hitler, the Soviets and the Chinese would be emboldened by small victories to grab for more. Resources gained in early conquests would strengthen them for subsequent rounds. U.S. allies would lose confidence and turn neutral; neutrals would cut a deal with the aggressor. Once tarnished, the United States' reputation for firm resistance could be recouped only through extremely costly, dangerous efforts. Thus, it was better and cheaper to nip aggression in the bud.[12]

When these justifications for global containment prevailed, two opposite kinds of consequences followed for the management of regional conflict. On one hand, the perception that every place on the globe was a vital interest left everyone hostage to the most reckless player. A reckless opponent could trigger a regional war at any time, and given the broad definition of interconnected vital interests, the defender would feel compelled to fight. Likewise, a reckless client could precipitate a crisis, and he would have to be backed up, even at the risk of direct military intervention by the protector, to prevent the loss of a vital ally. If every place was potentially vital, there would often be no choice but to back unsavory regimes pursuing aggressive policies. Perceived as indispensable, these regimes would have great bargaining leverage. Like Egyptian President Anwar el-Sadat in 1972–73, they might threaten to take their vital assets into the opponent's camp if they were not given the offensive weapons they desired. Like the Soviets, their great-power backers might perceive little alternative to accepting such a request, even though they had no desire to become embroiled in the risks of someone else's aggressive agenda.

On the other hand, the belief that every place is vital to the great powers in their mutual competition can have the advantage of clarifying commitments and making them highly credible. Especially when the great powers are nuclear-armed, this arguably enhances regional stability by sharpening the fear of nuclear retaliation for aggression. During the Cold War, this effect shaped the deterrent stalemate most clearly in Europe, which really was vital to both sides. The effect was attenuated elsewhere, since even the proponents of massive retaliation and the domino theory were loath to threaten nuclear war over peripheral setbacks.[13]

What are the chances that the competitive pattern, driven by relative gains concerns and the perception of an interdependent net of vital interests, could once again shape great-power intervention in regional conflicts? Such an outcome seems unlikely to become the main theme of international politics in the near future. Nonetheless, it could become a minor theme, with growth potential.

Today, a loose coalition of Russian nationalists, industrialists, the military, and opportunistic politicians are claiming that Western-oriented "new thinkers" have surrendered too much of Russia's military, economic, and ethnic security as the result of their naively cooperative approach to foreign affairs.[14] Ukraine, perhaps understandably, being a new state with an overweening neighbor, has been jealously guarding against real and imagined encroachments on its sovereignty, worrying that small concessions will lead down a slippery slope.[15] Japan has been pursuing narrowly competitive interests in its claims to the northern islands and, many would say, in its mercantilist economic strategy. Thus, relations among Russia, Japan, and Ukraine are already characterized by a competitive attitude, an orientation to relative rather than mutual gains, and fears that small concessions on regional issues would be exploited.

Beyond this, there is the possible drift toward the breakup of the open trading system into three partially closed blocs, centered on Japan, the United States, and Europe. Japan's bloc would be the smallest, the least self-sufficient, and the most vulnerable to pressure from the others. Conceivably, this situation could recreate what Kennedy calls "the crisis of the middle powers," where Japan might feel compelled once again to exploit the weakness of its Asian hinterlands to gain control over resources needed for a mercantilist policy vis-à-vis its larger competitors. If so, the competitive pattern of intervention in regional conflicts could reemerge.

What prescriptions flow from this unlikely but nonetheless conceivable possibility? The main prescription is to prevent the emergence of this competitive pattern by undermining the political coalitions in each country that would favor it. In Russia, the coalition basis of the foreign policy cleavage is beginning to take shape. A loose coalition, including elements of the military, industrialists, and nationalists, has begun to sketch out a rather coherent alternative in both domestic and foreign policy to the Westernizing, liberal, marketizing, dovish policies of former Prime Minister Yegor Gaidar and Foreign Minister Andrei Kozyrev. The nationalist-industrialist coalition is proposing a mutually reinforcing package of slow economic reform, continued state subsidies and central economic control, "nomenklatura privatization" benefiting old industrial elites, slowed economic integration with the capitalist world, a gradual reassertion of Russia's hegemony over its near neighbors, and the maintenance of Russian military power.[16] Insofar as this program risks triggering a number of regional conflicts, the West has an incentive to prevent the reemergence of this competitive pattern by helping liberals to stay in power by succeeding in their Westernizing reforms. Increased economic assistance to accomplish this should have sufficient conditions attached to bar its use to bankroll unproductive subsidies for the industrialists, yet the conditions should not cause such abrupt short-run dislocations that they play into the nationalists' hands.[17]

But what if competitive patterns of regional rivalry reemerge among some of the great powers despite such efforts? Four tried-and-true principles should be applied. First, spheres of vital interests should be recognized and respected. Second, where states have vital interests that extend beyond the spheres of their own control, other states should avoid threatening those interests, lest they trigger a casus belli. Thus, no matter how sharp the commercial competition with Japan, a reliable regime assuring Japan of the opportunity for free trade in oil must be maintained. Third, commentators and scholars must continue to remind politicians and the public of the dangers of erroneous arguments that exaggerate the strategic importance of nonvital interests, the reputational interdependence of commitments, and other variations on the domino theory.[18] Fourth, for the defense of important but nonvital allies and interests, states should adopt the habit of concluding conditional, defensive alliances. Thus, allies should be supported in regional conflicts if and only if they are the victims of attack and not the perpetrators.[19]

It should be noted that these prescriptions for regulating regional conflict in a competitive international system have little to do with the arenas of local conflict themselves. I have not mentioned peacekeeping, crisis micromanagement, or the creation of deterrent balances between the small-power rivals, although these might on occasion be useful measures. Rather, I focus my recommendations on preventing the emergence of political coalitions within the great powers espousing competitive ideas about grand strategy and, failing that, on general principles for the prudent conduct of a competitive great-power strategy. Only if these basics are handled properly can the details fall into place. If they are not, the cleverest tactics for managing regional disputes will be swept aside in the maelstrom of great-power competition.

▲ The Unilateral Hegemonic Pattern

A second pattern shaping the use of force is that of unilateral hegemony, in which a single strong state exerts decisive influence over a substantial region beyond its own core area. This includes the rare case of a state that faces no serious great-power rivals at all, as well as the case of hegemonic leadership within a sphere of influence that is not immediately contested by other great powers. The latter case is a hybrid, combining elements of the competitive and the unilateral hegemonic patterns.

Under unilateral hegemony, the essence of the problem is cost-effective domination within the sphere of influence. This is true regardless of the goals of hegemony. Hegemons out for economic plunder want to extract resources from their spheres of domination in the most cost-effective manner possible. Likewise, states that desire extensive empires as security buffers and sources of reliable strategic resources want to hold down the costs of protecting the empire. Even states with goals that include the psychological gratifications of ideological leadership must strive for cost-effectiveness in imperial management. Hegemons who ignore the imperative of efficiency in domination will soon find their sphere of control slipping away.

Some use of military force has always been indispensable in achieving and maintaining hegemonic domination, but force tends to be a comparatively costly instrument of statecraft.[20] As a result, successful hegemonic leaders usually employ military coercion as a last resort. Instead they try to develop cheaper means of everyday control. In part, they rely on their reputation for power, the memory of what they were able to do the last time they used force, and the prospect that, if pushed, they would do the same again. Sometimes they may rely on economic sanctions, which rarely get the direct short-run results of military force but can extract compliance as part of a long-run influence strategy. They also rely on economic inducements, which convince targets of influence that the benefits of remaining in the hegemon's sphere outweigh the attractions of revolt. When inducements are targeted on strategic elites or "swing" constituencies that decide which coalitions will rule, rather than distributed widely through the population, cost-effectiveness is increased.[21] Domestic coalitions can get hooked on economic, police, or ideological support from the hegemon and willingly help the hegemon exert its rule. Flexible bargains between the hegemon and its subject states can adjust the terms of vassalage, reducing the grievances of those most inclined to revolt. Ideologies can be developed to justify acquiescing to hegemonic leadership.[22]

Through all these means, the prudent hegemonic manager will try to adopt a strategy of low-cost, informal rule rather than resort to direct conquest and formal administration of subject peoples.[23] Especially in today's era of widespread political awareness, nationalism, and the diffusion of small arms, the use of force for direct hegemonic control comes at a premium.[24]

Despite the incentives to economize on the use of force, students of empires note a strong tendency for the costs of imperial security to rise over time. Often empires expand their sphere of control and commitment in times when they enjoy unusual advantages, such as when a major competitor has collapsed or when the empire has led the way in some military, organizational, or economic innovation that competitors have not yet succeeded in emulating. Then, when other states copy the innovations or simply return to their normal levels of relative power, the empire, without adding a single square mile to its holdings, becomes overextended. For example, the United States took on a global role after World War II when, owing to the devastation of the economies of all the other major states, it accounted for more than 30 percent of world Gross National Product (GNP) and more than 40 percent of world manufacturing output. Since the end of the 1960s it has struggled to maintain those commitments with just more than 20 percent of world GNP.[25]

Not only does the hegemon tend to decline relative to its would-be competitors but its hegemony often sets in motion social changes that cause conflict in the periphery of the empire. British penetration of traditional societies, for example, disturbed old political hierarchies, promoted new social groups, and spurred the development of intellectual and revolutionary elites that resented both imperial rule and the old elites of the traditional society. In places like South Africa, local economic development gave colonials the motive and the resources to break away from imperial rule and to engage in internecine squabbling. In Egypt, crushing debts of old patrimonial rulers weakened them in the face of revolutionary challengers. In short, hegemony promoted social change that created opposition to its domination, fostered turmoil among the locals, and eroded the hegemon's relative power.[26]

The instinct of most hegemons faced with this turmoil is to use force to reestablish order. Outright opponents of imperial rule must be resisted, even at a stiff price, according to the logic of the domino theory and reputational arguments. Even if turbulence is not directed at the hegemon, but simply at other locals, the empire may feel the need to reestablish order, on which efficient extraction and the legitimate right to rule depend. A decision to retrench from untenable positions will be difficult for an empire that has geared its self-conception, the prestige of its ruling elite, and its economic institutions toward the possession of an extensive empire.[27]

Coalition politics within the hegemonic leader affects the mix of instruments that the hegemon uses in establishing and maintaining its rule, as do the distinctive skills of the hegemonic state. "Trading states" will emphasize economic coercion and inducements, whereas great powers whose comparative advantage lies primarily in military force will have fewer options.[28] Commercial interests, like the City of London or the foreign-trading zaibatsu of the 1920s, tend to favor a different mix of instruments for imperial influence than do military or colonial bureaucracies. Likewise, in the Soviet Union after 1945, Communist Party ideologues tended to see revolutionary fifth columns as the best way to expand and consolidate Soviet hegemony, while other branches of the Soviet bureaucracy stressed their own instruments of power. Militaries are often ambivalent about the use of force to keep imperial order, especially those sectors of the military whose traditional mission is to fight other great powers in set-piece, conventional warfare. Nonetheless, states with a large military role in state ruling circles, as in the extreme case of imperial Japan, have tended toward the disproportionate use of military force in pursuit of hegemonic spheres.[29]

Beyond the effects of parochial interests, the broader ideological and constitutional character of the hegemonic regime also influences the instruments of imperial control available to it. Democracies are constrained from using methods of imperial control that result in many deaths of their own constituents and in large tax increases unless the government can persuasively explain why these costs are unavoidable. In the past they have usually justified interventions as a strategic necessity of competition with other great powers. At least in the near future, this rationale will often be unavailable.

In addition to being sensitive to costs, liberal democratic constituencies are sometimes concerned about uses of force that contradict liberal norms. Liberal regimes promoting a liberal world order would find it especially difficult to sustain strategies of control that involved civilian casualties in house-to-house combat in ethnically intermingled areas. Similarly, a regime with Japan's quasi-pacifist post-1945 constitution will not easily adopt military force as an instrument of influence.

Even during the belligerent Reagan period, the political preconditions listed by Secretary of Defense Caspar Weinberger virtually ruled out any use of force on a scale ranging from the total warfare of a possible World War III to a zero-casualty bombing raid. Thus, notwithstanding the recent Gulf War and Panama episodes, democratic leaders will rarely find the use of force attractive compared with other instruments of influence or with doing nothing in regional conflicts.

Strategic beliefs also affect the likelihood of adopting force as an instrument of imperial control. Whenever the domino theory is accepted, for example, it will seem cost-effective to use force to prevent the loss of the first domino, even in an intrinsically unimportant location, as an expedient to forestall the need to fight more costly battles in more important places in the future. The use of military force will look cost-effective when people can persuasively argue that a reputation for willingness to use force will deter future challenges elsewhere or that a key possession can be defended more cheaply if only barbarians on the turbulent frontier can be pacified once and for all. Such arguments are being used today to justify military intervention against the Serbs. Some Russian nationalists are concluding from the Serbian precedent that "ethnic cleansing" in ethnically mixed areas just beyond Russian borders would not be seriously opposed by the international community.[30] Conversely, it is sometimes argued that dealing with the spread of ethnic conflict and attendant migration problems would be more costly in the long run than using force to somehow solve the problem in Yugoslavia now. So far, such arguments seem far from persuasive.

For all of these reasons, any attempt at unilateral U.S. leadership of a hegemonic order would have to rely heavily on nonmilitary instruments like economic inducements, linked to the creation of Western-style institutions, and cooptation of local elites. In the absence of a very strong motive for involvement, however, the cost of even these lesser measures is likely to be too great.

▲ The Multilateral Hegemonic Pattern

In a multilateral hegemony, all the great powers agree on some basic principles of international order, on the legitimacy of the vital interests of the other great powers, and on the principle of acting in concert. Their motivation for the use of force in regional conflicts is the fear that if the dispute remains unresolved it will threaten the interests of one or more great powers, which might be compelled toward dangerous unilateral interventions.[31] Thus, in a multilateral hegemony interventions must be carried out by international forces like the U.N. blue helmets or, more commonly, by the national forces of great powers, designated to accomplish goals set by the great powers as a whole. Often this means that the nearest, most concerned great power receives authorization to use force, but under agreed limitations for agreed objectives only.

In the past this sort of arrangement has been rare. The Concert of Europe, which gradually unraveled between 1815 and approximately 1848, is usually considered the most successful example. It was associated with a very specific set of domestic coalitions and strategic ideas. After the defeat of revolutionary and Napoleonic France, conservative elites in all the great powers feared an expansion of political participation more than they feared each other, so they agreed to cooperate on a program to dampen political turbulence, which they thought would play into the hands of political radicals. They believed that political conditions across Europe were highly interdependent, that revolutionary instability in one region would cause a bandwagon elsewhere. Thus, each had an incentive to cooperate in managing political crises everywhere in and around Europe. The interlinked revolutions of 1830 and 1848 showed that they were right in this assessment.[32]

Any current revival of multilateral hegemony would have to recapitulate this combination of legitimist regimes with a belief in the global indivisibility of political stability. These conditions apply only imperfectly to the present. The advanced Western countries are firmly oriented toward maintaining the status quo, though Russia probably is not. These countries, riding high on a decisive and easy victory over a thoroughly discredited communist radicalism, do not seem to have a Metternichian fear of radicalism's revival. Thus, the motivation to band together to maintain a conservative social order is weaker.

Most importantly, only the United States believes in global strategic and political interdependence. Europeans, the Japanese, and the Russians see themselves as regional powers with regional interests. Europeans do not believe that Serbian aggression a few hundred miles away will significantly affect their security. The Japanese are standoffish in multilateral forums. The Chinese are wary of endorsing multilateral interventions, fearing a precedent for future international meddling in their own affairs. After a sour experience with proletarian internationalism, the Russians are in the mood for a Russia-first foreign policy. The Gulf War showed that the United States could mobilize the great powers to contribute to a multilateral use of force when obvious material interests were at stake; it is doubtful whether this could be repeated to counter less direct threats in a routine, effective manner.

Even if the preconditions for a multilateral hegemony were more firmly in place, other inherent problems would remain. The Concert of Europe was constantly plagued by divisiveness among the great powers. Some of these problems were geopolitical. Each power jockeyed to gain marginal improvements in its sphere of influence while trying not to violate Concert norms overtly. Sometimes the powers were even able to manipulate Concert norms in the service of unilateral gains. Under Prime Minister Palmerston, for example, Britain typically waited for Russia or France to take some aggressive, unilateral step unauthorized by the Concert; then, diplomatically isolating the transgressor of Concert norms, Britain would use or threaten force in order to consolidate its own domination over the disputed region. Several disputes involving Turkey between the 1830s and the Crimean War had this outcome. This is highly reminiscent of the manipulation of GATT (General Agreement on Tariffs and Trade) norms in seeking unilateral advantage in trade disputes today.[33] In a future world of incipient trading blocs, such tensions within the multilateral regime will surely remain.

Another source of conflict in the Concert of Europe was ideological divergence. Increasingly, British regimes found that the key to domestic stability was to accommodate pressures for expanded political participation rather than to maintain a solid aristocratic front against the rising middle classes. This also meant shifting the ideological legitimacy of the regime onto a more liberal foundation. Conservative governments like Palmerston's found that they could better restrain political change at home if they coopted radicals with support of liberalism abroad. This eventually destroyed the Concert, since Russia remained an archfoe of radicalism and liberalism in Europe. Throughout Europe, Britain and Russia increasingly tended to back opposite sides in regional and civil conflicts.[34]

However, this source of divisiveness may be less disruptive to a future multilateral hegemony. Apart from Russia, whose commitment to liberal ideology may be ephemeral, today's great powers seem much more unified and stable ideologically than those of the late Concert period.

Even if potential divisions among the great powers could be overcome, multilateral hegemony would still face many of the same problems that the unilateral approach faces. The exercise of hegemony is costly, especially through military force but also through economic coercion or cooptation. This is mitigated, as in the Gulf War, if costs are distributed among a number of states. Arguably, the advanced great powers might constitute what theorists of collective action call a "k-group" or "privileged group," in which each contributor to the provision of a public good receives sufficient private benefit to warrant paying its share. This was certainly true in the Gulf War.[35] Whether the benefits would be sufficient to sustain a k-group to police the Balkans or the Caucasus is highly questionable.

Only actors who believed strongly in the indivisibility of peace could warrant such a conclusion. They would have to argue convincingly that aggressors everywhere would be emboldened by a failure to punish them anywhere. But if this is true, then aggressors ought to have been well deterred by the example of the drubbing given to Iraq's Saddam Hussein. Somehow Serbia's Slobodan Milosevic failed to learn the right lesson. Too often, highly motivated aggressors conclude, whether for good reasons or wishful ones, that their case is different. Or, as in the Serbs' case, aggressors often perceive themselves as engaged in justifiable self-defense to which no one could possibly object. The post–Cold War U.S. public is likely to be justifiably skeptical about arguments for intervention based on upholding norms and teaching general lessons. As the Bush administration learned during the Gulf crisis, such arguments are hard to sell unless they can be tied to more tangible motives, such as the fear of a nuclear-armed Iraq.

Of course, multilateral interventions might nonetheless be acceptable if their costs were low enough. Costs in blood and treasure might be brought way down if eager, low-wage "gurkhas" were available in sufficient quantity to do the dirty work of policing the new world order. Similarly, it is possible that peacekeeping in ethnic disputes might be cheaper than the current Bosnian case makes it appear. Some social scientists believe that aggressive nationalists are motivated mostly by fear of attack by other groups.[36] Others believe that nationalism is highly malleable, depending on short-run changes in incentives and circumstances.[37] If these views are correct, preventive peacekeeping deployments might be highly effective in defusing the kind of security fears that arguably fueled strife in Croatia and Nagorno-Karabakh, thus shifting incentives away from nationalist mobilization. The preventive deployment of several hundred U.N. peacekeepers in Macedonia is serving as a test case of this view. On the other hand, if primordialist theories of deeply rooted ethnic hatreds are correct, multilateral intervention will be a quagmire.

Overall, multilateral intervention in regional conflicts has the major advantage of diffusing the costs of providing for a very expensive public good. For that reason, it may have somewhat greater viability than attempts to impose a unilateral hegemony. However, without the perception that peace is indivisible, the motivation to provide for the public good of keeping order may be too low to justify multilateral military interventions.

▲ Conclusions and Prescriptions

I have looked at the question of intervention in regional conflicts primarily from the standpoint of the various motivations that might spur or discourage the great powers' use of military force. Overall, I see some prospect for unilateral and multilateral interventions and less likelihood of competitive interventions. The future international "order" may be a hybrid that includes all of these types to varying degrees. There is some chance that Russia will use force to create a small unilateral hegemonic sphere along its immediate periphery. There is a good chance that the great powers will continue to intervene collectively in the Gulf to maintain the security of oil supplies. Competition for regional influence among the great powers is more likely to be economic, at least in the near term, than military. Dramatic domestic political changes would have to occur in Russia and Ukraine before a competitive military intervention in Crimea would occur.

The dominant pattern, however, is likely to be the refusal of the great powers to intervene in regional trouble spots. The interests engaged in most regional conflicts are too small to warrant even moderately costly interventions. Imperial political coalitions, which might invent interests in intervention, are not on the horizon for any of the great powers. Even the industrialist-nationalist coalition in Russia has a very limited imperial vision. Likewise, strategic beliefs that would justify widespread interventions—the domino theory, fears of a radical bandwagon, the notion that peace is indivisible, obsession with reputational precedents—are currently weak or absent among the great powers. Such beliefs are often crystallized by the emergence of a great geopolitical threat, but such a threat is nowhere in sight.[38]

Consequently, attempts to influence regional conflicts will in most cases have to rely on relatively inexpensive means. This will usually mean the use of nonmilitary instruments. However, some military strategies might be cost-effective and low in casualties for the intervening great powers. The deployment of peacekeeping forces before fighting breaks out might be inexpensive and effective in cases where the belligerence of both sides is driven by security fears. Also, peacekeeping to discourage a renewal of fighting after an aggressor achieves his main aims might be cost-effective. Although it may be ethically distasteful, a U.N. role in policing the internal borders of a Serb-dominated, cantonized Bosnia might speed the return to something like normal life in the region. In contrast, great-power peacemaking by force at the height of a regional conflict is likely to be ineffective and costly.

Other cost-effective strategies would include the sale or transfer of arms to the potential victims of aggression in local disputes. This would not necessarily prevent an outbreak of fighting, but it would help prevent the aggressor from achieving its aims at a tolerable cost to the great powers. Where possible, such transfers should be restricted to defensive types of weapons, such as anti-armor or antiaircraft weapons.

Moreover, defensive alliances might be concluded with threatened parties. The great powers might promise to provide air cover and transfers of defensive arms if and only if the ally were clearly the victim of aggression rather than the perpetrator. While not cost-free for the great powers, this strategy for deterring regional aggressors would at least place the burden of casualties on the local combatants.

Whether a strategy relying on arms sales and air power is attractive will depend on the great powers' goals. If the aim is to prevent the aggressor from threatening vital territories, as in the no-fly zone in Iraq, this approach might work very well, even if the aggressor decides to challenge the defensive alliance. But if the goal is to cause peace to avoid the unwanted migration of war refugees, the strategy will work only if it succeeds in deterring the would-be aggressor.

Finally, to reiterate my main point, the fate of attempts to create a liberal world order will not depend primarily on the devising of clever tactics for managing regional conflicts, whether by military or other means. Rather, the precondition for a stable world order is for the great powers to maintain peaceful, cooperative relations among themselves. To accomplish this, the most important task is to create conditions for the survival of liberal coalitions in those great powers where democracy is weakly institutionalized, especially Russia. First priority should be placed on the activities of Western financial institutions in Moscow, rather than on the efforts of the United Nations in Sarajevo.

NOTES

1. Francis Fukuyama, "The End of History?" *The National Interest* 16 (summer 1989): 3–18; John Mueller, *Retreat from Doomsday: The Obsolescence of Major War* (New

York: Basic Books, 1988); William Schneider, "The Old Politics and the New World Order," in *Eagle in a New World*, ed. Kenneth A. Oye (New York: Harper Collins, 1992), 35–70.

2. For the reasoning behind such an approach, see Jack Snyder, *Myths of Empire: Domestic Politics and International Ambition* (Ithaca: Cornell University Press, 1991), esp. 316–19.

3. Kenneth Waltz, *Theory of International Politics* (Reading, Mass.: Addison-Wesley, 1979).

4. Jeffrey Garten, *A Cold Peace: America, Japan, Germany, and the Struggle for Supremacy* (New York: Time Books, 1992).

5. Robert Gilpin, *War and Change in World Politics* (New York: Cambridge University Press, 1981).

6. For an example of this strategy, see David French, *British Strategy and War Aims, 1914–1916* (London: Allen & Unwin, 1986).

7. Paul Kennedy, *The Rise and Fall of the Great Powers* (New York: Random House, 1987), chaps. 4–6.

8. Michael Barnhart, *Japan Prepares for Total War* (Ithaca: Cornell University Press, 1987).

9. In addition to Kennedy, *Rise and Fall*, see Randall Schweller, "Hitler's Tripolar Strategy for World Conquest," in *Coping with Complexity in the International System*, ed. Jack Snyder and Robert Jervis (Boulder, Colo.: Westview Press, 1993), esp. 220–25.

10. Paul Kennedy, *Strategy and Diplomacy, 1870–1945* (London: Allen & Unwin, 1983), chaps. 1 and 8.

11. These arguments are discussed in John Lewis Gaddis, *Strategies of Containment* (New York: Oxford University Press, 1982), chap. 2.

12. Ibid., chaps. 4 and 7; Robert Jervis, "Domino Beliefs and Strategic Behavior," in *Dominoes and Bandwagons: Strategic Beliefs and Great Power Competition in the Eurasian Rimland*, ed. Robert Jervis and Jack Snyder (New York: Oxford University Press, 1991).

13. For a nuanced discussion, see Gaddis, *Strategies of Containment*, chap. 6.

14. Alexander Rahr, "'Atlanticists' versus 'Eurasians' in Russian Foreign Policy," *Radio Free Europe/Radio Liberty Research Report*, May 29, 1992, 17–23; Igor Torbakov, "The 'Statists' and the Ideology of Russian Imperial Nationalism," ibid., Dec. 11, 1992, 10–16.

15. Roman Solchanyk, "Ukraine and Russia," ibid., May 8, 1992, 13–15.

16. For background on Volsky and his supporters, see Philip Hanson and Elizabeth Teague, "The Industrialists and Russian Economic Reform," ibid., May 18, 1992, 1–7; and Elizabeth Teague, "Splits in the Ranks of Russia's 'Red Directors,'" ibid., Sept. 4, 1992, 6–10. For a statement on grand strategy by a group of the most moderate Russian nationalists, see Sergei Karaganov et al., "Strategiia dlia Rossii," *Nezavisimaia gazeta*, Aug. 19, 1992.

17. For elaboration, see Jack Snyder, "Nationalism and the Crisis of the Post-Soviet State," *Survival* 35 (spring 1993).

18. For a brilliant theoretical and empirical refutation of deterrence theory's exaggerated concerns about reputation for resolve, see Jonathan Mercer, "Broken Promises

and Unfulfilled Threats: Resolve, Reputation, and Deterrence" (Ph.D. diss., Columbia University, 1992).

19. For an evaluation of the contemporary utility of defensive alliances, see Stephen Van Evera, "Managing the Eastern Crisis: Preventing War in the Former Soviet Empire," *Security Studies* 1 (spring 1992), esp. 366–67. Since this calls for prudent political judgments, and not rigid legal ones, the infamous difficulty in defining aggression need not bar this salutary diplomatic practice.

20. David Baldwin, *Economic Statecraft* (Princeton: Princeton University Press, 1985).

21. For a fascinating case of oblique but effective influence on states' domestic coalitions, see Scott James and David Lake, "The Second Face of Hegemony: Britain's Repeal of the Corn Laws and the American Walker Tariff of 1846," *International Organization* 43 (winter 1989): 1–31.

22. G. John Ikenberry and Charles Kupchan, "Socialization and Hegemonic Power," *International Organization* 44 (summer 1990): 283–316.

23. J. A. Gallagher and R. E. Robinson, "The Imperialism of Free Trade," *Economic History Review* 6 (1953): 1–15.

24. For an argument that today's economic circumstances make force less useful, see Jeff Frieden, "The Economics of Intervention," *Comparative Studies in Society and History* 31 (Jan. 1989), 55–80.

25. Kennedy, *Rise and Fall*, chaps. 7 and 8; Joseph Nye, *Bound to Lead* (New York: Basic Books, 1990), chap. 3.

26. R. E. Robinson and J. A. Gallagher, *Africa and the Victorians* (New York: St. Martin's Press, 1961).

27. Gilpin, *War and Change*; Charles Kupchan, *The Vulnerability of Empire* (Ithaca: Cornell University Press, 1994).

28. Richard Rosecrance, *The Rise of the Trading State* (New York: Basic Books, 1986); David Lake, "Powerful Pacifists: Democratic States and War," *American Political Science Review* 86, no. 1 (1992): 24–37.

29. For elaboration and evidence on these points, see Snyder, *Myths of Empire*.

30. Paul Goble, "Serbians' Success Echoes in Russia," *New York Times*, Aug. 13, 1992, A23.

31. For conflicting views on collective security schemes, see Charles Kupchan and Clifford Kupchan, "Concerts, Collective Security, and the Future of Europe," *International Security* 16 (summer 1991): 114–61; and Richard Betts, "Systems for Peace or Causes of War? Collective Security, Arms Control, and the New Europe," ibid. 17 (summer 1992): 5–43.

32. In addition to Kupchan and Kupchan, "Concerts," see Richard Elrod, "The Concert of Europe," *World Politics* 28 (Jan. 1976).

33. Joseph Grieco, *Cooperation among Nations* (Ithaca: Cornell University Press, 1990).

34. Snyder, *Myths of Empire*, chap. 5; see also Kupchan and Kupchan, "Concerts."

35. Russell Hardin, *Collective Action* (Baltimore: Johns Hopkins University Press, 1982).

36. Barry Posen, "Ethnic Conflict and the Security Dilemma," *Survival* 34 (spring 1993).

37. See, e.g., David Laitin, Roger Petersen, and John Slocum, "Language and the State," and Charles Furtado and Michael Hechter, "The Emergence of Nationalist Politics in the USSR," in *Thinking Theoretically about Soviet Nationalities*, ed. Alexander Motyl (New York: Columbia University Press, 1992), 129–68 and 169–204, respectively.

38. Douglas J. Macdonald, "The Truman Administration and Global Responsibilities: The Birth of the Falling Domino Principle," in Jervis and Snyder, *Dominoes and Bandwagons*, chap. 5.

DAVID F. LINOWES

13 Privatization

*Problems of Implementation
and Opportunities*

After World War II, state-owned enterprises and central planning were widely adopted, being viewed as preferable to private ownership because they offered more government control and oversight. Government enterprises, it was believed, meant an end to involuntary unemployment, to problems of product excesses and shortages, and to inequalities and inequities in income distribution. In addition, projects involving large amounts of capital and significant financial risk were seen as requiring state control, as nationalist sentiments favored government ownership rather than intervention by foreign corporations.[1]

▲ Shortcomings of Central Planning

Owing to inherent inefficiencies of government control and central planning, state-owned enterprises were largely unable to provide an adequate quality of life for millions of people. Severe hardships were common, resulting in massive civil disturbances. Conflicts frequently erupted between the haves and the have-nots. Countries that relied on state enterprises and central planning saw their economies worsen while free enterprise societies thrived.

In central planning, an elite leadership group sets priorities for allocation, production, and distribution of goods and services with little or no input from the rest of society. These plans often are overly ambitious and have conflicting objectives. In the former Soviet Union, for example, each year the state planning committee would devise its Gosplan, comprising obligatory targets for more than two thousand groups of products. The plan was primarily based on the centralized material supply plan. At warehouses throughout the country resources would be assessed so that steel output matched plans for products to be produced; coal output matched steel requirements; and so forth. In all, seventeen thousand products were listed on the Gosplan in a system that required an enormous amount of information processing and manpower and resources beyond what the government could provide.[2]

Command economies always have difficulty monitoring production targets and getting specific information on operations to the decision makers.[3] There is always a lag or knowledge gap. Managers are required to meet production goals as outlined in the state's plan, without regard for supply and demand or changing economic conditions. Dieter H. Ambros, president and chief executive officer of Chemie AG Bitterfeld-Wolfen in the former East Germany, recently described for the Conference Board in New York City the problems associated with centralized planning: "For years, production targets and investment decisions were made by bureaucrats who had no interest in competitive pricing or net present value. Rather, decisions were politically motivated and had nothing to do with the needs of the consumer."[4]

The focus essentially is not to produce a quality product but to provide jobs for a nation's labor force, resulting in the need for massive state subsidies that drain government treasuries. Over time, government enterprises become associated with the economic ills that plague a nation. Contributing to these problems were the broad operational inefficiencies within the enterprises themselves.

▲ Inefficiencies of State-Run Operations

Operational inefficiencies take many forms. When General Electric acquired 51 percent of Tungstram, the Hungarian light bulb manufacturer, it discovered warehouses filled with obsolete and shattered light bulbs. The company employed seventeen thousand workers. General Electric's U.S. operation produced the same output with two thousand employees.

Since resources and equipment are not owned by any individual or specific group of individuals, assets are not managed judiciously. Shoddy and poorly maintained equipment is the norm, and frequent interruptions of services occur. Usually there is only one provider of a service. When the power plant breaks down, for example, there is no backup, so customers are forced to shut down their own operations until the state power is restored.[5]

Before Argentina sold its Entel phone system to private investors in 1990, phone service was so bad that businesses operating in the country were forced to purchase clandestine lines to connect indispensable numbers. Often these lines would be installed by Entel employees working on the side. The point-to-point lines would work until the enterprising installers sold them to someone else.[6] Then, of course, the phone would go dead.

Often government-operated businesses in developing nations do not follow "generally accepted business practices." In Malaysia, when the government's telecommunications firm, PTT, was privatized there were no books of account. It took months to determine PTT's value, and those working on the project discovered company-owned properties and buildings that had not appeared on any company records.[7]

▲ Consequences of State Ownership

Government ownership and operations were originally conceived as a way to give the people better goods and services at lower prices. The argument was that without the cost of profits, competition, and advertising, they could out-perform the private sector. The facts have been the reverse: without competitive stimuli and commercial pressures, government-operated facilities have been less effective as well as more expensive.

As markets increasingly became global, state industries found it increasingly difficult to compete. Economies of scale make it important for companies to work together across national boundaries. Nationally based government enterprises are at an inherent disadvantage in attempting to work cooperatively with private enterprises, for they cannot move expeditiously to take advantage of opportunities or adapt to changing market conditions. Because they are inefficient, they find global partners difficult to find.[8]

By the late 1970s and early 1980s, state-owned enterprises accounted for half of all outstanding domestic debt. In addition to producing goods, public enterprises were often responsible for building up a country's infrastructure and even for the distribution of subsidies to the people.[9] Such nontraditional uses of an enterprise's resources quickly drained national treasuries, putting great pressure on governing authorities.

In addition, countries relying on state-owned enterprises have seen their environments deteriorate dramatically. For example, in many areas of the former Soviet Union air and water pollution are at dangerous levels. Most Russian factories and ships dump waste without treatment, endangering fish populations in the Aral and Caspian Seas.

Frequently Soviet laws were contradictory. For instance, government five-year plans for housing and other construction programs called for cutting down forests around the Black Sea. Enforcing this law meant violating a law that protected Black Sea forests. Since all the land belonged to the government, it was easier and more cost-effective to clear-cut areas. Loggers saved no trees and left the beaches open to massive erosion. Now, the Black Sea's coast has been reduced by 50 percent, and as many as three hundred landslides occur annually, destroying hotels and other coastal buildings.[10]

Of late, these unfortunate consequences have triggered movements toward rapid privatization. When privatization is attempted too hurriedly, however, improperly designed programs lead to abuses. For example, Robert E. Anderson, an American management consultant on contract to what was the former Yugoslavian government, points out that managers were found looting the assets of their own companies. Managers arranged "sweetheart deals" with foreign companies through joint ventures in which assets of the state-owned enterprise were transferred to new corporations at low prices. In return, the managers received substantial payments or other benefits.

In Hungary, on the other hand, some government officials have been overly cautious. They fear that the high, 30 percent inflation and the interest rate of 35 percent could force newly privatized companies out of business. The largest Hungarian companies therefore remain in state hands. The government is reluctant to sell them off in separate parts, fearing that the smaller, private firms would not be able to compete in global markets.[11]

In addition, the Hungarian government is against widespread giveaway programs and instead wants to use the profits from privatization to offset its internal debt. Taking a more gradual approach, the country hopes to sell off many of its assets over three to five years. As a result, privatization in Hungary has moved slowly, even though the country has a large private sector and was the first Eastern European nation to permit foreign acquisition of domestic companies. Hungary's leaders, however, are under pressure to accelerate the privatization process.

It is interesting to note that the state's total proceeds from the sale of assets to foreign investors since 1989 have been more than $1 billion, and 82–85 percent of Hungarian enterprise sales have gone to foreigners. Sales that limit state ownership were spurred by the adoption of new laws in June 1992. The government has listed the names of specific companies in which it intends to maintain a 100 percent, 50 percent, or 25 percent interest. All other state assets must eventually be sold.

Once a nation recognizes the productivity benefits of private ownership, it sheds its ideological prejudice against free enterprise and proceeds to adopt a program of privatization. To do so effectively, certain elements must be taken into account.

▲ Considerations for a Privatization Program

Ownership

One of the first factors to consider in undertaking a program to transfer government assets to the private sector is who actually owns state industries. The national government, the republic, the local community, the workers, or the customers may assert ownership. It may be that the government wants to divest itself of a facility but finds that it lacks the authority. Reformers who take control from government ministries, therefore, find a multitude of competing ownership claims, sometimes based on unexpected reasoning. Workers' councils in the former Yugoslavia, for instance, had operated enterprises for forty years and felt they had a legitimate claim to the businesses. Workers said the past earnings that were reinvested in the enterprises should have been paid to them in the form of higher wages or other benefits, giving them ownership rights.

Political Considerations

Significant barriers to privatization that government decision makers must overcome are often political rather than financial or legal. In Poland, lack of government support for privatization has resulted in a lack of success in the nation's privatization program. There was a lack of consensus within the Solidarity Party on the best denationalization strategy, and the Warsaw government was not able to decide on general divestiture policies or goals. During the course of three administrations there was no determination of which assets to privatize, so the program stagnated. There was also public sensitivity concerning foreign acquisition of state industries and fear of unemployment resulting from the sales.

In general, opposition could be expected from

- political opponents who object on partisan or ideological grounds;
- bureaucrats within ministries who serve on boards of state-owned enterprises and managers who run the companies and are unwilling to give up perquisites;
- labor unions who fear a loss of jobs and therefore a weakening of union strength;
- those in the private sector who have benefited from special concessions through foreign exchange allocations or reduced tax rates.

In Greece, the New Democracy Party used the technique of putting its own people in key positions in government enterprises. These people then sought to block privatization so that they could keep their high salaries, free travel, and chauffeur-driven limousines.

Financing

Financing the sale of state-owned enterprises depends on the size of the enterprise being sold and the domestic capital markets that exist. Small state enterprises often can be financed locally. Occasionally private-sector buyers are able to pay the cost from their own resources or with limited assistance from domestic lending institutions. However, domestic commercial banks frequently are more interested in short-term loans with greater security than a recently privatized state enterprise would provide. Larger enterprises frequently must look to foreign banks or investors.

The extensive use of foreign capital, however, can be politically troublesome. Unrestricted direct foreign investment leads to charges of selling out to carpetbaggers from the West. Unfortunately, most developing nations have little choice but to invite foreign ownership. Poland, for example, only has enough gross domestic savings to buy 3 percent of the state assets currently being divested.[12] In Greece the government could not find buyers for thirty state companies that have a combined debt of more than $1 billion. Together, these firms account for 10 percent of the country's industrial revenues. They include Aget Herakles S.A., Greece's largest cement maker and the Piraiki— Pitraiki S.A. textile firm.

In addition to the lack of large pools of domestic investment capital, prices set for many companies may be considered high, and would-be buyers know they would inherit obsolete equipment useful only as scrap. In addition, as

John Carr reported in the *Wall Street Journal* in 1990, some of the firms have also been charged with falsifying production records in order to make sales more attractive to potential buyers.[13] As a result, outside investors are often unwilling to risk investing in state-run firms that have consistently lost money over the years.

Many governments, nevertheless, have turned to international or regional lending organizations and agencies. However, international financial institutions, such as the World Bank, have displayed ambivalent attitudes toward privatization. In the 1980s the World Bank's primary response centered on reforming state-owned enterprises instead of advocating privatization efforts. The World Bank's structural-adjustment loan program is designed to help borrowers who agree to a program of organizational reforms, including changes in management structure or accounting procedures and similar measures. Thus, the World Bank's record in privatization has been limited. Neither the World Bank nor the International Monetary Fund has enthusiastically embraced privatization; instead they have looked to other, less drastic reforms of the public sector. As a result, over a thirty-year period only 2 of the 197 projects financed by the World Bank were in the private sector.

Where a government is prepared to seek foreign investors, debt-equity swaps may provide an inducement to foreign businessmen. In these instances, foreign or local investors purchase international commercial bank debts at a discount, convert the debt to local currency, and buy all or part of the equity in the enterprise. Once the transaction is completed, the investor has acquired a company at a discounted price, and the government agency involved has successfully transferred one of its holdings to the private sector. Debt-equity swaps have the additional advantage of helping reduce external debt and stimulating the flow of capital.

Chile has used debt swapping effectively. First used in 1985, it has since then amounted to about 10 percent of Chile's outstanding debt to foreign commercial banks, stimulating the flow of capital into the country as foreigners sought attractive investment opportunities. In 1988, the best year on record for Chilean exports up to that date, manufactured exports grew by 35 percent.

Legal Barriers

Legal or regulatory constraints to privatization programs often inhibit entry or exit from a field of production. In addition, labor laws may impose hiring guidelines, adding overhead costs to operations. Complex licensing procedures associated with a business may add another hurdle. Rules designed to protect state firms by limiting competition do just that, restricting initiatives at the same time.

In Argentina a private airline, Austral, took passengers away from the state-run airline by offering better service and lower prices. The government retaliated by enacting a law that prohibited private carriers from servicing more than half of the passenger traffic and adopting regulations that prohibited Austral from providing service to other countries. The government moves forced Austral into bankruptcy.[14]

Public Support

Privatization can be hampered by a lack of public support, resulting from a lack of information about the process. While some countries deal with unemployment through an unemployment compensation system or through the use of a military draft, many leaders in developing countries tend toward state enterprises as a place to put their unemployed. As a result, widespread public opposition to privatization is not uncommon.

To engender public support, there should be a program to educate people about the likely benefits of the privatization process. At the outset, the government should avoid seeking to privatize companies that are substantial losers, as it is difficult for them to attract investors. Instead, the focus should be on firms that are sought after by investment capital. At the same time the public should be prepared through education and a program of public information. The key is to develop a constituency for privatization, while neutralizing or coopting self-serving opposing interests.

Autocratic Control of the Privatization Process

Too much reliance on the central government's authority to implement privatization can delay and complicate the entire process. One solution, which is being tried in Russia, is to reorganize the large state firms into smaller, shareholder corporations, thereby allowing various factions claiming ownership to own shares in smaller enterprise units. For instance, the Vaz Auto Works, a car manufacturer in Togliatti, is to be divided up among its 200,000 employees, its 150 managers, and a government ministry. Smaller firms can be purchased outright or leased by their managers through low-interest loans.

Scandals and Suspected Abuses

Early attempts at privatization in several countries have been marred by corruption as bureaucrats have sought to personally profit on the sale of state assets. In the sale of Hungary's Apisz stationery chain, it was revealed that managers sold the firm for a seventh of its actual value to Western investors and then absconded to Switzerland with a third of the shares in the newly privatized company. To combat this problem, many governments, including those of Hungary, Poland, and the Czech Republic, have established government watchdog agencies to oversee the privatization process.

When there are no markets to help determine a company's value, comparable prices for land, buildings, equipment, and other assets do not exist. Therefore, the privatization process is open to manipulation by government bureaucrats who are trying to strengthen their own positions. Through widespread publicity, responsible officials are now making every effort to avoid the perception of selling equities for less than their worth.

In spite of the many complex problems that accompany any privatization program, a willingness to be adaptable in responding to the needs and perceptions of the various parties is essential for keeping negotiations moving forward. Techniques vary depending on how a sale is contemplated.

▲ Privatization Techniques

Direct sales of assets to buyers might include private firms, local investors, multinational corporations, the general public through stock offerings, or the operation's own managers and workers by means of an employee stock ownership plan (ESOP).

In many countries, not all investors are politically acceptable to the government or to the general population. Not only are foreign investors suspect but local ethnic minorities are often excluded from the purchase of domestic firms. For example, Indians in certain African countries and Chinese in various Southeast Asian nations are not considered acceptable buyers. The sale of state enterprises to close friends or relatives of the country's leadership is highly resented. It has been shown that in such cases privatization often results in the replacement of a government monopoly with a private one.

The success of privatization movements throughout the world frequently depends upon the circumstances and cultures governing particular societies. There is no one set pattern for successful denationalization of state industry. However, creative initiatives in worker involvement represent one necessary constant. Broad equity ownership by way of public stock offerings helps create popular support for a sale and at the same time offers an opportunity to strengthen individual economic security. In Nigeria, the government strives to ensure regional and ethnic balance in the ownership of its privatized companies. Prior to the sale, each purchaser of company stock is required to list his or her state of origin and local government area. To date, progress on privatization in Nigeria has been slow.

Transfer of corporate equity to the employees themselves can be accomplished by creating a trust that holds the stock of the enterprise for the workers. In Guatemala, for example, 40 percent of the stock of the La Perla Coffee and Spice Plantation was transferred to an employee association, to be paid for out of the future earnings of the plantation plus employees' and employers' contributions averaging 3 percent of their pay. The funds generated through an ESOP allow the workers to purchase the state-owned enterprise and participate in management and policy decisions.

Europe

Britain has successfully used the sale of shares to employees as a means of reducing worker resistance. The government offered employees shares in several of the firms being denationalized, including the National Freight Corporation. In this sale, the work force purchased two-thirds of the corporate stock. Overall, nearly 90 percent of the employees in companies sold by public offerings are shareholders, and ten million British households, or 40 percent, own stock.[15] Privatization has been so successful in Britain that the Labor Party may abandon its longtime adherence to industry nationalization.

Former French Prime Minister Edouard Balladur stressed that one of the important provisions of his nation's privatization effort is worker participation. Under France's "preferential acquisition" arrangement, 10 percent of state-owned shares sold must be made available to the firm's employees. No employee may acquire shares valued at more than five times the amount of his social security contributions. The "popular shareholding" system has resulted in a threefold increase in the number of individuals holding stock. On average, more than half of those employed in privatized companies have become shareholders.

France has had a program of privatization since 1986. The former Chirac government scheduled sixty-five state-owned firms for privatization by 1991. Fourteen companies were sold in 1986 and 1987. However, the privatization movement essentially came to a halt in May 1988 under the new government of Prime Minister Michel Rocard with Pierre Beregovoy as finance minister; the government was responding to a public outcry of favoritism and unfair dealings in a number of the privatized projects.

France's new conservative coalition, elected in March 1993, has announced plans to renew the aggressive privatization effort. The country's extensive privatization plans include the sale of twenty-one companies, worth an estimated $68 billion. It has privatized Rhone-Poulenc, the nation's largest chemical and pharmaceutical concern. The initial six-million-share public offering was worth $550 million and was oversubscribed by a factor of four. Late in 1993, France sold one of its two large state banks, the Banque Nationale de Paris. The neo-Gaullist Rally for the Republic Party (RPR) has made supplementary privatization a mainstay of its platform.

Holland's proposed privatization of the chemical firm DSM includes plans to grant employees preferred rights to purchase shares and to allow workers to buy convertible bonds with loans from their employer. Although the Netherlands has few state-owned enterprises, it plans to sell Postbank, Schiphol Airport, and Nederlandse Waterschapsbank.

Israel has sold its largest importer and marketer of crude oil, and it plans to sell many additional firms in the future to raise as much as $6 billion. Currently, about 160 state-owned firms produce one-fifth of Israel's economic output. The Israeli government has sold some smaller companies and parts of larger firms, such as Bezeq, the telecommunications monopoly. In the proposed privatization of Israel Chemicals the government plans to sell 4 percent of the firm's stock to its employees. Fifty percent of the shares will go to a private investor, and the government will retain 26 percent. Israel hopes to raise $750 million from the sale.

Although political unrest has limited privatization efforts in Italy, Credito Italiano, the country's sixth largest bank, was sold in late 1993. Italy's three major trade union organizations, the Confederazione Generale Italiana del Lavoro (CGIL), the Confederazione Italiana Sindacati Lavoratori (CISL), and the Unione Italiana Lavoratori (UIL) have been involved in negotiating guarantees for the work force in the country's major *dismissioni*, or privatization efforts. The guarantees have generally been in the form of worker participation in production strategies and other labor relations issues. While the unions agree that any future privatization policy must include employment safeguards, whether privatization should continue without offering workers share options is still being debated. Therefore, major sales of state enterprises in Italy have not included the acquisition of shares by employees.

Republics in the former Soviet Union are promoting cooperatives and experimenting with leasing farms and factories in an attempt to reverse a seventy-year pattern of "collective irresponsibility." Currently, more than five hundred enterprises work under the collective leasing system in the Moscow area. The plan has led to a 25 percent increase in factory productivity and greater efficiency in service enterprises.

Under communist rule, Moscow told each farmer what to plant and when, regardless of local weather or soil conditions. Farmers were paid whether they worked or not. Farm children were guaranteed jobs regardless of need. In short, there was no incentive to do better, save money, or work diligently. By 1991 the situation had deteriorated to the point that it cost seven rubles to produce two rubles' worth of meat. The government hid its inability to feed its people by importing grain from the West. Some $70 billion worth was imported over a thirty-year period in a program Moscow bureaucrats called "bread exports."

A 1992 study by the World Bank concluded that no part of the collective farming system had ever worked. Russia lost 30–40 percent of its food en route from the fields to the markets. Grain rotted because of a lack of storage facilities while many in the population suffered from hunger and malnutrition. It took ten days for unrefrigerated cars traveling at six miles per hour to transport fruits and vegetables grown in the south to cities in the north, so that much of the load spoiled. Over the past sixty years, the only successful Russian farming was done in private gardens around homes and cottages. These fraction-of-an-acre plots produced more than 25 percent of Russia's food supply on just 3 percent of the nation's land. Some 90 percent of the former collective and state farms have been reorganized as limited-liability companies or partnerships. More than 270,000 privately owned farms now cultivate about 8 percent of the agricultural land.

In Hungary and the Czech Republic, collective farming operations are overstaffed and overly dependent on the government for subsidies. The farms are extremely large; one vegetable operation near Prague spans thirty-five hundred acres. These large holdings have to be broken up into more manageable, family-size farms. A problem to overcome, however, is finding individuals who want to be small farmers. After years of relying on the government for everything from seeds to fleets of machinery, farmers have to relearn how to manage entire operations on their own. The generations-old tradition of fathers passing on their farming knowledge to their sons has been lost.

In 1992 the United States spent nearly $21 million to help farmers in Eastern Europe and the former Soviet Union. Most of the money came from the U.S. Department of Agriculture's Model Farm Community program, which sent

American couples to the area to live with and teach modern farming methods to indigenous families. Equipment and supplies are procured locally; however, at this stage machinery, spare parts, and fertilizer are in short supply. Also, Russian entrepreneurs are gaining work experience with U.S. companies as the result of a 1993 agreement between the two countries.

Latin America

In Chile, as a result of the Pinochet government's aggressive privatization program in the 1970s and 1980s, three-fourths of the previously nationalized industries have been returned to private ownership. The success of the Chilean privatization efforts is due to the government's positive attitude toward the private sector, willingness to relentlessly pursue divestiture, and openness to foreign investments. Recent activities have included the complete privatization of the mining company Empresa Minera Aysen and the shipping entity Empremar Sur.

Chile's first privatization program involved the sale of about 350 enterprises between 1974 and 1977. Since 1982 the program has emphasized recruiting experienced and financially strong purchasers along with share sales to employees and small shareholders. Also, debt-equity swaps have been popular, with foreigners using such swaps to acquire portions of the telephone system and the national electricity grid.

Even though Chilean copper mines are a politically sensitive issue, new copper mines are being sold to private interests. One new copper mine is expected to produce revenues of $1 billion a year. Some functions of the old mines, such as engineering services, are currently being contracted out.

Although today it is among the most efficient steel companies in the world, for decades the Chilean steel manufacturer CAP was an example of a poorly managed state enterprise. CAP had been an unproductive white elephant since it began operations after World War II. To meet Chile's steel needs, CAP manufactured all types of steel instead of focusing on a specific segment of the industry. After shares were sold to private investors, major product realignments were made, and an austerity program was instituted. Results improved dramatically.

In the CAP sale, one-third of the shares were purchased by employees, with four thousand of the sixty-five hundred workers participating. The reprivatization was started in 1985, and the company became completely privately owned in 1987. When it was a state-owned enterprise, the government provided a $30 million annual subsidy to keep it operating. By 1991 CAP's annual sales exceeded $600 million, and the company had expanded into mining, real estate, and forestry. Today, the steel division is among the most efficient producers in the world. Net income in 1992 was $27.6 million.

In Argentina, the privatization concerns of both government officials and the public center on relationships with labor unions, which make up 40 percent of the private-sector work force. Unions exercise a most significant voice in the country. After years of clouded political commitment and ambiguous legal mandates, privatization action is finally under way. To date, Argentina has sold its telephone company, its state airline, two television stations, a grain-transporting railway, oil and gas concessions, and road maintenance concessions. Early in 1994 the banking and insurance company Caja Nacional de Ahorro y Seguro (CNAS) was sold. Now plans call for selling ten-year leases on the underground railways serving Buenos Aires.

The Spanish airline, Iberia, was the high bidder for 85 percent of the Argentine airline, Aerolineas Argentinas. To sell its Entel telephone company, the government divided the firm into northern and southern halves. Italy's STET and Spain's Telefonica purchased majority shares in the two companies for $650 million plus the assumption of outstanding debt.

Before its debt crisis in 1982, Mexico announced plans to privatize many of its 1,155 state enterprises. In all, some 500 companies in various industries have been sold. In the last few years, the divestiture of state enterprises has been a significant factor in the eradication of fiscal deficits. As late as 1986, foreign firms were excluded from strategic and priority areas and restricted to sectors where domestic investments would not be displaced. High valuations of the enterprises also hampered the privatization effort. Now the Mexican government has fully withdrawn from several sectors, with the result that there has been increased competition and increased private-sector investment in these areas. Small enterprise involvement in state-owned asset sales has been significant. The sales of some petrochemical firms, the government's interest in Renault (cement maker), and the national soccer team have involved scores of these small enterprises. Recently the Mexican government offered union workers shares in the proposed privatization of Cananea Copper, Mexico's largest copper mine. According to Maria Theresa Straffon of the Mexican Embassy in the United States, under the plan the current company would be liquidated and then employees would receive 25 percent of the corporate shares.

It should be noted that government officials sometimes oppose privatization programs because they fear a lack of control by the state over the provision of vital services for the people. This issue can be avoided through contracting-out programs, whereby the government contracts with a private enterprise for the actual production of goods or services but continues to be the provider and to set production guidelines.

▲ Superior Performance through Private Enterprise

Free enterprise clearly outperforms state-run entities. Hungary, Poland, the Czech Republic, Germany, and the People's Republic of China provide some examples.

Hungary

In Ozd, Hungary, part of the bankrupt state-owned Ozd Metallurgical Works was sold to a private investor. Janos Petrenko, a forty-nine-year-old coal miner's son, was able to buy the bankrupt steel mill where he had worked for twenty-five years as an electrician. Petrenko had left the Ozd plant ten years earlier to work on his own as an inventor and manufacturer of steel products. Eventually he headed his own seventeen-worker company. Based on his success as a private entrepreneur, Petrenko was able to get the financial backing to purchase the Ozd plant for more than $6 million. The mill, which had been destined for closure, was turned into a profit-making venture. Under state control the plant lost money for more than fifty years because of poor product quality and lack of research and development efforts, and most employees were forced to take second jobs to make ends meet. Recently the *Economist* reported that Janos Petrenko was able to transform the Ozd steel mill into a profit-making venture within a year of his return. Part of his strategy was to revise the product line to reflect Western tastes and markets. Now workers at the facility, who once faced imminent unemployment, are producing quality products competitively and enjoying high wages. Managers can afford to buy new Volkswagens, becoming the envy of their counterparts in state firms, and employees' jobs are secure.

Although state-owned Hungarian factories typically lose money from the day they open, the same is not true for private enterprises. Levi Strauss and Company recently opened a jeans plant in the southern Hungarian town of Kiskunhalas. The factory employs three hundred women, produces two million pairs of quality-made jeans a year, and earns profits of more than $1 million annually. It is now doubling its work force. More than a third of the production is shipped to markets in the West. Levi's wages of $200 a month are twice what workers earn in similar state-owned clothing factories; and absenteeism is 7 percent, compared with 25 percent in government-owned enterprises. Levi Strauss has just one supervisor for every forty workers. Its predecessor had a manager for every three workers and an oversized administration building.

Poland

In 1990 Poland privatized its Nowa Huta steel mill near Krakow, the largest of Poland's overstaffed and inefficient state enterprises. Over the years, the mill experienced extensive problems as a result of incompetent communist management. Built in 1953, it was operating with processing equipment dating from the 1960s and outdated, open-hearth technology that had been discarded by the West years before. The payroll had grown to twenty-eight thousand employees, while comparable Western plants operated more efficiently with half this number. The choking levels of pollution from the plant resulted in a deterioration of many medieval-style masonry buildings in the Krakow area. Under private enterprise, managers have added scrubbers to the Nowa Huta stacks to limit emissions and have modernized plant operations. The two oldest of the firm's five blast furnaces have been shut down. Today the mill is competing effectively on the world markets with quality products and is a profit-making concern.

Poland's commercial code has not been updated since the 1930s. To dig out of its morass, Poland is rewarding every adult Pole free "privatization bonds," which are exchangeable for shares in state-owned firms. Privatization minister Wieslaw Kaczmarek has advocated increased emphasis on sales of state assets for the foreseeable future. More than seventy-six hundred state enterprises are slated to be sold within the next few years. By 1992 more than four hundred Polish companies had been privatized, one-fifth of which had more than five hundred employees. Seventy percent of the nation's retail businesses once again had become privately owned.

In 1993 Poland's Sejm passed a new mass privatization program. The act covers about six hundred enterprises. All adults in Poland are able to buy share certificates issued by ten to fifteen national investment funds that will manage the companies. According to Janusz Lewandowski, the minister of ownership changes, the act will enable hundreds of enterprises to restructure and will facilitate access to Western markets and new technologies.

The Czech Republic

In what was the former Czechoslovakia, two hundred thousand small private enterprises have been established in light industry, electronics, and services. Private firms and joint ventures with Western companies are now beginning to compete in world markets. Czech citizens have been issued vouchers worth about thirty-five dollars to bid for shares in state firms. The voucher program has been so successful that some 8 million Czechs are now private shareholders. By the end of 1991, six thousand state-owned enterprises had been privatized and eleven thousand more were scheduled for imminent divestiture. At this writing the Czechs are divesting public utilities and services, including the national health service.

Tesla Electronics of Prague has joined with American Pacific Vista Systems of Vista, California, in a venture to produce computer capacitors. Prior to the 1990 joint-venture agreement Tesla had been ignoring research and development and had fallen twenty years behind the semiconductor industry. Now production components have arrived from America, and American technicians and scientists from America are assisting the Czechs in setting up new production lines with built-in quality controls. Tesla is once again ready to compete in the global marketplace with high expectations for the future.

Germany

Since 1990, Germany has privatized thirty-four hundred large state enterprises and twenty-two thousand small businesses in former East Germany. Sales have been overseen by the Treuhandanstalt, an agency with considerable power. Prior to that time, East German industry was mired in bureaucratic inertia. Incentives were lacking, products were ten to twenty years out of date, and payrolls were bloated. Production was guided by five-year plans instead of sound principles of management. All this is changing as hundreds of nationalized small business concerns in eastern Germany have been reprivatized and turned over to their original owners. The Treuhandanstalt has privatized entities at a rate of two hundred to three hundred firms per month.

One company that has thus become a private firm is Janetzki GmbH of Engelsdorf, near Leipzig, founded in 1945 by Heinz Janetzki. The company produces centrifuges for medical lab blood testing. Over the years, the Janetzki company grew from 11 to 330 workers and was one of the one hundred leading exporters among East Germany's eight thousand industrial firms. But in 1958 the government took over four-fifths ownership and taxed Heinz Janetzki's remaining share at a 92 percent rate. Then in 1972 the government nationalized the business in a broad campaign to eliminate private industry. Although the move was intended to improve efficiency through central planning, the result was nightmarish inefficiency, corruption, and incompetence.

In 1990 Heinz Janetzki returned to his factory after being banished for fourteen years. Not only had the plant failed to keep up with its competition, but no new centrifuge models had been introduced in nearly twenty years. The plant lacked the industry's standard Western technology, the operations were in shambles, junk was everywhere, and rubbish collected next to new raw materials. The payroll had expanded to more than twice the number needed. The Leipzig Chamber of Industry and Commerce reports that under Janetzki, who has recently retired, the company has returned to effective productivity under the name Geratebau Eppendorf GmbH.[16]

The People's Republic of China

In the People's Republic of China workers are being allowed to buy shares in enterprises that are slowly being freed from state and party control. Although public ownership of businesses is still the official party line, the government is contemplating privatization of about 250 state-run firms listed on the Shanghai and Shenzhen stock exchanges. Private concerns are on the rise in China even though budding entrepreneurs are forced to overcome some obstacles. One of China's richest private businessmen is Zhang Guoxi, who runs an international furniture exporting and property development empire. The thirty-nine-year-old businessman started his own company fifteen years ago in Yujiang, the county seat of Jiangxi Province, where his headquarters remains today. To raise capital for the venture, he sold his family home for $250. Today Mr. Zhang's net worth is estimated at $30 million. He maintains offices in a modern ten-story building, complete with direct international telephone hookups and fax service.

▲ The Superiority of Private Enterprise Operations

Private enterprise in a free market produces goods and services that are superior in quality and quantity to those of government-run operations and at the same time is more responsive to people's needs. There are a number of reasons why this is so.

First, the very nature of government operation injects a strong political dimension into economic decision making. This includes the nature of the goods and services to be produced, the level of capitalization and investment in facilities, and the kind of personnel policies adopted. When such decisions are based on political expedience rather than business needs, the results can be—and too often are—counterproductive. Government enterprise is often shackled by bureaucratic direction and may never be fully able to satisfy consumer needs and wants. In contrast, privately owned companies do not have to deal with government interference in decision making.

Second, a government operation is usually protected by a monopoly, so the drive and ingenuity that competition provides is usually missing. A government monopoly often becomes sluggish in its operations. Private firms, however, must constantly keep costs down and make products attractive or risk a competitor's taking the market. When a government enterprise fails to satisfy its customers, it does not risk going out of business as a private firm does. Government agencies cannot be dismissed if they fail to perform. In contrast, the private sector is customer-directed; the emphasis is on quality and customer satisfaction. Private companies are forced to become more efficient to survive. Consumers thereby benefit from higher-quality goods and services at lower prices.

Third, competition creates the opportunity for greater consumer choice. Replacing a single government service provider with competing private-sector suppliers increases people's options. Competition in a free market makes the fullest possible use of every economic and social activity. Consumers who require goods and services are given a choice and are not captive to the particular enterprise to which they happen to be assigned.

Fourth, in state-run operations, consumers' interests are subordinated to the interests of the producer, namely, the government. When goods and services are provided by the state, the recipients are obliged to accept what is offered whether it is of good or poor quality. When operations are in the hands of private business, however, customers' interests must be paramount or buyers will go elsewhere for their needs.

Fifth, the public sector is not compelled to keep abreast of the latest technology, to search out the latest cost-saving developments, or to innovate. Government operations are usually insulated from these pressures. While state-owned enterprises stifle innovation and creative problem solving, private firms open up their operations to bring in the talents and drive of a variety of individuals. As a result, production and profitability are maximized, stimulating the optimum use of resources.

Finally, wide ownership of an enterprise by stock distribution to large groups of people results in economic discipline through shareholder pressures on management through monitoring and motivating high-quality performance. Those owning stock demand corporate growth and profitable operations resulting in higher share values and dividend payments.

▲ The Process

Privatization of a government enterprise is a complex and drawn-out process if it is to be successful. In such an effort, the first elements for concentrated attention are a nation's administrative laws, its law enforcement mechanisms and judiciary system. National and local laws and regulations often have to be redesigned, establishing enforceable property rights and operational authority for individuals and corporate entities. The legal base of the particular enterprise itself may require change so that the corporate entity will be freestanding and will be recognized as such by all those with whom it interacts. Corporations and business entrepreneurs should be provided with due-process protection for property and should be given shelter from unreasonably discriminatory taxation.

Once the legal dimensions are clarified and redesigned where necessary, attention should be directed to the human resources in general and to management personnel in particular. Managers require orientation and guidance in understanding how a free-market economy works; how to seek raw materials and other supplies and then negotiate for the best price and quality; how to find and create markets for completed products; how to competitively hire, train, and fire workers; and how to negotiate for and obtain various levels of financing. Employees need explanations and assurances about how the employer-employee relationship functions in a competitive society.

With legal and human factors attended to, the transfer of ownership to the private sector may then be pursued. There are several approaches to the disposition of an enterprise, each having a number of variations. The outright sale of the complete project to one purchaser is a basic approach, but it applies most generally only to smaller and medium-sized entities. Very large enterprises may require a consortium of purchasers, or only a percentage of the equity might be sold. In such circumstances the government participates in whatever profits or losses are generated. Not infrequently, a facility may best be sold in parts. For example, an enterprise owning various plants — one manufacturing farm equipment, another hardware, and yet another small trucks — could be sold as three separate entities to different purchasers. Converting the enterprise to a stock company and then selling the shares to the public or to selected groups of people, such as customers, suppliers, workers, residents of a particular region, or domestic or foreign investors, is also a frequently used approach. It is also not uncommon to design a program to sell the company to the employees through an ESOP.

Another general approach for transferring operations to private hands is for the government enterprise to contract out the operations to private entrepreneurs while continuing to own the facility. In such an arrangement, the government continues to be responsible to the people for the furnishing of the goods or services, and the private contractor is responsible to the government.

A third approach for reducing government operations is somewhat indirect in that private entrepreneurs are invited to produce the goods or services in competition with the government enterprise. In such circumstance the greater efficiency of private operations ordinarily results in lower prices and better quality, competitively forcing the government facility out of business. Basic to this program is the removal of all government monopoly protection and subsidization.

A dramatic way transfer a state agency to private ownership is to give it to the people—to all the citizens of a country or only to the employees or other selected groups. This can be accomplished by distributing vouchers entitling the holders to shares of stock. (This device is presently being tried in Poland and Russia.) Under such an arrangement the government does not receive any proceeds from the disposition, but it rids itself of the burden of underwriting its losses.

▲ Conclusion

For privatization to flourish, there must be a relatively stable political environment, reasonable control of inflation, and a dependable currency. The existence of a capital market expedites transfers of government enterprises to private hands.

The world now faces the challenge of waging peace as economic issues dominate the international scene, and this effort is largely being led by the private sector. The potential for improving economic and government performance through private-sector initiatives is great. Through private local enterprises and multinational corporations, the quality of life of a people can be significantly improved. Privatization, by transferring state-owned entities to private hands, builds an economic foundation for freedom from want around the globe. No nation can have political democracy without economic democracy.

The modern business corporation is a superior economic tool for providing the material needs of life. It stimulates free trade and thereby serves as a catalyst for peoples of different cultures to know one another, encouraging cooperation and avoiding misunderstandings and conflict.

NOTES

1. Dennis J. Gayle and Jonathan N. Goodrich, "Exploring the Implications of Privatization and Deregulation," in *Privatization and Deregulation in Global Perspective*, ed. Dennis J. Gayle and Jonathan N. Goodrich (New York: Quorum Books, 1990), 1–23.

2. Alexander V. Kozhemiakin, "Russian Economic Reform" (seminar paper, Department of Political Science, University of Illinois at Urbana-Champaign, spring 1992), 2–3.

3. Jack Wiseman, "Privatization in the Command Economy," in *Privatization and Economic Efficiency*, ed. A. F. Ott and K. Hartley (Brookfield, Vt.: Edward Elgar, 1991), 260–61.

4. Dieter Ambros, "Privatization in Eastern Europe: The Farther East You Go, the Greater the Risk" (speech delivered at the Conference Board's strategic management meeting, New York, Jan. 21, 1993), *Vital Speeches of the Day* 59, no. 10 (Mar. 1, 1993), 296.

5. Madsen Pirie, *Dismantling the State* (Dallas: National Center for Policy Analysis, 1985), 8–16.

6. Thomas Kamm, "Argentina Kicks Off Privatization Drive," *Wall Street Journal*, June 26, 1990, A12.

7. M. Montagu-Pollock, "Privatization: What Went Wrong," *Asian Business* 26 (1990): 32–39.

8. John Vickers and Vincent Wright, "The Politics of Industrial Privatization in Western Europe: An Overview," *West European Politics* 11 (1988): 2.

9. Raymond Vernon, "The Promise and the Challenge," in *The Promise of Privatization*, ed. Raymond Vernon (New York: Council on Foreign Relations, 1988), 1–22.

10. Thomas DeLorenze, "Does Free Enterprise Cause Pollution?" *Across the Board*, Feb. 1991, 34–41.

11. Keith M. Rockwell, "Public Haggling Slows Hungarian Privatization Efforts," *Journal of Commerce*, May 9, 1991, 1.

12. Nicholas A. Vardy, "Eastern Europe: The Rocky Road to Privatization," *The World & I* 6 (1991): 83, 86.

13. John Carr, "Greece Has Trouble Finding Takers for Pricey, Risky 'Problem' Companies," *Wall Street Journal*, July 25, 1990, A9.

14. Manuel Tanoira, "Privatization as Politics," in *Privatization and Development*, ed. S. H. Hanke (San Francisco: International Center for Economic Growth Press, 1987), 59.

15. Calvin A. Kent, "Privatization of Public Functions: Promises and Problems," in *Entrepreneurship and the Privatizing of Government*, ed. C. A. Kent (New York: Quorum Books, 1987), 17–19.

16. J. E. Peterson, "Privatization by Storm: Lessons from the Eastern Bloc," *Governing* 5 (1992); F. Protzman, "Rebuilding East German Industry," *New York Times*, Nov. 10, 1989, 4.

EDWARD J. LAURANCE

14 | # The Role of Arms Control in Coping with Conflict after the Cold War

As this volume makes quite clear, armed conflict is alive and well in the post–Cold War world. A world featuring superpower rivalry marked by ideological struggle and the primacy of nuclear weapons has been replaced by one in which wars rage in many places and more are threatening to erupt at any moment. Does this new situation call for new thinking? Do any of the strategies of the Cold War apply to this new environment? Nowhere are these questions more relevant than in the area of arms control. This chapter concerns itself with the strategies that are associated with the concept of arms control, a term coined during the Cold War but one that in its larger meaning has always been used to cope with conflict.

The first step in this assessment of arms control and its applicability to the amelioration of regional conflict is to put to rest the post–Cold War "farewell to arms control" argument and reaffirm the role that arms control has continued to play since 1989. Second, the major systemic changes affecting the employment of arms control measures — increased cooperation between the two largest military powers, the decline of Russian military power, verification, and the rising importance of international organizations — are discussed. With this as background, I turn to those frameworks and dimensions that must be taken into account by strategic planners and policymakers as they develop and utilize arms control measures. The difference between collective and cooperative security, with stress on the latter, is emphasized so that arms control measures can be grounded on a solid understanding of what is possible. Also addressed is the relationship between the types of weapons systems used in conflicts and the arms control measures developed to deal with them. Also covered are global and regional efforts and the various approaches used to determine how weapons, including their accumulation, disposition, and use, may prompt or restrain conflict. A major section of the chapter outlines those factors that determine how the utility of arms control as a strategy must vary from region to region. Finally, these factors are applied to the U.N. Register of Conventional Arms to illustrate how an arms control measure can cope with regional conflict today.

▲ Arms Control: A Continuing Reality, Not a Potential Option

The rise in armed conflict, combined with greater media coverage, has focused more attention than ever before on the weapons of war. What caliber of mortar round was fired into that Sarajevo marketplace? Who fired it, and how can we know? How many fuel rods were taken out of the North Korean nuclear reactor? Which European companies helped Saddam Hussein expand the range of the SCUD missiles? It is commonplace to see not only diagrams of weapons systems but also maps of their placement in critical conflicts. In short, arms control, a strategy focused on weapons as a major determinant of conflict, is more relevant than ever.[1]

But arms control is not an apolitical strategy. Born at the height of the Cold War, it became the centerpiece of a major debate on how to deal with the nuclear arms race. Consequently, when the Cold War ended, there was no shortage of "farewells" to arms control. Colin Gray, perhaps the most vocal critic of this approach to ameliorating conflict, wasted no time in attacking arms control.[2] His argument asserts the primacy of politics and policy and dismisses a focus on weapons as a waste of time. Richard Betts is similarly skeptical about the use of treaty-based arms limitations to prevent or ameliorate conflict.[3] In its latest issue of *Strategic Survey*, the International Institute for Strategic Studies declares that "as 1993 came to an end, it was apparent that the traditional, bilateral arms-control agenda had virtually run its course."[4] As a final indicator, the journal *Arms Control*, born in the Cold War, has now changed its name to *Contemporary Security Policy*. This last example suggests a post–Cold War bandwagon effect to discard all Cold War baggage. The arms control agenda may indeed be alive and well, but the terms seem to be falling into disuse.

Arms control critics were not restricted to the realist end of the political spectrum. The peace and disarmament movement was uniformly opposed to an approach that not only legitimized nuclear weapons but also resulted in an overall increase in arsenals in the name of stability. Further, absent any empirical data on nuclear wars, most of the debate was theoretical. Those who criticized arms control in favor of approaches that dealt with the "real" causes of war—ambition, aggression, ideology, evil leaders, nationalism, territorial disputes, and so forth—pointed to such arcane indicators as the large Soviet civil defense budget as evidence of intent to launch a first strike. In the post–Cold War world we need theorize no longer. There are governments and peoples who are willing to go to war for all of the reasons that were suppressed during the Cold War. Based on this empirical reality, one could now make a very good case that it is indeed "people who kill people." The "guns" are not to blame. As for the Iraqi invasion of Kuwait, Saddam Hussein's behavior made it easy to focus on him, and not his weapons, as the problem.

But despite all of these reasons to discard arms control as a strategy, arms control *as behavior* has not disappeared. In fact, absent the rhetoric of the Cold War, national governments and international institutions are now more actively than ever using methods and approaches that can only be termed arms control to cope with conflict. The end of the ideological struggle in Europe led directly to the Conventional Forces in Europe Treaty (CFE), the Open Skies Treaty, and the overall invigoration of arms control and confidence-building measures within the Conference on Security and Cooperation in Europe (CSCE). Arresting the proliferation of weapons of mass destruction enjoyed the support of the major powers during the Cold War, and it enjoys even more support today. The Chemical Weapons Convention (CWC), outlawing chemical weapons, quickly became a reality, complete with its own international organization and verification procedures.

The host of actions that followed in the wake of the Gulf War made it clear that in order to prevent a reoccurrence of such conflicts, *weapons* matter. The International Atomic Energy Agency (IAEA), embarrassed by the situation in Iraq, has been revitalized and was a central player in the most recent crisis in North Korea. U.N. Security Council Resolution 687 established a U.N. special commission that to this day is hunting down and destroying Iraq's missiles and weapons of mass destruction. In the area of conventional weapons, the permanent five members of the U.N. Security Council have held meetings to restrict arms transfers into a volatile Middle East. In the fall of 1991 the U.N. General

Assembly created the U.N. Register of Conventional Arms, which called on all states to submit annual data on weapons exports and imports. In both 1992 and 1993 more than eighty states, including all of the major arms suppliers, submitted data. The Gulf War also saw a rebirth of the arms embargo as a tool of conflict control not only against Iraq but also against the former Yugoslavia, Somalia, Libya, Liberia, Haiti, and UNITA (the National Union for the Total Independence of Angola).[5]

In the United Nations, the well-documented increase in peacekeeping and peacemaking operations has been accompanied by a new emphasis on the role of disarmament in such operations. The Secretary-General has increasingly emphasized that the weapons themselves are an important factor: "It is my strong feeling that the time has come for the practical integration of disarmament and arms regulation issues into the broader structure of the international peace and security agenda."[6] Where factions involved in the armed conflicts have been disarmed, as in El Salvador, stability has been enhanced. In others conflicts, such as in Angola, where no such disarmament took place, negotiations have been frustrated because the weapons continue to flow into the region.

To summarize, arms control is not dead. Those responsible for stopping or reducing armed conflict have not bid farewell to arms control. Weapons do matter. In the introductory chapter to this volume, the global forces at work that frame regional conflict are introduced. The first of these is the "multi-lateralization of arms production and transfers, including military technology, which sustain, widen, and make regional armed clashes more destructive than ever before" (see chapter 1 above). In the final analysis, any discussion of coping with conflict must deal first with the causes of conflict. Arms control theory assumes that arms play a key role in conflict management. The remainder of this chapter addresses how these arms relate not only to the conduct of armed conflict but also to the outbreak of war itself.

▲ Systemic Factors Shaping Arms Control

Since arms control remains an important option for policymakers, we must focus on those systemic factors that will effect the success of arms control strategies in the new, post–Cold War environment. The first of those factors is the *verification* of arms control agreements and measures. While it was a major bone of contention during the Cold War and still is a barrier to arms control, the debate has diminished saliency today. This can be seen in the relative ease with which the CWC was concluded, despite the formidable task that lies ahead. The Open Skies Treaty also illustrates how far we have progressed. Although the U.N. monitoring of Iraq might be viewed as a special case, it is significant that the U.N. Special Commission (UNSCOM) has the authority to conduct aerial surveillance, irrespective of the wishes of Iraq *and* the major powers. The Intermediate-Range Nuclear Forces (INF), Strategic Arms Reduction (START), and CFE treaties seem to have broken the logjam and set new precedents for on-site verification. Verification problems have not disappeared, as can be seen in the current negotiations taking place in the Geneva-based Conference on Disarmament on a Comprehensive Test Ban Treaty (CTBT). While a tentative political consensus is emerging to ban nuclear testing, as evidenced by formal negotiations for the first time in the history of nuclear weapons, how such a ban is to be verified is as contentious as ever. While it is possible that verification might again be a major problem, it seems unlikely that the world will find it easy to slip back into the Cold War approach of national technical means as the sole source of verification.

A second important factor in assessing the efficacy of arms control approaches is the increase in importance of *international organizations* (IOs) in the area of international security, arms control, and disarmament. International organization scholars during the Cold War reached a consensus that the limited oversight enjoyed by IOs over technical areas, such as civil aviation, health, and economics, did not extend to security issues. This has started to change, as the peacekeeping activities of the United Nations attest (see chapter 6 above). But the changes go far beyond just the United Nations. New organizations have been created. With the signing of the CWC in 1993, the Organization for the Prohibition of Chemical Weapons (OPCW), based in The Hague, was established. It will have a large and technically competent secretariat with a level of autonomy that would have been inconceivable just a half-decade ago. U.N. Resolution 687 created UNSCOM with authority to conduct inspections, destroy weapons and production capabilities, establish intrusive monitoring systems, and in general behave as an independent IO that reports to the U.N. Security Council. Although this IO can be thought of as unique to a specific resolution, the precedent is very important when considering arms control approaches. UNSCOM controls its own aerial surveillance aircraft and maintains an independent intelligence operation. It has also ensured its longevity, as it will continue to monitor the importation of dual-use technologies and equipment into Iraq once the embargo is lifted.

Not only are there new IOs but those created during the Cold War are being strengthened as they adapt to the new international environment. The IAEA is weaning itself from the major nuclear powers and developing some independence for action, especially in the area of intelligence and information. The U.N. Center for Disarmament Affairs (UNCDA), almost dismantled at the end of the Cold War, is being reshaped from a conference support agency into an operational secretariat to support new approaches to arms control and disarmament. UNCDA is responsible for the new Register of Conventional Arms, including the maintenance of a data base and the promotion of the Register itself. At the regional level, Argentina and Brazil have renounced their ambitions for nuclear weapons status and set up a regional organization to verify their nuclear capabilities.

Not all change involves the expansion of IOs. Supplier cartels, such as the Missile Technology Control Regime (MTCR) and the Nuclear Suppliers Group (NSG), are under fire, especially from a newly resurgent South. One of the cartels, the Coordinating Committee on Export Controls (COCOM), has ceased to exist. In this period of transition and uncertainty national governments will experiment with a multitude of approaches to ameliorating conflict. In contrast to the situation in the Cold War era, the barrier to IO assistance has been breached. States are becoming increasingly more comfortable with the idea that in extending a measure of sovereignty to a global or regional IO they can enhance their security. This is especially true when it becomes clear that national capabilities alone will not accomplish national objectives. In the case of North Korea, U.S. behavior has been instructive. On the one (nationalistic) hand, the United States is dealing with the issue unilaterally, sending Patriot missiles, increasing troop levels, negotiating with the North Korean government, and so forth. On the other (internationalist) hand, the United States is making significant use of the independent nature of the IAEA and the international legal responsibilities of the United States, North Korea, and all of the other parties involved. None of this is possible without viable international organizations that no longer appear to be simply puppets of the major powers or captives of the nonaligned Group of 77.

These two factors, verification and international organizations, have the potential to significantly enhance the use of arms control in a variety of situations involving armed conflict. In the Balkans conflict, for example, all of the major actors have relied on IOs for verification. This reliance also means that arms embargoes are now much more likely to be put in place if the parties involved can identify weapons as part of the problem. This is clearly relevant in the case of the Balkans, and it is also of some importance in the conflicts in Rwanda and Somalia.

▲ Security and Conflict Frameworks for Developing and Utilizing Arms Control Measures

Cooperative versus Competitive Approaches

To succeed, arms control measures must be explicitly connected to the concepts, frameworks, and theories relied upon to explain conflict and cooperation among states. Much of the acrimonious debate over arms control in the Cold War was driven by the conflicting perspectives of the adversaries over these fundamental issues. Conflict theory and arms control practice must also be harmonized. With the passing of the superpower global conflict, regional and even locally specific factors assume greater importance; thus, there is a need for a new framework to shape arms control thinking. Indeed this volume is designed to do just that. Chapter 1 identifies six conceptually distinct levels of cooperation between antagonists, a six-rung typology that shapes in a very basic way the strategies used in coping with the conflict. These levels of conflict, in reverse order, are (6) intractable, (5) routinized and contained, (4) stabilized and in the process of reduction, (3) resolved, (2) consolidated, and (1) institutionalized consensual cooperation. This last level represents the Deutschian paradigm, the pluralistic security community. How can arms control measures be devised and employed to move the conflict up the rung toward a Deutschian condition?

Ivo Daalder's seminal article "The Future of Arms Control" provides some guidelines. He points out that at both ends of the conflict continuum framing the discussion of this volume, arms control performs no function. "At one end it is impossible, while at the other it is unnecessary. It is when political relations are somewhere between the extremes that there is a role for arms control."[7] He then distinguishes between "competitive" and "cooperative" arms control. In the former, which dominated most of the Cold War era, the objective is to stabilize the balance of military forces between adversaries and thereby reduce incentives for surprise attack and increase crisis stability. This approach also seeks to curtail military and technical developments that exacerbate the problem of counterresponse or reactive acquisitions (the arms race problem). In contrast, cooperative arms control has as its objective the creation of a set of norms and rules that govern the military dimension of interstate relations.[8] The mix of measures chosen will depend very much on where the adversaries are in terms of the six rungs of the conflict ladder.

But how do we move a conflict from levels 6, 5, and 4 toward the Deutschian paradigm in level 1, the pluralistic security community? Strategic planners and policymakers must do so through a refracted set of lenses, which alternately shift the focus from using force to controlling it. Chapter 12, by Jack Snyder, illustrates this shifting focus and the dilemmas of choice raised into view. Snyder outlines three patterns of great-power relations that shape the use of force in regional conflicts: competitive, unilateral hegemonic, and multilateral hegemonic. The implications for arms control of this typology emerge in his conclusion. Arms control is seen as inappropriate, and arms transfers are advocated as a way to control conflict. It would be useful to suggest an alternative to Snyder's security frameworks before advancing some specific arms control proposals.

Cooperative Security as an Alternative Framework for International Security

The notion of cooperative security offers an alternative to Snyder's options and their strictures on arms control and disarmament strategies. Illustrative are the proposals of Antonia and Abram Chayes, which assign a central role to arms control. The major objective of cooperative security is to move beyond a system based on deterrence to one based on "reassurance." As it relates to lower levels of armaments, "cooperative security contemplates an expanding network of generally applicable limitations on permissible weapons systems and force structures. . . . Compliance must be induced by the continuing sense that the limits imposed on military capabilities are consistent with the security requirements of the participants and that they are being generally observed." [9]

The Chayeses develop five principles for such a system. First is the need for a *strong normative base*. Without norms, accepted as firm and legitimate by states, compliance becomes problematic. "To be durable, international legal norms, whether or not treaty based, must meet broad tests of legitimacy. They must be the product of regular and accepted procedures, be applicable equally and without invidious discrimination and satisfy minimal notions of substantive fairness." "Most important in terms of enforcement of norms is that deviant action calls for explanation and justification. The actor when challenged must show that the facts are not as they seem to be, or that the rule, properly interpreted, does not cover the conduct in question, or that some other matter excuses the failure to fulfill the normative requirement." [10]

Inclusiveness and nondiscrimination, the second element in the Chayeses' framework, stipulates that the states affected by a security system participate in its operation. One of the best ways to overcome the lack of inclusiveness and nondiscrimination, especially in this time of transition, is to promote *transpar-*

ency, the third element in the scheme. Transparency involves "the availability and accessibility of knowledge and information, generated through the processes of the (international) regime." Transparency performs three functions in a cooperative security regime: it coordinates the independent decisions of actors; reassures members complying with regional norms that their security interests will not be jeopardized; and deters others from defection.[11]

Regime management, the fourth design element, involves several important information management functions: the collection, evaluation, verification, and analysis of relevant data and the review, assessment, and interpretation of noncompliance preparatory to dispute settlement. The final design element is that of *sanctions* and other coercive measures. Such measures, the Chayeses contend, "deter and if necessary redress egregious and obdurate violation." On the other hand, "unilateral military action for this purpose is inconsistent with the postulates of cooperative security."[12]

To summarize, cooperative security appears to be a more realistic goal than collective security. The five requirements — norms, nondiscrimination, transparency, regime management capabilities, and sanctions — are more likely to become a reality than are the more stringent requirements of collective security. We shall return to how arms control measures can and must be developed using this cooperative security environment. But first several other dimensions of the problem that will be crucial in shaping arms control measures must be addressed and defined.

▲ Global Arms Control Approaches and Their Effect on Regional Conflict

Aside from the theories of conflict and security addressed above and throughout this volume, other aspects of the global-regional nexus come into play in the development of arms control measures. The key tasks are, first of all, to fashion global arms control measures and, once these have been created, to determine their effect on regional conflict. Global measures must face the twin devils of universality and nondiscrimination; that is, a truly global measure must involve all or most actors on an equal and equitable basis. If a particular category of weapons — for example, chemical weapons — is outlawed, no advantage must accrue to one nation over another. Further, any verification regime to monitor compliance must not discriminate against any state.

In the post–Cold War era the major powers have increasingly supported global approaches to arms control. Evidence includes the widening consensus on outlawing chemical weapons and the likely extension of the Non-Proliferation Treaty in 1995. The former superpower rivals and their allies have readily agreed to these measures. Most other states are also willing to accept norms to preclude the use of these weapons. Verification and compliance problems certainly will arise, but one advantage of global measures is that they put into place norms that over time will have a dampening effect on states that would contemplate the acquisition and use of the weapons being outlawed or controlled. These subtle constraining effects can be seen at work throughout the crisis prompted by reported North Korean efforts to develop a nuclear device. North Korea's refusal to permit IAEA personnel to inspect its nuclear facilities in pursuit of its objections under the Non-Proliferation Treaty essentially defined Pyongyang's violation of international norms, rules, and procedures.

Global measures can have several additional effects on regional conflict.[13] The presence of weapons of mass destruction and their means of delivery by one or both adversaries in a regional conflict significantly alters the arms control agenda, in terms of both obstacles and opportunities. In South Asia, for example, both Pakistan and India have begun to integrate nuclear testing and preemptive strike issues into their security calculations, discussions, and negotiations. In the Middle East, Israeli nuclear capabilities and Arab missile and chemical capabilities create significant barriers to even the most benign of confidence-building measures. In Africa, Southeast Asia, and Latin America, where weapons of mass destruction are not a factor, it is possible for states to reach agreements on nuclear-free zones and other measures without risk of seriously undermining their security. Such an approach has the advantage of bringing parties together and "practicing" arms control in a low-risk area. In Latin America, Argentina and Brazil achieved a breakthrough in the nuclear arena by forming the bilateral Argentina-Brazil Accounting and Control Commission (ABACC) to monitor each other's civilian nuclear activities. This experience may lead to further efforts closer to the arms control measures involving conventional weapons being discussed in this chapter.

Global measures also allow regional actors to become better integrated into those IOs charged with arms control. In the case of chemical weapons, for example, the Provisional Technical Secretariat of the OPCW is in the process of recruiting the staff and expertise needed to operate this regime. Since it is a global organization, its international secretariat must include significant representation from the developing world. While the major industrial states, which possess chemical weapons and the capacity to build them, may attempt to control the OPCW, developing countries from the regions most likely to be the scene of armed conflict will have an equal voice in its decisions. The creation of the OPCW also encourages all members to act responsibly, including the developing states that heretofore confined themselves to criticizing the discriminatory policies of the major powers.

▲ Integrating Regional Factors into Arms Control Proposals

Regional specialists are quick to point out that arms control measures that work in one region may not work elsewhere. In the wake of the successful arms control agreements in Europe—CFE, Open Skies—it has become commonplace for both analysts and policymakers concerned with Asia and the Middle East to caution those who would apply the European model to their regions. These discussions have crystallized a set of criteria or preconditions for successful arms control that form a framework for the development and implementation of arms control measures in specific regions.

The first factor to be considered is the *level of conflict* in the region. Arms control will assume a different shape in Bosnia than it will in Latin America. Also important to consider is the culture of violence in a region. As indicated in the label assigned to the fifth rung of the conflict typology shaping this volume, conflict that is "routinized" is most likely a function of a shared view that conflict is an acceptable form of settling disputes and conducting diplomacy. But using arms control in a regional context involves much more than the level of conflict. The absence of arms control measures in the Middle East and the Korean peninsula might be explained by levels of conflict, but many more pacific regions have little more to show in the way of arms control.

This leads us to a second set of regional factors that will shape the use of arms control in ameliorating conflict. The first of these is the *balance of military power* in a region, especially between adversaries. Since the Cold War system of East-West client states collapsed, sovereign states have become much more conscious of military balances qua balance, especially in an era of uncertainty. Closely related are the overall *diplomatic relations* among states in the region. States accustomed to standard diplomatic relations possess the minimum necessary national and regional infrastructure for arms control, while those who do not (e.g, in the Middle East and the Korean peninsula) will find arms control more difficult to achieve. These states will have to develop such structures and expertise before they can engage successfully in developing reliable arms control regimes with their neighbors.

The status of *territorial disputes* is another factor that not only is related to the level and potential for armed conflict but also has implications for the implementation of arms control, even if the parties settle their political differences. In reaching the CFE accords, European states did not experience this problem, while in Bosnia and the Middle East disputes over territory represent a major obstacle to arms control. If arms control goes beyond mere limitations on inventories of weapons systems to include deployments, new maps will have to be drawn up. One is reminded of the difficulties involved in the rather specific agreement to remove the large-caliber weapons out of range of Sarajevo in the spring of 1994. The process was overlaid with the larger questions of who owned which territory and where U.N. inspectors could go. A somewhat related factor is the *strategic value of the real estate* involved. Arms control in regions possessing geography deemed critical to outside parties, such as the Golan Heights, occupied by Israel since the Six Day War in 1967, will be more complicated than in places where only the regional actors have a stake.

Another factor that must be considered is the level of militarization in the region. This has several components. The first of these involves the state of *civil-military relations* in the region. Arms control efforts are replete with examples of proposals and agreements issuing from foreign ministries but rejected by the militaries of the states involved. Measures such as transparency, hot lines, and arms limitations directly affect the security responsibilities of military organizations. So even in areas where conflict is low, such as Latin America, a political tradition that assigns a major role to the military ensures that arms control measures will be slow in getting started. This is another reason why progress in Europe, where the question of civilian dominance of the military was long ago decided, was so swift and dramatic. A second factor of militarization is the *capability of the states involved to indigenously produce the military hardware and support systems* required to enhance their military capability without dependence on outside suppliers. Dependency on this dimension acts as a barrier to arms control.

Arms control requires states to possess *bargaining skills, experience, and established negotiating frameworks,* like the CSCE in Europe. These vary widely across regions. Long before the European states finally negotiated the CFE and the Open Skies treaties, they set up the forums and associated procedures needed to hammer out an agreement. Other regions are just beginning to set up such mechanisms. The Association of Southeast Asian Nations (ASEAN), for example, despite its success as a political organization that has operated for years, is just now expanding its capabilities for dialogue to the security arena. Such bargaining skills are even more critical when it comes to the *culture of transparency.* Secrecy as a way of life, particularly for military organizations, dies hard. Transparency was long in developing in Europe and will take some time to develop in the developing world, the scene of most of the armed conflict.

One final factor is the *level of organizational stability and rationality* present among the states concerned with using arms control to ameliorate conflict. Scott Sagan's recent article on this topic, "The Perils of Proliferation," is most instructive. Sagan responds to neorealist pro-proliferationists such as Kenneth Waltz, who hypothesize that if all states were armed with nuclear weapons, the chances for nuclear war would decline to near zero. These arguments are based on the idea that it would be rational for these new nuclear states to avoid nuclear war. Sagan argues, in contrast, "that the actual behavior of new proliferators will be strongly influenced by the powerful military organizations within those states and that the common biases, rigid routines, and parochial interests of these military organizations will lead to deterrence failures and uses of nuclear weapons despite national interests to the contrary." [14] This argument can be applied as well to the development and employment of arms control measures such as arms limitations, transparency, and confidence- and security-building measures (CSBMs), which in the end have to be implemented by military organizations.

▲ Arms Control as a Function of Type of Commodity

In addition to competing frameworks of conflict and cooperation and the inherent baggage accompanying global and regional approaches, those planning arms control must also develop their strategies in accordance with the attributes of the particular type of weapons system involved in the conflict to be prevented or ameliorated. In essence, a typology of negative consequences associated with types of commodities to be controlled has evolved that has a significant influence on what can be done in the way of arms control.

At the top rung of this typology are *nuclear* weapons. Commencing with the signing of the Non-Proliferation Treaty in 1968, a regime was established around a set of norms that centered on the unacceptable cost of spreading nuclear weapons to more states than those those that possessed them in 1968. There was widespread agreement in both East and West that nuclear war would be the war to end all wars and that the commodities needed to fight such wars should therefore be outlawed, at least in terms of further proliferation. It was not a perfect regime, but a consensus emerged around its basic norms and rules. Despite the recent disclosures in Iraq and North Korea, it is still in place.

Moving down a rung on this commodities ladder to *chemical* weapons, we can see an immediate decline in the urgency to focus on the weapons per se. True, the use of chemical weapons in war was outlawed, and until Iraq used them against Iran and the Kurds in the 1980s they rarely found their way into armed conflict. But the United States and the Soviet Union continued to develop and deploy these weapons as part of the Cold War. The West virtually ignored the Iraqi gassing of an Iranian village in 1986, partly because the victims were from the Third World and partly because of a lack of concern about chemical weapons themselves. It was not until the Gulf War, with live pictures of the launching of SCUD missiles, purportedly with chemical warheads, that the West once again took serious the threat that chemical weapons posed to civilian populations. The Iraqi defeat and the U.N.-sanctioned destruction of its chemical weapons inventory served to move chemical weapons up on the ladder of arms control priorities. The end of the Cold War and subsequent U.S.-Russian cooperation further bolstered international efforts to outlaw chemical weapons a year later.

While regional conflicts that might involve either nuclear or chemical weapons (i.e., weapons of mass destruction) would clearly have an arms control component, most regional conflicts involve commodities below this level. No consensus exists on the negative consequences of the weapons per se. A good example is *military technology*. At the height of the Cold War the United States, Western Europe, and Japan created COCOM, designed to prevent the Soviet Union, its Warsaw Pact allies, and China from receiving any military or dual-use technology that could contribute to the development of those advanced weapons that could create instability and enhance the likelihood of conflict. Long before the Cold War ended, despite a surge in effort in the early Reagan years, the industries that were the subject of this supplier-cartel arms control approach were ignoring and even vigorously resisting such an approach. Why? Again the feasibility of arms control was a function of the consensus, or lack of it in this case, about the impact on conflicts of the commodity to be controlled. Firms often argued that the controlled item was not going to be used for military purposes. A second argument was that the target country already had the technology. A third was that such restrictions only open the market for competitors that are not part of the cartel. Another point often made was that industrial ties, being thwarted by such control measures, actually improve relations and thereby reduce the likelihood of conflict.

These controls quickly disappeared after the Cold War. COCOM itself was dismantled in the spring of 1994. The United States is currently leading a multilateral effort, using the same approach as COCOM, to prevent the so-called proliferator states from gaining the capability to make weapons of mass destruction. Citing Iran, the United States has been trying to convince its G-7 partners and Russia to prevent Teheran from importing sensitive dual-use items. Germany and Japan, which have extensive trade relations with Iran, balk at attempts to reinstitute Cold War controls. They do not see the evidence that Iran is like Iraq was in the 1980s, maintaining that the commodities in question can apply equally to economic development and that their import should be in the interest of all states.

COCOM did have some success in controlling dual-use commodities. The Western states agreed that their export could adversely affect their national security interests. No such accord exists today regarding *major and advanced conventional* weapons, such as tanks, ships, artillery, and those missiles not specifically designed to deliver weapons of mass destruction, that is, the commodities actually used in regional conflicts. Addressing weapons on this low rung of the ladder becomes difficult indeed. Unlike in the cases of the above three commodities, there is no international norm that shows that conventional weapons represent a threat to mankind. There is no perception that the use of conventional weapons is unacceptable in most cases. Despite the fact that during the Cold War all of the 20–30 million casualties in Third World countries occurred as a result of conventional weapons, the Third World–dominated United Nations insisted that nuclear weapons control remains the highest priority.

Another factor that explains the lack of arms control applied to conventional weapons is the inherent difficulties in constructing, monitoring, and verifying such agreements compared with doing the same in the nuclear arena. International discussions have been held for years on the banning of particularly "inhumane" weapons, but to no avail. Attempts are made to export only arms that are "nonlethal"; "offensive" weapons are to be limited, but "defensive" weapons are to be allowed. A consensus on all of these definitions, which is crucial if the negative consequences of using conventional weapons are to be addressed, is not likely to be reached in the near future. Presumably, one should be linking each type of weapon to its negative effects in conflict, which is inherently more difficult than estimating the effect of nuclear weapons. Additionally, assuming that some type of satellite photography is made available to the control regime, be it a national or international regime, it may be possible to detect the arrival of a fighter aircraft, helicopter, or tank prohibited by an agreement. But increasingly weapons systems are becoming smaller and harder to detect.

What of those *components*—so-called force multipliers—that, if transferred to actors in a regional conflict, can significantly shift the balance of military power? Upgrading a country's capability may take the form of a new target detection system or other "black box" totally hidden from the traditional means of monitoring or verification. Nuclear arms control suffers from similar verification obstacles, but the hurdle is much higher at the conventional level. Nowhere was this more clear than in Iraq's buildup of military capability prior to its invasion of Kuwait. While much of the evidence still is not public, enough has been revealed to show how Iraq acquired the dual-use technologies and equipment needed to develop and modify weapons systems, threatening to Israel and to the interests of the Western states.[15]

If it is difficult to develop a consensus on the negative consequences of major advanced conventional weapons, the task is even more daunting for those *light weapons* that have come to dominate the conflicts of the post–Cold War era. By all accounts, trade in light weapons—small arms, land mines, mortars, man-portable missiles, and so forth—has increased significantly.[16] The end of the Cold War has unleashed ethnic conflicts long dormant and controlled by the logic of the Cold War and the efforts of the superpowers to discipline their clients. Ironically, this increase in the trade of light weapons and its accompanying negative consequences are more visible today than before because of the greater use of U.N. peacekeeping and peacemaking operations, which expose conflicts to mass media coverage. These light weapons do most of the killing in armed conflicts, and there is no question that a growing number of such weapons are getting into the hands of established militaries, paramilitary forces, nonstate actors, and civilians involved in ethnic conflicts.

The characteristics of this trade and the nature of the commodities involved create significant challenges for arms control. First, light means small and less visible; satellites will not help much in detection and verification. This also means that monitoring and control efforts by national governmental officials, from desk officers down to customs officials, is inherently more demanding. Second, these weapons are inexpensive, ever more so given their increased availability. More participants are active in the trade, and financial transactions are less open to scrutiny. The world economic system fosters both increased legitimate free trade and the expansion of illicit markets in light weapons as well as drugs and laundered money. Third, these types of weapons are unlike major weapons in that they have little *political* significance. A possible exception may be the case of U.S. Stingers in Afghanistan and in the recent war in Rwanda.[17] But in the main, it takes major quantities of light weapons to have an impact on regime change. Given the international availability of these arms, a recipient state or nonstate actor has the option of multiple supply sources, thus effectively finessing the problem of single source dependency.

▲ From Weapons to Conflict: How Does It Happen?

Another problem that must be addressed in developing arms control measures, besides the commodities involved and regional influences, involves the linkages between the weapons themselves and the specific conflict being coped with. During the Cold War, with its focus on nuclear weapons, there was some consensus on the question of nuclear weapons. The fear of first-strike capability was based not only on presumed hostile intentions but also on military capabilities designed for a first strike. Fortunately for mankind, no empirical data were ever generated to test these propositions. But the relationship between the possession or accumulation of conventional weapons and the outbreak of regional conflict is not as clear.

The experience of several failed attempts to establish arms control in the area of conventional arms is instructive. In 1978 and 1979 the United States and the Soviet Union held several prenegotiating sessions called the Conventional Arms Transfer Talks (CATT). At that time the Carter administration had embarked on a unilateral policy of arms export restraint, coupled with a diplomatic effort to get the Soviet Union, Western Europe, and the developing world to join in. These discussions eventually centered around developing a list of those weapons systems that both sides could agree were inherently destabilizing and threatening to all suppliers. There was some preliminary consensus on weapons (e.g., naval mines), but the talks fell apart prior to serious negotiation when both sides could not agree on any regional applications of this approach. There definitely was no indication that they were about to agree on the weapons actually used in regional conflicts, most of which were being supplied by the United States or the Soviet Union. It should be noted that the other potential participants in this effort, Europe and developing states, resisted any controls. No agreement could be reached linking specific weapons to armed conflict nor about which conflicts should be controlled.

The CFE negotiations focused extensively on those weapons that either were most likely to be employed in surprise attacks or could be easily monitored and reported. They included the higher-caliber and longer-range weapons, omitting almost an entire class of weapons, mainly short-range anti-tank weapons. They also did not include ships and missiles or ammunition, commodities that would have applied arms control to the sacrosanct area of sustainability in combat, for which there was little political support.

While there have been attempts to generalize about the linkage between arms buildups and conflict and about arms transfers during conflict,[18] no consensus has yet emerged that can definitively guide arms controllers and policymakers. There are several data-gathering and analytical challenges that need to be faced. One of the most difficult is simply to acquire valid and reliable data on the inventories and acquisitions of the states involved. Assuming this can be done—a tall order in most cases, even with transparency measures—some sort of assessment of the military utility of these inventories must then be undertaken. At this point we enter the still unresolved offensive-defensive weapons debate.[19] The conflicting perceptions of states, especially opponents, poses another intractable problem. History is replete with misperceptions resulting in conflict, many of them involving misperceptions about military inventories and the capabilities of the items contained therein.

Should the analyst or policymaker get to the level of accurately determining military balances (i.e., a transparency regime worthy of the name), even larger analytical tasks remain, such as determining when an arms buildup is "excessive and destabilizing"; when a particular type of weapons system is destabilizing; or when a particular deployment of particular types of weapons, deployed in a particular manner, enhances the likelihood of conflict. The arms control task is nothing less than one of developing multilateral early-warning indicators and a consultative mechanism that can assess when these indicators point to conflict. This is exactly the objective of the U.N. Register of Conventional Arms, to which we now turn.

▲ The U.N. Register of Conventional Arms

The Iraqi invasion of Kuwait and the allied response resulted in an unprecedented international consensus that the accumulation of advanced weapons systems can be a major factor in the outbreak, conduct, and termination of armed conflict. It was a clear case of such accumulations' being destabilizing in themselves and leading to negative consequences even for the major powers. As a result, in the fall of 1991 the United Nations passed a General Assembly resolution by a vote of 150 to 0 to establish a Register of Conventional Arms. Its primary objective was to establish a step-by-step process that would eventually lead to the transparency of data on conventional arms acquisitions and inventories. The register was to be designed to reduce misperceptions and threats and, ultimately, to foster security at the lowest possible level of armaments.[20]

The Register requests states to submit data each year on the previous year's imports and exports of armaments in seven categories of weapons: battle tanks, armored combat vehicles, large-caliber artillery, combat aircraft, attack helicopters, warships, and missiles and their launchers with a range of at least

TABLE 14.1
Factors Affecting the Utility of Regional Arms Control Measures

International System Factors	Regional Factors
Verification technologies and techniques	Level of conflict
Role and capabilities of international organizations	Balance of military power
	Diplomatic relations
Security and Conflict Frameworks	Territorial disputes
Collective versus cooperative security	Strategic value of real estate
Effects of Global Arms Control	Civil-military relations
Universality and nondiscrimination	Indigenous military production capability
Global norms	Bargaining skills, experience, and established negotiating frameworks
Lack of global measures	Culture of transparency in military affairs
Presence of weapons of mass destruction	Level of organizational stability/rationality
Integration of regional actors into global IOs	Linkage between Weapons and Conflict
Type of Commodity	Calculating military balances
Nuclear	Determining excessive and destabilizing arms buildups
Chemical	Consultative Mechanisms
Strategic military technology	
Advanced conventional weapons	
Components and upgrades	
Light weapons	

twenty-five kilometers. As of the fall of 1994, more than eighty states had submitted data for both 1992 and 1993.

While the Register does not seek to limit arms per se, it clearly fits the definition of arms control as a transparency measure designed as a CSBM. It has developed to the point where it is useful to apply those factors put forth earlier in the chapter as a guide to examining the utility of the Register as an arms control measure that can move conflict toward the Deutschian paradigm (see table 14.1). In doing so we can gain insights into the employment of arms control measures more generally.

Verification, International Organizations, and Consultative Mechanisms

We start first with *verification*. One of the first questions asked of the Register is how we know that the data submitted by governments are true. Which international agency has verified the data? It is clear that the Register is a response to the Gulf War and the negative consequences of conventional arms buildups. In this sense it does concern, albeit indirectly, the traditional goals of arms control. However, the Register is different from classic arms control in that it has no provision for verification.

Despite this lapse, the demand for verification of data by *international orga-nizations* has not disappeared. During its first two years of operation, the Register has relied on several informal approaches that are more appropriate for a confidence-building measure. The first of these is the comparison of Register entries with public data. The second technique is a self-contained cross-checking within the Register itself. The Register asks member states to report both exports and imports. An exporting state may thus report a transfer of forty tanks, but the importer of these tanks may or may not report them. Not only did both of these situations occur in the Register's first two years but in some cases the exporter and importer reported different numbers for the same transfer. But the data submitted are made public each year in a report by the secretary-general, thereby giving any member state, and the public at large, the opportunity to assess the data submitted by governments to the Register, compare them with other public or governmental data, and identify apparent inconsistencies and inaccuracies.

If the Register is to develop into an arms control mechanism that can contribute to the amelioration of conflict, some sort of international organization or consultative mechanism must be developed. What would be the purposes of such a mechanism? First, the establishment of some permanent or established body would lower the political (and economic) costs of addressing excessive and destabilizing arms buildups, particularly if such a process is to be part of the U.N. system. A consultative mechanism would also regularize the determination of excessive and destabilizing buildups, eventually gaining the confidence of the states concerned. It might be possible for such a mechanism to serve as the focal point for the consideration of new categories and types of weapons to be added to the Register. Such a process would also allow the integration of perceptions into the determination of excessive and destabilizing accumulations, a particularly important point given that such accumulations only occur in specific regional contexts.

The Arms Register in a Cooperative Security Framework

If collective security ever becomes a reality, arms control will be much easier and in fact an expected component of the system. The formidable obstacles to collective security advise adoption of a framework of *cooperative security,* as outlined by Chayes and Chayes and summarized earlier. The five central elements in their schema can serve as a guide to how the Register and other arms control measures can develop into mechanisms that can more effectively ameliorate regional conflict.[21]

No arms control measure can succeed without being based on *norms* agreed to by the participating states. There are norms embedded in U.N. Resolution 46/36L that relate directly to the amelioration of conflict.[22] The first preambular paragraph states that "excessive and destabilizing arms buildups pose a threat to national, regional, and international peace and security, particularly by aggravating tensions and conflict situations, giving rise to serious and urgent concerns." The phrase "excessive and destabilizing" appears in paragraphs 2, 4(a), and 12 of the resolution. At this juncture in the history of the Register, there is support for the norm of preventing excessive and destabilizing accumulations: 150 countries voted for the resolution, and more than 80 countries have participated in submitting reports.

The Chayeses' schema then addresses the functions of *information management:* collection, evaluation, verification, and analysis. UNCDA has undertaken the function of data collection, recording exports and imports from the forms submitted by each participating country. But as the first year's experience demonstrated, even this simple task will take time to develop. Some states did not participate because the form and its associated procedures were not clear. Although UNCDA did conduct workshops on compliance, it resisted a proactive posture in soliciting submissions, citing the voluntary nature of the Register. Several major powers on the 1992 panel insisted further that the 1992 report outlining the procedures for the Register specifically limit the role of UNCDA, even in basic data gathering. The 1994 report gives more leeway to UNCDA to assist states in submitting data, but its potential role has yet to be fully exploited.

UNCDA's role is even more limited in evaluating and analyzing the data. This is partly a function of the "Cold War U.N.," in which the superpowers, especially the United States, ensured that any attempt by the United Nations to develop an independent analytical role, especially in security and disarmament matters, was squashed from the outset. Given this circumscribed role of the United Nations, the important management function of verification has been left to the cross-checking exercise previously described, performed by private institutions and national governments, and *not* by the U.N. Secretariat.

The groundwork for the other components of the management function that is so critical for effective arms control—*policy review, capacity building, interpretation, and dispute settlement*—has yet to be started. Even if UNCDA's role in information management should grow to the point where it can be more proactive in enhancing participation and conducting analysis, the large questions remain. What is to be done with the information? How will it be used to accomplish the consensus goals of 46/36L, preventing the excessive and destabilizing accumulations of conventional weapons? Which body will determine what is "excessive and destabilizing"? If the question can only be answered in relation to a specific region or context, how will this be done? One response is traditional diplomacy. However, it would seem that 46/36L pushes the international community beyond such an approach. If one assumes that most of the Iraqi arms buildup was generally known by states, the "traditional diplomacy" method failed. What is needed is some sort of consultative mechanism beyond traditional diplomacy to gather Register data. Confidence building, the major arms control objective in this case, is not possible without such a consultative mechanism to serve as a setting or venue for raising issues and building confidence. It must serve to resolve questions that states may have about buildups. And in the end, it must be able to accomplish the goals put forth in the Chayeses' model, those of interpretation and dispute settlement.

The Utility of a Global Arms Control Measure for Regional Security

Given that the 1994 U.N. deliberations on the Register produced an outcome that emphasized the importance of regional approaches, what can be the utility of a *global* arms control and confidence-building measure such as the Register? From the beginning the Register has been plagued by the fact that it was initially designed by industrialized states that normally are not the site of armed conflict. As a result, the initial focus was solely on arms transfers. This drew the immediate charge from key developing states such as Pakistan and Egypt, whose military capabilities depended on imports. The effect of a transfer-only Register was that these import-dependent states would be reporting their buildups, while their rivals, India and Israel, did not have to report arms acquired through national production. This discriminatory element of the Register still persists and poses a major obstacle to participation by key states.

Nevertheless, as a global CSBM the Register has brought together states that heretofore dealt with the arms trade through posturing and mutual recriminations. The panel of U.N. experts that created the Register came from seventeen countries, including the major supplier states—the United States, Russia, France, the United Kingdom, and China—as well as key developing countries, such as Egypt and India. The second group, which met in 1994 to evaluate and expand the Register, included representatives from twenty-three countries, with Germany, Australia, Israel, and Pakistan joining the group. Understanding about the relationship between global and regional factors has been broadened, and participating states have exhibited a rare seriousness and sense of responsibility in further developing the Register regime.

Regional Factors

All critical regions were represented on the two negotiating groups charged with developing the Register. As a result, one can gain insights from these negotiations into how regional factors affect state perceptions and participation and the effectiveness of the Register as an arms control measure. It was clear from the beginning that the *level of conflict* extant in a region greatly influenced participation. In the Middle East only Egypt and Israel submitted data on exports and imports for the calendar year 1992. This no doubt was a function of the special arms transfer relationship both have with the United States. Israel clearly opposes any expansion of the Register until the basic requirements referred to earlier in this chapter are satisfied, for example, the establishment of normal diplomatic relations among all regional states.

Western Europe and the former Warsaw Pact countries had the most complete participation: 96 percent of the countries reported. Participation was minimal in the new states of the former Soviet Union, owing in large part to the political and military instability in these states. Georgia, for example, reported that no official exports and imports had occurred in 1992, but the illegal arms traffic, fueling the various armed conflicts in the country, was significant. Adding to this reluctance to report is the sudden emergence of a significant number of *territorial disputes*. Arms control measures require some level of risk-taking and trust, especially in the absence of a verification mecha nism. The higher the level of conflict and territorial disputes and the lower the level of diplomacy as a tool of conflict resolution in a region, the less likely the states are to participate in arms control as a solution to these conflicts.

The *balance of military power* in a region has also determined Register participation. Pakistan insists that arms transfers, national production, *and* military inventories be included in the Register. The assessment of military balances, difficult in any case to calculate, is clearly impossible unless these three types of information are made transparent. In the Middle East, Egypt has sought to include weapons of mass destruction, a clear reference to the imbalance that is created by Israel's possession of nuclear weapons. The state of the military balance also affects how much information states are willing to make transparent. No state, not even in Western Europe, has been willing to make transparent its holdings of missiles. Only a few states provided details on their missile exports and imports. Many states — Sweden, Australia, Germany — object that for them missiles represent a critical tool of national security and that transparency is not possible if it inadvertently divulges combat sustainability to a potential enemy. As one representative put it, "We are not worried about creating an image of excessive armaments, but rather revealing just how under-armed we really are!"[23]

The *strategic value* of the region and its potential for arms purchases abroad also have shaped the effectiveness of the Register. Western governmental leaders' initial enthusiasm for limiting exports to the Middle East was quickly offset by stiff resistance from arms industries and their governmental allies. As the Cold War was winding down and national defense budgets were rapidly declining, arms producers were not keen on cutting back on arms exports anywhere, let alone the lucrative Middle East. By the time the Register was operative, governmental interest had cooled perceptibly. Some of the biggest of the Western states' clients—Saudi Arabia, the United Arab Emirates, Kuwait—have not participated. And none of their major suppliers—the United States, France, and the United Kingdom—furnished details on the precise types of equipment exported. Reports listed the number of tanks, missiles, and missile launchers but not their characteristics. In regions of less strategic importance, recipient states generally reported on types and models, creating more transparency and rendering the arms control measure more effective.

The status of *civil-military* relations has also played an important role in the implementation of the Register. At a 1993 UNCDA-sponsored workshop in Buenos Aires to introduce the procedures of reporting to the Register, attending states sent representatives from both their foreign ministries and their defense ministries. These representatives had not conferred prior to attending the workshop, evidencing just how far apart these two crucial ministries were on the issue in most states. It also became clear that no Latin American country could submit data until the military had approved. In some cases, such as in Venezuela, national law forbids the public release of any military information, precluding its participation in the Register.

In Southeast Asia, two major importers—Thailand and Indonesia—did not participate in 1992. In both countries, the military heavily influences security policies. At the opposite end of the spectrum, opposition to the U.N. Register was significant in the U.S. military, but the military's concerns were subordinated to a civilian national policy decision to participate in the Register. The minimal level of detail given by the United States suggests, however, that the military did have some influence on the final data submitted. Arms control measures by definition involve the weapons and armaments procured, maintained, and deployed by military forces. Secrecy is a mainstay of military security. As long as it remains so, the military clearly will have a major say in complying with these measures. The greater the preponderance of civilian control of the military, the greater the likelihood of participation in the Register.

As previously mentioned, *indigenous defense production* becomes critical in arms control measures for several reasons. First, it is critical in determining the military balances that are often the subject of arms control. Second, a state dependent on external suppliers for critical armaments is more subject to supplier' wishes. If the latter support the Register, compliance by these dependent arms states can also be expected to be greater. Israeli and Egyptian dependence on the United States for arms correlates, *grosso modo*, with their high-level, if reluctant, participation in the Register.

Sagan's point about *organizational stability and rationality* also comes into play. Formally expressed willingness to participate in the Register does not automatically translate into implementation. The Russian case is instructive. While the government strongly supported the Register on a political level, it only partially complied with the Register's reporting criteria. Some of the difficulty can be related to a hesitant military, which still controlled arms exports. But the more formidable impediment to compliance was the sudden collapse of the previous export control system. In a word, the Russian government does not fully know what is being exported. Furthermore, with the collapse of the Soviet Union, the expertise to determine and develop the data for submission has also disappeared. These problems are even more intractable for Ukraine, Georgia, and Belarus, which relied on Soviet controls.

Organizational capabilities vary significantly across states purely as a matter of bureaucratic efficiency, quite apart from any governmental intention to cheat, deceive, or mislead. The importance of regional factors was clearly demonstrated in the final report of the 1994 group of governmental experts on the first two years of operation of the Register. This group's mandate was to consider expanding the Register to include data on procurement through national production and inventories. The negotiations and discussions that generated this report broke down into two competing blocs of states. On one side were the major arms suppliers—the United Kingdom, France, and the United States—which challenged the recipient states to increase their participation in the Register to include such data. On the other side was a bloc of developing states—for example, China, India, and Israel—for which such an enlargement of transparency constituted a threat to national security interests. The impasse precluded further progress until the security interests of these resistant states could be assured or enhanced.

Types of Weapons and Their Linkage to Conflict

A final set of factors consists of the types of weapons being reported and how they are linked to the outbreak or conduct of armed conflict across regions. In the first two years of the Register's operation, more than 50 percent of states reported no exports or imports. While stagnant military budgets account partially for this outcome, most of the "nonreporting" arose from the inapplicability of the seven categories of weapons to many regions. Several developing countries made the point that the seven categories of weapons systems identified in the Register were at such a high level of capability that they excluded most of the conventional arms being actually "excessively accumulated" and used in regional conflicts, especially in places such as sub-Saharan Africa and Central America.

Even if it is assumed that the only arms related to conflict involve end items in the Register's seven categories, the Register still falls far short on missiles. Ground-to-air missiles are not included, and a range limitation of twenty-five kilometers for reporting excludes several classes of lethal missiles, such as anti-tank and air-to-air missiles. Other major systems, like electronic warfare systems or remotely delivered mines, remain outside the Register.

While the above assessment of the Register is rather sobering, it does give a clear picture of how arms control measures are likely to evolve in the post–Cold War era. The experience of the first two years demonstrates that while a *global* measure has proven to be an adequate start and will serve to maintain the momentum in dealing with the negative consequences of conventional arms, coping with *regional* conflicts must eventually rely on regional arms control measures.

The "regionalization" of the Register was foreseen from the start. Paragraph 17 of 46/36L "calls upon all Member States to cooperate at a regional and sub-regional level, taking fully into account the specific conditions prevailing in the region or sub-region, with a view to enhancing and coordinating international efforts aimed at increased openness and transparency in armaments." The submission of data to the Register in the first two years varied widely by region, providing further evidence that the regionalization of the Register process may well bring immediate dividends. In a recent address to the U.N. Advisory Board on Disarmament Matters, the U.N. secretary-general provided the strongest boost yet for this approach: "Regional registers should now be the next step. They have the advantage of allowing the categories of weapons to be registered to reflect the security concerns felt in the region." [24]

What would be the specific advantages of regionalization? [25] First, states in a particular region most likely share similar approaches to transparency and openness. In Latin America, for example, the role of the military has traditionally been strong, resulting in a reluctance to release military information. A process that focuses just on Latin America may well increase participation. Second, many regions already have mechanisms and organizations in place into which the register approach could be integrated. Many of these organizations are formally linked to the United Nations, which today stresses the role of regional security organizations as part of the new United Nations. Third, the causes and conduct of armed conflict vary significantly across regions. This is particular true of the categories and types of weapons whose excessive accumulation are the object of the Register process. Also, in those regions where security questions can be regionalized, the Register process can be easily integrated, a step that is critical if the Register is to go beyond mere collection and dissemination of data on conventional arms. Fourth, the culture of arms acquisition tends to be region-specific. In some cases the major arms-exporting countries play a crucial role and would have to be integrated into the process. In other regions this is not the case. In sum, both global and regional approaches are necessary.

▲ Summary

Using the U.N. Register of Conventional Arms as a tool to illustrate the general applicability of arms control in coping with regional conflict leads to several generalizations. First, an assessment of the conditions extant in a region that can support arms control, using the typology developed in table 14.1, is a critical first step. Such an assessment demonstrates that certain regions are more disposed than others toward such measures. Second, arms control measures will most likely develop in the cooperative security framework outlined by Chayes and Chayes. As indicated by the Register experience, this is a slow, incremental process. Third, global arms control efforts are important. The register approach is evolving into regional variants, owing largely to the presence of the global Register. Both the Organization of American States and ASEAN have recently adopted resolutions to enhance regional security through their participation in the U.N. Register process. Global exercises, even though they may not go as far as some would like, are important learning and confidence-building tools. Fourth, the development of international organizations and regimes will be crucial. The Register experience shows that even with global arms control measures, progress is still a function of the amount of sovereignty states are willing to consign to a neutral and independent international organization. And finally, much research needs to be done on the links between arms acquisitions and buildups, on the one hand, and armed conflict, on the other. Memories fade fast, especially when arms sales are at stake. What are the cases where buildups have led to armed conflict? They may arguably be few but disastrous, as in the Iraqi case. Those planning and promoting arms control measures must be able to demonstrate to skeptical participants that what has happened before can happen again.

It is also important to document and model those cases where arms buildups do *not* lead to conflict. Some buildups are benign, with acquisitions serving mainly to enhance prestige. Others are matched by rivals, and a stalemate ensues, which is costly but not necessarily lethal or fatal. Unconditional demands for disarmament as the only route to conflict reduction are likely to be irrelevant or self-defeating. There may be valid arguments for reducing armaments for economic reasons, and these of course are well taken and are being acted on today. But if the question is one of coping with conflict, analysts and policymakers must move beyond disarmament to arms control. This is not unlike the situation that created the concepts and approaches that became known as arms control in the late 1950s.

Now that regional conflicts have been freed from Cold War constraints, arms control is more important than it has ever been. As long as arms buildups occur and lead to or exacerbate conflicts, there is a place for arms control in the menu of strategies utilized to ameliorate differences between groups and states. All too often arms controllers rush headlong into a regional conflict, with prepackaged plans and policies, only to discover that the participants prefer to solve their differences by force and threats. Under these conditions arms control is no panacea. However, if it is applied with an informed appreciation of the complexity of modern arms and their variable impact on state security interests, arms control can be an important coping tool. The challenge is to know where and how to use it. As this chapter suggests, it is a precision tool that requires much thought and patience before positive results can be achieved.

NOTES

1. This chapter uses the standard arms control typology, summarized most recently by Richard Dean Burns in his *Encyclopedia of Arms Control and Disarmament* (New York: Charles Scribner's Sons, 1993). *Arms control* is defined as all forms of military cooperation between potential enemies in the interest of reducing the likelihood of war, its scope and violence if it did occur, and the political and economic costs of being prepared for it. The six techniques historically used to further these objectives include:

limitation and reduction of weapons; demilitarization, denuclearization, and neutralization; regulating or outlawing specific weapons; controlling arms manufacture and traffic; laws of war; and stabilizing the international environment through confidence- and security-building mechanisms (CSBMs), improved communications, and so forth.

2. Colin S. Gray, *House of Cards: Why Arms Control Must Fail* (Ithaca: Cornell University Press, 1992); idem, *Weapons Don't Make War: Policy, Strategy, and Military Technology* (Lawrence: University of Kansas Press, 1993).

3. Richard K. Betts, "Systems for Peace or Causes of War: Collective Security, Arms Control, and the New Europe," *International Security* 17 (summer 1992): 5–43.

4. International Institute for Strategic Studies, *Strategic Survey, 1993–1994* (Oxford: Brassey's, 1994), 50.

5. Karin Axell, Birger Heldt, Erik Melander, Kjell-Åke Nordquist, Thomas Ohlson, and Carl Åsberg, "United Nations Arms Embargoes," *SIPRI Yearbook 1994* (Oxford: Oxford University Press, 1994), 493–502.

6. Boutros Boutros-Ghali, *New Dimensions of Arms Regulation and Disarmament in the Post–Cold War Era,* U.N. Doc. A/C 1/47/7, Oct. 1992.

7. Ivo Daalder, "The Future of Arms Control," *Survival* 34 (spring 1992): 52.

8. Ibid., 52–53.

9. Antonia Handler Chayes and Abram Chayes, "Regime Architecture—Elements and Principles," in *Global Engagement: Cooperation and Security in the Twenty-First Century,* ed. Janne E. Nolan (Washington, D.C.: Brookings Institution, 1994), 65–130, quotation from 65.

10. Ibid., 71, 69.

11. Ibid., 81.

12. Ibid., 68.

13. For a treatment of this question applied to the Middle East, see Geoffrey Kemp, "Proliferation and Regional Security," in *The Control of the Middle East Arms Race* (Washington, D.C.: Carnegie Endowment for International Peace, 1992), chap. 5.

14. Scott D. Sagan, "The Perils of Proliferation: Organization Theory, Deterrence Theory, and the Spread of Nuclear Weapons," *International Security* 18 (spring 1994): 66–107, quotation from 102.

15. Kenneth Timmerman, *The Death Lobby* (New York: Houghton Mifflin, 1991).

16. For two excellent and recent accounts of increased trade in light weapons, see Aaron Karp, "Arming Ethnic Conflict," *Arms Control Today,* Sept. 1993, 8–13; and "The Covert Arms Trade," *Economist,* Feb. 12, 1994, 21–23.

17. For an excellent case study of the impact of small arms on the outbreak and conduct of armed conflict, see Stephen D. Goose and Frank Smyth, "Arming Genocide in Rwanda," *Foreign Affairs* 73 (Sept.-Oct. 1994): 86–96.

18. On the linkage between arms buildups and conflict, see Frederic S. Pearson and Michael Brzoska, *Arms and Warfare* (Columbia: University of South Carolina Press, 1994); on arms transfers during conflict, see Stephanie G. Neuman, *Military Assistance in Recent Wars: The Dominance of the Superpowers* (New York: Praeger, 1986).

19. For an in-depth treatment of these problems, see Edward J. Laurance, "The Conceptualization and Measurement of International Arms Transfers," in *The International Arms Trade* (New York: Lexington Books, 1992), chap. 2.

20. For in-depth description and analysis of the U.N. Register, see Hendrik Wagen-

makers, "The UN Register of Conventional Arms: A New Instrument for Cooperative Security," *Arms Control Today,* Apr. 1993, 17–19; Herbert Wulf, "The United Nations Register of Conventional Arms," in *SIPRI Yearbook 1993: World Armaments and Disarmament* (Oxford: Oxford University Press, 1993), 533–44; Edward J. Laurance, Siemon T. Wezeman, and Herbert Wulf, *Arms Watch: SIPRI Report on the First Year of the UN Register of Conventional Arms* (Oxford: Oxford University Press, 1993); Ian Anthony, "Assessing the UN Register of Conventional Arms," *Survival* 35 (winter 1993): 113–29; and Malcolm Chalmers, Owen Greene, Edward J. Laurance, and Herbert Wulf, eds., *Developing the UN Register of Conventional Arms* (Bradford, U.K.: University of Bradford, 1994).

21. For an application by Chayes and Chayes of their schema to the Register, see Antonia Handler Chayes and Abram Chayes, "The UN Register, Transparency and Co-Operative Security," in Chalmers, Greene, Laurance, and Wulf, *Developing the UN Register of Conventional Arms,* 197–224.

22. The question concerning the status of General Assembly resolutions in international law is controversial and beyond the scope of this chapter. There is some support for viewing such resolutions as customary law, especially if most states vote for the resolution and behave over time in accordance with its provisions.

23. Interview with participant in 1992 panel deliberations.

24. *Address of the Secretary General to the Advisory Board on Disarmament Matters,* U.N. press release SG/SM/94/3, 12 Jan. 1994.

25. For the pros and cons of regionalization of the U.N. Register, see Joseph DiChiaro, "The UN Register in a Regional Context: Basic Concepts," in Chalmers, Greene, Laurance, and Wulf, *Developing the UN Register of Conventional Arms,* 271–82.

Conclusion

EDWARD A. KOLODZIEJ

15 Thinking about Coping

Actors, Resources, Roles, and Strategies

▲ A Conceptual Template for Coping with Conflict

Coping with armed conflict remains one of the most impor-
tant challenges confronting the peoples and states of the post–Cold War world.
The end of the superpower conflict has hardly resolved the security problems arising from the use of force or coercive threats by groups and states to
get their way. As chapter 1 outlines, and as the succeeding chapters affirm,
most security threats arise today from within the boundaries of states, including separatist or subnational conflicts for self-determination, ideological
and group conflicts for control of central governments, and internal rivalries
over rank and power. These threats to security currently overshadow in scope
and intensity still important and unresolved interstate struggles, like those in
South Asia or those occasioned by the collapse of the Soviet empire and state.
Viewed from the perspective of an increasingly interdependent and emerging
global society, these multiple arenas of conflict and the diverse and disputed
stakes driving them underline the need to rethink how the states and peoples
of the globe might cope with them.

With the demise of the Cold War, there is little—certainly reduced—incentive for any one state to assume the security burdens previously assumed by Washington and Moscow in regulating regional conflict. These responsibilities, if they are to be exercised at all, devolve to the world community, principally to the major economic and military powers and international organizations that have emerged intact from the Cold War struggle. While persuasive reasons can be adduced for states and other international actors to discharge coping duties, the weakened political supports for coping in the post–Cold War world, particularly among the victorious powers of the West-centric system, must also be squarely faced if realistic goals are to be defined and effective strategies developed to ameliorate armed conflicts.

The problem of coping with conflict in the post–Cold War era resolves itself into the question of what actors, disposing what resources, playing what roles, and pursuing what strategies are best suited—and willing—to ameliorate a conflict. In other words, what mix is likely to move a conflict at one level of real, incipient, or potential armed conflict to one less disposed toward coercive resolution of differences between groups and states? What combination is likely to move a lethal struggle, particularly between enduring rivals, toward the Deutschian paradigm of a security community based on shared values and animated by principles, norms, institutions, and joint processes of decision in the service of peaceful change?

This ambitious, even heroic, understanding of a security community in a world divided against itself is an ideal and should not be viewed as a likely expectation to be realized sometime soon wherever political conflicts or armed clashes may be found. The strictures of this ideal, however, can be relaxed to provide a ready and more realistic guide for coping policies. Diverse conflicts can be usefully standardized, as chapter 1 allows, by reference to whatever progress can be made in ameliorating a conflict, defined simply by the degree to which the rivals have a lessened propensity to resort to coercive threats or force to get their way. Thus the Deutschian ideal is a normative aim rather than a reliable, real-time expectation, much less a plan, that the major states are prepared to intervene to preclude the outbreak of hostilities, to limit their damaging effects when they erupt, or to act quickly and decisively to stop the bloodshed. The sobering analyses offered by Morgan and Snyder suggest otherwise.

The constraints identified in this volume inhibiting states, international organizations, or groups from assuming coping roles highlight the distance between the Deutschian ideal of regular observance of norms of behavior and the actual efforts to attain it along two dimensions: the resistance of particular peoples and states to acknowledge their common humanity, with respect to either its biological and social origins or its universal fate, or to act on these assumptions in pursuit of OWL objectives. Absent a growing embrace of these ideals and the implied universal history and destiny underlying them, there is reason to be skeptical that movement up the Deutschian ladder is likely to be accelerated in the post–Cold War world. The pessimistic future seems especially predictable of those segments of the world society that are engaged in armed hostilities and have a long record of animosity and accumulated grievances, marked by tribal, ethnic, national, racial, confessional, and ideological splits. Yet progress has been made by some members of the global society at regional levels, as chapter 8 indicates, providing powerful evidentiary support for the gradual expansion of zones of peace and mutual welfare and the spread of universal values consecrated to the moral equality of humans on this earth.

Rather than assume that the security problems confronting peoples and states are essentially the same everywhere, it makes more sense to assume that the specific elements of the security dilemma inherent in the nation-state system and within the larger global society vary with actors, issues, conjunctural circumstance, and history across regions and locales. For some peoples and states, like the United States and Canada, Deutsch's notion of a security community is real and palpable. These members of the world society form an obvious set of actors who might be enlisted in coping efforts, since they need no assistance in addressing their differences through noncoercive mechanisms. At the opposite extreme, the political chaos that resulted in mass starvation in Somalia or that led to campaigns of "ethnic cleansing" in the former Yugoslavia and "tribal cleansing" in Rwanda destroy previous social and political restraints on force and thrust the rivals headlong toward a state of nature. Under these Hobbesian conditions, no civil society or security community exists to contain the self-help efforts of the opponents striving relentlessly to impose their will on rivals though violence.

Most states and peoples find themselves in security communities somewhere between these polar opposites, ranging from consensual cooperation — the United States and Canada — to coercive cooperation — the Somali warlords, the Lebanese factions, or North and South Korea. The six levels of cooperation, identified in chapter 1 provide rough diagnostic tools for arraying conflicts and, accordingly, for defining the kinds of security communities that have been established between politically differentiated and contesting peoples. What this volume attempts to show is that moving from a primitive to a mature security relationship, defined by the greater or lesser amount of violence and coercion characterizing the relationship, is very difficult, but still possible. Positive movement implies the contributions to peace not only of the principals to the conflict but of a large and disparate number of state and nonstate actors playing differing roles, disposing varied resources, and pursuing converging, if not always consciously articulated, military, economic, and political strategies to effect peaceful changes. Coping does not come cheap or easy; nor can one expect to devise a single set of coping measures that would be appropriate and effective in diminishing violence in all underdeveloped security communities in the post–Cold War era.

A significant part of the problem of developing a reliable template for the diagnosis of conflicts and prescriptions for resolution is that there exists no established consensus of what factors must be addressed, and within what international context, to explain why one group of peoples and states have achieved a relatively mature security community, while others are unable to progress beyond an immature relationship.[1] The tenuous status of security theory is revealingly illustrated by the failure of analysts to anticipate, much less predict, the end of the Cold War, the collapse of the Soviet empire, the disintegration of the Soviet state, or the turmoil and lethal clashes among peoples of the former Soviet Union in their efforts to create new states or reestablish old ones.[2]

The debate among analysts over the very meaning of security and security studies exposes the absence of a reliable theory to explain the evolution of security communities. Whether security studies should be reduced to examining the use or threat of force by states and theory building confined to that relationship or whether the notion of security should be expanded to include all factors that explain why peoples and states insist on or resist using force or coercion in pressing their claims on each other remain questions that are much at issue and unresolved. Within the enlarged perspective underlying the conception of security and security theory adopted by the editors of this volume,[3] it is not enough to confirm the importance and the continued saliency of force and threats in defining the security relations of peoples and states, as realists are inclined to do. Reliable theorizing about security communities and coping with conflict also obliges analysts to investigate the possibility that cooperation can be achieved by means other than by force or threats. In developing coping theory as a halfway house for a theory of war and peace that remains to be defined, the contributors to this volume neither rule in nor rule out the use of force as an effective coping tool that can be useful over time in moving a particular security community, say, the African Horn, from a primitive to a more mature level.

Rivals can learn to reduce the levels of violence that previously animated their security relations and can work together to institutionalize noncoercive ways of managing and resolving their differences. They can be shown to be responsive to varied noncoercive incentives, some created by third parties, to surmount or at least ameliorate the way they previously confronted their differences and defined their security relationships. A theory of war and armed conflict also implies a theory of peace; one cannot substitute for the other. Both are important patterns of a seamless cloth of coercive conflict and consensual cooperation.[4] It is not enough to confirm through observation that force still counts between enduring rivals, an insight tantamount to a tautology; it is also necessary to try to show that cooperation could not be progressively tilted, over time, toward noncoercive resolution of disputes.

▲ Developing a Template for Coping

Two examples may clarify the analysis and strengthen the case for the coping strategy advanced by this volume despite the absence of a reliable and generally accepted theory of conflict, conflict resolution, or cooperation. Gradual postwar Franco-German reconciliation and the sudden breakthrough in Israeli-Arab conflict, dramatized by the accords between Israel and the Palestine Liberation Organization (PLO) of September 1993 and 1995, illustrate the possibilities of long-term coping even in cases where obstacles to any reduction in the level of violence between such longtime bitter foes seemed impossible. An examination of these two conflicts and the slow evolution of a more mature security relationship between the antagonists in each case may also illustrate the usefulness of a common template to orient analytic thinking and international policymaking in coping with specific regional conflicts.

Several temptations should also be resisted: the search for a single solution to all security dilemmas; the assumption that all conflicts can be resolved; or the expectation that a security community that is moving toward the Deutschian ideal cannot slip and revert again to hostility and violence. The questions to be posed in diagnosing a conflict and prescribing for its amelioration are, arguably, the same, as this volume contends; the substantive responses of analysts and decision makers will necessarily have to differ depending on the specific circumstance and historical evolution of the rivalry. The same questions should be asked about coping; there should be no expectation that the same answers will be forthcoming when the questions are applied to a specific security community.

What seems clear is that both the European and Middle East conflicts have matured over time from primitive security relationships roughly conforming to the last two levels of security cooperation—intractable conflict or conflict that is at best routinized and contained—to a new status permitting a wider range and denser set of noncoercive interchanges and progressively lesser reliance on force or threats, open or veiled, to impose one party's will on the other. Most informed analysts would agree that France and Germany have reached the penultimate or top rung of security cooperation, characterized by the consolidation of their security policies within a common defense framework and by the progressive institutionalization of consensual cooperation between them.

For Israel and the PLO, let alone other Arab states like Syria and Iraq or fundamentalist Iran, the road toward consolidation and institutionalization will be long and hard and by no means assured. The Israeli-PLO conflict appears to be at rung 4, a reduction in force driving the conflict and the prospect that a process, guaranteed and supported by a rich mix of third parties, will be gradually installed to permanently reduce reliance on force and threats to resolve profound differences and to overcome still deeply felt hatreds, given to unexpected explosions of violence.

Resolving the Franco-German Rivalry

What actors, playing what roles, disposing what resources, and pursuing what strategies, have now brought France and Germany to their present level of security cooperation? This evolution is elaborated on in chapter 8. What remains to be highlighted is the mix of those elements that accounts for the success of these European peoples in surmounting their historical enmities and in creating a structure of shared power and pooled sovereignty that generates a synergism of incentives for consensual over coercive cooperation. This new political condition may be defined not simply as one of France or as Germany trying to get its way—each state will obviously press its preferences in bargaining over policy matters like interest rates and agricultural supports in the European Community (EC)—but as one of their jointly strengthening their mutually contingent and shared security relationship.[5]

The international context within which Franco-German postwar relations evolved toward consensual cooperation was, of course, that of World War II, a mutually devastating experience, and the Cold War, an occasion for cooperation to contain a common threat. For the noncommunist majorities of France and West Germany, covering the political spectrum from the conservative Right to the social democratic Left, the Soviet Union threatened the physical security of both states, the open economic systems to which both subscribed, the democratic regimes governing both states, and the free, pluralistic societies on which their domestic regimes depended for their support and legitimacy. The Soviet threat stilled past grievances between these traditional rivals and galvanized national efforts to construct a coordinated response to meet the Soviet challenge.

Key to fostering Franco-German reconciliation was strong and unwavering U.S. support for the Atlantic Alliance and the European Community as the pillars on which European security and economic development would rest. In retrospect, it is important to recognize that there was nothing automatic about U.S. Marshall Plan assistance for European recovery. The United States might well have imposed a punitive peace, which is what the Soviet Union actually did in East Germany; or, in granting assistance, Washington might have insisted that loans be repaid, the policy adopted after World War I toward Germany and the Allies. Instead, aid was outright, on the proviso that the European states agree to an integrated plan to solve the problems of postwar recovery and to Europe's return to a global capitalist system.

Similarly, the U.S. security guarantee under NATO, which facilitated direct Franco-German security cooperation within a common institutional framework, was not inevitable. Europe might have been compelled to do more for its own defense; the United States might have pursued a more unilateral national security policy in which the Europeans would have been more stakes than partners and allies; the United States might have withdrawn from Europe completely, as it did after World War I, or assumed an uncompromising hegemonic policy, as previous conquerors had done. Again, departing from historically sanctioned, if not successful, security practices, it championed European political integration not only to better fight the Cold War but also to surmount permanently Europe's civil wars, which had occurred since the inception of the modern state. The United States has continued to pursue a strategy of surmounting over balancing, at times more vigorously than the Europeans themselves, notably Gaullist France and Thatcher England.

The United States also acceded to the creation of a preferential economic zone in Western Europe at the expense of its own open trading principles embodied in the General Agreement on Tariffs and Trade (GATT), the International Monetary Fund (IMF), and the World Bank, all foundation stones of the postwar global capitalistic market system underwritten by U.S. military and economic power, for the sake of the anticipated security and political benefits of a united Western Europe. The United States might well have opposed such a trading block and the long-term goal of political union. Postwar history would have been different. Other victor powers, more vengeful than

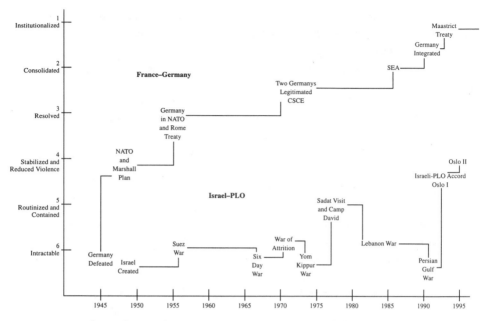

Fig. 15.1. The Evolution of Two Security Communities toward the Deutschian Ideal

visionary—France and Britain after World War I or imperial Germany after France's defeat in 1870—were not as prescient in the pursuit of their long-term interests.

In sum, U.S. military, economic, and diplomatic resources, Washington's decisive leadership role, and the adoption of elaborate and costly national security and economic recovery strategies, in cooperation with the European peoples, created a structure of power and internal incentives among the states and peoples of the Western coalition that contributed, as a necessary if not sufficient condition, to the reconciliation of significant elements of Europe's populations, most importantly the French and German peoples.

As figure 15.1 depicts, the consolidation of Franco-German reconciliation, the penultimate rung up the ladder toward consensual cooperation, has taken almost a half-century to reach and is still not fully assured. Along the way an impressive set of international institutions has been constructed within which the national policies of France and Germany could be collectivized and their sovereignties pooled. The very list of these structures testifies to the efforts of the European peoples to surmount the balance-of-power and narrow beggar-thy-neighbor mercantilist policies of the past that failed to ensure national security and domestic prosperity. Their creation and strengthening, realist expectations to the contrary notwithstanding, can be explained less as a response to some Kantian ideal of posited, preexisting harmony of national aims, interests, and values than as learned and sober responses to correct the failures of previous unilateral efforts to ensure national security and welfare. Multilateral and overlapping structures—NATO, the EC, the Western European Union (WEU), the Conference and Security and Cooperation in Europe (CSCE), the IMF, the GATT, the Group of Seven Industrialized Democracies (G-7), the United Nations, and others—institutionalized this learning process in cooperation and noncoercive bargaining, negotiation, and joint decision making. Taken together, they go a long way toward explaining the evolution of a mature security zone in Western Europe.

It is not without irony that the principal postwar force propelling Paris and Bonn to move from a coercive to a consensual security community—the Soviet threat—also contributed unwittingly to the process of consolidation and institutionalization. Dividing German power, the Cold War solution to previous German nationalism and expansionism, was, as Anton DePorte has argued, one of the few points on which the victorious Big Four could agree.[6] That implicit convergence of interests between the East and the West appeared so stable that few envisioned the collapse of the Cold War system anytime soon. The two Germanys were incorporated into two rival blocs, and their separate statehood and domestic regimes were legitimated by the Helsinki accords and by their admission to the United Nations.

With the end of the Cold War, the indispensable role played by the bloc system in advancing Germany's political rehabilitation and reintegration into the European state and economic system has been lost. Each Germany learned to cooperate with its respective alliance partners. The institutional structures created to foster security and economic cooperation were also the vehicles for Germany's gradual Europeanization. Within them, as Janice Stein's analysis of enemy images suggests, German national identity could be redefined in European terms. Although this process of Europeanization is far from complete in Germany and certainly is resisted even more so in other parts of Europe— witness the setbacks in Denmark, Britain, and France over approval of the Maastricht Treaty—Germany today bears little resemblance to imperial Germany a century earlier. If Thomas Mann's ideal of a Europeanized Germany is still beyond the grasp of Germans and Europeans, the prospect of a German Europe under Berlin's hegemonic control now appears absurd, while little more than a half-century ago it appeared to many as inevitable. Even a return to classical balance-of-power politics appears remote, since it reflects neither the institutional structures erected in Europe to coordinate German and European peoples' shared interests nor the psychological dispositions, economic needs, and political values pressing them toward union.

These observations also underline the importance of the self-help efforts of the European populations in moving toward a consensual security community. Third parties, principally the United States, and the multiplication of common institutions have been indispensable, but their positive contributions would hardly have been fruitful in the absence of the will and determination of the French and German peoples and their elites to bury the deeply felt hatreds of the past and to assume the risks of collective solutions to solve their shared security problems. Most European leaders drew important lessons from the damage and destruction of World War I and II and from the economic depression and dislocation of the interwar period. That learning process, defined by the failure of national solutions to national security and welfare problems, was incorporated in the French-led initiative to create the European Coal and Steel Community (ECSC) in 1950.

If the Marshall Plan prompted the ECSC, European planners gave particular shape and impetus to this forerunner of the EC.[7] The contribution of the ECSC to the evolution of a consensual security community in Europe can hardly be exaggerated. The ECSC treaty precluded solely national development of the coal and steel resources of the member states. Under the treaty, responsibility for this objective was communalized; German control of these resources, a precondition for its rearmament, was accordingly collectivized. After the failure of the European Defense Community, the ECSC became a model for the Rome Treaty and the Common Market. In turn, the EC has been drawn forward toward union in the Single European Act (SEA) and the Maastricht Treaty. The SEA has essentially been implemented, and the realization of a truly common market of 340 million inhabitants is all but complete. It was precisely the scope and the density of the interdependent economic ties achieved by the SEA that was a precondition for the Maastricht Treaty; if eventually realized, Maastricht would move Europe toward monetary and political union and a common foreign and security policy. A big "if" if analysis is fixed on current constraints; a relaxed "if" if attention is refocused instead on the considerable distance traveled by the European peoples toward the Deutschian ideal. Instead there is also the danger that too great an emphasis on constraints will become a prescription not only for projecting Europe's future condition — a danger that is especially acute with respect to the incorporation of Eastern European peoples in democratizing Europe from the Atlantic to the Urals — but also for lowering expectations, unduly and too quickly, of the prospects for progress toward more mature security communities in other regions of the world.

Reducing the Israeli-Palestinian Rivalry

The long process of consolidating and institutionalizing consensual co-operation in coping with conflict in western Europe, spanning almost a half-century—some might say four centuries—has just begun in the Middle East. The agreements between Israel and the PLO to undertake direct talks to resolve their differences moves the conflict from rung 6 of the security ladder in figure 15.1, where the rivalry has been essentially stalled since Israel's independence in 1948, to rung 4 and potentially to rung 3. Again, for almost half a century Israelis and Palestinians have been unable to move much beyond the routin-ization—some might even contend ritualization—of their conflict. Until now third parties, notably the United States, have been frustrated in their efforts to help. Not surprisingly, these efforts have focused primarily on containing rather than on resolving the rivalry. Mutual recognition opens the way to go further. If Israel and the PLO can successfully extend self-rule to Gaza and Jericho and then to the West Bank, both will be on the way toward reaching the fourth rung on the conflict resolution ladder, to which France and Germany had already ascended by the end of the first decade after World War II.

Whereas the Cold War and the Soviet threat were preconditions for Franco-German reconciliation, the reverse was true for lasting peace in the Middle East. The end of the Cold War and the collapse of the Soviet Union deprived the PLO of Moscow's arms, aid, and diplomatic support and narrowed access to its surrogates in the Middle East, principally Syria and Iraq. Even before the disintegration of the Soviet Union, Moscow had already joined the Western powers against Iraq and the PLO, which had badly miscalculated in support-ing Saddam Hussein. The creation of the Russian Federation and its depen-dence on the West foreclosed any reasonable expectation that the PLO, in an isolated political and increasingly vulnerable security and economic position, could persist in its opposition to the Israeli state.

The PLO's monumental blunders during the Kuwait crisis severely weak-ened its bargaining position vis-à-vis Israel and undermined its regional stance. It lost the extensive financial and economic support of the conserva-tive oil states, principally Saudi Arabia. It became exposed to the full force of U.S. and Western pressures in the peace process revived by the Bush adminis-tration. Pressures for peace could no longer be mediated and muted through Riyadh to bolster PLO resistance to Western insistence that it recognize Israel and enter into direct negotiations. The pillars of the PLO strategic position — indirect Soviet military support, conservative Arab financial assistance, and their implicit diplomatic convergence in support of PLO claims — had collapsed almost overnight. And the PLO's remaining Arab allies, principally Iraq and Syria, were shaky and unreliable reeds to lean upon. Iraq was a defeated and discredited power. Syria was preoccupied with shoring up its own eroding influence in the Middle East in the wake of the Iraqi debacle; in this recovery effort, the PLO was more a burden than a boon.

The end of the Cold War also compelled a rethinking of Israeli strategy and intransigence toward the PLO. If the collapse of Soviet influence and the defeat of PLO allies enhanced Israel's power position, sustained exterior support, principally from the United States, could not be confidently assured over the long run. The United States was increasingly concerned with domestic issues — budget, crime, welfare demands, and foreign economic challenges. Even if U.S. support was not in immediate question, Washington's ability to make economic and military resources available to bolster Israel's security and bargaining position as well as the Israeli economy was clearly in doubt. The mounting cost of maintaining Israeli rule in the West Bank and Gaza reinforced these pessimistic appraisals of Israel's receding power base. The Intifada was a constant drain on Israeli resources and a persistent security preoccupation. The rising strength of radical Palestinian groups, like Hamas, and Iranian fundamentalist support for Israel's opponents within the Palestinian and Islamic communities created an implicit convergence of interests between the ruling Labor coalition in Israel and an isolated and weakened PLO. The latter was driven to a moderate position in the Arab camp, pushed from above by the collapse of the Soviet Union and the end of the Cold War and from below by the rise of Muslim fundamentalism.

These global and regional structural changes in power relations, which essentially transformed the Israeli-Palestinian calculus of conflict, were further reinforced by the self-help efforts of the parties, the crucial role that third parties played in fostering the peace process, and the incentives of shared economic growth and development for both rivals if peace could be achieved. Each of these dimensions of the coping process warrants brief comment to identify the actors, roles, resources, and divergent strategies that had to converge to move the conflict up the coping ladder, when most observers despaired of any such progress just a few years ago.

As Janice Stein makes abundantly clear, neither side in the conflict could move toward negotiations in the absence of a long process of "de-demonization" of the images held by the elites and populations on both sides.

This process did not begin with the end of Desert Storm. It can be traced at least to Sadat's visit to Jerusalem in 1977 and to the Camp David accords between Israel and Egypt a year later. U.S. mediation and willingness to bear the heavy cost of guaranteeing the accords were indispensable if both rivals were to assume the risks of fundamentally revising their previous security relationship. The bitter experience of a generation of flawed efforts to resolve the conflict by imposing a solution on one or the other of the parties to the rivalry perforce slowly and indiscernibly prepared, as William Zartman suggests in his notion of the "hurting stalemate," the psychological and political ground for the reversal in the mutually hostile perceptions, fueled by unrelieved hatreds, held by both sides.

There is evidence also that both sides, at least those in control of the negotiation process, perceived their mutual entrapment and the need to escape the damaging effects of continued stalemate. Prospects that one or the other side would prevail appeared to be receding, particularly because both were confronted, although for different reasons, with an erosion of their long-term bargaining positions. The intervention of a neutral party (Norway), the guarded secrecy of direct bilateral talks between the principals, the willingness of both negotiators to assume the risks of exposure and attack from their own supporters at home and abroad, and, finally, a recognition of their alignment of interests with respect to opponents in their own camps—together, these factors essentially met Zartman's conditions for successful bargaining to end an enduring conflict.

The incentive of greater economic development for the Israeli and Palestinian peoples should also not be underestimated as a major contributor to peace, once the prospects of imposing a preferred outcome on the opponent were perceived as unfeasible. Moving from a zero-sum to a positive-sum relationship was not easy; nor should this transition be considered inevitable or irreversible once achieved. The Israeli-PLO process of constructing a security community that moves toward the Deutschian ideal has come about only after a long and difficult period of mutual learning in the wake of a century—some might argue several millennia—of costly trial and error by force of arms. The peace process also opens the way for the expansion of Israeli markets in the region, where Israel's advanced economic and technological development bolsters its comparative advantage. Peace also provides Palestinians with access to Arab and Western economic assistance that has been withheld since Desert Storm, with the promise of more support in the future. The leadership of the United States in gaining assurances for financial support of the peace process from other states within the Western coalition, including Japan, reinforces

welfare considerations salient in all security relations. The persistent and in-escapable preoccupation of states and peoples with bettering their material conditions and promoting their economic growth and prosperity also intro-duces into the analysis an economic dimension, which has had a crucial effect in narrowing differences between rivals whose conflict inhibits their mutual and interdependent economic development.[9]

Second, the template is not confined to the great powers, however impor-tant they are. Smaller states also play important roles, for example, Norway's role in the Middle East settlement and the Benelux states' role in the insti-tutional development of the EC. It also introduces other international actors, whether intergovernmental agencies like the United Nations and the IMF or private associations working within a state or across state boundaries, into the coping process.

The role and resource dimensions of the template are not biased for or against military force. Depending on circumstances, the use of force by third parties to regulate a conflict or the provision of external security guarantees to rivals as an alternative to their Hobbesian security relationship may move the rivalry toward the Deutschian ideal. For example, the defeat of Nazi Germany and imperial Japan opened both to peaceful paths after World War II. Their forced democratization also reinforced their revolutionary departures from previous imperialist solutions to satisfy their status, security, and welfare aims. The integration of both states into a global market system also contributed de-cisively to this pacification process. The institutionalization of Germany's and Japan's economic development and those of the other liberal democracies in the IMF, the GATT, the World Bank, and international financial markets was indispensable for the coping process in the post–Cold War era. NATO, the EC, the WEU, and the CSCE, moreover, were particularly relevant for Germany's integration into a free and democratic Europe.

Strategies for coping operate at many levels. These are not always con-sciously or deliberately planned by actors to move a conflict toward less co-ercive solutions and rules of peaceful engagement. In defeating Iraq, the U.S.-led coalition sought foremost to reaffirm the legitimacy and inviolability of national boundaries and to protect the developed states' access to oil. Few foresaw that the Iraqi defeat and PLO humiliation would lead to regional and global conditions conducive to peace, just as few expected the division of Germany during the Cold War to foster Franco-German reconciliation. The analyst is able to explain these developments ex post facto; the policymaker needs to be sensitive to such uncertainty, while planning for more systematic coping efforts.

What seems clear from the historical record is that hostile images of an adversary can, and do, soften and disappear. This process is long-term. Learning to cooperate with a rival through noncoercive means cannot be achieved easily or quickly. The security, diplomatic, and economic contributions of third parties—states and international governmental and nongovernmental organizations—are indispensable. Few rivals are able to ascend the Deutschian ladder alone. The workings of impersonal markets also link peoples across national boundaries in progressively denser and enlarging sets of interdependent welfare interests whose protection and promotion hinge increasingly on a security community that moves away from the Hobbesian limiting case. Such a setting prepares the ground for the pooling of power and interest of former rivals in the progressive institutionalization of their security relations as they move from unilateral to collective solutions of their mutual security concerns.

▲ Surmounting Coping Constraints

The contributors to this volume discharge their duties well, perhaps all too well. If their thoughtful and informed counsel is taken at face value, there would appear to be few opportunities in the immediate aftermath of the Cold War to make much headway in coping with conflict in the world society beyond what Max Singer and Aaron Wildavsky characterize as the "zone of peace," which comprises essentially the victor powers of the Cold War.[10] For several contributors, obstacles loom larger than opportunities for anything other than marginal efforts to mediate regional strife. Third-party interventions to cope with intrastate conflicts appear particularly troublesome. Hard-won international norms of national self-determination and sovereignty resist legitimating external interventions in the domestic affairs of a state even by international bodies. States are reluctant to create precedents that can be applied to them at a later date. China's abstention from authorizing U.N. resolutions for Desert Storm was purportedly motivated by this concern in the wake of the Tiananmen disaster.

As Paul Diehl's chapter suggests, even simple peacekeeping functions, not to mention more challenging peacemaking and nation-building missions, are difficult. In the current international environment, the stiff requirements of collective security to automatically underwrite international bodies' intervention in internal conflicts cannot be met. Except in cases representing wholesale attacks on the fundamental principle of the nation-state system, as the Iraqi-Kuwaiti crisis did, the convergence of security and political interests of the major states is likely to be as rare as their accord on appropriate means to address threats to international security. The failure of the Western states, principally the United States, Britain, Germany, and France, to harmonize their coping efforts in Yugoslavia suggests that neither the conditions of collective security nor the implicitly more relaxed criteria of a concert of states—which share similar conceptions of threats to international security, if not a common interest and will in doing something about it[11]—can now be met even among the victorious powers of the Cold War.

Several authors, notably Morgan and Snyder, foresee that the world's most capable and best-endowed actors are likely to exhibit decreasing interest in coping duties. The liberal democracies of the Western states and Japan are pictured as less interested than at any time since the end of World War II to intervene to manage conflict outside their borders. Now that the clear and present danger of the Soviet threat has evaporated, the outcomes of many regional conflicts no longer have real or perceived adverse implications for the Western states. Majorities among the Western democracies, which spent trillions of dollars and sent millions of their citizens to war in sustaining the Cold War effort—wildly beyond the expectations of democratic theorists[12]—are again reverting to norms of nonintervention and indifference. The very success of liberal democratic regimes in promoting domestic consensus and peace among themselves conditions them and their populations to resist risking their blood and treasure to solve what appear to be intractable security problems of distant and alien peoples. Humanitarian impulses evoked by media images of personal despair and tragedy may mobilize popular sentiment to intervene for brief periods, as in Haiti, but to withdraw quickly once the crisis has passed. Economic embargoes might also be organized, for example, against South Africa, to arrest the violation of human rights or to pressure recalcitrant domestic elements to democratize. Yet sustained and costly armed efforts to move enduring and chronic conflicts toward progressively more mature security regimes seems to have little appeal in the post–Cold War environment.

These disincentives of the post–Cold War era extend to economic and technical assistance to developing peoples. Thus, not even the long-run positive effects of economic development and modernization can necessarily be counted upon. As the liberal democracies turn inward and focus on their own problems, there is waning concern for the plight of the less fortunate. Free and open markets are the solution proffered to pull the impoverished out of their economic quagmires,[13] but there is less aid available to assist development and to facilitate the progressive incorporation of these peoples into global markets. Where freer trade proposals are actually suggested as a way to development, they are increasingly viewed as threats to jobs in the developed world; witness the debate in the United States and Canada over the North American Free Trade Agreement. As the turbulent transition to free markets by the peoples of Eastern Europe and the former republics of the Soviet Union reveals, the ascendant powers of the post–Cold War era are hardly prepared to underwrite the costs of coping or share the risk of failure.

But if constraints and disincentives for coping are always present and press upon the consciousness of analysts and decision makers alike, change that vaults these limits is no less a hard fact. Clearly, there are forces abroad in our increasingly interdependent global society that create incentives for learning among rivals, which makes for more mature security communities.[14] How else can the end of the Cold War, the Franco-German accord, and Israeli-PLO recognition be satisfactorily explained? If these conflicts could be reduced, why not others? Surely that expectation has some plausibility if the time frame for gradual reconciliation is extended into the future on the strength of the experience of past successes?

The division of Europe and of Germany appeared to be foreclosed questions, yet Germany is now united. The Eastern European states, which seemed permanently imprisoned by Soviet power, are now striving to meet the conditions for entry into the EC and are also bandwagoning on the West-centric security system. The principal republics of the Commonwealth of Independent States (CIS) are no less bent in the same direction, despite their internal turmoil. Indeed, the backlash to this trend—most notably the August 1991 and September 1993 crises, during which Russia passed through moments of truth on the way toward market and democratic reforms—evidences the compelling attraction of the West-centric solution to the problems of order, welfare, and legitimacy besetting the world society. No less did the Israeli-PLO conflict seem frozen and fixed. Yet now the enmities previously dividing the Russian and American, French and German, and Israeli and Palestinian peoples could not resist forces pressing for their relaxation and reversal. Only in retrospect do the revolutionary changes that have fundamentally transformed security politics around the globe appear inevitable and "post-predictable," although, and lamentably, analysts and decision makers still share no common explanation for these dramatic outcomes.

Meanwhile, it is useful to take stock of the strides that have been made in coping with global and regional conflict since World War II and to underline the importance of the nation-state, markets, and democratization in this process. If nationalism, particularly in its most virulent and atavistic forms, remains a powerful and potentially destructive force in some regions, it has also provided political anchorage for many peoples and elicited tested personal loyalties on which the overall security order of the world society can be progressively built.[15] If the nation-state remains the principal unit of security analysis, it is nonetheless susceptible to perfection and discipline, as the Western experience and, arguably, a recent turn toward peaceful change in the Middle East suggest, to meet the competing security needs of the world's diverse and contesting populations.

The warfare tendencies of the nation-state can also be blunted or redirected. Witness the emergence of the West-centric coalition. While it is neither a collective security system nor a concert, its members have at least settled their differences peacefully and continue to work together without any thought of war as an acceptable or viable way to settle differences. Similar movement up the Deutschian security ladder is feasible, at least for some regions and some conflicts, through the gradual coordination of national security policies. The evolution of the Israeli and Palestinian peoples cannot be explained without giving the force of nationalism its due. Nor can Middle East peace be assured unless national sentiment is relied upon as the foundation stone on which to build a mature security regime, paralleling Europe's progress or the U.S.-Canadian and U.S.-Japanese relationships. The end of the Cold War, and with it the passing of the specter of nuclear war, can also be attributable in no small measure to the demands for self-determination of the peoples of the republics of the former Soviet Union, the Eastern European members of the Warsaw Pact, and the German people. Nationalism can be enlisted in the service of global and regional consensual learning and in the multiplication of mature security regimes.

If nationalism as well as ethnic and culture differences, ideological splits, and racial hatreds are still vital forces, it does not follow, as the evolution of more mature security regimes sketched above suggests, that they cannot be tempered and tamed. Specifically, nationalism need not always be expressed, as it so often was in the past, in militaristic and self-destructive ways. The security dilemma rooted in separate nation-states may not be fully and satisfactorily resolvable on theoretic grounds,[16] but this formidable barrier to confident consensual cooperation has not stopped states and peoples from creating impressive and workable mature security communities. Political learning curves concerning the costs of armed conflict and the psychological, material, and political debility of preciously guarded hatreds are not all flat or downward-sloping. Some leaders and some peoples that were once hostile under some circumstances, circumstances that this volume attempts to specify, have learned that these burdens are as intolerable as they are inconclusive. The mounting exchange costs of lethal rivalries can be estimated by several reinforcing measures, including loss of life and property, the foreclosure of a better future for a rising generation, and lost opportunities for economic development, technological progress, and modernization. Bitter feelings and hostile enemy images die slowly, but they can be gradually blurred and blunted. Institutions can pool rather than polarize the aims, interests, and values of the states and peoples they comprise. They can codify this learning process of mutual coping; and once it is set in motion, this process can become self-propelled with the result that the scope for consensual cooperation can widen as it deepens.

Creating Coping Incentives for the West-centric States

If the very ascendancy of the West-centric system of liberal, market-oriented democratic peoples and states as the dominant grouping of the world society is one of the major obstacles to progress in coping, how can incentives be generated that might induce the West-centric peoples to assume greater coping responsibilities? The disincentives should be squarely faced in building a case for coping. Why should the victorious Cold War states act as a policeman for the world now that their principal superpower opponent no longer exists? Why should they contain or constrain recalcitrant and often well-armed opponents from seeking to advance peacekeeping, peacemaking, and even nation building where external intrusion is resented in favor of traditional coercively based security regimes and where ethnic and communal strife is enduring? Since Western military power is unrivaled and no grouping of non-West-centric states can challenge the primacy of the West-centric states, why should the latter and their distracted peoples bother with coping duties?

The outcomes of local rivalries like those in Yugoslavia or Rwanda no longer have either real or perceived negative implications for the security of the West-centric system. Nor do the members of this coalition see their vital interests immediately at risk in these controversies. Even if Iraq's attempted absorption of Kuwait—the most significant challenge to the West-centric system in the post–Cold War era—had proved successful, it would be difficult to argue that, at least in the short run, Western security and welfare interests had been dealt a fatal blow. Thus, insulation and disengagement would appear to be the appropriate watchwords for Western capitals. Certainly this is a new condition for these states.

If the Western states and peoples can learn to resolve their national differences and create security regimes resistant to internal and external challenge, then others involved in conflict are not necessarily locked into interminable strife except by their own choosing. These mature security regimes, however anarchical their internal structure, rest solidly enough today on the learned principle that unilateral solutions to national security problems are essentially ruled out under conditions of massively destructive weapons and growing economic interdependence among democratic peoples. Similarly, if states and their peoples can be led to accept the view that there are no lasting unilateral solutions for national welfare, then this learning process and the cooperative institutions that this conceptual revolution begets—such as the GATT, the IMF, and the EC—can relax the security dilemma confronting all states. Cooperative learning, transparency, and shared institutions work over time to make states more permeable and to dispose them to consensual ways to meet their security and welfare needs.[17] Finally, the cooperative effects of this learning and institutional process have the potential to be harmonized through the convergence of domestic governments based on democratic majorities to legitimate their authority and to ensure the rule of law, the protection of civil liberties, and respect for minority and human rights.[18]

These long-term trends frame the post–Cold War coping process. Although they do not guarantee the extension and internal strengthening of the coping process—erosion is always a possibility—they do afford the West-centric segment within the emerging global society incentive to resist the temptations of isolation and withdrawal. Experience suggests that coping with conflict is not inevitably fraught with failure and that the costs of timely intervention are not higher than those of indifference or inaction, when a crisis, like that in Rwanda, gets out of hand. For the first time since the formation of the nation-state system, as early as the fifteenth century, large bodies of nationally disparate peoples live within a self-made security community that approximates the Deutschian ideal.

Several additional considerations also encourage the post–Cold War ascendant coalition to adopt an outward, proactive strategy based on self-interest. First, the West-centric states and peoples cannot ensure their long-term security, prosperity, or open societies unless key powers currently outside this grouping, most notably a reforming Russia and Communist China, are fully integrated and made satisfied members of the post–Cold War system.

The problem confronting Russia and the Western states is similar to that of France after the Napoleonic wars, Germany after World War I, and Germany and Japan after World War II. Russia's successful incorporation into a post–Cold War, West-centric concert requires, as Paul Schroeder suggests, that the post–Cold War balance of power satisfy elite and popular concerns in Russia, particularly those bearing on external security and economic reconversion within a global market system.[19] The first order of business is the preservation of the Russian state and the strengthening of its capacity for economic reform and democratization. As Jack Snyder argues, the West has been slow and tentative in addressing these imperatives either by providing sufficient economic assistance to underwrite the transition to a market economy and democratization or by defining Russia's security role in its region of Europe and how Russia might contribute to multilateral peacekeeping missions. None of these tasks will be easy, but neglecting them or only halfheartedly confronting them essentially creates a vacuum in which forces working for a return to Russia's communist past or to an even older nationalistic and xenophobic tradition in Russian history would be bolstered. Unchecked, these forces would create disruptive forces capable of incalculable harm not only to the interests of the Russian people (why return to failed solutions for OWL problems?) but also to those of the West-centric peoples.

No less important is China's eventual inclusion in the West-centric coalition. This aim is not as far-fetched as it may appear, despite obvious differences in history, culture, and political experience between the West and China. The process of a working, cooperative relationship acceptable to the peoples of the West and China has been in train for over a century and a half. What began as a coercive relation—the Opium War—can be transformed, if Western relations with Japan are any guide, into increasingly cooperative relations across security, economic, and even cultural domains. There is no reason to believe that progressively greater East-West compatibility is impossible. Chinese Communist leaders, with little prompting or prodding from the West, took a major and irreversible step toward the Western world by launching what have now proven to be the remarkably successful market reforms of the Chinese economy as early as 1978, shortly after the death of Mao Tse-tung. While it would be naive to minimize the obstacles barring a satisfactory resolution of Western and Chinese differences, impressive progress has been made. Irredentist territorial claims are being met. Hong Kong will revert to Chinese rule in 1997. Settling the Taiwan question will obviously take longer, but fears of war to forcefully integrate Taiwan with the mainland, prevalent during the Cold War, are now muted and distant. Open talks between Taiwan and Beijing to address their common problems strengthens optimism that China, like Germany, will also one day be peacefully united.

There is also room for cautious optimism that an increasingly greater Western-Chinese accord can be encouraged if market forces, in league with continued and progressively denser contact with the West, are permitted to work fully. In turning to markets to spur Chinese economic and technological development and to open China to the world, China's leaders have relinquished, or at least relaxed, their hold on China's future economic and internal development. In abandoning the high exchange costs of a planned economy, they have been forced to bow increasingly before regional demands for increasing economic freedom from Beijing's control. This process of economic liberalization infects politics too. The Tiananmen Square massacre is witness to this liberalization process, which was temporarily arrested but hardly squashed permanently, as China's economic and social modernization proceeds forward. Authoritarian government may well persist for sometime in China; more problematic is the prospect that its continuance is without substantial cost to long-term economic growth, which depends on a free, open Chinese civil society, increasingly independent of state control. The anticipated convergence of the Taiwanese and Chinese markets and their integration in a larger global system also set the stage for their parallel political liberalization and harmonization. These trends are not easily sustainable unless China and the West pursue an open-door policy and refuse to isolate the presently embattled Chinese leadership and the Chinese people.

The proliferation of both nuclear and conventional weapons of mass destruction and the diffusion of long-range delivery systems around the globe also urge arms control and disarmament regimes responsive to the needs of the West-centric states. The Iraqi experience, as Edward Laurance persuasively argues, pointedly illustrates the threat of rogue states' or terrorist groups' coming into possession of nuclear weapons. Such fears can no longer be dismissed as imagined if credence is given to reports of Russian fissionable materials illegally reaching foreign markets. The post–Cold War era is not without the threat of nuclear or conventional war. New nuclear players are not susceptible to the same deterrent threats that kept the superpower struggle in stable balance. Several states are either undeclared nuclear powers — India, Pakistan, and Israel — or, like Iran, moving toward nuclear status. Others, like China, France, the United Kingdom, and the United States, continue to modernize their forces.

The Strategic Arms Reduction Treaty cannot be implemented unless three of the four nuclear states of the CIS — Ukraine, Belarus, and Kazakhstan — can complete the transfer of their nuclear weapons to Russia as the inheritor of the Soviet Union's international obligations under the accord. Nor can the deep cuts agreed to by Presidents Bush and Yeltsin in 1992, which would reduce the nuclear arsenals of the United States and Moscow to thirty-five hundred weapons on each side, be implemented in the absence of the denuclearization of these three states. All of these nuclear contingencies imply political and strategic understanding among the nuclear and would-be nuclear powers that advise an active Western antiproliferation policy. The assistance offered to Russia and the nuclear CIS states to better control and reduce their nuclear arsenals is evidence of pressures, however much states concerned with arms proliferation may resist them, to penetrate the decision-making processes of weapons-producing and -purchasing states.

In the long run, the economic well-being of the West-centric peoples depends both on the political stability of the developing states, principally the major powers, and on their future economic and technological advancement. The first is a precondition of the second, since economic growth must rely on stable political conditions to ensure continuing and expanding economic interchange and encourage long-term investment. While the bulk of trade and economic exchange today occurs principally between the peoples of the developed states, the expansion of economic activity to the Southern Hemisphere promises the fastest growth potential for these economies and is critical for the support for their economic health. While it would be too much to argue that the developed states have an equal interest in economic growth for all peoples throughout the globe, opportunities for market expansion are attractive, especially in those regions of the globe where political stability has been achieved. Part of the explanation for U.S. reluctance to impose sanctions on China and to withdraw most-favored-nation status arises from the damaging effects such moves would have on jobs and economic growth in the United States. In any event, access to raw materials, especially oil, argues against indifference to the political instability of those regions, like the Middle East and the Persian Gulf, where West-centric interests are deeply engaged.

As a negative incentive for an outward strategy, slow or slipping economic growth in the developing world or wholesale dislocation will inevitably have damaging effects on the developed world's economic prosperity and social cohesion. As Paul Kennedy argues, the developing states are poorly positioned to address the needs of their rapidly expanding populations.[20] These needs may well double in the next century. Whereas the countries of the Northern Hemisphere were able to rely on the industrial revolution and technological advancements to escape this Malthusian dilemma, the peoples of the developing world lack the resources and access to modern technology to solve this problem without outside assistance.

One obvious implication of this dilemma is the relentless effort of disadvantaged peoples to escape their misery through emigration to the wealthy North. Economic and social stagnation and retrogression in the developing world spur emigration to developed regions and incite internal ethnic, national, and communal strife in the affected states. The Western states, with perhaps the exception of Japan, have lost control over their immigration policies, as France and Germany have discovered in their relations with the Mediterranean peoples of the southern littoral and as the United States has discovered in its failed efforts to stem the flow of immigrants from the Caribbean and Central America.

There is also the growing problem of global environmental and ecological security. Forests, grazing fields, and croplands available for sustainable growth are rapidly shrinking. Unbridled exploitation of these resources further diminishes the earth's life-support system. Heavy industrialization pollutes the world's ground and water resources. The former states of the Soviet Union and its Eastern European allies created monumental ecological damage in their determined drive to industrialize. The developing states risk making the same debilitating mistakes, the repercussions of which are likely to be no less global. Fish and wildlife stocks are being rapidly depleted around the globe. Overfishing and pollution have contributed to an alarming decline in the seafood available to the world's population. The mounting demand for energy around the world, coupled with the destruction of the earth's capacity to offset harmful carbon emissions (e.g., the destruction of rain forests), threatens global warming and the greenhouse effect, with potentially damaging effects on world agriculture and habitat. These are only some of the more important environmental problems collectively confronting the world's populations. There is, accordingly, no technical solution to their abatement or resolution short of a political accord of the principal states contributing to these problems to share the costs and burdens of solving them.

The relationship between growing global environmental problems and armed conflicts is dual-edged. On the one hand, many conflicts, particularly those that encompass large numbers of peoples and multiple states, set limits to international accords on environmental issues. Negotiations aimed at achieving cooperative agreements to arrest environmental damage are hardly encouraged where states and peoples are otherwise in armed dispute. These conflicts, if widespread, deadly, and damaging, also result in large-scale ecological harm. Illustrative is the scorched-earth policy of the Iraqi army in setting fire to Kuwaiti oil fields in the wake of its retreat. On the other hand, as industrialization and consumer demand rise in the developing world, cooperative accords to protect the global environment will become increasingly difficult to achieve. Burden sharing, already complex, will become increasingly thornier and resistant to solution. Currently, for example, the United States, with only 5 percent of the world's population, produces almost 20 percent of

the world's greenhouse gases (carbon dioxide, methane, chlorinated fluorocar-
bons), an imbalance resented by many and a source of international conflict
and mistrust. As environmental and ecological problems become more urgent
and threaten economic development and world public health, they will inevitably generate new sources of tension, marked by threats, embargoes, and
even external intervention, as states and groups take matters into their own
hands to protect their local environments.

Large, influential, and vocal elements within the West-centric states continue to sustain pressures for democratization along the Western model and to
induce their governments to actively pursue these aims as moral duties and as
political imperatives. Spurred too are calls for humanitarian interventions by
the world community where natural (Bangladesh floods) or human-created
disasters (Somalia and Rwanda) produce large-scale suffering. Because of the
instantaneity of world communications and television broadcasting, virtually
no repressive state escapes external review and virtually no people's plight goes
unnoticed, nor their pleas unheeded. Simply to preclude interventions abroad
or to refuse assistance when there is an opportunity to advance economic or
democratization goals — and, by implication, the management and resolution
of security problems — will raise debate among the Western democracies over
what to do about these crises. If past is prologue, some kind of piecemeal
efforts to cope with conflict will be mounted when these crises are seen as
impediments to economic development and humanitarian assistance, continuance of repressive regimes, or threats to global and regional security. Instead
of piecemeal, why not planned efforts that offer some promise of success and
sustainability?

Finally, there is the possibility of the infection and spread of local conflicts
that could adversely affect the cohesion of the West-centric coalition. If the
Western states are able to resist intervention in the Yugoslav civil war and
to work together fitfully to contain the crisis, important security issues loom
elsewhere as sources of division. Western inaction essentially tolerated ethnic
and tribal cleansing in Bosnia and Rwanda. Toleration invites other groups to
resolve their grievances by toughening their bargaining postures and giving
vent to their hatreds by force and violence. Failing to contain such potentially
infectious conflict promises to be costly and risky. If Russian peacekeeping
efforts in Azerbaijan and Armenia may be applauded, intervention on behalf
of the Russian minorities in the Baltic states or elsewhere in the republics of
the former Soviet Union would raise apprehensions and would pose serious
problems for the preservation of a zone of peace among the major powers,
not to mention the fatal blow that such unilateral Russian initiatives would

have on Russian's eventual incorporation into a post–Cold War concert. These misgivings are also deepened by the bloody, coercive force used by Moscow to suppress nationalist movements like that in Chechnya. There is also the rise of communal strife, evidenced in Muslim fundamentalist demands from North Africa to the northern tier in Afghanistan, which are not easily squared with the power, privileges, and interests of the West-centric states. Small and weak states, like Afghanistan, Panama, Haiti, and Somalia, are also subject to take-overs by local thugs, warlords, or drug dealers, who oppress their populations and traffic in illicit dealings while enjoying the immunities of sovereign states.

The dilemma facing the Western states is that immunization from these various forms of infection is not possible and thus nursing these conflict zones to health will not be easy or assured. If solutions for these many problems are not clear, the argument of this volume is that they must be addressed, since there is no foolproof scheme available to escape them as some suggest.[21] Rightly understood, the self-interest of the West-centric states and peoples advises them to cope with conflict beyond their immediate borders if for no other reason than that their long-term security, material welfare, and open, democratic ways of life depend on the progressive development of a global security community in pursuit of the elusive Deutschian ideal and the dif-fusion of shared values and wealth on which such a community necessarily rests. The West-centric states and their allies in the world society ignore these coping challenges at their own peril. That current populations may be able to limit damage to their interests in pursuing a withdrawal strategy cannot be gainsaid; but that is not the point of this volume. Over the long haul the peoples of the world will hang together, not separately. The question facing the Western peoples is essentially the same as the one posed by Alexander Hamil-ton at the opening of the Federalist papers. In arguing for the creation of a stronger federal government and for the development of a larger American community, Hamilton asked "whether societies of men are capable or not of establishing good government from reflection and choice, or whether they are forever destined to depend on political constitutions, on accident, or force."[22] This question is now a global one owing to the emergence of a world society whose future depends on the resources and will of the West-centric peoples.

The massive destructiveness of modern warfare, both nuclear and conven-tional; the globalization of solutions for national and local welfare demands; the unquenchable thirst for ever greater technological development and eco-nomic growth; the transparency, permeability, and interdependence of states and societies as a consequence of their confrontation of these security and wel-fare imperatives, expressed daily by increasingly dense and ever-multiplying information, communications, and transportation networks — all these forces have created a world society of peoples and states for the first time in history. International conflicts between states or peoples, within or sprawling across borders, are threats to the preservation and peaceful evolution of a global society of 5 billion diverse and contentious peoples, with more on the way. The surface signs of societal turbulence and turmoil, often erupting in violence and sustained armed conflict, obscure the deeper and ever-widening mutual interdependencies that define the political conditions of state, group, or regional decisions and behavior. These interdependencies occasion choices to pursue cooperation by force or by other means, or by some combination of these instruments.

If armed conflicts are treated as separate and isolated events, analysts and decision makers risk minimizing the threat that these conflicts pose to the peace and prosperity of the world society. It is precisely this world society that has now emerged and that is at risk. Its arrest or devolution threatens, ironically, the realization of local and national preferences about how the world should be ordered, how its wealth should be distributed, and on which moral and political principles of governance such crucial issues should rest for authoritative decision. For the many reasons advanced in this volume, a world society does not imply one world. History and local circumstance, the nation-state and markets, and the varying cultural experiences, values, and visions of the world's populations preclude realization of a unified and integrated utopian state. What does seem feasible is continued coping with conflict that yields steady movement along a broad, if irregular, front toward the Deutschian Ideal. Conflict between peoples and states will surely continue, but resort to violence or threats can become increasingly less useful and persuasive in deciding matters of mutual interest, even where differences of values and aims persist. Coping can count.

NOTES

1. For a review of different schools of thought and the essentially inconclusive state of the debate, see Jack S. Levy, "The Causes of War: A Review of Theories and Evidence," in *Behavior, Society, and Nuclear War,* ed. Philip E. Tetlock et al., vol. 1 (New York: Oxford University Press, 1989), 210–333. Barry Buzan relies on a theory of strong states as an essential condition for international security, but this approach begs the question how they are to reconcile their differences, a problem magnified by the fact that big-power struggles have accounted for most wars since the rise of the nation-state. See Buzan's *People, States, and Fear,* 2d ed. (Boulder, Colo.: Lynn Reinner, 1991); and Barry Buzan, Charles Jones, and Richard Little, *The Logic of Anarchy* (New York: Columbia University Press, 1993).

2. For a review of this debate, consult John Lewis Gaddis, "International Relations Theory and the End of the Cold War," *International Security* 17 (winter 1992–93): 5–58; Stephen Walt, "The Renaissance of Security Studies," *International Studies Quarterly* 35 (1991): 211–39; Edward A. Kolodziej, "Renaissance in Security Studies? Caveat Lector!" ibid. 36, no. 1 (1992): 421–38; Charles W. Kegley, Jr., "How Did the Cold War Die? Principles for an Autopsy," *Mershon International Studies Review* 38 (Apr. 1994); and Richard Shultz, Roy Godson, and Ted Greenwood, eds., *Security Studies for the 1990s* (Washington, D.C.: Brassey's, 1993).

3. The contributors to this volume are hardly agreed on this enlarged conception of security and security studies. See, for example, the exchange between Patrick Morgan and Edward Kolodziej in a symposium on this subject in two issues of *Arms Control:* Edward A. Kolodziej, "What Is Security and Security Studies? Lessons from the Cold War," and Morgan's rejoinder, "Safeguarding Security Studies," *Arms Control* 13 (Apr. and Dec. 1992): 1–31 and 462–79.

4. This point is explored in Kolodziej, "The Renaissance of Security Studies"; and idem, "What Is Security and Security Studies?"

5. Until World War II, the French and German security relationship was dominated by a conception of power consistent with realist thinking of *Macht* politics, in which power was conceived in binary terms. The relationship was built essentially on Robert Dahl's classic conception of power as "How can A get B to do x?" (Robert A. Dahl, "The Concept of Power," *Behavioral Science* 2 [July 1957]: 201–15). France and Germany still differ over many important issues, ranging from Desert Storm and the Gulf War to European Community policies toward Yugoslavia. The decisive change is that common security, economic, and political institutions have been created and increasingly denser relations of intergovernmental and people-to-people contacts have developed that radically diminish resort to direct assertions of power in favor of defining common rules for economic competition and for developing integral policies and institutions to coordinate shared aims, including security policy. This latter conception of power is fundamentally social and structural and depends on the will of the parties to sustain it through the pooling of their power. Within these shared structures of power, incentives for cooperation are posed differently than within the isolated, particularistic framework suggested by realist thinking or, more formally, by Dahl's conception of power. For an elaboration of this alternate view, see Kenneth Boulding, *Faces of Power* (Berkeley: Sage, 1989). David Baldwin also suggests, as do several chapters in this volume, that positive "sanctions" or rewards can be viewed as forms of power to induce otherwise divergent individuals and groups to coordinate their preferences and to cooperate on joint projects or in making common institutions work for their mutual benefit (see David A. Baldwin, "Power Analysis and World Politics: New Friends versus Old Tendencies," *World Politics* 33 [Jan. 1979]: 161–94).

6. Anton DePorte, *Europe between the Superpowers,* 2d ed. (New Haven: Yale University Press, 1986).

7. Irwin M. Wall, *The United States and the Making of Postwar France, 1945–1954* (New York: Cambridge University Press, 1991).

8. See Levy, "The Causes of War"; and Jack S. Levy, "The Polarity of the System and International Stability: An Empirical Analysis," in *Polarity and War: The Changing Structure of International Conflict,* ed. Alan Ned Sabrosky (Boulder, Colo.: Westview Press, 1985), 41–66.

9. E. L. Jones, *Growth Recurring* (Oxford: Oxford University Press, 1988).

10. Max Singer and Aaron Wildavsky, *The Real World Order* (Chatham, N.J.: Chatham House, 1993).

11. Charles Kupchan and Clifford Kupchan, "Concerts, Collective Security, and the Future of Europe," *International Security* 16, no. 1 (1991): 114–61.

12. See Alex de Tocqueville, *Democracy in America*, ed. Phillips Bradley (New York: Vintage, 1956), vol. 2, bk. 3, chaps. 21–26, 265–303; and Walter Lippmann, *The Cold War* (New York: Harper, 1947).

13. On the renewed interest in markets to motor economic development in the developing states, see the special report in the *Economist*, Sept. 25, 1993.

14. James N. Rosenau, *Turbulence in World Politics* (Princeton: Princeton University Press, 1990), reviews these forces.

15. Buzan, *People, States, and Fear*, esp. chaps. 2–5, pp. 57–185.

16. See Kenneth Waltz, *Theory of International Politics* (Reading, Mass.: Addison-Wesley, 1979); and for a critique, consult Robert O. Keohane, ed., *Neorealism and Its Critics* (New York: Columbia University Press, 1986).

17. Mark Zacher, "The Decaying Pillars of the Westphalian Temple: Implications for International Order and Governance," in *Governance without Government: Order and Change in World Politics*, ed. James N. Rosenau and Ernst-Otto Czempiel (Cambridge, Mass.: Cambridge University Press, 1992), 58–111.

18. For evidence that democracies do not fight, see Bruce Russett, *Grasping the Democratic Peace: Principles for a Post–Cold War World* (Princeton: Princeton University Press, 1993).

19. Paul Schroeder, "The Nineteenth Century System: Balance of Power or Political Equilibrium," *Review of International Studies* 15 (1989): 136–53; idem, "Did the Vienna Settlement Rest on a Balance of Power?" *American Historical Review* 97 (June 1992): 683–705.

20. Paul Kennedy, *Preparing for the Twenty-First Century* (New York: Random House, 1993), esp. 3–136.

21. Singer and Wildavsky, *The Real World Order*.

22. *The Federalist*, no. 1 (New York: Modern Library Edition, n.d.), 3.

Contributors

ARTHUR J. ALEXANDER is president of the Japan Economic Institute of America (JEI) in Washington, D.C., where his specialty is Japan's economic and security relations, including the defense industry and technology. Prior to joining JEI in 1990, he was a staff member of the RAND Corporation in Santa Monica, California, where he first focused on Soviet affairs before turning his attention to Japan. His RAND studies include *Perestroika and Change in Soviet Weapons Acquisition* and *Of Tanks and Toyotas: An Assessment of Japan's Defense Industry.* His current research includes an examination of Japan's global role, especially as influenced by civilian technology with defense potential.

MOHAMMED AYOOB is professor of international relations at James Madison College, Michigan State University. During 1993–94 he was a Ford Foundation fellow in international security at the Watson Institute, Brown University. He is the author, coauthor, or editor of eleven books and approximately sixty published research papers. He has published in leading journals, including *World Politics, International Studies Quarterly, International Affairs,* and *Foreign Policy.* His latest book is *The Third World Security Predicament: State Making, Regional Conflict, and the International System.*

NICOLE BALL is director of the Program on Enhancing Security and Development at the Overseas Development Council in Washington, D.C., which examines the ways the international development community can support conflict resolution and postconflict reconstruction and reconciliation. She has been a consultant for the International Labour Office, the Swedish Ministry for Foreign Affairs, the World Bank, the International Development Center of

Japan, and the Global Coalition for Africa on demobilization, military expenditure reduction, and defense-industry conversion. Her publications include *Security and Economy in the Third World* and *Pressing for Peace: Can Aid Induce Reform?*

PAUL F. DIEHL is professor of political science at the University of Illinois at Urbana-Champaign. He is the author of *International Peacekeeping*, coauthor of *Territorial Changes and International Conflict*, and editor of *Reconstructing Realpolitik, Measuring the Correlates of War, The Politics of International Organizations*, and *Through the Straits of Armageddon*, as well as the author of more than forty articles on peace and security affairs.

ROGER E. KANET is professor of political science and a member of the Program in Arms Control, Disarmament, and International Security, as well as director of international programs and studies and associate vice chancellor for academic affairs, at the University of Illinois at Urbana-Champaign. He is the editor of *The Soviet Union, Eastern Europe, and the Developing States;* and coeditor, with E. A. Kolodziej, of *The Limits of Soviet Power in the Developing World: Thermidor in the Revolutionary Struggle* and *The Cold War as Cooperation: Superpower Cooperation in Regional Conflict Management*, and, with D. N. Miner and T. J. Resler, of *Soviet Foreign Policy in Transition*. His current research focuses on emerging relations among Russia, the other Soviet successor states, and the countries of Central Europe.

SAMUEL S. KIM, formerly a professor at Princeton University (1986–93), is senior research scholar at the East Asian Institute of Columbia University. He has written widely on Chinese foreign policy, East Asian international relations, and world order. He is the author or editor of more than a dozen books, including *China, the United Nations, and World Order* (1979), *The Quest for a Just World Order* (1984), and *China and the World: Chinese Foreign Relations in the Post–Cold War Era* (1994).

EDWARD A. KOLODZIEJ is research professor of political science and a fellow at the Center for Advanced Study at the University of Illinois, Urbana-Champaign. He is the author of *Making and Marketing Arms: The French Experience and Its Implications for the International System* and, most recently, coeditor, with Roger E. Kanet, of *The Cold War as Cooperation*. Author of more than one hundred articles on foreign and security policy, he is currently working on a book about global security after the Cold War.

EDWARD J. LAURANCE is professor of international policy studies at the Monterey Institute of International Studies (MIIS), where he teaches courses on international organizations, military proliferation, and public policy analysis and is also the associate director of the Program for Nonproliferation Studies. He is the author of *The International Arms Trade* (1992), coauthor of *Arms Watch: SIPRI Report on the First Year of the UN Register of Conventional Arms* (1993), and coeditor of *Developing the UN Register of Conventional Arms*. He is a member of the International Advisory Committee of the Arms Project of Human Rights Watch, a consultant to the *Human Development Report,* and a consultant to the United Nations Centre for Disarmament Affairs and the U.N. Register of Conventional Arms.

DAVID F. LINOWES is professor of political economy and public policy; Boeschenstein Professor Emeritus; and senior adviser to the Institute of Government and Public Affairs at the University of Illinois at Urbana-Champaign. He has served as chairman of the U.S. Privacy Protection Commission, the President's Commission on the Nation's Energy Resources, the U.S. Commission on Fair Market Value of Coal Leasing, and the President's Commission on Privatization. His books include *Managing Growth through Acquisition, Strategies for Survival, The Corporate Conscience,* and *Privacy in America.*

PATRICK M. MORGAN is the Thomas and Elizabeth Tierney Professor of Peace and Conflict Studies in the Department of Politics and Society at the University of California—Irvine. His special interests are national and international security and theories of international politics. Among his publications are *Deterrence: A Conceptual Analysis*; *Security and Arms Control,* coedited with Edward A. Kolodziej; *Strategic Military Surprise,* with Klaus Knorr; and *Theories and Approaches to International Politics.*

JACK SNYDER is professor of political science at the Institute of War and Peace Studies, Columbia University. He is the author of *The Ideology of the Offensive* and *Myths of Empire.*

JANICE GROSS STEIN is the Harrowston Professor of Conflict Management and Negotiations at the University of Toronto and a fellow of the Royal Society of Canada. She is the coauthor of *Rational Decision-Making: Israel's Security Choices* and *Psychology and Deterrence* and has just completed *We All Lost the Cold War.* She is the coeditor of *Getting to the Table: Processes of International Prenegotiation* and *Choosing to Cooperate: How States Avoid Loss.*

I. WILLIAM ZARTMAN is the Jacob Blaustein Professor of International Organization and Conflict Resolution and director of the International Relations Program at the Johns Hopkins University School of Advanced International Studies in Washington, D.C. He is the author of a number of books on conflict management and negotiation, including *The Practical Negotiator,* and the editor of, and contributing author to, *The Negotiation Process, The 50% Solution, Positive Sum: Improving North-South Negotiations,* and *International Multilateral Negotiations.* He has also written extensively on African politics and relations, his latest works being *Ripe for Resolution: Conflict and Intervention in Africa* and *The Politics of Trade Negotiations between Africa and the European Economic Community.*

Index

Abboud, Ibrahim, 280
Abduh, 236
Abkhazia, 67, 71, 78
Adenauer, Konrad, 203
Afghani, Jamal-al-Din al-, 236
Afghanistan, 4, 7, 52, 64, 75, 148-49, 155, 162, 228, 231, 257-58, 265, 346, 390
Aflaq, Michel, 235
Africa, 4, 9-12, 340
African Development Bank, 176
African Leadership Forum, 192
aid ministries, national, 171-73
Akashi, Yasushi, 105
Albania, 122
Algeria, 5, 10-12, 237, 280, 287-88
Aliyev, Heydar, 72
All-African Council of Churches, 9
Ambartsumov, Evgenii, 84 n.38, 85 n.58
Ambros, Dieter H., 310
Anderson, Robert E., 312
Angola, 4, 7-8, 12, 52, 75-76, 155, 164, 190, 277, 281, 285-86, 334
Arab-Israeli conflict, 5, 152, 154, 273-74, 276, 373-76
Arab Maghrib Union (UMA), 288
Arab nationalism (pan-Arabism), 232-35, 239
Argentina, 11-12, 180, 311, 316, 322, 336, 340
Aristide, Jean-Bertrand, 178
armed conflict: assumptions about, 21; over boundaries, 9-11, 156-57, 287, 341-42, 353; in the developing world, 5; diagnosis of, 21-25, 35; and enemy imagery, 247-70;

foreign intervention in, 15-16; historical permanence of, 23-25; levels of, 353; management of, 35-37, 188, 231-32, 287-88; mediation of, 7, 161-64, 186-93, 271-90; prescriptions for, 21-30; ripeness of, 276-79; saliency of, 23-24; solutions for, 13-21; and standardized cooperation, 25-28, 188; over structural rivalries, 11-13; threat of, 3-7; tractability of, 23-24, 26, 337; types of, 7, 363; understanding relevant parties to, 28-30, 170-78, 226-44
Armenia, 4, 11, 24, 68-70, 162, 389
arms control and disarmament (ACD), 130-31, 130-60, 184, 331-60, 386-87
arms production and transfers, conventional, 14-15, 53, 76
Art, Robert, 51
Asia, 4; democratization of, 20; economic growth in, 88; regional power balancing in, 43-44
Asian Development Bank, 176
Assad, Hafez el-, 233-35
Association of Southeast Asian Nations (ASEAN), 29, 58 n.21, 128, 139, 177, 342, 357
Atlantic Alliance, 199, 208-9, 214-15, 220, 369
Australia, 353
Austria, 213
Azerbaijan, 4, 11, 24, 68-70, 72, 162, 389

Baker, James, 131
balance, of regional powers, 42-44, 191, 291-308, 341, 353-54
Balkan conflicts, 4, 26, 47, 336

Balladur, Edouard, 318
Baltic states, 63, 68, 80, 389
Banda, Kamazu, 280
Bangladesh, 39, 230, 389
bargaining (third-party mediation), 271–90
Belarus, 72, 79, 111, 179, 355, 386
Beregovoy, Pierre, 319
Betts, Richard, 332
Biafra, 39, 230
Biden, Joseph, 57 n.18
Biological Weapons Convention, 176
Bitar, Salah-al-Din, 235
Boigny, Felix Houphouet, 281
Borodai, Iurii, 78
Bosnia (and Bosnia-Herzegovina), 42, 54,
    73–75, 148, 152–53, 175, 217–18, 242, 305,
    342, 389
boundary disputes, 9–11, 156–57, 287, 341–42,
    353
Boutros-Ghali, Boutros, 134, 150, 162, 165
Brazil, 336, 340
Brezhnev, Leonid, 257
Brunei, 127
Buchanan, Patrick, 57 n.14
Bull, Hedley, 17, 22
Bundesbank, 211–12
Burma, 99, 105
Burundi, 8, 24
Bush, George, 39, 44–45, 52, 116, 133–34,
    166 n.6, 373, 386
Buzan, Barry, 13

Cambodia, 4, 7, 13, 26, 29, 64, 75–76, 105–6,
    128, 133, 147–48, 155, 158, 164, 182–83, 285
Camdessus, Michel, 179–80
Cameroon, 10
Camp David accords, 281–82, 375
Canada, 23, 39
Carr, John, 315
Carter, Jimmy, 282–83
Central America. *See* Latin America
Central Asian Republics, 29, 66–67, 69, 72,
    80
Chad, 7, 11–12, 29
Chayes, Antonia and Abram, 338–39, 350–52,
    357
chemical weapons, 343–44
Chemical Weapons Convention (CWC),
    333–35
Chile, 11–12, 38, 315, 321–22

China, People's Republic of: alternating
    national roles in, 118–21; arms transfers to
    and from, 53, 76, 115, 131–32; comprehen-
    sive national strength of, 114; conception
    of world order in, 116–17, 136; dialectic of
    conflict and cooperation in, 122–30; eco-
    nomic growth of, 136–37; future of, 135–39;
    human rights in, 42; maxi-mini strategy
    of, 130–35; military strength of, 138; as
    nuclear power, 119, 130–31; opposition to
    Japanese military intervention in, 98, 114;
    as party to collective great-power man-
    agement, 45, 111–12; political legitimacy in,
    87; post-Cold War position of, 112–17; pri-
    vatization in, 326; regional security policy
    of, 115; rival Communist party factions in,
    24–25; support for U.N. in Cambodia, 29;
    in West-centric coalition, 385–86
Chirac, Jacques, 318
Civic Union, 78–79
Clausewitz, Carl von, 26
Clinton, Bill, 42, 45, 48, 166 n.6
collective security, 44–51, 149–54, 193, 350–52
Colombia, 7, 9, 285
Commission of the European Communities,
    177, 184
Committee of Permanent Representatives
    (COREPER), 207
Common Agricultural Policy (CAP), 203–4
Common Foreign and Security Policy
    (CFSP), 209–10
Common Market, 202–4, 372
Commonwealth of Independent States
    (CIS), 63, 68–69, 81 n.6, 381
competition: in arms control, 337–38;
    for military force, 292–97; for natural
    resources in the Middle East, 192
Conable, Barber, 179
Concert of Europe, 301–2
Conference on Disarmament on a Com-
    prehensive Test Ban Treaty (CTBT),
    335
Conference on Security and Cooperation in
    Europe (CSCE), 39, 47, 63, 177, 188, 199,
    214, 220, 333, 342, 371, 378
confidence- and security-building measures
    (CSBMs), 343, 352
conflict. *See* armed conflict
conflict prevention, 27, 37, 194
conflict reduction, stabilization, and resolu-

tion, 26–27, 37, 149, 165, 186–94, 260–65, 271–90, 337
Congo, 154
Conventional Arms Transfer Talks (CATT), 347
Conventional Forces in Europe (CFE) Treaty, 333, 335, 341–42, 347
cooperation: as alternative to superpower hegemony, 107; in arms control, 337–39; and collective security, 350–52; definition of, 22; as goal of conflict resolution, 288; levels of, 25–28, 36, 337
Coordinating Committee for Multilateral Export Controls (COCOM), 174, 336, 344–45
Council for Foreign and Defense Policy, 86 n.62
crisis management, 36, 259–60
Croatia, 9, 15, 65, 73, 79, 217, 303
Crocker, Chester, 286
Cuba, 75
Cyprus, 7, 39, 73, 132, 149, 154, 163, 230, 276, 278
Czech Republic (Czechoslovakia), 7, 213, 317, 320, 325

Daalder, Ivo, 337
de Gaulle, Charles, 203–4, 208, 216
de Klerk, F. W., 162, 274–75, 280
Delors, Jacques, 205, 216
democratization, viii, ix, x, 3, 6, 17, 19–21, 38, 87, 193, 241, 381, 389
Deng Xiaoping, 121, 130, 135, 139
DePorte, Anton, 371
Deutsch, Karl, 22, 200, 219, 365
developing countries: armed conflict in, 5, 227–28; arms sales to, 184; definition of, 84 n.43; Russian intervention in, 60–61, 75–77. *See also* Third World
Development Assistance Committee (DAC), Organization for Economic Cooperation and Development (OECD), 169, 179, 181, 192
Diehl, Paul, 379
Doe, Samuel, 8–9
Dominican Republic, 154
Dulles, John Foster, 263

Eastern Europe: control of aid to, 173; democratization of, 20; economic reform in, 218, 220; great-power intervention in, 49–50, 71; Soviet withdrawal from, 265
East Timor, 104
Economic Community of West African States (ECOWAS), 8–9, 177, 188
economic sanctions, 165 n.5, 174–75, 380
Ecuador, 12
Egypt, 5, 11–12, 233–34, 237–38, 257–58, 281, 299, 353
El Salvador, 7, 182–83, 185–86, 189–90, 334
employee stock ownership plan (ESOP), 317, 329
Eritrea, 7, 9–10, 276, 285
Estonia, 82 n.17
Ethiopia, 4, 7, 10–11, 280, 288
Euratom, 27, 202–3
European Bank for Reconstruction and Development, 176
European Coal and Steel Community (ECSC), 27, 202, 372
European Community (EC), 15, 27–28, 93, 148, 164, 185–86, 198–225, 368–69, 371, 378
European Council, 205, 207
European Defense Community (EDC), 203, 207–8, 372
European Economic Community (EEC), 203
European Exchange Rate Mechanism (ERM), 212
European Monetary System, 206
European Political Cooperation (EPC), 207–8
European Union (EU), 39–40, 49–50, 185–86
Excess Defense Articles Program, 184
Expanded International Military Education and Training Program (U.S. Department of Defense), 191
export credit facilities, 174–75

Fahd (king of Saudi Arabia), 280
Federalist Papers, 390
Finland, 213
Five Principles of Peaceful Coexistence (FPPC), 117, 124
Foreign Ministry, Japanese, 97, 205
Fouchet Plan, 208
France, 53, 318–19, 368–73
Franco, Francisco, 29
Frente Farabundo Martí para la Liberación Nacional (FMLN), 185
Funabashi, Yoichi, 99

Gaidar, Yegor, 296

General Agreement on Tariffs and Trade (GATT), 49, 102, 107, 137, 199, 302, 369, 371, 378

Georgia, Republic of, 4, 66, 69, 80, 355

Germany: arms sales by, 53; development assistance to Africa from, 191–92; economic assistance from, 181; military power of, 353; postwar supervision of, 202, 216; privatization in, 325–26; restraints on military intervention by, 99; rivalry with France, 368–73

Global Coalition for Africa, 188

global markets, viii–ix, x, 3, 6, 17–19, 21, 87, 381

good offices, of the U.N., 162

Gorbachev, Mikhail, 62–65, 69, 75, 126, 150, 255–60, 264–65

Grachev, Pavel, 68

graduated reduction in international tension (GRIT), 264

Gray, Colin, 332

Great Britain: arms sales by, 53; in European Community, 213; military force of, 294; privatization in, 318

Greece, 174, 213, 314

Grenada, 154

Group of Elders, 281

Group of Seven Industrialized Democracies (G-7), 49, 218, 371

Group of Seventy-Seven (G-77), 126, 336

Guatemala, 318

Guinea-Bissau, 10

Gulf War (Operation Desert Storm), 44, 75–76, 132, 150–51, 153, 179, 189, 217, 221, 228, 234, 242, 274, 278, 285, 291, 300, 302–3, 334

Haile Selassie, 280

Haiti, 42, 50, 178, 334, 380, 390

Hamilton, Alexander, 390

Heraclides, Alexis, 229

historical permanence of conflict, 23–25

Hitler, Adolf, 21, 46, 248, 293–94

Hoffmann, Stanley, 221

Hong Kong, 88, 385

Horowitz, Donald, 228–29

Hosokawa (Japanese prime minister), 98, 102

Human Development Report 1991, 184–85

humanitarian aid, 159–60, 380, 389

Human Rights Monitoring and Mediation Efforts program, 189

Hungary, 213, 310, 312–13, 317, 320, 323–24

India, 4, 7, 12, 23, 26, 29, 76, 119, 152, 154, 163, 193, 231–32, 241, 340, 386

Indonesia, 98, 104, 236, 354

institutionalized consensual cooperation, 27–28, 37, 337, 365

Inter-American Development Bank (IDB), 169, 176

Inter-Governmental Agency on Drought and Development (IGADD), 280, 288

Intermediate-Range Nuclear Forces Treaty (INF), 130, 264–65, 335

International Atomic Energy Agency (IAEA), 264, 333, 335–36, 340

International Bank for Reconstruction and Development (IBRD), 195 n.9

International Court of Justice, 11, 161

International Development Association (IDA), 195 n.9

International Finance Corporation (IFC), 195 n.9

international financial institutions (IFIs), 176, 179–81, 187, 315

International Institute for Strategic Studies, 332

International Labor Organization (ILO), 177, 184–85, 190

International Monetary Fund (IMF), 49, 169, 173, 176, 179–80, 186–87, 199, 220, 315, 369, 371, 378

Iran, 4–5, 7, 24, 71, 76, 80, 132, 161–62, 236–38, 345, 386

Iran-Iraq War, 43–44, 52–53, 234

Iraq, 7, 12, 48, 50, 53–54, 75–76, 79–80, 151, 334, 344, 374, 386

Islamic fundamentalism (political Islam), 24, 66–67, 80, 215, 232, 235–39, 278, 390

Israel, 7, 10, 12, 14–15, 26–27, 163, 192, 242, 281, 283, 319, 353, 368, 373–76, 386. *See also* Arab-Israeli conflict

Israeli-Egyptian conflict, 23, 261–63, 275

Italy, 213, 319

Jamiat-ul-Ulema-i-Hind, 236

Janetzki, Heinz, 325–26

Japan: economic assistance from, 181; economic growth of, 88–89, 101–2; forces for

change in, 100–104; future of, 106–8; in global economic system, 87–88, 91–94; impediments to international political involvement by, 97–100; influence in East Asia, 104–6, 114; influence of the United States in, 89, 106–8; military competition by, 293–95; and regional power balance in Asia, 44, 88–91; restraints on military intervention by, 95–99; support for global and regional security, 94–97
Jiang Zemin, 115–16, 128
Jordan, 11, 15, 174

Kaczmarck, Wicolaw, 324
Kaifu, Toshiki, 125
Kampuchea, 52
Kanemaru, Shin, 103
Kashmir region, 7, 12, 24, 152, 154, 157, 228, 231, 241
Kaunda, Kenneth, 280–81
Kazakhstan, 79, 110, 179, 386
Keita, Modibo, 280
Kellogg-Briand Pact, 39
Kennan, George F., 43, 57 n.15
Kennedy, Paul, 19, 36, 296, 387
Keohane, Robert, 22
Khasbulatov, Ruslan, 78
Khieu Samphan, 133
Khmer Rouge, 133
Khomeini, Ayatollah, 20
Kissinger, Henry, 57 n.17, 123 24, 282
Kohl, Helmut, 211–12, 216
Kolodziej, Edward, 35–36, 38, 42, 112
Korea, North and South, 87–88, 98, 104, 118, 126, 133–34, 150–51, 184, 333, 336, 340–41
Korean War, 5, 122, 149, 154
Kozyrev, Andrei, 62–63, 65, 67–68, 71, 73–74, 77–79, 296
Kravchuk, Leonid, 67
Kurds, 13, 15, 50, 153, 229–30
Kuriyama, Takakazu, 90
Kuwait, 7, 11, 15, 64, 75, 111, 147, 150–52, 215, 333, 346, 348, 354, 373, 383. *See also* Gulf War

labeling, of the enemy, 249
Lall, Arthur, 125
Latin America: arms control in, 340; boundary disputes in, 9, 12; democratization of, 20; economic growth in, 88; military power in, 357; nuclear-free zone in, 159; privatization in, 321–23; U.N. intervention in, 64, 154–55, 158
Latvia, 82 n.17
Laurance, Edward, 386
League of Nations, 39, 150, 164
Lebanon, 7, 11, 15–16, 23, 47, 156, 163, 231, 241
Lebed, Lt. Gen. Aleksandr, 67
legitimacy, political, 40, 50, 125, 228, 284–85
Lenin, V. I., 95, 121
Levi Strauss and Company, 323–24
Lewandowski, Janusz, 324
Lewis, Anthony, 57 n.18
Lewis, Bernard, 237
Liberal Democratic Party (LDP), Japanese, 92, 98, 102
Liberia, 8–9, 188, 334
Libya, 11–12, 76, 80, 334
Li Daoyu, 135
Li Luye, 127
limited security regimes, 260
Li Peng, 124
Lodge, Juliet, 208
London Club, 174

Maastricht Treaty, 199, 202, 206–7, 209–11, 214, 216, 219–20, 371–72
Macedonia, 303
Malaysia, 11, 127, 311
Mali, 10–11, 281
managerial internationalism, global, 38
Mandela, Nelson, 274–75
Mann, Thomas, 371
Mao Zedong, 21, 121, 123–24, 130, 385
markets. *See* global markets
Marshall Plan, 29, 201, 369, 372
Maull, Hanns, 99
Mauritania, 7, 11
McNamara, Robert, 180
mediators: as communicators, 279–80; as formulators, 280–81; leverage of, 282–83; as manipulators, 281–84. *See also* armed conflict, mediation of; conflict resolution
Mehdi Bazargan, 238
Mexico, 322
Middle East, 4; arms control in, 340–42; arms sales to, 333; boundary disputes in, 10; competition for natural resources in, 192; mediation in, 281, 285; structural

Middle East (*continued*)
    rivalries in, 12; terrorism in, 24; U.N.
    intervention in, 162–63
military force: competitive, 292–97, 341; level
    of, 342; multilateral hegemonic, 301–4;
    unilateral hegemonic, 297–300
Milosevic, Slobodan, 303
Ministry of Foreign Affairs, Russian, 62, 79,
    257
Missile Technology Control Regime
    (MTCR), 131, 174, 336
Mitchell, George, 57 n.18
Mitterand, François, 216–17
Miyazawa, Kiichi, 103
Mobutu Sese Seko, 8
Modelski, George, 36
Moi, Daniel Arap, 280
Mojahedin-e-Khalq, 238
Moldova, 66, 68–69, 71, 78, 80
monetary union, European, 211–14
Monnet, Jean, 202
Montenegro, 63
Morgan, Patrick M., 364, 380
Morocco, 9–12, 280–81, 283, 287–88
most-favored-nation (MFN) status, of
    China, 131, 134–35
Mozambique, 4, 7, 12, 182–83, 185, 277, 280,
    285
Mueller, John, 18
Mugabe, Robert, 280, 285
Muiannad Aimad (Mahdi of the Sudan), 236
multilateral development agencies, 177,
    184–86
Multilateral Investment Guarantee Agency
    (MIGA), 195 n.9
multilateralism, 51–52, 177–78, 193, 301–4
multipolarization, 113–16, 119–20
mutually enticing opportunities, 277–78
mutually hurting stalemates, 276–77, 375

Nakasone, Yasuhiro, 97–98, 102–3, 107
Namibia, 4, 52, 64, 148, 158, 182, 274, 277, 281,
    283, 285–86
Nasser, Gamal Abdel al-, 233–34, 257
nationalism: as cause of armed conflict,
    7–8, 157; in Europe, 199, 221; pan-Arab,
    232–35, 239; restraint of, viii; and self-
    determination, 7, 39, 363
nation-states, viii, ix, 3, 6, 17–18, 21–22, 87,
    219, 379, 381–82

NATO, 15, 24, 39, 48, 118, 151, 160, 199, 204,
    208–9, 214–17, 369, 371, 378
naval peacekeeping, 159–60
Nazarbaev, President, of Kazakhstan, 69
neoisolationism, 41–42
neoliberal internationalism, 41–42
neorealism, 41
Nepal, 29
Netherlands (Holland), 183, 319
Neutral Military Observer Group (NMOG),
    188
New International Economic Order (NIEO),
    40, 118. *See also* global markets
new international political and economic
    order (NIPEO), 117
Newly Industrializing Economies (NIEs), 184
New World Order, 52, 116–17, 291
Nicaragua, 7, 182, 185, 189
Niger, 12
Nigeria, 10, 230, 318
Nixon, Richard M., 123
Non-Aligned Movement (NAM), 126
Nordic Ministers of Development Coopera-
    tion, 181
North American Free Trade Agreement, 381
North Atlantic Consultative Council
    (NACC), 215
Norway, 278, 375, 378
Nuclear Non-Proliferation Treaty, 131, 176,
    179, 340, 343
nuclear proliferation, 15, 52–54, 110, 119, 343
Nuclear Suppliers Group (NSG), 336
Nye, Joseph, 57 n.18
Nyerere, Julius, 280–81

OAS. *See* Organization of American States
    (OAS)
OAS International Commission for Support
    and Verification (CIAV-OAS), 189
Obasanjo, Olusegun, 281
Ogaden region, Ethiopia, 7, 10
Open Skies Treaty, 333, 335, 341
order, welfare, and legitimacy (OWL), 21,
    38–40, 47, 87, 112, 240, 365
Organization for Economic Cooperation
    and Development (OECD), 169
Organization for the Prohibition of Chemi-
    cal Weapons (OPCW), 335, 340–41
Organization of African Unity (OAU), 8, 12,
    148, 177, 188–90, 280, 288

Organization of American States (OAS), 51, 177–78, 357
Organization of Petroleum Exporting Countries (OPEC), 54
Orientations on Participatory Development and Good Governance (PDGG), 181–84, 192
Owen, David, 74
Ozawa, Ichiro, 98, 103

Pahlavi, Mohammad Reza (shah of Iran), 236, 238
Pakistan, 11–12, 23, 26, 29, 53, 131, 152, 154, 163, 176, 193, 238, 340, 386
Palestine, 7, 278
Palestine Liberation Organization (PLO), 10, 14–15, 26–27, 163, 242, 275, 368, 373–76
Palmerston, Lord, 302
Panama, 300, 390
parties, to mediation, 275
peace: economic considerations for, 168–69; threats to, 3–7; and U.N. peacekeeping role, 154–60; and U.N. peacemaking role, 161–64, 279. *See also* armed conflict, mediation of; conflict resolution
peacemaking, 161–64, 279, 291
Pereira, Aristides, 281
Pérez de Cuéllar, Secretary-General, of U.N., 165
Persian Gulf, 4, 76, 157
Persian Gulf War. *See* Gulf War (Operation Desert Storm)
Peru, 7, 12, 285
Petrenko, Janos, 323
Pfaff, William, 57 n.18
Philippines, 115, 127
Piscatori, James, 236
Poland, 213, 313–14, 317, 324
Pol Pot, 21, 133
Portugal, 213
Preston, Lewis, 180
Primakov, Evgenii, 64
privatization: advantages (superiority) of, 326–28; versus central planning and state ownership, 309–13; considerations for, 313–17; and performance, 323–26; process of, 328–29; techniques for, 317–23
protectionism, Japanese, 91
Punjab, 241
Pyle, Kenneth, 106

Qian Qichen, 133–34
Quemoy conflict, 122

Reagan, Ronald, 283, 300
regional power balancing, 42–44, 191, 291–308, 341, 353–54
requitement, establishment of, 273–74
Resolution of the Russian Federation toward the Yugoslav Crisis, 74
Rhodesia, 29
Rida, 236
Rocard, Michel, 319
routinized and contained conflict, 26, 36–37, 42, 149, 165, 259–60, 337, 341
Russian Federation, 4, 11, 53; arms sales by, 76–77; conception of world order in, 62–66; future role of, 61, 77, 80–81; global conflict management by, 60–62; intervention in developing world, 60–61, 75–77; intervention in Europe, 60–61, 73–75; intervention in regional conflict, 60–61, 66–73; military competition by, 296; nuclear capability of, 110, 179
Rwanda, 4, 7–8, 20, 24, 182, 188, 201, 221, 336, 346, 365, 383–84, 389

Sadat, Anwar el-, 238, 255–63, 275, 295, 375
Saddam Hussein, 44, 64, 75, 132, 233–35, 254, 303, 332–33, 373
Sagan, Scott, 343, 355
Sahara, dispute over, 7, 12, 64, 285, 288
Sahrawi Arab Democratic Republic, 10
Salafiya movement, 236
Salame, Ghassan, 237
Saudi Arabia, 11–12, 184, 238, 354
Savimbi, Jonas, 285
Sawyer, Dr. Amos, 8–9
Schelling, Thomas, xii
Schroeder, Paul, 384
Schuman, Robert, 202
Second Special Session on Disarmament (SSOD-II), 130
security community, Deutschian, 22, 200, 219, 221–22, 364–65, 367, 375, 390
security dilemma, 250
Senegal, 11
Senghor, Leopold Sedar, 281
separatist movements, 7, 228–30, 363
Serbia, 47, 61, 63, 79–80, 175, 219, 300, 303
Shaba province, Zaire, 8, 11–12

Shaposhnikov, Marshal Evgenii, 69, 71

Shevardnadze, Eduard, 62–65, 77

Shuskevich, Stanislav, 72

Singapore, 87

Singer, Max, 379

Single European Act (SEA) of 1986, 202, 205–6, 208–9, 219, 372

Sino-Indian border conflicts, 122

Sino-Soviet border conflicts, 122

Sino-U.S. rapprochement, 123–24

Six Day War (1967), 152, 342

Skokov, Iurii, 78

Slovenia, 9, 15, 73, 217

Snyder, Jack, 338, 364, 380, 385

Somalia, 4, 9–11, 20, 26, 42, 53, 55, 76, 148, 153, 159–60, 221, 280, 288, 334, 336, 365, 389–90

Somaliland, 9–10

Soseki, Natsume, 100

South Africa, 4, 12, 20, 148, 152, 162, 273–75, 283, 298, 380

South African Development Community, 188

South America. *See* Latin America

South Asian Association for Regional Cooperation (SAARC), 28

South China Sea, 114–15, 122, 127–28, 139

Southeast Asia, 4; arms control in, 340; democratization of, 20; structural rivalries in, 13

South Ossetia, 78

Soviet Union: central planning and state ownership in, 310, 312, 316; collapse of, ix, 4, 10, 39, 60, 66, 110; democratization of, 20; privatization in, 319–20. *See also* Russian Federation

Spain, 213; democratization of, 29

Sri Lanka, 4, 7, 228, 231–32

stalemates, mutually hurting, 276–77, 375

Stalin, Joseph, 21

Stankevich, Sergei, 70, 78

state-owned enterprises, 309–13

Stein, Janice, 371, 374–75

Stockholm International Peace Research Institute (SIPRI), 227

Straffon, Maria Theresa, 322

Strategic Arms Reduction Talks (START) treaty, 179, 264–65, 335, 386

Sudan, 4–5, 7, 9, 11–12

Suez Crisis (1956), 154, 233

superpowers: collective great-power management by, 44–51; demise of bipolarity, 3–4; management of global conflicts by, 35–37, 147–48, 227–28; military competition between, 293–94

support: for mediation, 274–75; for privatization, 316

Sweden, 183, 188, 213, 353

Syria, 12, 15, 131, 192–93, 234, 237, 374

Taiwan, 53, 87–88, 127, 134, 184, 385

Tajikistan, 66–67, 69, 71

Tamamoto, Masaru, 89, 99

Tanganyika, 11

Tanzania, 11

Taylor, Charles, 8–9

Thailand, 99, 106, 354

Thatcher, Margaret, 206

Third World: armed conflict in, 5, 227–28; China's role in, 126, 129, 132; debt crisis in, 54; Russian Federation intervention in, 60–61, 75–77. *See also* developing countries

Tocqueville, Alexis de, 293

tractability of conflict, 23–24, 26, 337

Transdniester Republic, 66

Tunisia, 11–12, 237

Turkey, 24, 71, 76, 193, 217, 302

Turkmenistan, 68

Uganda, 181–82, 185–86, 190

Uganda Veterans' Assistance Board, 185

Ukraine, 4, 11, 66, 68–69, 71, 79–80, 110, 179, 295, 355, 386

UNESCO, 127

United Arab Emirates, 354

United Nations: and arms control, 158–60, 333–34; awarded Nobel peace prize, 148; China in, 120, 132–33; collective enforcement by, 149–54; economic role of, 177–78; humanitarian assistance by, 159–60; military capability of, 53–54; naval peacekeeping by, 159–60; peacekeeping by, 154–60; peacemaking by, 161–64, 279; post-Cold War intervention by, 147–67; superpower support for, viii, 39, 48, 61, 63–65; supervision of elections by, 158, 160

United Nations Angola Verification Mission (UNAVEM), 155

United Nations Center for Disarmament
Affairs (UNCDA), 335, 351
United Nations Children's Fund (UNICEF),
177, 184–85
United Nations Conference on Disarmament
and Security Issues in the Asia-Pacific
Region, 129
United Nations Conference on Trade and
Development (UNCTAD), 126
United Nations Department of Humani-
tarian Affairs (DHA), 190
United Nations Development Programme
(UNDP), 177, 184–85, 188
United Nations Emergency Forces (UNEF):
I, 163; II, 154
United Nations Good Offices Mission in
Afghanistan and Pakistan (UNGOMAP),
155
United Nations High Commissioner for
Refugees (UNHCR), 177
United Nations Interim Force in Lebanon
(UNIFIL), 156, 163
United Nations Military Staff Committee
(MSC), 150
United Nations Observer Group in Central
America (ONUCA), 155
United Nations Register of Conventional
Arms, 334, 336, 348–57
United Nations Special Commission
(UNSCOM), 335
United Nations Special Committee on
Peacekeeping Operations, 132
United Nations Transitional Authority in
Cambodia (UNTAC), 133, 155, 158
United States: arms sales by, 184, 283; con-
ception of world order in, 38–42; eco-
nomic aid from, 188–89; global conflict
management by, 36–38, 42–55; managerial
internationalism in, 38
United States Agency for International
Development (USAID), 183, 190
United States–Japan Mutual Security Treaty,
94
Upper Volta (Burkina Faso), 10, 281
uti possidetis juris, doctrine of, 9

Vance, Cyrus, 74, 162
verification, of arms control, 334–35, 349–50
Vietnam, 4, 41, 118, 127–28, 139, 148
Vietnam War, 5, 104, 122, 228
Volsky, Dmitry, 71
Vorontsov, Iulii, 73

Waldheim, Kurt, 162
Waltz, Kenneth, 343
war, decline of, 111, 291
Warsaw Pact, 24, 71, 204, 213
Weinberger, Caspar, 300
welfare, U.S. aid for, 38–40
West African Military Observer Group
(ECOMOG), 188–89
West-centric coalition, 382–91
Western European Union (WEU), 199,
208–10, 216–17, 220, 371, 378
Wildavsky, Aaron, 379
World Bank, 49, 118, 133, 169, 173, 176, 179–81,
186–87, 190, 193, 220, 315, 369, 378
World Council of Churches, 9
world food production, 55
World Food Programme (WFP), 177, 184–85
World Trade Organization (WTO), 93, 121,
199. *See also* General Agreement on Tariffs
and Trade (GATT)

Yeltsin, Boris, 61–63, 65, 67–71, 74, 77–79,
386
Yom Kippur War (1973), 154, 158, 162, 277
Yoshida, Shigeru, 94–95, 98, 100, 103
Yugoslavia, 4, 7, 10–11, 16, 20, 23–24, 39, 48,
50, 61, 63, 65, 73–76, 79, 135, 152, 159, 162,
164, 183, 201, 221, 300, 313, 334, 365, 383,
389. *See also* Balkan conflicts; Bosnia;
Croatia; Macedonia; Serbia; Slovenia
Yu Mengjia, 132

Zaire, 7–8, 11–12
Zambia, 12
Zanzibar, 11
Zartman, William, 375
Zhang Guoxi, 326
Zimbabwe, 12, 285

Library of Congress Cataloging-in-Publication Data

Coping with conflict after the Cold War / edited by Edward A.
    Kolodziej, and Roger E. Kanet.
        p.   cm. — (Perspectives on security)
    Includes index.
    ISBN 0-8018-5106-8 (hc : alk. paper)
    1. International relations.   2. Low-intensity conflicts (Military
science)   3. Developing countries — Relations.   4. National state.
I. Kolodziej, Edward A.   II. Kanet, Roger E., 1936–
III. Series.
JX1391.C666   1996
327.1'7 — dc20   95-30674